PROMISES
TO KEEP

PROMISES TO KEEP

On Life and Politics

★ ★ ★ ★ ★

JOE BIDEN

RANDOM HOUSE TRADE PAPERBACKS

NEW YORK

2008 Random House Trade Paperback Edition

Published in the United States by Random House Trade Paperbacks,
an imprint of The Random House Publishing Group,
a division of Random House, Inc., New York.

RANDOM HOUSE TRADE PAPERBACKS and colophon are registered trademarks
of Random House, Inc.

Originally published in hardcover in the United States by Random House, an imprint of
The Random House Publishing Group, a division of Random House, Inc., in 2007.

Grateful acknowledgment is made to Henry Holt and Company, LLC,
for permission to reprint four lines from "Stopping By Woods on a
Snowy Evening" from *The Poetry of Robert Frost,* edited by Edward
Connery Lathem, copyright © 1923, 1969 by Henry Holt and
Company. Copyright © 1951 by Robert Frost. Reprinted by
permission of Henry Holt and Company, LLC.

Library of Congress Cataloging-in-Publication Data
Biden, Joseph R.
Promises to keep : on life and politics / Joe Biden.
p. cm.
ISBN 978-0-8129-7621-2
1. Biden, Joseph R. 2. Legislators—United States—Biography. 3. United States Congress.
Senate—Biography. 4. United States—Politics and government—1945–1989. 5. United
States—Politics and government—1989– I. Title.
E840.8.B54A3 2007
328.73092—dc22
[B]   2007019603

Printed in the United States of America

www.atrandom.com

2 4 6 8 9 7 5 3 1

Book design by Victoria Wong

For Mom and Dad,
who kept their promises

The woods are lovely, dark and deep.
But I have promises to keep,
And miles to go before I sleep,
And miles to go before I sleep.

—ROBERT FROST

CONTENTS

PROLOGUE

THE FIRST PRINCIPLE OF POLITICS, THE FOUNDATIONAL principle, I learned in the 1950s in my grandpop's kitchen when I was about twelve or thirteen years old. My parents had recently moved us to Delaware, but most Friday nights Mom and Dad would load me, my sister, Val, my brother Jimmy and the baby, Frankie, into our car and drive up to Scranton, Pennsylvania, to spend the weekend at Grandpop Finnegan's house. I'd have Saturday to play with my old friends from the neighborhood—baseball, basketball, cops and robbers. Between games, we'd head down toward Green Ridge Corners, stopping in at Handy Dandy for caps for our cap guns, or to Pappsy's or Simmey's for penny candy. Simmey's was right next to Joseph Walsh's storefront insurance agency, so we'd pass right by the crucifix in the window. It wasn't unusual or at all odd to us to see a crucifix in a place of business. A lot of the people who shopped at the Green Ridge stores were Irish Catholics like us. We never thought about it one way or another. Seemed to us like most of the kids in our neighborhood were Catholic, and we all knew what was expected of us. If we saw a nun on the street on our way into Simmey's on a Saturday we'd tip our caps—"Good afternoon, Sister"—and we'd always hold the door for her. The priests were a presence around the neighborhood, too, and they warranted respect. My grandpop might complain about Monsignor Vaughan, who was always asking for more money, but nobody in Green Ridge passed a priest without acknowledging him: "G'dafternoon, Father."

Many of the businesses in Green Ridge dated back fifty years, when the coming of the first electric trolley lines sprouted these tightly packed neighborhoods where the bootstrap Irishmen could move their families for fresh air and a little patch of green lawn. My mom had been to some of these stores when she was a little girl.

Once we'd spent our limit on penny candy from Simmey's, Charlie Roth, Larry Orr, Tommy Bell, and I would head toward the Roosie Theatre for the twelve-cent double feature—usually a pair of westerns or Tarzan.

If we had time to spare after the movies let out, we might stop in at Thompson's market. Mr. Thompson kept a live monkey in the store, so even if we couldn't afford more candy, it was worth the stop. We might linger in front of Evelyn and E-Paul's, too, waiting for the aroma of homemade candy and ice cream to waft by. But when the sun started to drop, Charlie, Larry, Tommy, and I began to make our way home, heading down East Market Street to the Lackawanna River. Stunted little eight-foot trees lined the bank on our side of the river, so we'd swing on the branches, reenacting scenes from the Tarzan movie we'd just seen. The bigger adventure was crossing the river at a gallop on top of sixteen-inch pipes. We knew we probably shouldn't; the Lacky was a sewage dump in the fifties, and filthy. Our parents were always warning us away from it. But as long as we didn't fall in, who would know? Running the pipe was hardly a mortal sin.

When we'd finished at the river, it was usually supper time, so we'd pick up the pace—through the alley behind Richmont Street, which was a string of one-story garages. Tommy and I would run the roofs of the garages, leaping from one to the next. "Ground's the swamp. Touch it and you die—eaten by alligators!" Charlie and Larry usually took their chances with the alligators. Sometimes one of the Richmont Street residents would open a back window and give a holler— "You boys get down off those garages!" Anyway, it was usually near dark on Saturday evening before Charlie, Larry, Tommy, and I made it back home.

Sunday was different; that day was reserved for family. It started with Mass. My attendance was not optional. The entire Finnegan clan rode over to Saint Paul's Catholic Church together, and church always felt like an extension of home. I had already worked my way through the questions in the Baltimore catechism: Who made us? . . . Who is God? . . . What is a Spirit? . . . What do we mean when we say that God is all good? And the answers: For the word of the Lord is right; and all His works are done with faithfulness. He loveth mercy and judgment: the earth is full of the mercy of the Lord. I could practically recite the entire catechism. I'd memorized the Lord's Prayer and the Apostle's Creed. I'd been to my first confession. My grandpop Finnegan had taught me to say the Rosary. And every night when I went in to kiss my grandpop good night, he'd remind me: "Three Hail Mary's for purity, Joey." It was a long time before I understood he was talking about chastity. In the beginning I thought he meant nobility or purity of cause, ideas that tracked with the sermons we heard at Saint Paul's. It was more about doing good than being good.

After Mass, the Finnegans and their friends would gather at my grandpop's house at 2446 North Washington Avenue, out at the end of the trolley line. Dinner was already cooked, warming in the oven, so the women took their ease in the dining room, thumbing the lace tablecloth, having tea.

Meanwhile, Grandpop, his pals from the neighborhood, maybe a crony from the *Scranton Tribune,* and my Finnegan uncles, Jack and Boo-Boo, settled in at the kitchen table. They'd sit in the spreading afternoon light talking sports and politics. These men were educated, informed, and eclectic—and they loved to debate. They'd argue local politics, state politics, world events, Truman against MacArthur, Truman against the steel companies. They were Truman Democrats, working men, or sons of working men, but they had to admit Truman might have gone too far when he tried to take over Youngstown Steel. Probably the Supreme Court was right when they knocked him back. A president's a president, not a dictator. It seemed un-American. Still, at least he was up front about it. That's the thing they liked about Harry Truman: no artifice. He knew where he stood, and he wasn't afraid to say it. The fellows at Grandpop's table didn't trust the new Democratic standard-bearer, Adlai Stevenson. They thought he might be a little soft. They were willing to give Eisenhower the benefit of the doubt; he was a hero of the war, after all. My dad, who didn't join in the talk much, trusted Ike because he had been able to win a war while negotiating the competing national prerogatives of the western allies and the substantial egos of Franklin Roosevelt, Winston

Churchill, Charles de Gaulle, Field Marshal Montgomery, and General Patton. Dad thought Eisenhower was a man with ballast, a leader. But the Finnegans wanted to argue Ike's policies.

I found myself drawn to my grandpop's kitchen by the pace and power of the volleys, and although I was too young to merit a regular place in these arguments, the men didn't mind if I stayed around to listen from time to time. Even when it turned to local politics—the doings in Scranton and Lackawanna County—and the talk got heated, they never shooed me. One Sunday, as I remember it, they were on the case of a local pol they called Patrick, a slick Irish operator, friend to the diocese, friend to the working man, friend to his neighbors, friend to his family—maybe too good a friend. I guess Patrick's political favors, even in the days of patronage, had often caught the attention of the local newspapers. Some of the younger guys thought it was time for Patrick to move aside, time to put a more modern sheen on the Democratic machine in Scranton. But I noticed my grandfather was defending Patrick even when his friends kept attacking him. After a while my grandfather stopped defending and did something he'd never done in these Sunday talkathons: He turned to me and said, "Joey, you're wondering why Pop likes Patrick."

"No, no, no, Pop. No."

"You like Mr. Scranton, don't you, honey?"

What was I supposed to say? You didn't lie at Grandpop Finnegan's table. To me William Scranton was the epitome of an upstanding citizen. He was the sort of man my dad respected. Mr. Scranton was descended from the town's founding family. He'd been a flier in the war, like my hero uncle. He was a well-educated man and a civic leader.

"Well, yeah. Yeah, Pop. I like him."

"Joey, let me tell you the difference between Patrick and Bill Scranton. When I ask Patrick for a favor, he might say yes and he might say no. He might look at me and say, 'I'm sorry, Ambrose. I'm gonna cut your heart out.' I can deal with that. Whatever Patrick has to say, he's gonna say it to my face. I might not agree with him, but he thinks enough of me to tell me to my face."

My grandpop called me over to his chair, and as I moved beside him, he put an arm around my waist and pulled me closer. "You know where Mr. Scranton's family lives, Joey?" I could picture the kind of home the Scrantons would live in; it'd be a mansion. He said, "I could call right now and say, 'Mr. Scranton, it's Ambrose Finnegan from the *Tribune*. I have a problem. Can I come and see you?' He'd say, 'Sure. Come on over, Ambrose.' Couldn't be more polite. I'd walk up that big flight of stairs and knock on the door, and his man Jeeves would answer the door. Jeeves would invite me in. He'd take my coat. Then he'd take me to the library and offer me a sherry." I didn't know what a sherry was, and my grandpop didn't slow down to explain, but it sounded like a good thing to get. "Then Mr. Scranton would come in and say, 'Ambrose, what can I do for you?' And I'd tell him my problem. And he'd say he'd be happy to help."

And just then Grandpop reached up and hit me in between my shoulder blades. He hit me so hard, it startled me. I thought he might be angry at me, that somehow I'd disappointed him. I could feel the heat rise in my face. But my Grandpop was still talking. " 'Ambrose,' he'd say, 'I'd be happy to help.'

"Joey, it wouldn't be until I got my coat, got out the door, and reached the first landing that I felt a warm trickle of blood down my spine."

"You know what we Irish call that, Joey?" one of my uncles said. "We call that a silk stocking screw."

My grandpop didn't even look at my uncle. He held my gaze and he said, "Joey, remember this: Men like Mr. Scranton would never do to their friends at the country club what they would do to us on the street. They think politics is beneath them. They think politics is only for the Poles and Irish and Italians and Jews, so anything goes."

I knew that Ambrose Finnegan was a Democrat, with a bit of a chip on his Irish shoulder about the Scranton elite, but I still didn't see the wisdom of dismissing the Mr. Scrantons of the world outright. My dad always said you couldn't blame a guy for being rich. But I understood that my grandpop was trying to instruct me in something more elemental than class.

He wanted me to understand two big things: First, that nobody, no group, is above others. Public servants are obliged to level with *everybody,* whether or not they'll like what he has to say. And second, that politics was a matter of personal honor. A man's word is his bond. You give your word, you keep it.

For as long as I can remember, I've had a sort of romantic notion of what politics should be—and can be. If you do politics the right way, I believe, you can actually make people's lives better. And integrity is the minimum ante to get into the game. Nearly forty years after I first got involved, I remain captivated by the possibilities of politics and public service. In fact, I believe—as I know my grandpop did—that my chosen profession is a noble calling.

FROM THE TIME I was little I had a picture in my head of the sort of man I wanted to become, a picture filled in by my mom and dad, by the teachings of the Catholic schools I attended, by stories I heard about our family hero, Uncle Bosie, a pilot who was shot down in World War II, and by a faith in the size of my own future. During my adolescent and college years, men and women were changing the country—Martin Luther King Jr., John F. Kennedy, Robert Kennedy— and I was swept up in their eloquence, their conviction, the sheer size of their improbable dreams. I knew I wanted to be a part of the change. I didn't know how. I had no plan, but I knew. And as it turned out, surprising political opportunities opened up for me when I was a young man. When they did, I was not shy about pursuing them, because I already had a picture of what I had to do—how I had to conduct myself—to take advantage of them.

When I look back at my earliest political speeches, I see it was much more than the inspiration of Dr. King or the Kennedys that animated my entrance into public life. It was as much my grandpop's simple, straightforward belief that the welfare of our country depends on having leaders who call it like they see it: "People don't know who or what to believe in—and, most of all, they are afraid to believe in politicians," I told the crowd at the Hotel du Pont in Wilmington when I announced my candidacy for the Senate in 1972.

> We must have public officials who will stand up and tell the people exactly what they think. . . . Our failure in recent years has *not* been the failure of the people to meet the challenges placed before them, but rather the failure of both our great political parties to place those challenges honestly and courageously before the people, and to trust the willingness of the people to do the things that really need to be done. . . . We all know—or at least we are told continually—that we are a divided people. And we know there's a degree of truth in it. We have too often allowed our differences to prevail

among us. We have too often allowed ambitious men to play off those differences for political gain. We have too often retreated behind our differences when no one really tried to lead us beyond them. But all our differences hardly measure up to the values we all hold in common. . . . I am running for the Senate because . . . I want to make the system work again, and I am convinced that is what all Americans really want.

I believed that in 1972; I still believe it today. Our nation's founders framed a political system of uncommon genius, and generation after generation of Americans has used that system to make the country more fair, more just, more welcoming, more committed to individual rights. The United States has the finest and fairest system of governing the world has ever known. There is nothing inherently wrong with the system; it's up to each of us to do our part to make it work.

It's been my privilege to serve that purpose. I've been a United States senator from Delaware more than half my life. And after almost thirty-five years I'm more passionate about the job and more committed to what I'm doing than I've been in my entire career. Any day of the week you can read or hear about the lamentable state of our nation's politics, about our bitter and partisan party divisions, about the regrettable coarseness of the discourse. I don't deny it, but from inside the arena none of it feels irreversible or fatal. We can always do better. I believe that, or I wouldn't still be in politics. In fact, I sense a greater opportunity today than any time in my career. Maybe it's because after all these years, people actually listen to me.

Only a few dozen men in history have served in the Senate longer than I have. When I was elected in 1972, I was twenty-nine years old, not yet old enough to be sworn in. There were giants still standing in the Senate then. They may have been no better or worse than the people who serve today, but from Dixiecrats to Progressives, they were incredibly well known: James O. Eastland, Sam Ervin, John Stennis, Barry Goldwater, Warren Magnusson, Stuart Symington, Jacob Javits, Henry "Scoop" Jackson, Abraham Ribicoff, Philip Hart. And the best of them—men like Mike Mansfield and Hubert Humphrey—endowed that body with esteem in the eyes of the American people. It felt like a sacred place when I got there, and I've never lost that feeling. Thirty-five years later I still get goose bumps when I come out of Union Station and see the Capitol dome.

I started at the bottom, dead last in seniority, with an office so small that people on my staff had to get up and stand sideways just so somebody could open the front door. At the time I had no intention of serving more than six months. But I lasted long enough to serve, at different times, as chairman of the Judiciary and Foreign Relations committees. Things have changed in my six terms, for better and for worse. I served with the last of the southern segregationists, but I was there to see Carol Moseley Braun and Barack Obama sworn in. There was not a single woman in the Senate in 1973. Today there are sixteen, and one of them has a real shot at the presidency. In committee rooms, conference rooms, the cloakroom, and on the floor of the Senate itself, I've witnessed the decline of common decency and a growing unwillingness of colleagues to try to see the world through another's eyes. I've seen a rise in partisanship and the rising power of money in both campaigns and governance. But I've also seen a thousand small kindnesses from one side of the aisle to the other and hundreds of acts of personal and political courage.

The rules and traditions of the Senate have a way of asking the best of the men and women who serve. Back in the early days of my first term, when the courts ordered President Richard Nixon to turn over the Watergate tapes, the government appeared headed toward a constitutional crisis. The president asked Senator John Stennis to run interference for him, to listen to the tapes, summarize them for his colleagues, but keep them away from the full Senate. Stennis demurred. He would not run interference for the executive branch; the tapes should be available to all. John Stennis acted on principle to uphold the Constitution. I remember what he said in the Democratic caucus that day: *"I've thought long and hard on what my obligation is. I've decided what I'm honor bound to do . . . and I've decided I am a Senate man. I am not the president's man. Therefore, I will not listen to the tapes. I am a man of the Senate."* I'm proud to say I am a Senate man, too. The job plays to my strengths and to my deepest beliefs.

I serve the citizens of Delaware, but I also serve the Constitution and the nation. George Washington called the Senate a "cooling" institution, conceived to operate outside the political expediencies of the moment. The nation's founding documents impel United States senators to take the long view in both national and international affairs; to offer on every issue what wisdom and intelligence we bring collectively and individually; to protect the minority from destructive passions of the majority; and to keep an eye fixed on any president who reaches beyond the limits of his or her power. The Senate was designed to play this independent and moderating role, and it is a solemn duty and responsibility that transcends the partisan disputes of any day or any decade.

AS A UNITED STATES senator I've watched (and played some small part in) history: the Vietnam War, Watergate, the Iran hostage crisis, the Bork nomination, the fall of the Berlin wall, the reunification of Germany, the disintegration of the Soviet Union, 9/11, two wars in Iraq, a presidential impeachment, a presidential resignation, and a presidential election decided by the Supreme Court. I have been in war zones across the world and have seen genocide up close. I have sat face-to-face for hard talk with Kosygin, Khadafy, Helmut Schmidt, Sadat, Mubarak, and Milosevic. I've seen Nixon, Ford, Carter, Reagan, Clinton, and two Bushes wrestle with the presidency. I ran my own race for president and had to pick up the pieces after the train wreck . . . then nearly died from a cranial aneurysm. In the aftermath I had to remake my health, my reputation, and my career in the Senate. The years since then have been my most rewarding. I count my role in helping to end genocide in the Balkans and in securing the passage of the Violence Against Women Act as my proudest moments in public life. If I had accomplished nothing else (and if I accomplish nothing more), for me those two efforts redeem every second of difficulty and doubt in my long career.

I've learned plenty about myself over the years, but I believe I've learned even more important lessons about the American people—about their point of particular pride. Just after I won my first election to the Senate in 1972, I used to say I had great faith in the American people—and I really meant it. I wasn't just saying it in speeches; it was pillow talk with my wife. I was so proud of the race we ran in 1972; it was honest, straightforward, and clean. I really believed I had lived up to my grandpop's admonitions. The Biden for Senate campaign meant to preserve the integrity of politics, and I felt that we'd been vindicated for that effort. I'd talk about it with my wife, Neilia, in our big new house: "I do, Neilia. I really do. I have great faith in the

American people." Neilia was always more clear-eyed than I am. "Joey," she said, "I wonder how you would have felt if you lost?"

Full disclosure: I do not have absolute faith in the judgment and wisdom of the American people. We're all human, and we can all be misled. When leaders don't level with citizens, we can't expect them to make good judgments. But I do have absolute faith in the *heart* of the American people. The greatest resource in this country is the grit, the resolve, the courage, the basic decency, and the stubborn pride of its citizens. I know thousands of ordinary Americans, faced with burdens that would break many of us, who get up every single day and put one foot in front of the other and make it work. Most do it without demanding special favors or pity, even while the more fortunate among us stand willing to help ease those burdens. I'm convinced of the generosity, determination, and capabilities of our fellow Americans. I've seen it over and over, but it came home to me dramatically in the hours after the attacks on the World Trade Center and the Pentagon on September 11, 2001.

The planes hit while I was on the train from Wilmington to Washington, and when I came out of Union Station that morning, I could see a haze of smoke rising from the Pentagon across the Potomac. It was a morning of surreal stillness. There was almost no breeze. It was so quiet, I could hear myself breathe as I walked toward the Capitol dome. I was struck by the warm glow of sun on my face and the sharpness of the cobalt blue sky, which was strangely unmarred by air traffic. But beneath the calm there was a gathering feeling of panic on the ground in Washington. The Capitol building had already been evacuated. Senators, House members, and their staffs were milling around the park between the Capitol and Union Station. Some were talking on cell phones. Some were already arguing about the need for funding Reagan's Star Wars missile defense system. The Capitol police refused to let anybody back into the building, but they were offering briefings for a select group of elected officials at a command post on the top floor of a four-story building behind the Senate offices. Most members were camping out on the floor below. So I was shuttling back and forth between floors, trying to persuade anyone who would listen that we should get back in session and show the American people we were taking care of business. Nobody would budge; leaders in both parties were being told they should be prepared to leave town. Congressman Bob Brady, who had also been pushing our colleagues to get back in session, finally gave up in disgust. He thought he might be able to do some good back in his home district in Philadelphia, and he offered to drop me in Wilmington on the way. On the way out, Brady and I could sense the panic rising as we walked through scores of reporters outside the building; they were understandably anxious to get some word of what was happening. "Senator Biden," a reporter from ABC said to me, "senators I've spoken to and members of Congress as well have said we are now at war. Senator Shelby, who is the ranking member on the intelligence committee, has said we are now essentially at war. We have to be on a war footing. And Senator Chuck Hagel says we have to start securing our borders, locking down our airports, revisiting the way we protect our public institutions. What about that?"

"I hope that's not true," I told her and her listening audience.

I would say it another way. I would say we've come face-to-face with a reality. A reality we knew existed and we knew was possible. A reality that has happened to varying degrees in other countries. But if in fact, in order to respond to that reality, we have to alter our civil liberties, change the way we function, then we have truly lost the war. . . . The way to conduct the war is to demonstrate that your civil liberties, your civil rights, your ability to be free and walk and move around in fact are not fundamentally altered. . . . There are a lot of things we can do though to diminish significantly the possibility of this happening again without changing our character as a nation. . . . This nation is too big, too strong, too united, too much a power in terms of our cohesion and our values to let this break us apart. And it won't happen. It won't happen.

By then the Senate and House leadership had been convinced to board helicopters for a flight to a secure location in West Virginia. The vice president had been spirited away to an undisclosed hideaway. The president was flying from safe spot to safe spot on Air Force One; he'd been convinced it was too dangerous to come back to D.C.

The Twin Towers had collapsed by the time we got on the road toward Wilmington, and the death estimates in New York were five, six, seven thousand—maybe more. But when I got home and put on the television, I saw that the American heart was still beating strong. Doctors and nurses were standing by at hospitals in New York City, ready to treat the wounded. Snaking through the streets and up the avenues were long lines of New Yorkers waiting to give their blood, even though word was being passed that no more blood was needed. I could see it in their faces: They were hungry to do something, *anything*. Nobody was talking about war footings or payback. They just wanted to do their part. That was the day that reminded me that even in a moment of almost total silence from their leaders in Washington, Americans would rise to the occasion. Watching those people on the blood lines, I was convinced the country would get up off the mat, face the new challenge head-on, and emerge stronger for having done it.

To me this is the first principle of life, the foundational principle, and a lesson you can't learn at the feet of any wise man: *Get up!* The art of living is simply getting up after you've been knocked down. It's a lesson taught by example and learned in the doing. I got that lesson every day while growing up in a nondescript split-level house in the suburbs of Wilmington, Delaware. My dad, Joseph Robinette Biden Sr., was a man of few words. What I learned from him, I learned from watching. He'd been knocked down hard as a young man, lost something he knew he could never get back. But he never stopped trying. He was the first one up in our house every morning, clean-shaven, elegantly dressed, putting on the coffee, getting ready to go to the car dealership, to a job he never really liked. My brother Jim said most mornings he could hear our dad singing in the kitchen. My dad had grace. He never, ever gave up, and he never complained. "The world doesn't owe you a living, Joey," he used to say, but without rancor. He had no time for self-pity. He didn't judge a man by how many times he got knocked down but by how fast he got up.

Get up! That was his phrase, and it has echoed through my life. The world dropped you on your head? My dad would say, *Get up!* You're lying in bed feeling sorry for yourself? *Get up!* You got knocked on your ass on the football field? *Get up!* Bad grade? *Get up!* The girl's parents won't let her go out with a Catholic boy? *Get up!*

It wasn't just the small things but the big ones—when the only voice I could hear was my own. After the surgery, Senator, you might lose the ability to speak? *Get up!* The newspapers are calling you a plagiarist, Biden? *Get up!* Your wife and daughter—I'm sorry, Joe, there was nothing we could do to save them? *Get up!* Flunked a class at law school? *Get up!* Kids make fun of you because you stutter, Bu-bu-bu-bu-bu-Biden? *Get up!*

PROMISES
TO KEEP

* 1 *

Impedimenta

JOE IMPEDIMENTA. MY CLASSMATES HUNG THAT NICKNAME on me our first semester of high school when we were doing two periods of Latin a day. It was one of the first big words we learned. *Impedimenta—the baggage that impedes one's progress.* So I was Joe Impedimenta. Or Dash. A lot of people thought they called me Dash because of football. I was fast, and I scored my share of touchdowns. But the guys at an all-boys Catholic school usually didn't give you nicknames to make you feel better about yourself. They didn't call me Dash because of what I could do on the football field; they called me Dash because of what I could not do in the classroom. I talked like Morse code. Dot-dot-dot-dot-dash-dash-dash-dash. "You gu-gu-gu-gu-guys sh-sh-sh-sh-shut up!"

My impedimenta was a stutter. It wasn't always bad. When I was at home with my brothers and sister, hanging out with my neighborhood friends, or shooting the bull on the ball field, I was fine, but when I got thrown into a new situation or a new school, had to read in front of the class, or wanted to ask out a girl, I just couldn't do it. My freshman year of high school, because of the stutter, I got an exemption from public speaking. Everybody else had to get up and make a presentation at the morning assembly, in front of 250 boys. I got a pass. And everybody knew it. Maybe they didn't think much of it—they had other things to worry about—but I did. It was like having to stand in the corner with the dunce cap. Other kids looked at me like I was stupid. They laughed. I wanted so badly to prove I was like everybody else. Even today I can remember the dread, the shame, the absolute rage, as vividly as the day it was happening. There were times I thought it was the end of the world, my impedimenta. I worried that the stutter was going to be my epitaph. And there were days I wondered: How would I ever beat it?

It's a funny thing to say, but even if I could, I wouldn't wish away the darkest days of the stutter. That impedimenta ended up being a godsend for me. Carrying it strengthened me and, I hoped, made me a better person. And the very things it taught me turned out to be invaluable lessons for my life as well as my chosen career.

I STARTED WORRYING about my stutter back in Scranton, Pennsylvania, in grade school. When I was in kindergarten, my parents sent me to a speech pathologist at Marywood College, but it didn't help much, so I went only a few times. Truth was, I didn't let the stutter get in the way of things that really mattered to me. I was young for my grade and always little for my age, but I made up for it by demonstrating I had guts. On a dare, I'd climb to the top of a burning culm dump, swing out over a construction site, race under a moving dump truck. If I could visualize myself doing it, I knew I could do it. It never crossed my mind that I couldn't. As much as I lacked confidence in my ability to communicate verbally, I always had confidence in my athletic ability. Sports was as natural to me as speaking was unnatural. And sports turned out to be my ticket to acceptance—and more. I wasn't easily intimidated in a game, so even when I stuttered, I was always the kid who said, "Give me the ball."

Who's going to take the last shot? "Give me the ball." We need a touchdown now. "Give me the ball." I'd be eight years old, usually the smallest guy on the field, but I wanted the ball. And they gave it to me.

When I was ten, we moved from the Scranton neighborhood I knew so well to Wilmington, Delaware. My dad was having trouble finding a good job in Scranton, and his brother Frank kept telling him there were jobs in Wilmington. The Biden brothers had spent most of their school days in Wilmington, so it was like going home for my dad. For the rest of us, it felt like leaving home. But my mom, who was born and raised in Scranton, determined to see it as my dad did; she refused to see it any other way. This was a wonderful opportunity. We'd have a fresh start. We'd make new friends. We were moving into a brand-new neighborhood, to a brand-new home. This wasn't a hand-me-down house. We'd be the first people to ever set foot in it. It was all good. She was like that with my stutter, too. She wouldn't dwell on the bad stuff. *Joey, you're so handsome. Joey, you're such a good athlete. Joey, you've got such a high IQ. You've got so much to say, honey, that your brain gets ahead of you.* And if the other kids made fun of me, well, that was their problem. *They're just jealous.*

She knew how wounding kids could be. One thing she determined to do when we moved to Wilmington was hold me back a year. Besides being young and small, I'd missed a lot of school the last year in Scranton when I'd had my tonsils and adenoids removed. So when we got to Wilmington, my mom insisted I do third grade over—and none of the kids at Holy Rosary had to know I was being held back by my mom. That was just another of the ways Wilmington would be a fresh start.

Actually, we were moving to the outskirts of Wilmington, to a working-class neighborhood called the Claymont area, just across the Pennsylvania state line. I still remember the drive into Delaware. It all felt like an adventure. My dad was at the wheel and my mom was up front with him, with the three of us kids in back: me, my brother, Jimmy, and my six-year-old sister, Valerie, who was also my best friend. We drove across the state line on the Philadelphia Turnpike, past the Worth Steel Mill, the General Chemical Company, and the oil refineries, all spewing smoke. We drove past Worthland and Overlook Colony, tightly packed with the row houses that the mills had built for their workers not long after the turn of the century. Worthland was full of Italians and Poles; Overlook Colony was black. It was just a mile or so down the road to Brookview Apartments and our brand-new garden unit. A right off the Philadelphia Pike, and we were home.

Brookview was a moonscape. A huge water tower loomed over the development, but there wasn't a tree in sight. We followed the main road in as it swept us in a gentle curve. Off the main road were the "courts." One side was built, but the other was still under construction. We could see the heavy machinery idling among the mounds of dirt and red clay. It was a hot summer day, so our car windows were rolled down. I can still remember the smell of that red clay, the sulfurous stink from the bowels of the earth. As we arced down the main street toward a new home, my mom caught sight of these airless little one-story apartments. They were the color of brown mustard. My dad must have seen my mom's face as she scanned her new neighborhood. "Don't worry, Pudd'," he told her. "It's not these. We have a big one."

He pulled the car around to the bottom of a bend, and without getting out of the car, he pointed across an expanse of not-quite lawn, toward the big one. Our new home was a two-story unit, white, with thin columns in front—a hint of Tara, I guess—and a one-story box off each side. "There it is," he said.

"All of this?" Mom asked.

"No, just the center," my dad said. Then, "Don't worry, Pudd', it's only temporary."

From the backseat I could tell my mom was crying.

"Mom!? What's the matter, Mommy?"

"I'm just so happy. Isn't it beautiful? Isn't it beautiful?"

ACTUALLY, IT DIDN'T seem bad to me. It was a miniature version of a center hall colonial, and we had bedrooms upstairs. I had the bedroom in back, which meant from my window I could gaze upon the object of my deepest desire, my Oz: Archmere. Right in the middle of this working-class steel town, not a mile from the mills and directly across from the entrance of Brookview Apartments, was the first mansion I had ever really seen. I could look at it for hours. John Jacob Raskob had built the house for his family before the steel mills, chemical plants, and oil refineries came to Claymont. Raskob was Pierre du Pont's personal secretary, but he had a genius for making money out of money. He convinced the du Ponts to take a big stake in General Motors and became its chairman of finance. Raskob was also a Catholic hero. He used part of his fortune to fund a charitable foundation, and he'd run the campaign of the first Catholic presidential nominee, the Democrat Al Smith. In 1928 the Democrats had political strategy sessions in his library at Archmere. Raskob went on to build the Empire State Building.

The mansion he built in Claymont, the Patio at Archmere, was a magnificent Italianate marble pile on a property that sloped down to the Delaware River. Archmere—arch by the sea—was named for the arch of elms that ran on that slope to the river. But after the working man's families, not to mention the noise and pollution from the mills, began to crowd the Patio, Raskob cut his losses and sold the mansion to an order of Catholic priests. The Norbertines turned it into a private boys' school. Archmere Academy was just twenty years old when I moved in across the street.

When I played CYO football that year, our coach was Dr. Anzelotti, a Ph.D. chemist at DuPont who had sons at the school. Archmere let Dr. Anzelotti run our practices on the grounds of the school. From the moment I got within the ten-foot-high wrought-iron fence that surrounded the campus and drove up the road—they actually called it the yellow-brick road—I knew where I wanted to go to high school. I didn't ever think of Archmere as a path to greater glory. When I was ten, getting to Archmere seemed enough. I'd sit and stare out my bedroom window and dream of the day I would walk through the front doors and take my spot in that seat of learning. I'd dream of the day I would score the touchdown or hit the game-winning home run.

I ENTERED THIRD grade at Holy Rosary, a Catholic school half a mile down the Philadelphia Pike where the Sisters of Saint Joseph eased me into my new world. They were the link between Scranton and Claymont. Wherever there were nuns, there was home. I'm as much a cultural Catholic as I am a theological Catholic. My idea of self, of family, of community, of the wider world comes straight from my religion. It's not so much the Bible, the beatitudes, the Ten Commandments, the sacraments, or the prayers I learned. It's the culture. The nuns are one of the reasons I'm still a practicing Catholic. Last summer in Dubuque, Iowa, a local political ally, Teri Goodmann, took me to the Saint Francis Convent—a beautiful old building that looked like it belonged on an Ivy League campus. On the way over we'd stopped by the Hy-Vee to buy some ice cream for the sisters, because Jean Finnegan Biden's son does not visit nuns empty-handed. It reminded me of grade school, of the last day before the holidays when all my classmates would be presenting their little Christmas offerings to the nun. The desk would be a mound of little specialty soaps. (What else do you get a nun?) The sisters smelled like lavender the rest of the year. I don't remember a nun not smelling like lavender.

So I walked into the Dubuque convent with several gallons of ice cream and immediately began to worry we hadn't brought enough. Teri was expecting ten or twelve of the sisters to show up for the event, but there must have been four dozen nuns—many of them from the generation that taught me as a boy—sitting in a community room.

I was there to give a talk about the situation in Iraq, and the sisters really wanted to understand the sectarian conflict there. They peppered me with questions about the Sunnis, the Shi'ites, and the Kurds. They wanted to know about the history of the religion the Kurds practice, and they wanted to know how I educated myself about the concerns of the Iraqi people. Many of these nuns had been teachers; knowledge mattered most. We also talked about our own church, then about women's issues, education, and national security. Whether they agreed with my public positions or not, they all smiled at me. Even after we opened up the ice cream, they kept asking questions. And as I was getting ready to leave Teri asked if the sisters would, in the days ahead, pray for Joe Biden's success in his public journey. But they did more than that. The sisters formed a circle around me, raised their arms up over my head, and started singing the blessing they give to one of their own who is going off to do God's work in the next place. "May God bless you and keep you." The sisters were so sweet and so genuine that it made me feel the way I did when I was a kid, like I was in touch with something bigger than me. It wasn't any epiphany, wasn't any altar call. It was where I've always been. The Sisters of Saint Francis in Dubuque, Iowa, were taking me home.

The nuns were my first teachers. At Holy Rosary, like at Saint Paul's in Scranton, they taught reading and writing and math and geography and history, but embedded in the curriculum also were the concepts of decency, fair play, and virtue. They took as a starting point the biblical exhortation that man has no greater love than to lay down his life for another man; in school we were about ten clicks back from that. You didn't give your life, but it was noble to help a lady across the street. It was noble to offer a hand up to somebody who had less. It was noble to step in when the bully was picking on somebody. It was noble to intervene.

One day at Holy Rosary our teacher, Sister Michael Mary, had to step out of the class. When she walked out of the room, Sonny Deramo threw an eraser, and when she came back, it was still on the floor. "Who did that?" Sister Michael Mary wanted to know. Silence. Nobody said a thing. "Well, you're all staying after school until whoever did it admits it." So I raised my hand. "Sister, I did it." And when the day was done, she sent everybody home except me. "Mr. Biden, you stay after school." I knew what that meant—a hundred times on the blackboard, I'd have to write *The road to hell is paved with good intentions.*

When the rest of the class was gone, she sat me down. "You admitted to doing something you didn't do," she said. I nodded, figuring I was going to be let go. "It's admirable," Sister Michael Mary said, "but you still have to pay for it. You still have to stay after school." Sister made her point, one I never forgot. When you intervene, you have to stand up and take the consequences.

While the priests were for Sunday, the nuns were there every day. Sister Lawrence Joseph would play baseball with us, pulling up her habit and running the bases. I was an athlete, but even held back a grade, I was still one of the smallest boys, and Sister Lawrence Joseph knew I was bothered by my size. So she'd say, "You know, my brother was small too, Joey, but he was a really good athlete." They were always building me up. Almost every teacher I ever had tried to help me with the stutter. Like my mom, they'd remind me I was a good boy, a smart boy, a good athlete. If my classmates made fun of me in class, they stood up for me. They even tried to give me suggestions about how to work through the stutter.

I had devised my own strategies, what I called gaming it out. It required me to anticipate what other people were thinking. In 1955, after my parents bought a new house in a development called Mayfield, I had the neighborhood paper route. I lived in dread of Saturday mornings when I had to go collect from people I was just getting to know. I learned to anticipate the conversation to come. My next-door neighbor was a big Yankees fan, and I'd always check the Yankee box score, because I knew he'd ask, and I knew I'd have to say something without making a fool of myself. I had played out the entire conversation before he opened his front door: "D'ja see Mantle hit two homers yesterday?"

Because reading aloud from the page always made me panic, I'd memorize long passages I knew I'd have to read in school. And one of the nuns suggested I learn to keep a cadence, sort of singsong, so I didn't get stretched out, so the muscles in my face didn't seize up. The nuns were always trying to help. That's why the Sir Walter Raleigh incident surprised me.

After we moved to Mayfield, I transferred to the grade school at Saint Helena's. Seventh grade, like all the years, we sat in rows, in alphabetical order, which meant I was always in the first row, a few chairs back. And when I knew I'd have to read in class, I could anticipate which paragraph would fall to me. If I was the fifth person back, I'd get the fifth paragraph. The one I knew was coming this particular day was this: "Sir Walter Raleigh was a gentleman. He took off his cloak and laid it over the mud so the lady would not dirty her shoes." That day it hit just right. I got the right paragraph. I had it memorized. I had my cadences down. "Sir Wal-ter Ral-eigh was a gentleman—" The nun stopped me short. "Mr. Biden, what is that word?" I could feel myself panic. I couldn't read the words on the page. I just blanked. She wanted me to say gentle-muhn, and I couldn't. "Ju-juju-ju . . ." She cut me off again. "Mr. Bu-bu-bu-Biden . . ." And I could feel a white heat come up through my legs and the back of my neck. It was pure rage. I got up from my desk and walked out of the classroom, right past the nun. I left the school and walked the two miles to Wilson Road in Mayfield. My mom was waiting for me when I got home. The school had already called.

I didn't even get in my front door. "Joey, get in the car." She loaded me and my brother Frank—who was barely walking—into her car and drove toward Saint Helena's. I could tell she was mad. I knew I was in trouble. "Joey, what happened?" she asked.

"Mom, she made fun of me. She called me Mr. Bu-bu-bu-bu-Biden."

When we got to Saint Helena's, Mom grabbed me by the hand and picked up Frank. We headed toward the office to see the principal, Mother Agnes Constance. The principal's office looked like one of those old film noir private eye offices, with wood paneling four feet high and then frosted glass. My mom sat me down in the anteroom, put Frank in my lap, and went in. The sun was shining through, and I could make out the figures. I could hear, too. I heard my mother say, "Can Sister come down?" And she did, and when the nun started to explain what I'd done, I heard my mother cut her off: "Yes, I know that, Sister, but what did you say?"

"Well, Mrs. Biden, I didn't really say any—"

"Did you say Bu-bu-bu-bu-Biden?"

"Well, that's irrelevant," I heard Mother Agnes Constance say. But my mom kept pressing: "Did you say Bu-bu-bu-bu-Biden?"

"Yes, Mrs. Biden, I was making a point."

I could see my mother pull herself up to her full height, five foot one. My mother, who was so timid, so respectful of the church, stood up, walked over in front of the nun, and said, "If you ever speak to my son like that again, I'll come back and rip that bonnet off your head. Do you understand me?"

Then the door flipped open, and my mom grabbed Frankie from my lap. "Joey," she said as she left, "get back to class."

THE ONE THING my mother could not stand was meanness. She doesn't have a mean bone in her body, and she couldn't stand meanness in anybody else. She once shipped my brother Jim off with instructions to bloody the nose of a kid who was picking on smaller kids, and she gave him a dollar when he'd done it. Religious figures and authority figures got no exemption. They abuse their power, you bloody their nose.

You respect the habit, she used to say, you respect the vestments, you respect the uniform, but you do not have to respect the person in it. Years later, when I told my mother I was going to have an audience with the Queen of England, the first thing she said was "Don't you bow down to her." When I told her I was going to see the pope, it was "Don't you kiss his ring." "Remember, Joey," she'd say, "you're a Biden. Nobody is better than you. You're not better than anybody else, but *nobody* is any better than you."

Even when money was so tight the electric company would send a collector to the house to dun us, or when I had to put cardboard in an old shoe until Dad's next payday, nothing flustered my mom. When I was in eighth grade, I got invited to the Presbyterian church for a mixer for all the kids in the public school. I was the Catholic kid; in Mayfield there weren't many Catholic families. I had to wear one of my dad's dress shirts, which were too long, so Mom rolled up the sleeves twice, French cuffs, and then we couldn't find any cuff links. It was Friday night, and my dad was working late, so my mother went to the basement, grabbed the toolbox from on top of the washing machine, and emerged with two nuts and bolts. When she started trying to secure my shirtsleeves with the hardware, I pulled away. "I'm not doing this, Mom!" I said. "I am not going to wear this. The kids will make fun of me."

"Joey," she said, "look at me."

"I'm not doing this. I am not doing this."

"Now look, Joey, if anybody says anything to you about these nuts and bolts, you just look them right in the eye and say, 'Don't you have a pair of these?'"

I said, "Mo-oo-oom! Moo-oom! Don't make me do this."

But in the end I wanted to go to the dance. So I went. And when I was standing at the punch bowl filling a glass, somebody caught a glimpse of my makeshift cuff links. He grabbed me by the arm, held my sleeve up, and yelled, "Look at Biden! Nuts and bolts!"

I could feel the embarrassment in my face, and then the anger. But I remembered what my mom had told me. "You don't have a pair of these?" I said.

There was dead silence . . . until my tormentor said, loud enough for everybody nearby to hear, "Yeah. Yeah, I got a pair of these. I got a pair of these."

About ten years ago my sister, Val, gave me a set of Tiffany's sterling silver cuff links shaped like nuts and bolts to commemorate that dance, and to remind me.

When any of us had a problem, we'd go to Mom and she'd set us straight. I was having a hard time on the school bus one year. I would be the first one on the bus, and then six or seven stops later we'd make a stop and on would get this chubby little girl from a not-so-great house who had freckles and smelled like she came right out of her grandmother's attic. The bus would be nearly empty, but she'd sit down in my seat, right next to me. It was a source of overwhelming embarrassment to me. Everybody made fun of me because everybody made fun of her. I went home one day and took it up with Mom. "I don't know what I'm gonna do, Mom. I mean, the bus is empty, and she sits down next to me, and everybody thinks she's my *girlfriend*."

My mom looked at me and said, "Does she like you?"

"Yeah, Mom. She likes me. *That's* the problem."

And my mom said, "Well, like her back. Anybody who loves you, love them back."

That was the constant lesson in the house, treating people with respect. The other constant lesson was watching out for the family. There's a saying in our family: "If you have to ask, it's already too late." In our house Val, Jimmy, Frankie, and I were expected to look out for one another. "No one is closer," my mom used to tell us.

"You're blood. You're closer to one another than you are to your dad and me. You have the same blood."

We could fight among ourselves inside the house, but we were not allowed to say a single syllable against a sibling on the outside. It was never, ever, under any circumstances—no matter what my brothers or sister had done—appropriate to do anything other than side with them. Going against them would have been like giving secrets to the Russians in the middle of the Cold War. It was traitorous. In grade school the nuns made me a lieutenant on safety patrol and gave me a shiny blue badge. My job on the bus was to report bad behavior. Val transgressed on the bus one day, and at dinner that night I asked my dad what to do. "Everybody knows it," I explained. "I'm supposed to report her."

"She's your sister, Joey."

"But Dad, they gave me the blue badge. I'm supposed to report her."

"Well, Joey, you know that's not your only option."

I knew what I had to do. The next day I turned in my badge.

THERE WAS NO daylight between my mom's philosophy of life and my dad's. She was just more vocal about it. Dad was always quieter; you got the lessons by watching him. The thing he couldn't stand was people who lorded it over the less fortunate. Don't ever talk about money, he'd tell us. And he couldn't stand people who abused power of any kind. He never laid a hand on any of us. "It takes a small man to hit a small child," he'd say. "No man has a right to raise a hand to a woman under any circumstance." Dad worked long hours, but most nights he'd take an hour to drive home and have dinner with us. Dad was the keeper of the rules at the table—our manners were to be impeccable—and he liked to nudge the conversation toward big issues like morality, justice, and equality. From time to time he'd talk about the Holocaust. My dad could never understand how people could be persecuted just for being who they were. "The world was wrong—failing to respond to Hitler's atrocities against the Jews—and we should be ashamed." We each had a personal responsibility, he told us, to speak out when we saw that kind of wrong.

My parents didn't go out much, so it was a big deal when they did. And one year they left Val and me home to babysit Jim and Frank while they went to the Christmas party at the car dealership Dad was managing at the time. The owner of the dealership was a big guy in every way—over six feet tall, with a drawl, big bank accounts, and political connections around the state. He was a self-made man whose billboards advertised him as "the workingman's friend." His trademark was the silver dollar; he'd give silver dollars to all his good customers. That was fine by Dad, but he cringed when the guy paid his employees with sacksful of silver dollars they'd have to lug home. That didn't seem so friendly to the workingman. Dad was cheered when the owner decided to host a Christmas party for salesmen, secretaries, and mechanics. The plan for the party was to clear out the showroom and have a big band there. My dad loved big band swing music. He had been a pretty fair clarinet and saxophone player back in the thirties, and he was a graceful ballroom dancer. So my mom put on her best dress, and they headed out.

My parents had been gone only a few hours—the party should have just been getting going—when they came back through the door. Dad was silent as they went off to their bedroom. We found out the next day that Dad no longer had a job. Mom told us later what happened. During dinner they were seated up at the head table overlooking the dance floor. And before the dancing even started, the owner took a bucket of silver dollars, threw them on the floor, and watched from above as the salesmen, secretaries, and mechanics scrambled around the dance floor scrounging for change. Dad sat frozen for a second, then he stood up, took my mom's hand, and walked out of the party. He'd quit his job in protest.

I DIDN'T NECESSARILY get it at the time, or I didn't acknowledge it, but my father was sort of a fish out of water in Mayfield. We were just the fourth family to move into the neighborhood in 1955, and as three- and four-bedroom split-levels rose around us, they filled with the families of young professionals just starting at the DuPont company. They were all young, college-educated men—chemists, accountants, lawyers. Mayfield was another treeless new development, a big move up from Brookview, but still just a way station for these young men working their way up the corporate ladder to bigger jobs, bigger cars, bigger houses. DuPont meant security for today and better times in the future. The other dads all wore tie clips imprinted with the company trademark: a little oval with DuPont in the center. There was a saying among the DuPont dads: "The oval will take care of you." Like that old saw "You're in good hands with Allstate." "The oval will take care of you."

I always knew my dad was not a company man. He was more or less on his own hook. But he seemed just as confident of his future as the other dads. This is only temporary, he'd say of our house on Wilson Road. My brothers and sister and I never felt any less secure in those days, and America seemed to be remaking itself for our postwar generation. There were new houses, new schools, new car models, new gadgets, new televisions, and new television shows with people who looked just like us. And it all seemed perfectly safe. The threat of Communism sweeping into Mayfield seemed about as likely as Nikita Khrushchev showing up for dinner at the Cleavers' kitchen table.

Mayfield was mostly Protestant, so we had to go a little farther to get to Mass on Sunday, but as a family we were pretty much like everybody else. After Sunday dinner Dad would give me a dollar, and I'd pedal off to Cutler's Pharmacy to fetch a half-gallon of Breyer's ice cream. I'd ride back and we'd all six sit around the living room to watch *Lassie* and *Jack Benny* and *Ed Sullivan*.

But I always had a sense my dad didn't quite fit in Mayfield. I never asked him much about his life, and he didn't offer, but it was strange to open a closet door and see my dad's polo stick, his black leather equestrian boots, his tan riding breeches, and his hunting pinks; to see the home movies of his cousin's big estate on Long Island where Dad had boarded his horses, or the pictures of his favorite jumper, Obediah. There were a lot of things I only heard about later. Once when Jimmy was about eight, Dad took him to the Wilmington airport, rented a Piper Cub, and flew it solo—just the two of them up in the air above the city. They'd go skeet shooting at the Delaware River. When I was in college, my dad took the rest of the family out on a forty-five-foot boat he borrowed, and Jimmy was shocked that Dad knew how to sail. Legend was, my dad once swam *across* the Delaware River. I did see him get on a diving board and do a perfect swan dive. He was the most elegantly dressed, perfectly manicured, perfectly tailored car sales manager Wilmington, Delaware, had ever seen. He was a great dancer. He loved to sing, and he had a thoroughgoing grace; I never saw him flustered in a social setting. But my brother Jimmy—who used to ask my father about his past—always sensed a little melancholy in him.

I remember how my dad used to say to me, "You've got to be a college man." It was so like him, the phrase from another time. "You've got to be a college man." It almost makes me fill up when I think about it. He always regretted not having a college degree, and he felt held back for not having one. He never said it directly, but his message was clear: Joey, they can never take away your degree. There are powerful people who can get you on a string. They can take your job and they can take your money and they can take your pension. But they can't take away your education. My dad and his brother Frank never even started college. No Biden I knew had ever been to college. But the way things had started for him, it didn't look like Joseph Robinette Biden would need a college degree.

My dad was born in Baltimore in 1915, around the time his dad, Joseph H. Biden, had fallen in with a family called the Blausteins, helping them deliver kerosene door-to-door from a special tank rigged on a horse-drawn wagon. When the company anticipated the coming of the automobile age, they turned to gasoline and made a nice little company called American Oil Company (later Amoco). Joseph H. was shipped to Wilmington to run the American Oil operation there. Most summers, though, my father went to stay with his cousin, Bill Sheen Jr., who was like a brother to him. Old Man Sheen, Big Bill, was a tough, hard-drinking Irishman who—we were told—had invented a sealant used for cemetery vaults. The Sheens had an estate in Baltimore hunt country and—without putting too fine a point on it—they were wealthy. Every couple of years Big Bill would go out and buy new Cadillacs for himself, his wife, and his son. For his favored nephew, Joseph Biden, he'd buy the newest Buick roadster. My dad grew up well polished by gentlemanly pursuits. He would ride to the hounds, drive fast, fly airplanes. He knew good clothes, fine horses, the newest dance steps.

So when his own father, Joseph H. Biden, was transferred from Wilmington to Scranton, my dad drove his beautiful new four-hole Buick to Scranton for his last year of high school. He was something the Scranton Catholic schools had never seen, and his classmates gave him a pretty hard time for being such a swell. But my mom—Jean Finnegan of North Washington Avenue—fell head over heels in love. They were married in Scranton in May 1941.

With the war on the way, the Sheens got a big contract to put their sealant on merchant marine ships that left from American ports, and my dad was swept into the new business. Big Bill ran the operation at the Norfolk, Virginia, shipyard; Bill Jr. ran New York; my dad took over the Boston operation. Bill Jr. and my dad lived high. They'd pilot their private planes up and down the eastern seaboard, run over to the Adirondacks to hunt elk, and appear in the kitchen of Manhattan's Barclay Hotel with a brace of quail for the chef to prepare. The Sheens did exceedingly well during the war, and my dad went along for the ride. He ended up with a little money of his own and plans to use it to stake his own future in business. When the war ended I was not yet three years old. We were living comfortably in a nice house in the Boston suburbs, and Dad went into partnership with an old friend to buy a building downtown. They'd planned to have a furniture store. But before the deal was completed, the partner ran off with all the money. And my dad refused to press charges. The money was already gone; besides, the guy had been his friend. "I can't do that," he told my mother. "I'm the godfather to his daughter."

Dad took what money he had left and went into business with another friend who had been a pilot in the war. They bought an airfield on Long Island and started a crop-dusting business. They'd spray the apple orchards in upstate New York and the potato farms on Long Island. We had barely settled in Garden City when that business went bust, too, and Dad had nowhere to turn. His own father and mother had both died. His uncle Bill Sheen was dead also. And his cousin Bill Sheen Jr. had run through his war-won fortune living too well on his Long Island estate.

By the time I was ready to start school in 1947, we were back in Scranton—and broke. Mom, Dad, Val, and I moved to Grandpop Finnegan's house on North Washington, the house where Mom had grown up. Her brother Edward Blewitt (Boo-Boo to us) was still living there, and so was an old maiden aunt, Grandpop's sister-in-law, Aunt Gertie Blewitt. It was not an easy house for my dad. The Finnegan boys used to be pretty hard on him when he was making money, but they didn't let up when he'd lost it. The Finnegans were fond of their Irish grudges, and they didn't easily let one go.

I remember being up in Aunt Gertie's musty room on the third floor one night. She was beside me, scratching my back. "Now, honey," she said, "your father is not a bad man." This, of course, had never occurred to me. "Your father's not a bad man. He's just English. But he's a good man."

My dad was a remarkable man in this way: He understood the world didn't owe him a living. Whatever his past, he was willing to take any kind of work if his family needed money. For almost a year he commuted from Scranton to Wilmington to clean boilers for Kyle Heating and Air-Conditioning. To make extra money he worked in a booth selling pennants and other knickknacks at a weekend farmer's market in New Castle, Delaware. One Saturday my mother decided to surprise my father and take him his lunch. And when she found him at his booth in his pressed tweed jacket, with his elegantly knotted silk tie and his pocket square folded to four crisp points, selling pennants, he was humiliated. It was bad enough that he was doing it; it was worse that my mom had to see it. But she walked up to him, put her arms around him, and said, "I am so proud of you."

My dad taught me the value of constancy, effort, and work, and he taught me about shouldering burdens with grace. He used to quote Benjamin Disraeli: "Never complain. Never explain."

That's how I went about getting into Archmere. My dad wasn't too sure about the Archmere thing because tuition was $300 a year. He'd say, "Sallie's is good, too, you know, Joe. Sallie's is good, too." Salesianum was good, and it was about a third the tuition. There was nothing wrong with Mount Pleasant, either; it was a free public school and about the best high school in Delaware. But I had my heart set on Archmere, and I found out they were willing to do work-study programs for students whose families couldn't swing the tuition. No student had to work during the school year, so they didn't embarrass the boys who didn't have money. But when I passed the entrance exam and got accepted to Archmere, the school put me to work for the summer. There were about ten of us on the Archmere grounds crew, which was run by a raspy-voiced guy named Dominic. So I gave up some of my summer to work on Dominic's crew, eight in the morning to four in the afternoon every day. Dominic lived on the grounds, and worked under the supervision of the headmaster, Father Justin Diny. Dominic was always in a bad mood that summer. *"Goddamn Father Diny!"* The first job Dominic assigned me was weeding the formal gardens next to the big mansion. I weeded the garden for days. Then I washed every window in the mansion. This was not a Windex job but vinegar cut with water, mixed in a bucket . . . and a rag to wipe it and newspaper to dry. There must have been two hundred windows. After that I found myself painting the wrought-iron fence. But when September rolled around, I had earned my place at Archmere.

THE FIRST DAY of school was like a dream. Everything was new. I had new clothes—we wore jackets and ties every day—new notebooks, a new Parker fountain pen, and a dozen new No. 2 pencils sharpened to a gladiatorial point. The bus rolled down past the wrought-iron fence (which gleamed with fresh black paint), through the big stone pillars that formed the front gate, and down the yellow-brick road to Raskob's mansion where the windows shined in the morning light. Upperclassmen were parking their cars down by the old garages and servants quarters, and walking up past the formal gardens toward the front entrance. They looked like college men.

We entered Archmere under the front portico and walked straight into the square central foyer, all marble, ringed with marble columns, under a retractable stained-glass *ceiling*. From the main entrance I could see through to the back patio, then the arch of elms that ran to the Delaware River. Off the foyer were classrooms, a dining room we used for meals and Mass, the office of the headmaster, and the library. I think I gasped the first time I walked into the library. Like the other rooms, it was paneled with rich, dark wood, but it was lined floor to ceiling with books. I thought I'd died and gone to Yale.

Downstairs were the locker rooms—Archmere was a big sports school—and doors of wonder to a fourteen-year-old kid who lived in a split-level in Mayfield. One door led to a bowling alley built by John Jacob Raskob, another to a passageway to the servants' quarters and garages. In the winter we would walk through the secret passageway to the classrooms housed in Mr. Raskob's old garages and servants' quarters. One of my first days at Archmere I got a pass to leave my study hall and go downstairs to the bathroom, and when I got back to the top of the staircase and turned the corner, I heard Father Diny call to two upperclassmen. He was on the raised walk on the outside of the foyer, and the students were a step below. I froze behind one of the pillars to watch. They never knew I was there. Father Diny was in his white habit, with a white cape, and I could hear him say, "A jug for you both." They had walked out of class without a pass to have a smoke, and they were each getting a demerit. Neither one spoke, but one of them must have given Father Diny a look. "You're angry at me, aren't you, Mr. Davilos?" Father Diny said. "You'd like to take a swing at me, wouldn't you, Mr. Davilos?" I was shaking, but Davilos didn't even look flustered. He was on the football team, had to weigh two hundred pounds. Father Diny was about fifty-five years old at the time. But Davilos wasn't stupid.

"My father would kill me if I did," he said.

"Well," Father Diny said, "I'll give you permission."

"Father, you don't want to do this."

"Mr. Davilos," he said as he stepped down off the raised walk to Davilos's level, took off his cape, and handed it to the other boy, "yes, I do. Go ahead, son. Take a shot." Then Father Diny slapped Davilos on the face.

Davilos could not have been thinking. He wound up and took a swing, which Father Diny blocked with his right arm. The headmaster followed with a straight left and a right hook. Davilos went down. Father Diny put his hand out to get his cape back. "Pick up Mr. Davilos and take him to class."

I didn't waste any time getting back to class.

THE START AT Archmere was a hard one for me. I was the second smallest boy in the class, five feet one inch, and just over a hundred pounds. And it didn't take long for my fellow students to pick up on my stutter or the fact that I was the one kid who didn't have to stand up for public speaking our first year. But I didn't want any exemptions, and I didn't want any excuses. I prayed that I would grow out of the stutter, but I wasn't going to leave this to chance. I was going to beat the stutter. And I went at it the only way I knew how: I worked like hell. Practice, practice, practice. I would memorize long passages of Yeats and Emerson, then stand in front of the mirror in my room on Wilson Road and talk, talk, talk. *"Meek young men grow up in libraries . . . Meek young men grow up in libraries . . . Meek young men grow up in libraries . . ."* I'd stare at myself as I talked to make sure I kept the muscles in my face from contorting. That's what really made the other kids laugh, and made me freeze. So if I saw my jaw start to clench, I'd pause, try to go slack, smile, then pick it up again. *"Meek young men grow up in libraries, believing it their duty to accept the views which Cicero, which Locke, which Bacon, have given, forgetful that Cicero, Locke, and Bacon were only young men in li-*

braries, when they wrote these books. Hence, instead of Man Think-ing, we have the bookworm."

At home I had constant encouragement from my mom, but I had a second spur there, too: Uncle Boo-Boo. My mom's brother, Edward Blewitt "Boo-Boo" Finnegan, came to visit us in Wilmington just after Grandpop Finnegan died in 1956, and he stayed for seventeen years. Blewitt was a traveling salesman for Serta, the mattress com-pany, but when he'd come off the road, he bunked in Mayfield with me and my brothers. Boo-Boo could be a great pal. He was a brilliant guy—the only person in the house with a college degree. He'd make me read the *New York Times* editorial page, then sit and argue poli-tics with me and my friends. One day he drove Val and me to Wash-ington, D.C., just to see the Capitol. He walked right up to Senator Everett Dirksen and introduced us.

Like my father, Blewitt could not stand vulgarity. When Jimmy or I started trying out curse words we'd picked up at school, Uncle Boo-Boo would scoff: *Vulgarity is a sign of a limited mind trying to ex-press itself, Joey. Why don't you come up with something more creative in trying to express your displeasure?*

But Uncle Boo-Boo had a terrible stutter his entire life, and he used it as a crutch, an excuse for everything he didn't accomplish. He never married, never had children, and never made a home of his own. He had so much talent, and he squandered it. The day after Pearl Harbor my mom's four brothers went down to sign up for war service. Three of them got in. My uncle Ambrose Jr. was a flier killed in New Guinea. Jack and Gerry did their part. But the army wouldn't take Blewitt. Was it because of his stutter? With a few drinks in him, he would tell me how he really meant to be a doctor. He would have gone to medical school if it weren't for his debilitating stutter. "That's a damn lie, Edward Blewitt Finnegan," my mom would say for all of us to hear. "You could have gone to medical school if it took twenty years." My mom wouldn't accept excuses.

Even as kids we noticed Uncle Boo-Boo drank a bit heavily. And as time went on, he became more and more bitter. If he was being made fun of—"Hu-hu-hu-hu-hey Bu-bu-bu-bu-Blewitt"—he'd hit back hard. "My n-n-n-name i-i-i-i-s F-f-f-f-f-finnegan, ya know. I bet you n-n-n-n-never even heard of *F-f-f-f-Finnegans Wake*! I'll w-w-w-w-wager you don't even know wh-h-h-h-h-o wrote it." Then he'd turn to somebody else and say, "I-I-I-I-I'll w-w-w-w-wager he's never even r-r-r-r-read J-j-j-j-Joyce." He could not stand rich guys. When my dad was making money during the war, he used to remind him he'd never been to college, that no Biden had. "B-b-b-b-Biden's have money, L-l-l-l-Lord Joseph, but the Finnegans have education." He grew more bitter with age and sometimes would even go lax on his own rule about vulgarity. "Money talks, Joey, and shit walks."

I loved Uncle Boo-Boo, but I knew I never wanted to end up like him. So I'd stay in front of my mirror at night, studying my face as I talked: "*A foolish consistency is the hobgoblin of little minds, adored by little statesmen and philosophers and divines.*" "Joey, it's time to go to bed!" "*With consistency a great soul has simply nothing to do. He may as well concern himself with his shadow on the wall. Speak what you think now in hard words, and to-morrow speak what to-morrow thinks in hard words again, though it contradict every thing you said to-day.—'Ah, so you shall be sure to be misunderstood.'—Is it so bad, then, to be misunderstood? Pythagoras was misunderstood, and Socrates, and Jesus, and Luther, and Copernicus, and Galileo, and Newton, and every pure and wise spirit that ever took flesh. To be great is to be misunderstood.*"

I once even tried the old Demosthenes trick. Demosthenes, the greatest of all the Greek orators, I'd read, had been a stutterer, but he taught himself to speak by putting pebbles in his mouth and practicing elocution. The legend, as I remember it, was that he put these pebbles in his mouth, ran along the beach, and tried to make himself heard above the "roar of the sea." We didn't have any beaches or oceans nearby, but I was desperate, so I gave it a try. One of our neighbors in Mayfield was putting a little garden in their backyard, with little paths made of pebbles. So I grabbed about ten of these pebbles and went to the side of our little house, stuck them in my mouth, and tried to throw my voice off our brick wall. For the record, it doesn't work. I nearly swallowed half the pebbles. So it was back to my room, back to the mirror.

I BEGAN TO grow into myself at Archmere, literally. By my junior year I was a foot taller than when I entered. My grades were never much better than solid B's, but I was popular with the girls and with my classmates. In almost any group I was the leader. I was class representative my sophomore year and class president my junior and senior years. I might have been student body president, but Father Diny wouldn't let me run—too many demerits. And I knew not to cross him. If I was going to be a leader, I meant to lead the right way. I made sure to look out for the kid who was being made fun of. I knew how that felt. I'd pick up some freshman who was being razzed and give him a ride home, maybe stop by the Charcoal Pit so he could be seen with me. I took one younger kid to the prom along with my date.

Where I really worked to excel was sports. I was the leading scorer on our undefeated and untied football team my senior year, and I didn't lack for confidence on the field. I still wanted the ball. In our last game in high school, at Friends Central in Philadelphia, we were coasting to an easy win when we got the ball back with just a few minutes remaining in the fourth quarter. I remember our quarterback, Bill Peterman, saying, "This is it, guys. Last possession of our career. We each get the ball once, one chance to score." Counting the quarterback there were four of us in the backfield. He turned to me. "You first, Joe." We were forty-five yards from the goal line. I guess Peterman figured whoever got the ball last had the best chance to score, and he was calling the plays. "Okay, I'll take it first. But you're not getting the damn ball back, Peterman." I must have run 110 yards, zigzagging from sideline to sideline, but I wasn't going down until I got to the end zone.

But my proudest accomplishments at Archmere came where I had the least confidence. My sophomore year, I got up in front of the morning assembly and did my five-minute public speaking requirement—no excuses, no exemptions, just like everybody else. And at our graduation in June 1961, when I stood up on the stage and made the welcome to friends and parents without a single stammer, it was the final confirmation that the stutter was not going to hold me back.

I beat that stutter with a lot of hard work and with the support of my teachers and my family. But I have never really let go of my impedimenta. It's not a heavy load, but it's always with me, like a touchstone, as a reminder that everybody carries his or her own burdens—most of them a lot bigger than mine—and nobody deserves to be made to feel smaller for having them, and nobody should be consigned to carry them alone.

⋆ 2 ⋆

Neilia

SO MANY THINGS ARE COMMUNICATED WITHOUT WORDS, or between words. Being a single parent taught me that. I have never believed that the panacea of parenting was the planning and execution of "quality time." The best memories I have of raising my children are the moments that happened out of the blue, in the quiet spaces of just being together. I remember pulling up to a park near our house in North Star. I was driving my '67 Corvette—top down—and my son, Hunter, who was then four years old, was riding in my lap. Before I gathered him up to head for the swings, I reminded him as I had hundreds of times and for no reason in particular, "I love you, honey."

Hunter looked right at me and then raised his arms and opened them wide. "I love you more than the whole sky, Daddy."

And it wasn't only affection and esteem communicated in the simple act of being there. Kids mirror and mimic the adults they see. They breathe the values of their family as they breathe air. As my own mom likes to say, "Children tend to become what you expect of them."

There's another vivid memory I have of Hunt. It was maybe two years later. In the middle of one of our hang-around days, I put the question to him: "So, Hunter, what do you want to be when you grow up?"

"I want to be important." I knew what he meant.

WHEN I STARTED the University of Delaware in the fall of 1961 and had to declare a major, I chose the subjects that interested me: political science and history. But my plan was to go to law school. I got the idea in the library at Archmere in the spring of 1960 when John F. Kennedy, junior senator from Massachusetts, was heading toward the Democratic presidential nomination. If he made it, he'd be the first Catholic nominated since Al Smith, and while plenty of people said Americans would never elect a Catholic, Kennedy was undeterred. "I refuse to believe that I was denied the right to be president the day that I was baptized," he told a crowd just before he won a decisive victory in the West Virginia primary. My Irish mom was thrilled.

It's not like the Kennedys had a lot in common with the Bidens. Kennedy's father was one of the richest and best-known men in the country. I'd seen the pictures. I knew Hyannisport didn't look much like Mayfield. Senator Kennedy appealed to me in spite of his money. My family never associated with the notion that good works assure a good life. We were always skeptical of the old Calvinistic saw that the righteous are rewarded with earthly spoils.

Kennedy's grace and confidence, his beautiful wife, and his perfect children were not what captivated me, either. That seemed normal. It wasn't his youth or the vigor he projected. It wasn't even the novelty of his ideas. In fact, the thing that struck me about his inaugural address in January 1961 was not the newness of the ideas but how much those ideas rhymed with the lessons I'd learned at Saint Paul's and Holy Rosary and Saint Helena's and Archmere—and especially in my own home. We have to do good works on earth, Kennedy reminded us, because it is our duty: "With a good conscience our only sure reward," he said in closing that day, "with history the final judge of our deeds, let us go forth to lead the land we love, asking His blessing and His help, but knowing that here on earth God's work must truly be our own."

What he said was a powerful public confirmation of the things I'd learned growing up: What we valued most—equity, fairness, and simple justice—were ours to protect, not God's. President Kennedy reinforced for me, as I'm sure he did for many others of my generation, that it was our obligation to try to make our world a better place. It was something I was already thinking about.

Like a lot of teenagers, I had a pair of outlandish Walter Mitty–esque daydreams that filled my head in high school. One was to play professional football. The other was to become an esteemed public figure—who would do great things and earn a place in the history books . . . on the good side. It was a toss-up as to which dream was more ridiculous. In my junior year in high school I weighed 140 pounds, and my family's political connections did not extend to the local school board.

But those sobering facts on the ground did not mute my teenage ardor. During a study hall near the end of my junior year at Archmere, I went to the library, pulled down the Congressional Directory, and started reading through the biographies. I wanted to know who these men and women were who had made it to Washington. How did they get there? What struck me while thumbing through their personal histories was that a lot of them were from wealthy and well-established families. The ones who got there on their own hook were almost all lawyers. So that set my course.

I probably started my first year of college a little too interested in football and meeting new girls. There were a lot of new girls to meet. And after the rigors of Archmere, college was not difficult. Whatever it was, I did not distinguish myself as a scholar. When my first semester grades came out, my mom and dad told me I wouldn't be playing spring football. My dad didn't want me to blow it—"Remember, Joey, you gotta be a college man. They can never take your degree from you." My dad walked into my dorm room one afternoon and found me sprawled out on the bed, wearing a baseball cap. The room was a mess and littered with stolen road signs. There wasn't an open textbook in sight. "So," he said, shaking his head, "this is college."

The first two years, I just didn't buckle down; I was even put on probation for hosing down an RA with a fire extinguisher. I spent a lot of time in the lounge with my friends, where I could always find a good argument. Sometimes it was politics: the civil rights movement, the Bay of Pigs, Kennedy's meeting with Khrushchev, the Cuban Missile Crisis, the future of the free world. But more than that we were focused on our own future. One day I posed this question: "*You guys could be guaranteed—upon graduation—a job at the DuPont company, with a nice starting salary and a job for life, but you would never make more than $40,000 a year (which was no small salary in 1962). Or you could take a job at half the salary, no guarantees, but there would be no limit to the money you could make. Which would you take?*" Most of them chose the security of the sure thing. Spoken just like engineers, I'd tell them. I'm taking the risk.

I was in the lounge arguing when I should have been studying. But I figured all I had to do was graduate in four years, do well on the Law School Admissions Test, and I'd be in law school. I knew I was smart enough. But what good was calculus going to do me? Or physical science?

In the first semester of my junior year I started to get a little worried. I was no longer sure, given the state of my academic transcript, that I could talk my way into a good law school. So I went to see a young professor in the political science department, David Ingersoll. The only way I was going to impress the schools now, he told me, was to demonstrate my abilities. I'd put myself in the hole and had three semesters to make it up. I had to take big loads and do well.

Once I made that commitment, I did it. I carried thirty-seven hours the next two semesters with decent grades, even while taking another run at the football team. I hadn't played for two years, but I surprised the coaches by moving up the depth chart fast. After the annual spring game that April, it looked like I had a shot to start at defensive back. I couldn't wait for next September; I could almost see the fall season unfold in my head. So I was feeling pretty good when I headed to Florida for spring break after our last practice. That trip changed everything.

I drove down to Fort Lauderdale with some friends; I was a little short on cash, so a big group of girls from the University of Delaware agreed to let me stay at their rental house. But after two days on the beach, I was bored. Half the campus was there. It was the same people with fewer clothes, and drunk. And I didn't drink. So the second day I was talking on the beach with a Wilmington friend of mine who was about to graduate, Fred Sears, and another guy from the football team. Fred must have been bored, too. "Hey, Joe, you ever been to Nassau?"

"Uh, no." I'd never been in an airplane.

"Well, for twenty-five bucks we can get a round trip on Caribe Air."

What was left of my $89 tax refund was burning a hole in my pocket, so the three of us decided to go. If we couldn't find a free place to stay, we figured we could just spend a day, turn around, and head back. The next morning we flew to Paradise Island, in Nassau, the Bahamas.

On the way out of the airport we met another group of college guys who agreed to let us stay at the house they were renting. But we didn't hang around there. First day in Nassau, we headed straight to the beach. Paradise Island has beautiful white sand beaches, but we had no passes for any but the public beach. We were the only college students on that beach, and right next to the public beach—cordoned off by a chain-link fence that ran all the way to the water's edge—was this luscious pink pile called the British Colonial Hotel. Through the fence we could see dozens of beautiful young college girls sunning themselves on the British Colonial beach. You had to be a hotel guest to go to that beach, but we were determined to get in. The three of us liberated three towels that guests had hung on the fence to dry, wrapped them around our waists so the British Colonial insignia was in plain sight, and walked past the guards at the main entrance. We walked like we belonged, and it worked.

I'd never been in a place like the British Colonial—it was the Archmere of leisure. We walked out through the breezy atrium toward the back of the hotel and onto the deck of a swimming pool that overlooked the beach. There were college kids roaming all over the place, but we spotted two girls sitting poolside on the chaise longues nearest the beach. One was a brunette, the other a blonde. "I've got the blonde," I said.

"No," said my buddy. "I've got the blonde."

"I've got a coin," Sears said. "You guys can flip for it."

I didn't wait to see who won. I approached the blonde. My other buddy took the brunette. She was very attractive and wore a tight leopard-skin bathing suit, so he didn't seem to be really disappointed. I walked up and sat down on the edge of the blonde's chaise. Over my shoulder I heard my friend hit the wall.

"I'm Mike."

"You're in my sun, Mike."

"Hi, I'm Joe Biden."

"Hi, Joe. I'm Neilia Hunter."

When she turned toward me, I could see she had a beautiful smile and gorgeous green eyes. She was lit by the unforgiving glory of a full afternoon sun, and I couldn't see a single flaw. Basically, I fell ass over tin cup in love—at first sight. And she was so easy to talk to. She was in school at Syracuse University, right down the road from her hometown, Skaneateles, New York. She was just two months from graduation and hoped she'd be teaching at a junior high school in

Syracuse that September. We talked about our parents; her father owned restaurants. We talked about our siblings; she was the oldest, too. While we made small talk, I caught a glimpse of this big boat that was slowing to a stop right in front of the British Colonial beach. I'd never seen a boat that big in person; it must have been forty feet long. I guessed it was a yacht. And as I told Neilia about myself, my family, where I lived—I was sort of fascinated by the yacht. My focus was on Neilia, but I was keeping one eye on this guy on the yacht while he dropped anchor about forty yards offshore. The figure on board dropped a dinghy, hopped in the boat, and began rowing toward shore. With perfect ease he steered the boat right up onto the beach, got out, and started walking toward the British Colonial pool. It looked like he was coming right at me. He was all in white, with a little white yachter's cap and his pant legs rolled up. As he came trudging up the beach in his bare feet, it became increasingly clear he was walking right toward me. And then he was standing over us, squinting into the sun. "Hi, Neilia," he said, and my heart sank. I'm done. This is over. And then he said it: "Are we on for tonight?"

She looked up at him, then at me. "Oh, John, I'm sorry," she said. "Say hello to Joe."

"Hey, Joe."

He was about our age, maybe a bit older.

"Hey, John."

"I'm really sorry about tonight," Neilia said, almost in a whisper, so we both had to bend in closer to hear, "but Joe and I are going to dinner tonight."

I felt my heart go *thumpa-thumpa*, like it was going to jump out of my chest. I mean, I thought we were just talking.

John didn't stick around for explanations. And after he was gone, Neilia started to apologize to me, too. "I hope you don't mind me saying that, but I did not want to go out with him. He's a nice boy—I know him from school—but I really did not want to go out with him tonight." I heard her, but her earlier words were still echoing in my head: *Joe and I are going to dinner tonight.*

"Well," I said, "would you like to go to dinner?"

"I'd love to," she said, again in a whisper, but she said it like she really meant it. "There's a neat little place right around the corner from the hotel."

I had $17 left. And that had to get me home. "Uh, how about somewhere we could get a hamburger?"

"That would be fine, Joe," she said. And I could tell she meant it.

I PICKED HER up at the hotel that night, and she guided us over to the restaurant. It didn't look fancy, thank God; you could order a hamburger from the menu. We talked some more about school, about what we wanted to do when we got out. Mainly we talked about family. After a few hours the dinner was done and the bill came. Nobody had warned me about the island's prices. The bill was $20—with no drinks. This was 1964. The waitress was looming over me, waiting to collect. I could feel myself sweating . . . until I felt a tap on my knee. It was Neilia's hand, and when I put my hand down to meet hers, she handed me two twenties. She must have seen the look of panic on my face. When the waitress walked away to make change, I apologized. "I'm so embarrassed."

"Oh, don't be," she said. "Don't be. That happens a lot to my dad. You shouldn't be embarrassed."

And I wasn't. That was her special touch, the way she made everybody feel okay about themselves. Nobody ever felt smaller around Neilia.

We didn't feel like splitting up after dinner, and Neilia knew of a club where we could see a young Broadway star promoting her new album. Neilia assured me we could go for free because Neilia's friend in the leopard-skin bathing suit was dating the club's owner. So we went to a live show at a little club, and then I walked Neilia back to her hotel. I don't remember my feet touching the ground. At that time of night the parking attendants had put up a chain to keep cars off the service road. Did I pick up the chain so we could walk under it?

No.

I tried to scissors-jump it, caught my foot on the way up, and fell flat on my ass. I could hear Neilia laughing behind me. Then she caught herself. "Are you okay?"

I got up and dusted myself off. "I'm fine. Just embarrassed again."

"Oh, no, don't be. It was so dark you couldn't possibly see."

How could I not love this girl?

I dropped her at the front of the hotel, and on the walk back to my accommodations, I just kept thinking: This Is The One.

I stayed in Nassau the last four days of the vacation, and Neilia and

I saw each other every day and every night. On the fourth day I told her I really didn't have any plans for the following weekend. "Can I come see you in New York?"

"I hope so."

"You know we're going to get married," I told her.

She looked me right in the eye. "I think so," she said in the whisper. "I think so."

WHEN I GOT back to Delaware, I didn't head straight for my dorm room. I stopped by our house in Mayfield instead to deliver the news. Val said I started yelling as soon as I opened the door, before I even walked across the threshold. "Val! Val! C'mere. I found her."

"Found who?"

"I met the girl I'm going to marry."

I told everybody about Neilia. I couldn't quit talking about her. I told Val and Jimmy and Frankie; I told my teammates, my classmates, my parents. My dad could see how it was, and he let me borrow a car off the lot. The next Friday I drove the 320 miles to Skaneateles to see my new girlfriend. The first time I pulled up to Neilia's house on the lake, I realized the Hunters were different from the Bidens. Her dad had done well in the restaurant business. Even in the dark I could see the outlines of the house, and it was huge by my standards. As I walked to the door, I could hear my heart beating. I knocked. The door opened—and there she was in a yellow V-neck sweater. There was music playing, and she was smiling. Over her shoulder I caught a glimpse—through the leaded glass—of the lake. Soft lights sparkled from the docks on the other side. I felt like Fitzgerald's Gatsby—only my vision, my dream, was standing right there within reach.

Being with Neilia at her home was just as easy as being with her in Nassau. We could talk all day and all night, and the talk got to be less and less about the past and more and more about the future. We'd leave off on Sunday night and pick up the next Friday evening. I went up every weekend for the rest of the school year. Mr. Hunter had a boat on the lake. "You water-ski, don't you, Joe?"

"Well, I never tried it," I said, "but I think I could do it."

Neilia told me she could water-ski "a little bit," which I soon found out meant she was a local phenom. So the week before Mr. Hunter took the boat out of winter storage was the only weekend I missed in Skaneateles—because one of Val's friends, Jean Ferry, had agreed to teach me how to water-ski at Harveys Lake in the Poconos. I must have used up twelve gallons of gasoline at Harveys Lake, and I was out on the water for six hours straight one day. "C'mon Joe," Jean would yell. "You had enough?"

"Just a little longer. . . . Let me slalom."

My legs felt like rubber when I finally got out of that lake, but when I went back to Skaneateles the next weekend, I could slalom. By the end of the summer I could take the jump.

I did most of the travel, but Neilia came to Wilmington one weekend to meet Val and Jimmy and Frankie and my parents. My parents threw a big barbecue, and I invited everybody to meet Neilia. Things were a little tight at our house, so Neilia stayed in Val's room, and they hit it off right away. And it wasn't just Val. Everybody in the family approved. Even in a new place, surrounded by strangers, Neilia didn't rattle. She was completely at ease. "This is a great barbecue pit, Mr. Biden," she said to my father. "Oh, it's wonderful."

My parents could tell we were in love—it wasn't hard to see—and they were thrilled for me . . . for us. The Hunters could see it, too, but they weren't quite so sure about it. I could tell her dad liked me, but I think he was getting pressure from his sister, who was a prominent figure in the Presbyterian church in Auburn. One Friday night after the long drive from Wilmington, Neilia met me at the door like she always did, but she pushed me outside. "Wait, Joey," she told me. "Daddy doesn't want me to see you anymore."

I thought I was going to die on the front porch. This is over?

"It's about your being Catholic. But I told him, 'Don't make me choose, Daddy. Don't make me choose.' "

And Mr. Hunter hadn't. He never said anything to me, and he never again said anything to her. If there was any doubt before, now I was sure. I knew we were going to be married. I got a job pumping gas at a nearby marina so I could spend the last month of the summer break in Skaneateles. Then I had to decide about football.

We were expected back for practice two weeks before the fall semester started, which meant I'd have to leave Skaneateles two weeks early. And I realized that if I played football, my weekends were taken. I wouldn't see much of Neilia in September, October, November . . . into December if we made the playoffs.

I called the coach a few weeks before preseason started. "Coach, I'm not coming."

"Who is this?"

"It's Joe Biden, Coach. I'm not going to play this season."

"Biden!? You realize you've got a shot to play this year?"

"I know, Coach, but I'm not coming. I'm not playing. . . . See, I met this girl, and she's at Syracuse—"

Bzzzzzzzzzz was all I could hear. He'd hung up.

I managed to keep my fall semester schedule free of classes on Friday so I could get a jump on the weekend every weekend. When I couldn't borrow a car, I'd hitchhike. I even found a way to finance my trips to visit Neilia. I organized a group of guys to ferry cars for my dad and some of the other dealers around Wilmington—$10 a car. So I'd borrow a station wagon and drive six or seven guys up to the Manheim Automobile Auction near Lancaster, Pennsylvania, every Friday and pay them $5 each to drive a car back down to the dealer lots in Wilmington. They'd hitchhike back to school, and I'd pocket at least $30 every weekend; on a great weekend I'd net $100.

On the drives to and from Skaneateles I'd be alone, and even when I was breaking my own speed record—320 miles in five hours; I was in a hurry now—I had plenty of time to game out the future Neilia and I talked about. Graduation in a year. Law school. The wedding. The children. She wanted five, and that was okay by me. She said she wanted to have them early in the marriage so we'd still be fairly young when they were grown. We talked about a big Tudor-style house with real trees, what the real estate professionals call "mature plantings." I'd be a trial lawyer and build my own firm, then run for public office. Once I had Neilia with me, it became more of a plan than a daydream. Nobody outside my family had ever believed in me the way Neilia did; seeing myself through her eyes made anything seem possible. Now I could see the picture whole, the law firm, the campaign announcement, the speeches, the travel, the victory night, and being in office, being of service. Seeing it meant seeing it all the way to the end. And I could see the moves. I knew how Neilia and I would look, what I'd say, what I wanted to do in office. When I told Neilia, I didn't just talk about holding office, I talked about using the office to make things better for people. And Neilia agreed. We agreed on almost everything. Our life together would be an adventure. "We can do this" was how she'd say it. "I promise you."

The next step was getting into law school, and since Neilia was already teaching in Syracuse, I applied to Syracuse University College of

Law. With Neilia part of my future, I was even more focused; I took my schoolwork more seriously than ever. And I wrote my senior thesis on a congressman from the Hunters' district in New York State. I figured it was prudent to get to know the political landscape in upstate New York in case Neilia really wanted to stay home.

My grades were up the next two semesters, and I did just fine on the Law School Admissions Test. When I shipped my application off in January, I had decent test scores and letters of recommendations from my professors. "Mr. Biden was a late bloomer, but in his last year has shown great promise. . . . Mr. Biden has shown outstanding ability in his recent work. . . . I believe he is coming along better now. . . . I have formed an increasingly high opinion of his general ability and rapidly growing maturity. . . . I would expect him to improve steadily in law school. . . . He seems to be a 'natural' lawyer, able and argumentative, ready to take a position and defend it with strong and well-presented arguments." My want must have been hard to miss. The faculty member who interviewed me at Syracuse a few weeks later deemed me admissible, but what he made note of wasn't so much my academic record as my hunger. "Motivation," he wrote, "seems potent."

In March 1965 the letter arrived at my parents' house in Wilmington—"Dear Mr. Biden: We are glad to notify you that you are admitted to this College of Law to enter September 1965. You will be welcome . . ."—and the first step was complete. But when I sat down and figured out what the first year was going to cost, I came up with $3,600. I had $600 saved up from my summer job, but my dad was strapped. Jimmy was at a public high school, but Val was at the university and Frank was in private school. And Dad had medical and dental bills to contend with. So I applied for financial aid, and my dad had to explain our situation. "I find it almost impossible to contribute more than five to six hundred dollars to his graduate school education. My only regret is that I find this request necessary." The alumni fund picked up half of my first year's tuition, and the State of Delaware picked up the other half, but I'd have plenty of other expenses, which meant I'd have to work, too.

The dean of the law school arranged a job for me as a resident advisor in an undergraduate dorm, and that covered my room and board. In the dorms I became a mentor to a freshman who had a terrible stutter; he also had the worst name I could imagine for a guy with a stutter—Bruce Balmuth from Ballston Spa. I spent a lot of time trying to build up Bruce's confidence; I'd take him to Neilia's and include him with our friends. And I showed him how I beat the stutter, in front of the mirror. By the end of the first term, Bruce could quote as much Emerson as I could.

I still regretted having given up football the previous year, so with some of my classmates I got together a team from the law school and entered the intramural league. My teammates said I went at it like it was an Olympic sport. They must have thought I was over the top when I asked a friend in Wilmington to buy me some Rydell spikes and ship them to me. I couldn't find them anywhere in Syracuse.

The social life was great; most of my classmates were married or, like me, about to be. So we'd get together as couples at somebody's apartment on Friday night. My classmates were pretty good guys, and smart. I was meeting new people from all over the Northeast. One of my best friends at Syracuse was Jack Owens, a Catholic guy from Long Island. Jack had style; I mean he had different clothes for every season. We called him Hampton Jack. If we were going to a football game on Saturday, he'd wear a camel hair cashmere sports coat—and the lining of the jacket matched his pants!

Jack wasn't dating anyone seriously, so Neilia and I talked it over . . . and we agreed. He would be a perfect date for my sister, Val, who was coming to visit for homecoming weekend at Syracuse. Wouldn't it be neat if Jack and Val hit it off? So I put the rush on Jack. *My sister is the greatest. She's so smart. She's so funny. She's drop-dead gorgeous. She was the homecoming queen at the University of Delaware.* Jack agreed to try a date. Val was less sure. I didn't know it at the time, but my sister was secretly pinned to a guy at Delaware. I had to put Neilia on the phone to her. "Val, you'll really like him."

"I'm really not interested, but I'll go out with him one night I'm there—not both nights."

"I promise you, Valerie," Neilia said, "if I could pick any guy in the world for you, it would be Jack Owens."

"One night."

The plan was to go in a big group, five or six couples, from the law school: the homecoming game, dinner, then back to Neilia's parents' house on the lake. The minute Jack and Val met, the sparks flew. Jack was, in Val's felicitous phrase, an arrogant SOB. Jack later told me he thought he could still make out the indentation of Val's homecoming crown. At around eight o'clock that Saturday night he took his leave, explaining that he needed to go to the library to study. "It was nice to meet you," Jack said to Val. He was always polite. "I hope I'll see you again."

"Not if I see you first," Val said.

Joe Biden wasn't hitting the library on very many Saturday nights. To me, law school was like college; all I had to do was get through to graduation, and I could get moving on real life. The work didn't seem so hard, just boring, and I was a dangerous combination of arrogant and sloppy. I'm not sure I even bought all the textbooks I was supposed to have first semester. And I was a less-than-frequent visitor to class. Once a week I'd ride home with Clayton Hale, and he'd hand me his notes to copy.

About six weeks into the first term I botched a paper in a technical writing course so badly that one of my classmates accused me of lifting passages from a *Fordham Law Review* article; I had cited the article, but not properly. The truth was, I hadn't been to class enough to know how to do citations in a legal brief. The faculty put my case on the agenda of one of their regular meetings, and I had to go in and explain myself. The deans and the professors were satisfied that I had not intentionally cheated, but they told me I'd have to retake the course the next year. They meant to put the fear of God in me; the basic message was that I had better show some discipline or I'd never get through the first year. But the dean of the law school wrote a note to the dean who oversaw my work as a resident advisor: "In spite of what happened, I am of the opinion that this is a perfectly sound young man."

I should have been worried, but I found most of the work tedious, and when the grades came out for the first semester, I was in good shape. These were just pencil grades, given as a measure of how we were doing halfway through our yearlong classes. Only the final test at the end of the year would really count. But I'd done well enough that I knew I wouldn't have to be a grind. There was work. There was play. There was Neilia. I thought I could have my time with Neilia, work as a resident advisor at the dorms, help Bruce, spend hours practicing touch football, and then play frantic catch-up before exams. I was always a quick study, and I liked the romance—the rush—of being able to keep all the balls in the air . . . until I panicked. It was ten days before the final exams—the only thing that really counted the whole year—when I realized I had put myself in too big a hole. I had ten days to cram for the entire year. It was the first time in my life I ever drank coffee.

Neilia devised the strategy. There were four big classes I had to pass: Contracts, Property, Torts, and Criminal Law. I would do the notes and study sheets for Contracts and Property. Neilia would take my notes—and Clayton's—and do study sheets for Torts and Criminal Law. Her study sheets were so detailed, and the mnemonic devices she invented so clever, that I cruised through the exams in Torts and Criminal Law. I flunked Contracts; I might have done the same in Property, but the professor died and they passed everybody in the class. Jack, who did well in law school, told me later he would have flunked, too.

So, together, Neilia and I had made it through the first year, and several weeks later we had a big wedding in Skaneateles; the Hunters made it an event. My entire family came up—Dad, Mom, brothers and sister, Uncle Boo-Boo, Uncle Frank, cousins—and my closest friends from law school, college, and Archmere. Two of my running buddies from Scranton—Larry Orr and Charlie Roth—were ushers in the wedding. After the ceremony Mr. Hunter had a catered reception for close friends and family at their big house on the lake. That afternoon there was a big reception at the country club for the wider circle of the Hunters' friends. But the most generous thing Mr. Hunter did for me was at the church itself that day. Neilia understood how important it was to me to be married by a Roman Catholic priest, and she'd agreed to it. Mr. Hunter acquiesced, but I don't think it was easy for him. I've never seen a man so nervous going into a church as Mr. Hunter was. He's there in our wedding movies, standing in his tails at the threshold of the Catholic church, holding his hands behind his back. They were in a constant and terror-stricken tremor. His daughter was marrying a Catholic, a guy with almost no money . . . and a Democrat. But Mr. Hunter showed me in a hundred small ways that if Neilia had endless faith in me, his faith in me would match. If she was willing to take a chance on me, he was, too.

I continued to have trouble keeping a focus on the most tedious of the classwork, but where I was engaged—federal jurisdiction, legislation, international law—I got high marks. The closer I got to graduation, the surer I was about being a trial lawyer. I won a small-fry moot court competition in Kingston, Ontario, and I fondly remembered getting an ovation from classmates after giving an answer in Torts. What had terrified me in grade school and high school was turning out to be my strength. I found out I liked speaking in public. With all that practice quoting Emerson, I could memorize long passages; I never had to look down and read a text. So when I talked, I could watch an audience for their reaction. If I felt myself losing them, I would extemporize, tell a joke, focus in on a single person who wasn't paying attention and call him out. I fell in love with the idea of being able to sway a jury—and being able to see it happen right before my eyes.

But as my last year was winding down, Neilia and I still hadn't settled on where we were going to live, so I hadn't accepted a job. And when we visited my parents in Wilmington that Easter break, my dad seemed anxious . . . and anxious to help. A friend of his in the car business had a son who was a superior court judge. And Judge Quillen, my dad said proudly, was willing to give me some advice. So on that Saturday morning I put on a suit, grabbed a couple of my law school résumés, and went to see the judge at his office downtown. Bill Quillen was Harvard Law, class of '59. He'd been a special assistant to Delaware governor Charles Layman Terry, who named him—at age thirty-one—to the judgeship. In 1968, Judge Quillen was still only in his thirties. In his chambers that morning the judge asked me what I wanted to do, and I told him I wanted to try cases. I wanted to be a litigator. "The best trial firm in Delaware is Prickett, Ward, Burt & Sanders," he said, picking up the phone. "My college roommate at Williams was Rod Ward. He's a partner there." A few hours later I was sitting in Winkler's Restaurant, looking across a white tablecloth at Rod Ward. As I handed him my résumé, he was all smiles. And why wouldn't he be? He was young, too, and he had an air that said he'd never been knocked off his pins, and he never would be. He was Old Delaware, with a big house in hunt country.

Ward took a long look at my résumé, which didn't sparkle with academic achievement, and noted my photograph in the right-hand corner. "Obviously you're hoping to get a job based on your good looks," he said. He was a wise guy, but he was still smiling. "So, Joe, why should we hire you?"

I smiled back, but I couldn't hold my tongue. "Enamored as you are of prestige," I said, "you'd probably want to hire me." What the hell? I knew they weren't going to hire Joe Biden.

Several weeks later I got a letter in the mail from William Prickett, Esq., senior partner of Prickett, Ward, Burt & Sanders. Mr. Prickett was famous for numbering every paragraph. The letter went something like this: *(1) Mr. Biden, your credentials are not very impressive, but we'll take a chance on you. (2) We will offer you a job at $5,200 per year. If you pass the bar, we will pay you $8,000 a year. (3) Please let us know.*

I've wondered over the years why William Prickett was willing to take a chance on me. He was hiring from Georgetown, Harvard, Yale. Why should he even consider a guy about to finish seventy-sixth out of eighty-five at Syracuse? Did Rod Ward think I cut such a fine figure at Winkler's that day? Was my intellect and drive so unmistakably remarkable? Probably not. But all my life I'd been surrounded by people who expected big things of me, and I believe I carried the best of those expectations with me.

Years after I got that unlikely job offer, I had occasion to look back at my law school files and came across letters of recommendations from my professors. "Mr. Biden has shown himself to possess the confidence and capabilities which would enable him to become an outstanding trial attorney," Dean Robert Miller wrote. "He is endowed with the ability to think quickly in a logical manner while on his feet and then articulating those thoughts. He is also capable of doing penetrating, analytical research and formulating this on paper."

"In recitation, [Mr. Biden] exhibits a sharp and incisive intellect and a knowledge of the particular subject under inquiry," wrote Professor James Weeks, who taught the technical writing course that nearly sunk me my first semester. "He knows what he is doing and appears to possess a highly developed sense of responsibility. He is the type of individual one is more than willing to take a chance on, for he is unlikely to sell short your expectations."

Something That Will Last

WHEN I TOLD FRIENDS I WAS GOING TO ACCEPT THE JOB offer in Wilmington, one of them pulled out the old joke: "If you can get Mr. Biden to *work* for you, you will be indeed fortunate." I saw the humor, but this wasn't fooling around time anymore. This was real life now, and I was ready to work. I studied hard for the Delaware bar, cramming three years of law school into three months. By then Neilia and I knew she was pregnant—due in February 1969. We were going to be a family, and I had to start thinking about what kind of home we wanted to live in. Actually, I'd thought about houses quite a bit already. My idea of Saturday fun was to jump in the Corvette with Neilia and drive around the Wilmington area scouting open houses, houses for sale, land where we could build.

Even as a kid in high school I'd been seduced by real estate. When the school bus to Archmere turned off the main road, Marsh Road, to pick up the kids from the upscale neighborhood, I was always impressed by the beauty of the homes. To me there was no place more alluring than Westwood Manor. The houses in my neighborhood, Mayfield, had sprouted just a few years earlier from what had been a flat and treeless farm field. There wasn't a spot of shade in the neighborhood. The streets were smooth, fast, and narrow—built for speed. They were great for bike races and whiffle ball. But everything there felt squared off, as if in perfect obeisance to the new suburban God of Right Angles. Uniformity ruled. Every roof had the same pitch. But

Westwood Manor had wide looping streets dappled by light from morning to evening. Sixty- and seventy-foot elms and oaks stood in quiet splendid grandeur. The lawns were green and manicured and sloping. The houses weren't all square boxes of brick and wood. There were slate roofs, bowed windows, rounded turrets, generous arcs of cut stone, and what must have been thousands of square feet of stucco. My dad always talked about our house on Wilson Road in Mayfield as just temporary, a way station. The houses in Westwood Manor looked like forever. I drive through there today and it looks like a nice middle-class neighborhood, nothing special. But in 1955, Westwood Manor felt like a place with a special connection to history and tradition, a place with a past, a place of perfect shelter. In the cold, damp winters I could almost picture the hearth in one of the Tudors I liked best, and I could almost imagine my own family in front of a great stone fireplace, in the warm glow of comfort.

When Neilia and I arrived back in Wilmington in the summer of 1968, I knew we couldn't afford Westwood Manor, and I wasn't going to take any chances buying a house until I passed the bar. So we rented a little yellow farmhouse on Marsh Road. Neilia and I started looking at houses in Wilmington right away, and the kind of house I'd been pining for since high school seemed within our reach.

I COULD TELL from the day I entered the offices of Prickett, Ward, Burt & Sanders that this was a firm that could afford to take a chance on a guy from Syracuse with lousy marks. Prickett, Ward represented big insurance companies, railroads, construction companies, and oil companies. Their clients had enormous resources. They could pay for squads of investigators on any big case. And I started with a full head of steam. I meant to make their gamble pay, and I think Mr. Prickett saw something in me. He asked me to be in charge of the Christmas party that the firm hosted every year for Delaware's Young Republicans. Some people at the firm started suggesting I join the Young Republicans. I didn't tell them I could never join a party that was headed by Richard Nixon or that I wasn't comfortable representing the firm's bread-and-butter clients, which were big corporations. I wasn't at the firm long.

The break came in the federal court on Rodney Square in downtown Wilmington when Mr. Prickett invited me to watch him make an argument in a civil suit one morning. Our firm was representing a company that was being sued by one of its workers. The plaintiff was a welder who had been badly burned on the job. But in his testimony the afternoon before, the welder had apparently admitted that in order to squeeze into a tight work space he had decided not to put on his safety clothes.

Mr. Prickett's argument the morning I was with him was straightforward: the welder had been negligent. And under the law, his contributory negligence meant that the judge could simply find for our client without our putting on a defense before a jury. When Mr. Prickett made his argument for the directed verdict that morning, he was using the relevant law and representing our client well. But as he spoke to the bench, I couldn't take my eyes off the plaintiff's family. The welder and his wife were about the same age as Neilia and I. And I remember his wife simply stopped looking at the bench and stared down at her feet while Mr. Prickett made his argument. The judge didn't grant Mr. Prickett's motion right away, but asked Mr. Prickett to write a brief and then called a recess in the trial.

I walked alone down the steps of the federal courthouse and across Rodney Square, with a pit in my stomach. I didn't think Mr. Prickett had done anything immoral or unethical. In fact, he was doing his job. But I couldn't get the picture of that young family out of my head. The plaintiff had been disabled and permanently disfigured and there was a possibility he would get *nothing*. I wasn't built to look the other way because the law demanded it. The law might be wrong. I felt like I should have been representing the plaintiff, that my place was with people who were outside the reach of the system. By the time I got to the center of Rodney Square, I had decided to quit Prickett, Ward. And it was liberating. I was confident Neilia would back me. I didn't feel like I was walking away from something; I felt like I was walking toward a purpose.

Downtown Wilmington was a strange place at the end of 1968. The city had been under martial law for nearly six months. The Democratic governor, Charles Terry, had called out the National Guard when rock and bottle throwing escalated to sniping, looting, and arson in the days following Dr. Martin Luther King's assassination the previous April. Every day I went to work at Prickett, Ward, I walked by six-foot-tall uniformed white soldiers carrying rifles. Apparently they were there to protect me.

Even seven months after the rioting ended, Governor Terry refused to call off the Guard. The mayor of Wilmington asked him, but still Terry refused. That fall the national news cameras would show up occasionally to do stories about the only American city where the National Guard was still out patrolling predominantly black neighborhoods. The white citizens the TV reporters interviewed were almost all happy to have the Guard there. They were afraid riots might ignite in the ghetto and then spread from there. They were afraid Wilmington's police force wasn't big enough to keep it contained. Generally, they were afraid. So they agreed with Governor Terry when he said the National Guard was about maintaining law and order, and citizens might have to give up a little freedom to secure the peace.

But in the black neighborhoods of East Wilmington, residents were afraid, too. Every evening National Guardsmen were prowling their streets with loaded weapons. Curfews were in effect from dusk to dawn. Mothers were terrified that their children would make one bad mistake and end up dead. The locals called the nightly National Guard reconnaissance rounds "rat patrols." "They patrol our streets like we're animals," black citizens would say. "They take away our pride."

The nightly news had a way of making these stories seem like a conversation between the races in Wilmington, but I knew blacks and whites weren't talking to one another. Most white people out in Mayfield or Westwood Manor or Ardencroft probably never spoke to a black person in 1968. And I'm sure only a minuscule percentage of the forty thousand black citizens of Wilmington had any significant interaction at all with white people. I knew that from my experience at a swimming pool in an inner-city neighborhood where I worked as a lifeguard one summer.

I'd worked there back in the early sixties, when freedom rides, sit-ins, and Bull Connor's dogs and fire hoses were starting to get people's attention. Like everybody in America in those years, I was getting dramatic lessons about segregation and civil rights from newspapers and television. But I'd say my most valuable lessons about what divides people—and what unites them—I learned as a nineteen-year-old college kid at Prices Run Swimming Pool in the summer of 1962.

Prices Run was always packed in the summer. There wasn't a lot of air-conditioning in the nearby housing projects in those days, so the

pool was the one place to cool off in the blazing Wilmington summers. Of the dozen lifeguards working at the pool that summer, I was
the only white guy. Of the hundreds of people who swam at Prices
Run every day, few were white—with one notable exception. At some
point almost every day an old Navy salt named Bill Wright would
show up to service the big machinery of the pool works. So I was a
fascination to everybody at Prices Run. Most of the people I got to
know there had literally never really talked to a white person.

The younger children liked to splash water on my legs, then sit and
watch my hair curl as it dried in the sun. (Some of those boys came to
visit me the next year when I was a park director in an Irish neighborhood. They got the hell beat out of them for drinking out of a water
fountain.) The other lifeguards invited me to play on their basketball
team. We'd drive over the Third Street Bridge to play the guards from
the Riverside Pool, and I'd be the only white guy on the court. Sometimes my friends would tell me about being forced to sit in the bal-
conies at the segregated movie theaters downtown.

Every day at lunchtime we'd sit in the key room and talk. The guys
would ask me what white girls were like or if they could borrow my
Bass Weejuns for their date that night. But most of all I remember the
stories they'd tell about how they were treated by whites day in and
day out. Every day, it seemed to me, black people got subtle and not-
so-subtle reminders that they didn't quite belong in America. It was a
dozen small cuts a day. The stories my friends at the pool told were always tinged more with confusion and pain than outright anger. I
thought about it the next year when Dr. King's letter from a Birmingham jail was published in answer to the sympathetic local clergy—
white and black—who were asking him to be less confrontational, to
show a little patience:

> When you suddenly find your tongue twisted and your speech
> stammering as you seek to explain to your six-year-old daughter
> why she can't go to the public amusement park that has just been
> advertised on television, and see tears welling up in her eyes when
> she is told that Funtown is closed to colored children, and see omi-
> nous clouds of inferiority beginning to form in her little mental sky,
> and see her beginning to distort her personality by developing an
> unconscious bitterness toward white people; when you have to con-

coct an answer for a five-year-old son who is asking: "Daddy, why do white people treat colored people so mean?"; when you take a cross-county drive and find it necessary to sleep night after night in the uncomfortable corners of your automobile because no motel will accept you; when you are humiliated day in and day out by nagging signs reading "white" and "colored"; when your first name becomes "nigger," your middle name becomes "boy" (however old you are) and your last name becomes "John," and your wife and mother are never given the respected title "Mrs."; when you are harried by day and haunted by night by the fact that you are a Negro, living constantly at tiptoe stance, never quite knowing what to expect next, and are plagued with inner fears and outer resentments; when you are forever fighting a degenerating sense of "nobodiness," then you will understand why we find it difficult to wait.

I understood better what Dr. King was saying for having talked to my friends in the key room at Prices Run Swimming Pool.

The only real trouble I ran into that summer was early in the season. A couple of "gangs" hung out at the pool, including one I thought I heard calling themselves the Romans. The Romans, like everyone else who wore pomade in their hair, were required to use bathing caps when they went in the pool. They were typical teenage guys who spent a lot of time at the diving tower in the deep end. And one day a Roman called "Corn Pop" wouldn't stop bouncing on the high board. That was one of the clear rules at the diving boards, and I guess I wanted everybody to know I wasn't an easy mark. So I whistled to him and told him to stop the bouncing. He didn't stop. So I whistled again. "Hey, Esther! Esther Williams!" I yelled, loud enough for everybody to hear the joke. Esther was the queen of the fifties water spectacular movies. "Get off the board, man. You're out of here." And I threw him out of the pool.

The other guards told me Corn Pop would be waiting for me outside the chain-link fence and that he'd probably have a straight razor to use on me when I went for my car. The story was that a few years earlier the former white captain of the lifeguards had been cut so badly that he'd required forty stitches to close up his back. So I decided to call the park police to escort me to my car. But Bill Wright was there that day, and he told me that if I made that call, I'd never be able to come back to the pool again. He pulled out a piece of chain from the pool room and cut a six-foot length, wrapped it around my arm, then wrapped a towel over the chain. He told me exactly what to say when Corn Pop came at me: "You might cut me, Corn Pop, but I'm going to wrap this chain around your head before you do."

And that's exactly what I said to him when he confronted me at my car. But I didn't stop talking there. I really did not want to get cut. And I thought I had learned something inside that key room: I thought I knew what Corn Pop deserved to hear. "By the way, I owe you an apology," I said, again loud enough for everybody to hear. "I should have never called you Esther Williams. That was wrong. And in front of all your friends, I sincerely apologize. But if you bounce on the board like that again, I'm still going to throw you out."

We both put our weapons away, and we ended up being friends. Corn Pop and the Romans looked out for me the rest of the summer.

So in 1968 when I heard the people from the inner-city complain about the way they were being treated by Governor Terry and the National Guard, I knew what they were saying. Did they have the same constitutional protections as the folks in Westover Hills or Mayfield? Did they have the same freedom of movement as the people in the white neighborhoods nearby? Did they have the same right to a sense of security in their own neighborhood as white America did? I thought the folks in those neighborhoods deserved at least that much. I didn't think I could change the world in 1968 or even what was happening, but I thought I could make a difference. So I walked across Rodney Square and into the basement of a three-story building, and applied for work in the public defender's office. The Supreme Court decision in *Gideon v. Wainwright* five years earlier had said that no defendant should be forced to go to trial without a lawyer. If a defendant couldn't afford one, the state would foot the bill. This seemed like God's work to me. Being a public defender was never easy, but it was the first time I felt like I was an actor in upholding the Constitution. Most of the clients I drew were poor African Americans from East Wilmington, and whether they were guilty or innocent, I did my best to make sure they were well represented at trial.

But I got a real lesson in the criminal justice system from day one. While I was still in the middle of my orientation at the criminal courts, a judge assigned me to a case the next day. I protested that I was not even officially on board yet, that I didn't know anything about the case and I wouldn't have any time to prepare. The judge looked at the robbery defendant, who was in handcuffs and ankle chains, and asked him if I'd be okay. "Ones's as good as another," he said.

BUT IT TURNS out that God's work wasn't full-time work in 1969. The new public defender's office wasn't well funded yet, so they could use me only about half-time. But they suggested I check in at a law firm called Arensen & Balick. Sid Balick was one of the most respected criminal defense lawyers in the city, but he was known as a soft touch. He did a lot of pro-bono work and a lot of hard cases. As long as I was doing public defender work, I couldn't try any criminal cases for Arensen & Balick. But he was overwhelmed with civil litigation, and most of it was on a contingency basis, which meant that if we won, we got paid, but if we lost, we didn't.

I learned how to be a good lawyer watching Sid Balick. By the time clients got to Sid, they were probably really, really desperate and in trouble. We were representing people who didn't have much margin. Something had gone wrong, and now they had their backs to the wall. If they'd lost their car in an accident and the insurance company wasn't going to cover it, they couldn't get to work. Any injury or illness that affected their ability to work would upend an entire family. Most of them weren't covered by unemployment insurance or workers' compensation. They had no way to pay the bills. Sid taught me how to help people in the toughest spots in their lives. Beyond good legal help, they needed to be reassured enough to get them past the panic. Sid showed me the importance of putting my arm around clients and letting them see that somebody was on their side. If it was a guy in a conservative dark suit and tie, all the better.

The other thing I learned from Sid was how to focus a jury, or an audience. In criminal cases he'd often be defending men who must have really frightened some of the jurors we drew, but Sid knew to make a jury bear down on the facts of the case. "Now folks," he'd tell the jurors at the beginning of a criminal trial, "you've got to keep your eye on the ball. The prosecutor is going to try to tell you a lot of bad things about my client that aren't particularly relevant to the case at hand. Now, if you just look at my client, you might think he's not a particularly attractive guy. Maybe he's not someone you'd invite home to dinner. Maybe he's not someone you would want your daughter to go out with. But that's not the issue. The issue is, did he commit this robbery? I want you to keep your eye on the ball. The prosecutor is going to continue to focus on why you shouldn't like this guy. But that's not your sworn responsibility. Your sworn responsibility is to determine whether the evidence proves—beyond a reasonable doubt—that my client committed this particular crime."

Sid Balick also swept me into an organization called the Democratic Forum, which was trying to reform the Democratic Party in Delaware. Governor Charlie Terry's martial law in Wilmington was a symptom of a bigger problem. The state party wasn't keeping up with the mainstream national Democrats who were becoming more and more progressive on race. A lot of Democrats in Delaware were still fighting school integration and open housing for blacks. So every Wednesday night I'd leave my office on Market Street and walk half a block to the Pianni Grill to meet with a group of people who believed they could remake the Delaware Democratic Party. I was practicing law I believed in, and I was getting involved in politics. I was right where I wanted to be.

JOSEPH ROBINETTE BIDEN III—we called him Beau—was born in February 1969, and three months later Neilia was pregnant again, so it seemed like the right time to focus on looking for a house. But I found that the more involved I got in real estate, the more complicated my life became. First I borrowed some money from Neilia's dad and bought a little house in Newark, Delaware, but that was just a rental property, to make some money and flip. But before we could do that, Neilia and I found a house on Woods Road in Wilmington—it wasn't a Tudor like we'd wanted, and it might have been a bit too expensive, but we thought it would be a shame to lose it. So I talked to my dad, and we decided that he'd buy the house on Woods Road, and he and my mom would move there. I'd buy his house on Wilson Road in Mayfield, and Neilia and I would move there to save up more money. My parents did move to Woods Road, but before we moved to Mayfield, I heard about a deal on a little cottage on seventeen acres. We could live there rent free! All we had to do was manage the private swimming club on the grounds. So I rented out the house in

Mayfield to a doctor and his wife and took over management of the Country Club Swimming Pool.

The cottage was a little cramped, especially after Robert Hunter Biden was born in February 1970. But I convinced the board of the swim club to allow me—at my own expense—to expand. And with help from the rental income from Newark and Mayfield, I was able to make a little addition on the cottage. Alas, Beau was still sleeping in a closet, so we kept up our hunt for the perfect house. And the more we looked, the more Neilia and I thought we might like to have some land. So when we found a farm twenty-five minutes away in Elkton, Maryland, we jumped. That was going to be our estate: eighty-five acres to grow on, with a half-acre pond and a long dirt road leading to a small, beautiful old stone house. The house was going to take some work—well, a lot of work . . . but there was room on the property to make a Biden family compound. I was going to line the drive with trees to make a leafy overhanging canopy, like Archmere. Val could build a home there. Jimmy and Frankie, too. It would be a perfect spot for Mom and Dad to retire. We paid $55,000 for the farm, which was a stretch, but I sold off about thirty acres to an old high school friend who wanted to make a Christmas tree farm. Then I shipped Jimmy out to do some painting and general clean-up before I got the money together for the big renovation. In the meantime, Jimmy found me a group of college students who were looking to rent a place. The University of Delaware was just down the road.

Now Neilia and I had three rental incomes to finance a future renovation of the Elkton farm. She was teaching at a local Catholic grade school. And we were still living in the rent-free cottage and managing the pool. I was probably the only working attorney in Delaware who lifeguarded on Saturdays.

I HURRIED HOME to Neilia and the boys most nights, but I tried not to miss the Democratic Forum's Wednesday meetings at the Pianni Grill, and I guess I hung around enough that I seemed useful. One of the senior members showed up at my office one day to ask if I'd consider running for the New Castle County Council. The district I lived in, he told me, was almost 60 percent Republican—it included Westover Hills—but it had Democratic strongholds in the working-class precincts. The guys at the Forum thought I might be an attractive candidate.

I had no great interest in being a county councilman. I wasn't even sure what the job was. And I had been talking to Neilia about starting my own law firm. "I can't do it," I told the envoy from the Forum. "I just don't have time to be running to Dover." I assumed the council met in the capital city.

He looked at me like I must be joking. Then he walked to my window, pulled back the curtain, and pointed to an office building. "On the other side of that building is where New Castle County Council meets on Tuesday and Thursday nights."

"Oh."

So I went home that night and told Neilia I thought I'd like to run for county council. I explained it was a Republican district, so I probably wouldn't win, but I'd be doing the party a favor and I'd learn a lot, which had to be a good thing for somebody who wanted to make a more serious run later on. She had only one question, as always: "Joey, do you think you can do this?"

"Yeah."

"I think we can, too. Let's try it."

I asked my sister, Val, if she'd run the campaign, and she said, "There's a county council?"

Valerie Biden did not go into any race to lose, Republican district or no. She was a methodical organizer. She got voter records going back several elections, had an index card for every block in every neighborhood, and started recruiting block captains. I spent most of my time in heavily Democratic precincts such as Elsmere, Newport, and Stanton. But I also spent a great deal of time going door to door in the middle-class neighborhoods like the one I grew up in. They were overwhelmingly Republican in 1970, but I knew how to talk to them. I understood they valued good government and fiscal austerity and, most of all, the environment. I promised them to try to check the developers and fight to keep open space. And those middle-class voters were key for me. The November 1970 elections were a washout for the Democratic Party in Delaware, but I won election to the county council by two thousand votes.

NEILIA AND I could both feel our life beginning to pick up speed. Everything was happening faster than I expected, but I wasn't going to stop the rush. County council took up two full nights a week, and the prep work took up more and more time as I got involved in issues I really cared about and where I thought I·could have impact. Growth in New Castle County had been accelerating for decades. The television show *Candid Camera* had recently had a little fun with the state. "The people of Delaware are doing something about population explosion," the host explained as the camera showed two official-looking guys at an intersection on Delaware's northern border. They held up a big sign, DELAWARE CLOSED TODAY, and they were stopping motorists at a roadblock and turning them back. *Try New Jersey. It's open.* A lot of drivers did turn back. One poor guy pleaded to be allowed to wait until somebody left and then be let in, like a fair trade. But by 1971 things weren't that funny. There was almost no check on development in New Castle County. In the unluckiest neighborhoods, overloaded sewage systems were backing up, filling up residents' bathrooms and basements, blowing manhole covers on the streets. Christina Marsh was being threatened by raw sewage. Shell Oil had quietly bought fifty-four hundred acres on the water near Delaware City, and they were racing to build a second oil refinery on the coast. The federal highway department was handing over money for huge projects to turn arterial roads into federal superhighways. While very little federal money was being set aside for the sort of mass transit that would reduce air pollution, the state was perfectly willing to pave over porches, tree houses, sidewalks, flower gardens, and grocery stores to make a ten-lane superhighway to speed big trucks from Pennsylvania and New Jersey through the county and then to Maryland and points beyond.

My first year on the county council I became known as the guy who took on the builders and the big corporations. I was all for businesses creating jobs and wealth, but I thought the companies that would profit owed a fair accounting of the real costs. "Let Shell prove to us they won't ruin our environment," I'd say. "If they can't prove it, we'll rezone them right out of here." Years later my stance would have made me a "smart-growth guy." What a lot of people called me in 1971 was a no-good SOB who was stopping progress.

The county council took time at night, but my days were spent trying to build a law firm. I borrowed money through the bank that financed all the cars where my dad worked, brought in two other lawyers, leased offices on Market Street in downtown Wilmington, and became a small businessman.

Neilia, Beau, Hunter, and I were still living in the cottage, and I was still managing the pool. Even in the winter there were things that had to get done. Neilia and I had to arrange for new drinking fountains, get the phone company to do a hookup in the guard shack, find a contractor to replace gutters and downspouts, and another one to locate and repair the leak in the pool, and another one to repair the railings at the men's end of the bathhouse.

Each of the properties we owned had its own separate headaches. The tenants at the farm in Elkton were complaining that the well went out, so I had to put that back on line, even though I didn't have the $600 to spare. Besides being in debt to Neilia's dad for the seed money on the first house, we were carrying three mortgages. I was in constant danger of falling behind, especially when the college guys who were renting the house in Newark didn't pay their rent. I'd spend otherwise billable hours every month on letters to tenants. "It puts me in a precarious financial position when you fellows don't pay" was a typical plea. "To get right down to it, I need money quickly. Please get in touch with me this weekend so that we can make some definite arrangements and I can get myself out of the hole."

The Joe Biden family was spread thin in every way, but the way Neilia and I saw it, it was just temporary. This was an adventure of our own making. We were building something big, something permanent. And I was running hard to put everything in place. On a free Saturday, Neilia and I would pack Beau and Hunter into the back of the Corvette in Moses baskets and go looking for the perfect house. And on one of those drives, on a winding country road up near the Pennsylvania state line, we saw it: The House of Our Future. The minute we saw it, we both knew we had to have it: 228 North Star Road was a sloping and wooded four-acre lot in the village of North Star, Delaware, about twenty minutes north of Wilmington. There was the house, and there was an old barn with a pool and a bathhouse in back. The house itself was a center-hall Colonial—literally, a Colonial—built in 1723, stucco over stone, with high ceilings, and in move-in condition. We wouldn't have to do a thing. Neilia and I didn't hesitate. We made an offer the last week in February 1971 and had the papers for the loan the first week in March.

There were two key snags to the North Star purchase. First, I had to sell some combination of the Elkton, Mayfield, and Newark houses in a hurry to raise cash for the down payment on North Star. And second, North Star Road was out of my county council district, so we couldn't really move until my term was finished.

We never had a second of buyer's remorse. When our offer was still pending that spring, we'd drive by the house just to look, and the entire back end of the driveway was a sunburst yellow bloom of forsythia. Neilia was pregnant again, and there was no way we could fit three children in the pool cottage. Now was the time. Nothing was going to stop us from getting this house.

FRANKLY, MY IMMEDIATE political future didn't look all that bright. The Delaware Democratic Party was in a sorry state in 1971, the measure of which was that Joe Biden, New Castle County councilman, a twenty-eight-year-old political novice, was the highest-ranking Democrat to win a truly contested district in the most recent elections. We'd lost nearly everything. Out of near desperation, the party leaders set up the twenty-five-person Democratic Renewal Commission. They invited a former governor, former congressmen, a former Supreme Court justice—the most prominent Democrats in the state . . . and me. I was the token youth, the youngest member by nearly fifteen years. I was the guy who kept the notes and turned off the lights. But I took it seriously because the other commissioners took it seriously. We knew we had to modernize our organization, our campaign techniques, and our substance. In the winter and spring of 1971 we held hearings all over the state and met every Democratic committeeman and committeewoman in Delaware. Neilia saw the advantages of my being on that commission even before I did. She was a more instinctive pol than I was, so it was Neilia's idea to have "Blue Ribbon" dinners at my parents' house on Woods Road. My mom and my sister, Val, would help Neilia cook and clear out the living room to make space for the commission members.

My friend Bob Cunningham and a few other guys asked me to help them recruit a strong candidate for the U.S. Senate seat in 1972, somebody to lead the new charge. We asked Bert Carvel, who'd been governor. We asked Judge Joe Tunnell, a Rhodes scholar and chief justice on the Delaware Supreme Court. We went to the few corporate leaders who were Democrats. That was the perfect candidate for Delaware, a corporate leader who was a Democrat. Everybody we asked said no. For one thing, the race looked unwinnable. The Republican incumbent, J. Caleb Boggs, hadn't lost a statewide race since 1946.

I HAD MY own worries that spring of 1971. I found a buyer for the Mayfield house and managed to close on it the day before our closing on North Star. I had buyers for the Newark house and the Elkton farm, but those deals wouldn't close for months. Our third child was due in November. And one big problem remained: I didn't feel right about moving out of my council district. Even though we owned North Star, I didn't think we should move yet. So Neilia and I talked it over . . . and we decided there was only one thing to do. The next weekend we went to my parents' house for dinner—my parents' house on Woods Road, right in the middle of my council district. We sat in our usual places at the table—the boys were both in their high chairs—and I decided to get right to it. I looked at Neilia, and before I could even open my mouth, my mom said, "What, Joey?"

My mom missed nothing.

"Oh, this house we bought." I turned to my dad. "You'd really love this house, Dad. It's got land. Got a pool. You'd really love this home, Dad."

"Yeah, sounds great, Champ."

I could see my mom squinting her eyes at me.

"You know, Dad, the thing is, it's outside my district."

"Okay." He didn't see why that should concern him.

"Well, Dad, I'd like to ask you a favor."

And Dad said, "Yeah, sure."

"Now, Joe," Mom said to Dad, "be careful."

"Well, Dad, would you mind moving into the house in North Star, and we could live here?"

"Jesus Ca-rhist! Joey!" My dad didn't raise his voice often. "You just moved us in *here*."

"You'd really like this place, Dad. You'd really like it. It'd just be for a year or so. The Republicans just redrew my district anyway, and I have to run next year. It's almost two-thirds Republicans in the district now. No way I can win again."

"All right," he said, "but dammit, Joe . . . Yeah . . . Okay."

"You've got to give us some time on this, Joey," Mom said. She knew me pretty well.

I took Dad out to show him the place, and I could see he loved it, so three days later, while my dad was at work, Jimmy showed up at Woods Road with a moving truck. (In all the moves the Biden family has made, we've never once hired a moving company. We do it on our own.) Anyway, Jimmy took the bed first. "Not the bed, Jimmy," Mom pleaded. "Let your father come home to his bed."

"Don't worry, Mom, we're going to set up the bed first at North Star. You'll be in it tonight."

So Mom called Dad at the car dealership. "Oh God, Joe," she told him. "Don't come home to Woods Road tonight."

"What!?"

"Don't go to Woods Road. They're moving us today."

"Damn those kids. What's the matter with them?" And after work he drove to North Star where his bed was set up.

Neilia and I had committed to managing the pool through the summer season, but when we shut it down that fall, we moved into my parents' house on Woods Road. Neilia and I were twenty-eight years old, and things were already falling into place. We were finally in the nice, comfortable house I'd always wanted. And before I was thirty, I was sure, we'd be at the house in North Star. Neilia was an absolute anchor. She was completely easy in the world, almost without insecurity or self-doubt. I could be impatient, brash, and off-putting, but Neilia had a way of smoothing my rough edges. She looked after our three children, the houses, and the politics. She somehow kept our life humming so that family, work, and politics were a seamless whole. She didn't have the need to compartmentalize, to separate out one part of our life from another. She made them all fit without apparent effort.

Largely because of Neilia, my new law firm was a success, too. When we won our first big case, I got a check for $5,000, made out to Joseph Robinette Biden Jr. That was the first big check that I ever, ever, ever had for anything. The check didn't put us beyond financial worries, but Neilia and I felt like we could buy the world. So we went to the finest furniture store in the state and bought a four-poster bed, a dining room set, and a big desk for my office downtown. The bill was substantial—maybe more than the check—but so was the furniture. The bed and the dining room suited a place like North Star. And Neilia said I deserved a desk befitting a senior partner in a successful law firm. A more practical young family might have played it safer. But this was our adventure, and Neilia was so sure of our future. "We should buy something of quality," she said to me in the store that day. "We should buy something that will last our entire life.".

✶ 4 ✶

The Doors Swing Open

WHEN OPPORTUNITY KNOCKS, YOU DON'T EXPECT IT TO BE at a place like the Hub Motel. There was nothing regal or romantic about the Hub, a typical roadside motel in Dover, Delaware. My room had a couple of beds with polyester spreads, a too-smooth wood-laminate desk built into the wall, and a little bathroom. This was home base for a couple of days in the summer of 1971; the Hub was hosting most of the state Democratic Party at our off-year convention. I was in my room getting ready for a meeting at a local junior high school—in my skivvies, at the bathroom sink, shaving—when I heard the knock. As I opened the front door, Henry Topel and Bert Carvel, both elders of the Delaware Democratic Party, brushed by me and sat down on the beds to have a talk. I thought I must have done something terribly wrong, so I asked their forbearance while I took a second to put on my pants.

As I stood there half-dressed in the Hub with a fistful of shaving cream, Topel and Carvel turned the tables on me. *Joe, you've asked all of us to run for Senate. We think you should run.* Now nobody in my family had ever known a United States senator; I'm not sure anybody in my family *knew* anybody who had known a United States senator. My initial reaction was: I don't think I'm old enough. I had to do the math. The election would be November 1972. I'd turn thirty at the end of that month, which qualified me to be sworn in when the new session opened in January 1973. I'd qualify with five weeks to spare.

Topel and Carvel knew I wasn't going to be running for county council again; the Young Turks in the Republican Party had seen to that. I think they saw me as a rising star, so after the 1970 census the Young Turks managed to redraw my district. My new district seat was up in 1972, and the district had gone from about 55 percent Republican to more than 60 percent Republican. I heard them kid about it at the time. They thought it was very funny. I had no place to go. It was up or out.

Still, there were plenty of reasons not to run for the Senate. I was building the law firm. Neilia and I had three children. I needed spare time to fix up North Star. I planned to paint the barn, plant around the pool, and make little repairs, I had told Neilia I could do most of it myself with help from my brothers and a few friends. And the race itself was an uphill battle. If J. Caleb Boggs, the Republican incumbent, ran, he'd be nearly impossible to beat. Early polls had Boggs crushing Bert Carvel, who had twice been the Democratic governor of Delaware. The two possible heirs to Boggs, United States congressman Pierre S. "Pete" du Pont IV and Wilmington mayor Hal Haskell, were also outpolling the best-known Democrats. I'd begun to meet the important players in the party in Sussex and Kent counties, but I had only ever run for New Castle County Council in a small district in the suburbs of Wilmington. So I told the delegation sitting on the twin beds at the Hub that I'd have to think about it.

And from that moment forward I couldn't *stop* thinking about it. How many twenty-eight-year-olds ever get in the position to even consider such a move? As a senator I knew I could have an effect on the issues that mattered to me: war and peace, the environment, crime, civil rights, women's rights. As a senator, I believed, I could help make Delaware and the rest of the country a better place. I could really help people in the way I believed I was supposed to. So I started talking to people about running. One night after a commission meeting I caught a ride home with my friend and fellow party reformer Bob Cunningham, who was about a dozen years older than me and knew his way around Delaware politics. I wanted to know what Bob thought because I respected his opinion. We were sitting in his car in front of the Hotel du Pont. "Hey, Bob, some people have been talking to me about running for the United States Senate," I told him. "You think I should take them seriously?" He looked me right in the eye and said, "I think you should take them very seriously."

Neilia thought we could do it, too. We'd been talking about it since the Hub, but she quickly grew tired of talk. In her heart of hearts Neilia wanted me to stay in law, build the practice. Her dream for me was to be a Supreme Court justice. But she knew I had no interest in being a judge. And she knew it was time for us to focus. The time for keeping every option open was gone. "Joey, I think you should be all the way in or all the way out. You're working forty-plus hours a week building your law firm. You're working forty-plus hours a week on the county council business. You're going to kill yourself trying to do both jobs. If politics is what you want to do, let's do it—full-time."

THE BIG THING I had going for me in the Senate race was the big thing I had going for me my whole life: the Bidens . . . especially my brothers and sister.

Val had run every campaign I was ever in, from high school to college to county council, and she would manage the Senate campaign, too. I didn't have to ask. Frankie was still in high school, so he could help bring in the young volunteers. Jimmy, who was in his last year at the University of Delaware, took on the toughest job: He had to raise money.

At our family meeting in the summer of 1971, my mom voiced the only reservation in the family. "Joey," she said, "Judge Quillen says you're such a good young lawyer. You're not going to run for Senate and ruin your reputation, are you?" But the way I saw it—and the way I could explain it to her—the race for the Senate was risk-free. Only a handful of people outside the family thought I had a real shot to win, so I figured even if I lost, people were going to say, "That's a nice young guy. That's a serious young guy." I couldn't see anything about the race that could hurt me. I was confident I could be a solid candidate. And I actually believed I could win. And once Mom was reassured that my future was safe, win or lose, she would do anything. In the first months she pitched in on the "coffees," which were modeled on the old Kennedy family campaign technique. We actually brought in an old Kennedy hand, Matt Reese, who had helped organize their coffees. We had hundreds of coffees around the state; held ten coffees a day, twice a week, for the half year before I announced my candidacy. Smart guys used to say, "Why don't you let the press know what you're doing? Put out press releases." But I wanted to meet as many voters as I could, to let them see me and hear me, before I ever announced. All through 1971 and early 1972 it was coffee under the radar. We'd start at eight o'clock in the morning, Mommom, Neilia, Val, and I. Val made sure we had thirty women at every coffee, which was easier then because fewer women worked. She'd find a neighborhood hostess and make sure she gave us the names and phone numbers of at least forty neighbors. Then, as Val followed up on whether or not they were coming to the coffee, word circulated down the block; women started inviting themselves. We'd bring the coffee and the doughnuts and set them up in the host's living room. I'd walk into the first one at eight o'clock with my mom. My sister would go to set up the second one, which would begin at nine, and Neilia would start to set up the ten o'clock. I'd leave my mother behind at a quarter of nine and go to Val's. My mother would stay for another half hour, then move on to the eleven o'clock. Mom-mom, Val, Neilia, and I leapfrogged through the day like that, sometimes doing ten coffees a day. We'd often have our children with us; we just carried them from house to house like footballs in wicker baskets. If we were downstate, it might be near midnight before I nosed our station wagon into our driveway. Neilia, Beau, Hunter, and my new daughter, Naomi, would all be with me, sleeping peacefully in the car. By the end of those long days I would have seen and gotten to know more than three hundred people. For forty-five minutes at each house I really talked to them and really heard them.

I made sure to make time in the schedule to drive over to the Democratic meeting places like the Polish Library to show the bosses there that I understood their neighborhoods; that Hedgeville and Browntown were just like Green Ridge in Scranton. It was easy to demonstrate that I felt at home at Mass at Saint Hedwig's and Saint Elizabeth's and that my family knew what it was to work for a living. When the esteemed boss of those Polish neighborhoods introduced me around like I was a member of the family—"I likadaboy," they'd say—I knew that was good.

When the political reporters around Delaware started to find out how hard I was working to win over voters, none of them called my running for the Senate ridiculous. I was "one of the bright young men of the Democratic Party . . . one of the few rising stars in the Democrats' rather dismal sky . . . a joyous campaigner, his whole family joining in the effort." I think they liked fresh blood to write about. At the same time, the smart guys covering Delaware politics didn't give me a snowman's chance in August. They'd note my lack of a real war chest, Senator Boggs's long-standing popularity, his quarter century of serving Delaware, and the slew of Democratic challengers he'd left by the roadside over the years. I tried to agree with the punditocracy where I could. "If I were a bookie, I'd give five-to-one odds right now that Boggs will be reelected," I'd tell them. But I wanted to let them know I was running to win. "If I can get to the people, I can beat Boggs." I'd also explain that I needed to raise only about a fifth of the money Congressman Pete du Pont had spent on his last statewide race to have a shot. I'd need $150,000 and a squad of volunteers to get my name and message out.

Even with a modest goal of $150,000, my brother Jimmy struggled to raise money. Our chairman of finance was Roy Wentz, a DuPont company lawyer who made the renegade move of backing a Democrat. Roy was a great attorney, but he had one flaw as a fund-raiser: He was constitutionally unable to ask people for money. So Jimmy made the asks. The money people were the surest gauge of what the political establishment thought about Biden for Senate. To this day Jimmy will say they didn't think we had a prayer, and they reminded him a hundred times a week: *Boggs, was unbeatable. He was a Republican . . . who had once been endorsed by labor! He'd been congressman, governor, and senator. He'd been running statewide in Delaware for twenty-six years and never lost.* People pointed out to Jimmy that Joe Biden was four years old when Boggs was first elected.

When we first started, the state Democrats were happy just to have me fill out the ticket and put their money into the governor's race, where we had a real shot to unseat the Republican incumbent. They figured getting me to take on the Senate race was win-win. The party would get a lost cause off its plate, and I could run without embarrassing anybody. I understood from the jump that the state party wasn't going to put up any money for my race. Jim's job was to find money outside the state, to get the national party and national Democrats to take a chance on my campaign. It was up to him to go hat in hand to beg campaign contributions—a twenty-three-year-old kid with long hair and a tie as wide as the Potomac. From start to finish we were short on money. I occasionally lost track of Jimmy, but then there would be a $1,000 wire from a Western Union office in Texas or California or Alaska to the Biden for Senate campaign fund.

Our first real money break was at the Democratic Senatorial Campaign Committee in Washington. In 1972 the committee was staffed by Nordy Hoffman, who had been one of Knute Rockne's all-American down-linemen at Notre Dame. Nordy was a big, tough, and stubborn slab of a guy. Nothing scared him. And he didn't think much of my chances. Years later Nordy would say the committee had handpicked me in Delaware; they'd done polling in the state, and my name kept coming up. But the truth was that when Jim and I first went to see him, he didn't want to give us a dime. I was a bad investment. He didn't want to waste time on races he couldn't win. He started in on me right away. "Look, Joe, I'm sure you're a nice kid, but I go to a dentist up in Wilmington and I've been talking to him and he doesn't think you can win. You're twenty-nine years old, and you don't have a chance. Nobody in Delaware thinks you can win. I don't think you can win. My dentist sure as hell doesn't think you can win." He kept going on about his dentist. I think Jimmy could see my jaw clench and my chin start to jut out. I stood up and started for the door. "Look, I don't have to take this malarkey," I told him. "I don't need you or this committee. And another thing . . . I'm gonna win."

Jimmy trailed out behind me, trying to get me to calm down, to go back and try again. Nordy followed us, too. He stopped us in the hallway and said he thought maybe the committee could do something after all. Nordy said he still didn't think I could win, but I guess he liked the way I stood up to him.

He also suggested we go and get a big-time campaign consultant. The only political operative we knew who had done a statewide race anywhere was my old friend from law school, Jack Owens. Jack had gone to work in Pittsburgh after law school and worked on Pete Flaherty's underdog race for mayor, which Flaherty won. After that race, Jack had run most of western Pennsylvania for Milton Shapp and helped him become the first Jewish governor of the state. I invited Jack down to help us on the campaign. From the moment Jack walked into the kitchen cabinet meetings at our house on Woods Road, he and Val picked up where they had left off on their disastrous blind date. When Jack said *black*, Val said *white*. Jack said *this* and Val said *that*.

"He walked in the door and we looked at each other and it was like *uh-oh*," Val recalls. "I remember one time he came in, and I said, 'Jack, take a memo.' He looks at me like 'If you ever . . .'" I was not pleasant. And we continued to butt heads."

Jack had been at the campaign two months when Val came to me one day and said, "Joe, look, you gotta pick. I'm not working with him. We just can't seem to get along."

"Don't worry, Val. That's easy," I told her. "Jack told me last night he's leaving. He said he realizes that blood is thicker than water."

I DID TAKE Nordy's advice and signed on a young campaign consultant, John Marttila, out of Boston, who was also running John Kerry's congressional campaign that year.

I was walking out of my law practice one day just before my official announcement when an older attorney I knew grabbed me on Market Street. "Joe," he said, "listen. I'm a Democrat, but I'm telling you: You will never, ever beat Cale Boggs." At that very moment, as if on cue, Senator Boggs's car—with the special license plates—rolled by. And as it did, the guy kept talking: "Joe, let me tell you about Cale Boggs." Then he told me the story of a recent regular poker game he'd hosted. There had been an argument among his friends about which hand was the winner. Nobody could agree. "You know what we did, Joe? We called Cale Boggs to settle it."

Even if few others did, the Bidens knew I could win, and in the beginning that was enough. By the time I was ready to announce my candidacy in March 1972, I was saying to everyone who would listen, "I have every intention of winning the upcoming election."

The plan for the announcement was to start at the Hotel du Pont in downtown Wilmington, then go downstate to Sussex County, do a second event there, and then on to Kent County. No one had ever done that before. We still didn't have much money, but we had an organization and we had a message. Creating them was one of the greatest times of my life. Neilia, Val, Jimmy, and I planned the whole campaign from our living room. On Sunday nights we'd convene meetings with the issues gurus and spend hours and hours talking them through. Especially on the issues most important to me—civil rights, women's rights, the environment, crime, and the Vietnam War—I could feel the world was turning on its axis, and I wanted to give it a little shove. I knew I had to be sure-footed about the issues I was talking about. When you're twenty-nine years old, who the hell is going to think you're credible? It wasn't enough to have ideas; I had to know my facts. I had to demonstrate command from the minute I started running. I understood that was the test I had to pass. So Neilia would cook spaghetti, and we would invite professors from the University of Pennsylvania and the University of Delaware for Sunday night dinner. We'd send them questions ahead of time and then talk through the tax code, the Vietnam War, drugs, the environment, crime, and rehabilitation. Those nights in our home we gathered bright, dedicated people. Bob Cunningham was a Fulbright scholar. Arlen Meckler was a lawyer with a Ph.D. in chemical engineering; Jack Jacobs is now a judge on the Delaware Supreme Court, and his wife, Marion, was just as bright. They were all willing to help me sharpen my policy on issues.

By the time I gave my announcement speech, I felt great. I knew what I meant to do, and I said it. I was absolutely sure. I reread the speech recently, and I feel the same way today as I did in 1972. What I said that day was what I believed, and it came from my life. I was only twenty-nine, but I'd seen a lot. I'd been in judges' chambers, at the all-black pool in inner-city Wilmington, at parks in the poorest white working-class neighborhoods. I'd grown up in middle-class homes. I understood the size of the gulfs that separated people in Delaware, but I also knew the hopes they held in common. "The Brandywine Hundred housewife and the mother on Wilmington's East Side both want their homes to be secure, their streets to be safe, and their children to be educated," I said at my announcement at the Hotel du Pont. "The Sussex County parent worries as much as the Newark production-line worker about the drugs that threaten the children of both. The fabric of our complex society is woven too tightly to permit any part of it to be damaged without damaging the whole."

After the Wilmington event I jumped into the copilot's seat of a Piper Apache airplane and headed for Sussex County, trailed by two other planes. Even when I was racing through the sky, 2,500 feet over Delaware, my entire family was behind me that day. Mom, Dad, Val, Jim, and Frank were there. And Neilia's parents had come all the way from Skaneateles to show their support, though they remained registered Republicans.

In Georgetown, with four hundred people in attendance, I said the same things I had in Wilmington. My issues were voting rights, civil rights, crime, clean water and clean air, pension protection, health care, and the war in Vietnam. That day in 1972 I called for a comprehensive national health care program to protect families from the financial disasters of coping with catastrophic illness: "We can no longer allow the wealthiest nation in the world to be a second-class citizen in providing health care for those who need it." Above all, I said that day, I still believed in the system, I wanted to make it work, and I could be trusted to try.

That was the nut of my campaign from day one: winning back trust. I was holding fast to Grandpop Finnegan's first principle. *Tell them what you really think, Joey. Let the chips fall where they may.* "You may not agree with me, but at least you'll know where I stand," I said on announcement day and at every event after. I was convinced that voters in Delaware thought like I did and what they really wanted was for somebody to be straight up about what was going on. We made one unscripted campaign ad that drove the professional political guys crazy. John Marttila came down from Boston with a boom mike and a recorder and followed me into the Prices Corner Shopping Center. "Just record this, John," I told him. I'd walk up to people and say, "My name is Joe Biden. I'm the Democratic candidate for the United States Senate. Do you trust me?" They'd look at me across their shopping carts like I was an alien. "Hell, no! . . . Huh? . . . Why should we trust you?" We did that with ten or fifteen people and wrote an ad around their responses, saying, "That's what's wrong with America right now. I promise you if you elect me, you'll know exactly where I stand. You'll be able to trust me."

Marttila kept saying, "You can't put an ad on the air having people testify they don't trust you!" But I knew it would work. It wasn't hard to figure it out. People felt like they were losing control. Nixon didn't invent the law-and-order issue out of thin air. People in neighborhoods all over Delaware were genuinely fearful of crime. We were being told the war in Vietnam was winding down, but the casualties were arriving at Delaware's doorstep. Every week young American men were being shipped to the mortuary at Dover Air Force Base in body bags. How many mothers lay awake at night wondering how their own sons might return, and wondering what exactly they were risking their lives for?

I kept reminding people that Caleb Boggs was a nice guy, but he hadn't been willing to make a tough choice on much of anything. And maybe now we needed somebody to stand up to Nixon when he ordered the mining of North Vietnamese harbors, escalating American military operations even as he promised to withdraw troops. I didn't argue that the war in Vietnam was immoral; it was merely stupid and a horrendous waste of time, money, and lives based on a flawed premise. We were spending a billion dollars every two weeks, jeopardizing our entire international posture, and spending so much energy in Southeast Asia that we had left truly vital interests unattended. The president kept talking about how American honor was at stake, which I resented. If that was all we were now fighting for in Vietnam, I said, I couldn't see how that was worth anybody else giving up his life.

Still, the message was nothing without nuts and bolts. Politics is not just smart people dreaming up big ideas and ways to sell them. Real campaigning is organizing, and organizing is effort, every day. It requires exactly the sort of constancy my dad taught. It requires working at it every day—on the good days but especially on the bad days. We already knew a little something about nuts and bolts. Val had run a very modern campaign for my council race in 1970. We got the motor vehicle registration and voter records and organized block by block. We had every development, every street in it, and every house on it on file cards. We had recruited block captains and put them to work. And for the Senate race we just built on that; Delaware wasn't that big—only one congressional district. We just used volunteers and made the file cards statewide. We went to the useful Democratic Party regulars I'd met on the renewal commission and backfilled the rest of the areas with kids. This was the first year eighteen-year-olds could vote, and Val turned them into a small army of thousands.

I also made it a point to go into the high schools to talk to students. A lot of watchers thought I must be doing this because 1972 was the first year eighteen-year-olds could vote, and they thought I was wasting time. But I could count as well as they could; I understood that only a handful of high school students were already eighteen, but I had a theory—one that nobody else seemed to be buying: that fifteen-, sixteen-, and seventeen-year-olds have more influence on their parents than their parents have on them. I believed that if a high school student went home and sat down at the dinner table and actually talked to his or her parents—"You know, Dad, I met a really neat guy today. His name was Joe Biden, and I really liked him"—that Dad and Mom might be rock-ribbed Republicans, but guess what, they really wanted to show respect for the opinion of their children. They might take a second look at Joe Biden. So I went primarily to the high schools in Republican areas.

By the time the voters really started paying attention to the race, Biden for Senate had a message; we had a clear position on every issue, and we had organization. We even had a little money coming in from unexpected contributors—namely the people I had angered as a county councilman fighting irrational growth. They knew I had introduced an ordinance in the council that stopped Shell Oil from getting a quick start on their new refinery in Delaware City, and that gave the state legislature the time to put the kibosh on it for good with the Coastal Zoning Act a few years later. They also knew I had introduced legislation that would effectively cut off the federal highway funding to divert Route 141 and widen the Concord pike. The construction unions were not happy with me; they argued that this was costing jobs. And the Association of General Contractors was spitting nails. So when a couple of builders wrote a check to the Biden for Senate campaign, Val couldn't figure out why. "We'll do anything," they told her, "to get your brother out of New Castle County."

THE POLLS TWO months out had me behind Senator Boggs, 47–19. So I was nearly thirty points down on Labor Day when we first stood in the same room together at the Hadassah debate. I was sure I'd stack up against him. Cale Boggs was an avuncular fellow. He was a decent, gentle, and honorable man who'd served his country well, but I never thought he was going to make a difference in where this nation was headed. Standing next to him during the first debate, I wasn't intimidated. I thought I could be a better senator. In fact, I wondered if he really wanted this race. There was talk when I was first exploring the run that Boggs was ready to retire, and the GOP bosses were worried that a primary between leading contenders Pete du Pont and Hal Haskell would be bloody, expensive, and wounding.

I learned later that Boggs really did want to leave office, and his wife badly wanted to be out of public life. But President Richard Nixon had flown to Delaware and told Boggs he needed to run for the good of the Republican Party. I believe Boggs agreed to run again in part because the race looked so easy. Still, there were rumors that Boggs would win the seat and then hand it over to du Pont. At the time I didn't know if there was a grain of truth to any of it, but I did believe that if people saw Boggs and me together in the same room, I wouldn't remain thirty points down. I got my first opening at the debate. Actually, the senator was late, so I spent much of the debate sparring with one of his aides. But Boggs was there at the end.

During the question-and-answer session at the close of the Hadassah debate, a man in the audience asked Boggs about his position on the Genocide Treaty. The treaty had been written in response to the Holocaust, but for years the radical right-wing John Birchers had blocked its ratification. The Birchers said it threatened our national sovereignty. The treaty was a big issue in the Jewish community, and the guy in the audience had lobbed Boggs a softball. But Boggs was flummoxed. "I'm sorry," he said. "I'm not familiar with the specifics of the Genocide Treaty. I'll check on the details and get back to you." So the guy said I should answer the question, which was contrary to the rules of the debate. But the moderator agreed. I knew the treaty, and I knew the answer cold. This was an opportunity to hit Boggs hard. The truth was, I was surprised that a two-term United States senator was unfamiliar with the Genocide Treaty. But I didn't even have to think about the answer; I probably had better political instincts then than I do now. Like anybody who's been in politics three decades, I've built up barnacles. Today I'd probably win the point but lose the match because I'd be too busy ripping somebody's head off with the facts. But I knew enough in 1972 to know that nobody in the audience wanted to see Boggs embarrassed—it would have been like clubbing the family's favorite uncle. So I said, "I'm not sure. I promise I'll get back to you as well."

NO MATTER HOW hard and how fast I ran, the age question stayed on my heels. People would come up to me at campaign events and say, "Hey, I'm going to vote for your dad!" And I'd jokingly say, "I am, too!" One Delaware newspaperman was fond of pointing out that Senator Boggs probably had shoes older than me. But the problem was real. On Election Day I would literally not yet be constitutionally eligible to be sworn into the Senate. And that was a pretty big hurdle. We knew that if we had support from Democratic senators in Washington, it would lend our campaign much needed gravitas. Val wanted them to appear in one of our campaign brochures under the banner headline: "He's not even in the Senate yet, and Joe Biden is already creating a stir." The Senate majority leader, Mike Mansfield, was reluctant. Tradition in the Senate held that a member didn't campaign against a colleague even if he was from the other side of the aisle. The leader finally agreed to say something positive about me, but he wouldn't say a word against Boggs. So Mansfield, along with Frank Church, Adlai Stevenson, Fritz Hollings, Ted Kennedy, and Henry "Scoop" Jackson, agreed to have their pictures taken with me . . . and say something nice.

I rode down to Washington one day with Val and a photographer, and we met Mansfield in the grand reception room off the Senate floor. He was friendly, but he had a schedule to keep, so he was all business. While the photographer was clicking away, Val suddenly blurted out, "Oh my God! That's it!" Mansfield looked startled. "That's what, Val?" I asked. She was pointing over our shoulders at one of the paintings hanging in the reception room—portraits of solons of earlier Senates. "Henry Clay!" she yelled. "Henry Clay. Henry Clay was under thirty. From now on when anybody says to you, 'Isn't it true you're not old enough to be a senator?' You just look at them and say, 'You know, not since Henry Clay has anybody my age joined the Senate.' " We found out later that there were a couple of others, but invoking the Great Compromiser worked.

Biden for Senate still didn't have a lot of money, and we were completely outmatched in fund-raising. Nixon's biggest financial supporter in Delaware, Big John Rollins, was giving big money to Boggs and the state GOP. So we had to play to our strength. We had youth, we had energy, and we knew how to improvise around money shortages. A single statewide mailing cost $36,000, which we couldn't afford. The first campaign brochure we printed sat on the shelf, getting stale. So Val invented the Biden post office. Once a week, either Saturday or Sunday, her army of volunteers hand-delivered our private campaign newspaper to about 85 percent of the households in the state. By the middle of October people would be waiting on Saturday mornings for a kid to come to the door. If it rained and we were late, a few people would call the campaign headquarters to complain. There were little signs we were breaking through. A staff worker got a call one day from a woman who wanted to know if she'd be allowed to vote for just one Democrat or if she was bound to vote a straight Republican ticket because of her party affiliation.

Donations were trickling in, enough to run our radio ads. But money was still hard, and if we ran out, the campaign was lost. So it was hard to stay out of Jimmy's business. In the beginning of the campaign I was always on his case. He was working night and day, but it wasn't good enough: "C'mon, Jim," I'd tell him, "if you can't do it, I'll hire some pros." Neilia finally blew. "Joey," she said to me in front of Jim, "get off his back. If you want him to do it, let him do it. If you don't, hire somebody else. But leave him alone. You do your job. Let Jim do his."

A few weeks after Labor Day, Jimmy said he had some good news from the international machinists union. He'd been dutifully showing up at their national headquarters in Washington for nine months. The president of the union would keep him waiting for hours, sometimes make him come back three or four times before he'd finally usher him in at the end of the day to have a chuckle at our internal poll numbers. But when our numbers started creeping up in the weeks leading up to the election, he said, "Tell you what, Jim. I'm gonna give you $5,000. But I want to meet your brother."

"Uh, Bill," Jimmy said, "I really don't know if you want to meet him. He's good. I showed you his position papers."

"Yeah, I know, Jimmy. But for $5,000 I want to meet him. I want to give him the check."

Jimmy knew what was coming. He knew I could screw it up. He always said the smartest thing to do when raising money for me is to keep me away from money people. But the guy was insisting that he put the check in *my* hand. So Jim brought me to Washington to meet the president of the machinists union. Jim still remembers it to this day: "We walk into his office and we sit down in front of his desk and he's bigger than life and smoking a cigar and he's got the $5,000 check sitting on his desk. He says, 'Listen, Joe. This is an uphill battle. Boggs looks unbeatable. I really don't know why we're doing this. But I like you. So let me pose you a question. Let me give you a hypothetical. Let's say the Lockheed bailout comes up again in the next session, and you're a sitting United States senator. My guys are losing jobs, ya know, Joe. How do you vote?'

"Joe looks at me like he could put a dagger in my chest and turns to the union guy and literally says, 'If you're asking me how I'm gonna vote on a particular issue, you can take that check and stick it.' Joe gets up and walks out the door. The campaign was desperate for money. How could I leave a $5,000 check sitting on a desk? Now I am Fredo in *The Godfather,* in the scene in the hotel room. I'm trying to stop Joe from going down the elevator and then running back to the union guy to say, 'Joe's not a bad guy. He didn't mean that. I know you didn't mean what you said. He didn't mean what he said.' Then I'm back at the elevator begging Joe to come back. Then I'm back in the president's office. 'Please apologize. My brother really takes offense.' Finally, they make up . . . and he hands Joe the check and Joe still refused to take the check from the guy's hand. I had to take it."

THE CAMPAIGN WAS spending what money we had on the radio spots, and as long as they were on the air, I felt like we were closing the gap on Boggs. I think everybody did. I would check in at the campaign office on Market Street in Wilmington late at night after my day's speeches and events were done, and the kids were always there organizing mailings or working the phones. When I stopped in the next morning before I hit the road, the office was still full. Thursdays were the mornings I waited for; first thing I wanted when I got there on Thursday was the new poll numbers, straight from Cambridge Research in Boston, which was really just a brilliant twenty-two-year-old numbers cruncher and strategist named Patrick Caddell. His tracking polls that autumn had us closing every week. I could feel it in the size of the crowds and the numbers of new volunteers showing up at Market Street to ask what they could do. In the first week in October, Bob Cunningham put a poll in my hand as I walked into headquarters. I stared at the numbers and could feel the heat on the back of my neck. I was not happy.

"Dammit!"

"Joe," Bob said, "what are you talking about? We're two points up."

"This can't be right. We're going to have to do the whole damn poll over again. This can't be right."

But the next day every major Republican candidate from Claymont to Delmar was running against Joe Biden. They had the same numbers, too. It was a dead heat. The Delaware Republican Party had been so fixated on holding the governorship, they hadn't seen me coming. And Boggs's advisors had been telling him all along that the race was a lock and he didn't even have to leave Washington. But now they were frantically calling him to Delaware for the final push. Some of the Young Republican Turks who had redistricted me out of the county council started telling reporters that I was only going to be using the Senate as a stepping-stone . . . to the White House. I knew they were worried when the Boggs people shipped out a mass mailing of their new campaign literature. It was a tabloid like ours, with a kitchen sink on the cover. "This is the only thing," it said, "that Joe Biden hasn't promised you."

We were ten days out and still even in the polls when Jimmy came into the office to deliver bad news. "The radio stations have told us they're going to cut off our ads, Joe. We gotta come up with the money for next week's ads." The spots were costing us $20,000 a week. We were out of cash. If we couldn't keep the ads up, we didn't have a chance.

Val had an idea. Her friend Ted Kellner was working at a Delaware firm that was managing money for very wealthy clients, and Ted thought some of the investment counselors and their clients would be willing to take a look at me, maybe even consider contributing to the Biden for Senate campaign. So Ted set up a meeting and Jimmy drove me out to Centerville, Delaware, and we walked into this beautiful investment firm inside a bank in this beautiful little town. Jimmy and I had barely settled into our chairs when the men started offering us drinks. These were not my regular sort of contributors; these men were worth millions. They were all Greenville Republicans who had supported Senator Boggs. But they were all very gracious, and it seemed to us like they might be willing to help—and Jimmy and I knew they could save our radio spots. Jimmy figured they had the capacity to raise twenty grand for me overnight. Alfred I. du Pont Dent said he could raise the money himself if he had to. But at one point in the discussion they asked me what I thought about capital gains. Maybe they were just trying to make small talk, but it didn't seem like a small question to me. I had the same feeling I'd had with the president of the machinists union.

Nixon was calling for a reduction in the capital gains tax. It was a big issue in 1972, and I had come out against it. I was wondering if these men expected me to say something in private that I wouldn't say in public. I knew the answer I thought they wanted to hear, and I knew that the right answer could be worth a lot to my campaign fund. All I had to say was that I'd consider it . . . and I couldn't say it. I wasn't thinking about macroeconomics, and I wasn't staking out the moral high ground. I just couldn't lie to their faces. "I'm not for changing capital gains," I told them. "I wouldn't change it."

Jim and I finished our lemonades and walked to the car in silence. He was not happy. That money was a big get for Jim, and he thought I'd blown it. Jim drove us—in perfect silence—back toward Wilmington. As we neared home, he finally said to me, "Joe, I sure in hell hope you feel that strongly about capital gains because you just lost the election."

As it turns out, most of the guys in that room did become supporters. They gave me money despite my hardheadedness. But just to be sure I could get the radio ads up, I decided to take a chance. I had one thing of value besides my family: the house in North Star. So I wagered it. Our finance chairman, Roy Wentz, agreed to cosign a note, and I took out a $20,000 loan that we used to keep the radio spots on the air the last seven days. We had some good luck, too. There was a newspaper strike the week before election day, so Boggs's new mailing—a flyer with the picture of the moon and the headline "The Only Thing Joe Biden Hasn't Promised You"—never got distributed. When seagull droppings landed on my head at a campaign event at Bowers Beach two days before Election Day, I chose to read it as a sign of a coming success.

Neilia's parents came to town in the last days of the campaign to help out. Actually, Mr. Hunter had been helping all the way. The hardest thing in the campaign, I can say without equivocation, was being able to run and eat. I was getting a little share from my new law firm, but things were tight. Neilia's father, a good Republican, became a quiet provider for the Joe Biden Jr. family. If we were down to nothing, Neilia would reach in her pocket, and there'd be a hundred dollars. "Where'd you get a hundred dollars, Neilia?!" But I always knew. Her father's faith in me actually flattered me. Six years after he stood trembling at the door of the Catholic church in Skaneateles, Mr. Hunter was still ready to take a chance on me.

Election Day was like a dream; the weather cleared, and we got the big turnout we needed. By the time I got to the suite at the Hotel du Pont for the election night party, I was pretty sure we stood a shot to win the Senate seat from Boggs and the Republicans. When the returns began to come in, it looked promising. I'd done much better than expected in conservative downstate Sussex County where voters made their judgments more on being personally comfortable with the candidate than with his positions. I'd done much better than expected in the heavily Republican Brandywine Hundred, too. But the race was close, and we had to wait for the final returns from a working-class Polish neighborhood and a part of my county council district. I'd gone door-to-door in that neighborhood for three years. Everybody there knew me, and they all knew Neilia. They thought of her as a favorite daughter. As I'll always remember it, they put me over the top. I won huge margins in Browntown and Hedgeville. I'd won by 3,000 votes out of 230,000 votes cast statewide. I was still upstairs in the suite with my family and Neilia's parents when Senator Boggs called to concede. "Good race, Joe," he said.

And when he said it and I knew I'd won, it felt nothing like I thought it would. It was supposed to feel great. I was supposed to be elated. But when Senator Boggs started to talk, I could feel myself filling up, like I might cry. I could feel the back of my throat constrict. It was like my old stutter was back. I didn't think I'd be able to talk. So Boggs spoke again: "You ran a good race, Joe."

"I'm sorry, Senator" was all I could say. "I'm sorry."

In my head was a picture of the two of us on Returns Day, two days later. Returns Day is an old custom we still practice in Delaware. The Thursday after an election, both parties gather in the town circle in Georgetown, and the town crier reads the election results from the courthouse balcony, literally buries a hatchet, and then the winner and the loser of each race parade around the town square in a horse-drawn buggy. So I begged off. I told Boggs I had bronchitis and didn't feel up to showing up for Returns Day. But he hadn't been undefeated for twenty-six years without being able to read people. "Joe, I rode many times as a winner," he told me. "I'd be proud to ride with you."

When I put down the phone, nobody in the room said a word. I think we were all stunned. The whole thing felt unreal. Finally, Neilia's father spoke up. "Well, Joe, if my daughter has to be married to a Democrat, he might as well be a United States senator."

People were gracious and honest. Big John Rollins called with congratulations and compliments, too: "Goddamn it, kid, you won," he drawled. "If I'd known you had a chance, I would have spent a lot more money to beat you."

Jimmy was ecstatic. He was fielding calls from all over the country that night. Suddenly I had a whole lot more supporters. "Jimmy! Didja get my check? . . . No? . . . Don't know what could have happened. . . . I mailed it a week ago. . . . Probably be there in a coupla days." I guess I was feeling my oats that night. I told Jimmy I wasn't taking money from people who wanted to jump on the bandwagon only after we'd won. "Joe," Jimmy pleaded, "we've got a deficit. You've got a second mortgage on your house. We need the money."

"To hell with them. Tell 'em we're sending them back."

Jimmy listened to me that night. But he didn't send back any checks, thank God.

I don't remember staying long at the party that night. Neilia and I planned to start our thank-yous at a plant gate in Delaware City early the next morning so we went upstairs while the party still raged. It was impossible to sleep, so in bed that night, in the darkness, we started filling in the picture of our future. We had a whole new life to make in Washington, D.C. There would be a new house. We'd have to entertain, right? New schools for the boys. We'd be away from family in Wilmington. Would we need babysitters for our daughter? Best of all, we talked about being a United States senator. I could actually *do* what we'd been talking about all these months. We weren't just going to be a vote, we'd say; we were going to be a voice. Part of me wondered, though I didn't say it out loud that night: What did I do to deserve this?

LOOKING BACK ON IT, I probably should have been intimidated by the idea of entering the United States Senate, of stepping into the well to debate with William Fulbright or some other luminary. But I wasn't. There was excitement—and anticipation—like the rush I used to get before a big fourth-down play when I'd taken the measure of the linebacker I had to block, and I knew I could do it.

Senator Church set me up with a chief of staff, Wes Barthelmes. Wes had been press secretary to Bobby Kennedy and a metro editor at the *Washington Post*. When Katharine Graham needed somebody to arbitrate between labor and management at the *Post,* she called Wes. He knew his way around Washington and around the Senate. He'd also jumped into Normandy with the 82nd Airborne in 1944, so he had a pretty clear sense of proportion. The first order of business was hiring a staff. We had about thirty-five jobs to fill—and about 2,500 applicants, most of them from Harvard Law or the University of Chicago or Stanford. I couldn't even make a paper cut. Should I hire a Rhodes scholar to be a receptionist?

I was assigned offices tucked away in the corner of the sixth floor of the Dirksen Senate Office Building. (There are people who don't even know Dirksen has a sixth floor. Maybe they'd heard a rumor of its existence, but they'd never seen it.) But I couldn't expect much. I was literally last in seniority, which is determined by the highest office a newly elected senator had attained—and, if that didn't settle it, by the size of your state. As a county councilman I was behind former congressmen, governors, state legislators, and mayors. I might have been able to lord it over a city dogcatcher, but that was about it. Worse yet, I wouldn't even be able to take the Dirksen office until a few months into the new session of Congress. But Senator Robert Byrd of West Virginia offered me space in his majority whip's office in the Capitol so I'd have a place to interview job applicants.

When I wasn't interviewing people, I made the rounds to pay my respects to the senators who were in town between sessions. It was tradition, and I wanted to let them know how honored I was to be there with them. Part of it was upbringing, part of it was my age, but I didn't presume familiarity with any of my new colleagues. I couldn't imagine calling Senator Church "Frank" or Senator Magnusson "Warren" (or "Maggie") or Senator Jackson "Scoop." To me they were "Mr. Chairman" or "Senator." One day I walked into the office of Senator John Stennis of Mississippi to pay my respects. Stennis was a formal and formidable man who had spent more than twenty-five years in the Senate and held the chairmanship of the Senate Armed Services Committee. When I was still in grade school, Stennis had stood on the Senate floor and heroically pummeled Senator Joe Mc-Carthy for denying citizens their constitutional liberties; Stennis had also been a committed segregationist. He was sitting at the end of a big mahogany conference table he used as his desk as I walked in and he patted the leather chair next to him. "Sit down. Sit, sit down here. . . . Tell me, what made you run for the Senate?"

"Civil rights, sir," I said before I remembered, with a start, the senator's segregationist past.

At the time I wondered if I might have overstepped, but he just smiled. "Civil rights? Good," he said. "Good. Good. Glad to have you here." That was it.

I HAVE NEVER since wished away any time, but I could hardly wait to be thirty, the constitutionally required age for entering the Senate. We threw a big party at the Pianni Grill in downtown Wilmington on my birthday, November 20, two and a half weeks after the election.

That was the big event for me, turning thirty, like my election was finally official. There was a cake, and Neilia and I cut it together, standing over it like we did our wedding cake, except that Beau and Hunt were there—and a television news crew, and newspaper photographers. The next day there would be a story in a local paper that I was surely headed for the White House. I wasn't even sworn into the U.S. Senate yet! I remember thinking that this wasn't good. This couldn't be good. Maybe it was nerves finally kicking in, but it seemed like my future was coming at a full rush, and I wasn't sure if I was ready. I'd always remember the funny feeling I had standing beside Neilia, cutting that cake.

MY ELECTION TO the Senate meant I was no longer on the county council, which meant we could move into the house in North Star. Jimmy and I rented the trucks, and we did the move ourselves. Moving Mom and Dad's stuff back to Woods Road took some time, but moving Neilia and me to North Star was easy. The only real furniture we had was our four-poster bed, a dining room set, and a big wing chair that we set up in the living room in front of the fireplace. It did look a bit ridiculous. The living room was a big room, eighteen feet by thirty, with high ceilings, shiny wood floors (we didn't have rugs yet), a stone fireplace, and a wing chair. But we didn't have much time to do anything about that yet. We hadn't even had time to shop for Christmas or to put up a tree. I was back and forth to Washington, and for the three weeks after my birthday, Neilia came with me whenever she could. If I got free from staff interviews, we'd run out to look at houses. We planned to live in Washington. We weren't going to give up North Star, though it would be tough for us to keep up two separate houses on a senator's salary of $42,500, but we needed a home in Washington and schools for the boys. Neilia's dad volunteered to give us the down payment for a second house, and when we found a small colonial near Chevy Chase Circle, right down the street from a Presbyterian church where the boys could go to kindergarten, he was more than happy to help. Our offer was accepted on a Friday, December 15, and we planned a closing for the middle of the next week. That weekend Neilia and I were back in North Star, and it felt like we had finally arrived at the future we had so long envisioned. The Washington house was going to be nice, but North Star already felt like home—Thanksgivings and Christmases, Easters and birthdays and anniversaries, would all be celebrated at North Star. We planned on spending most weekends at North Star. When Beau and Hunt and Naomi thought of home, they'd think of North Star. And that Sunday night, with the children asleep over our heads, Neilia and I sat on our lone wing chair, in front of the warm glow of a fire, in our stone fireplace, in a moment of near perfect repose. The moment exceeded all my romantic youthful imaginings. I was a United States senator–elect at age thirty. Our family was together under one splendid roof. The doors were just beginning to swing open on the rest of our lives. Neilia and I had done this amazing thing together, and there was so much more we would do. Neither of us was sure exactly what the rest of our lives would bring, but we couldn't wait to see.

✳ 5 ✳

Give Me Six Months

THE NEXT MORNING I HEADED OFF TO WASHINGTON TO
interview staff, but Neilia decided to stay home in Wilmington.
Christmas was a week away, and we hadn't had time to do anything,
so Neilia was going to have breakfast with Jimmy, then do some big
shopping, then get a tree. She wasn't going to come home without a
Christmas tree.

Val and I were sitting in the office Senator Byrd had lent me when
Jimmy called from Wilmington. He wanted to talk to Val. When she
hung up the phone, she looked white. "There's been a slight accident," she said. "Nothing to be worried about. But we ought to go
home."

Was it something in the way Val's voice caught? Something in the
way she set her mouth? What I felt was something jarring, something
stronger than a premonition. It was a physical sensation, like a little
pinprick at the center of my chest. I could already feel Neilia's absence.

"She's dead," I said, "isn't she?"

Val said nothing. I remember walking out of Senator Byrd's office
and finding myself beneath the hollow expanse of the Capitol ro-
tunda. Under that soaring dome I felt . . . small.

They flew us to Wilmington, but I didn't know anything for sure
until I got to the hospital. All the way up, I kept telling myself that
everything was going to be okay, that I was letting my imagination
run away with me, but the minute I got to the hospital and saw

Jimmy's face, I knew the worst had happened. Beau, Hunt, and Naomi had been in the car with Neilia when the accident happened. Neilia had been killed and so had our baby daughter. The boys were both alive, but Beau had a lot of broken bones and Hunt had head injuries. They doctors couldn't rule out permanent damage. I could not speak, only felt this hollow core grow in my chest, like I was going to be sucked inside a black hole.

The first few days I felt trapped in a constant twilight of vertigo, like in the dream where you're suddenly falling . . . only I was *constantly* falling. In moments of fitful sleep I was aware of the dim possibility that I would wake up, truly wake up, and this would not have happened. But then I'd open my eyes to the sight of my sons in their hospital beds—Beau in a full body cast—and it was back. And as consciousness gathered again, I could always feel at least one other physical presence in the room—and there would be Val, or my mom, or Jimmy. They never left my side. I have no memory of ever being physically alone.

Most of all I was numb, but there were moments when the pain cut through like a shard of broken glass. I began to understand how despair led people to just cash it in; how suicide wasn't just an option but a *rational* option. But I'd look at Beau and Hunter asleep and wonder what new terrors their own dreams held, and wonder who would explain to my sons my being gone, too. And I knew I had no choice but to fight to stay alive.

Except for the memorial service, I stayed in the hospital room with my sons. My life collapsed into their needs. If I could focus on what they needed minute by minute, I thought I might stay out of the black hole. My future was telescoped into the effort of putting one foot in front of the other. The horizon faded from my view. Washington, politics, the Senate had no hold on me. I was supposed to be sworn into the Senate in two weeks, but I could not bear to imagine the scene without Neilia. I tried to be up front about it. Delaware could always get another senator, I told people, but my boys can't get another father. I told the Senate majority leader, Mike Mansfield, that I wasn't going to be a senator. But Senator Hubert Humphrey, the former vice president of the United States, called almost every day. He just wanted to know how I was doing, but usually he never got past Jimmy who was screening my calls and knew I didn't much feel like talking to anybody outside the family. Jimmy was also talking to Delaware's governor-elect, who would have to appoint a new senator.

But Senator Mansfield would not give up on me. He kept calling to check on me. He reminded me that he had put me on the Democratic Steering Committee, the group that chose the committee selections, which was unheard of for a freshman senator at that time. There was a fight brewing over a new slot on Finance, and he needed my help. I really did not care.

There was good news: The doctors assured us that Beau and Hunter would make full recoveries. Beau's bones would mend. Hunter had no brain impairment. But Christmas passed with the boys in the hospital, and I began to feel my anger. When the boys were asleep or when Val or Mom was taking a turn at their bedside, I'd bust out of the hospital and go walking the nearby streets. Jimmy would go with me, and I'd steer him wordlessly down into the darkest and seediest neighborhoods I could find. I liked to go at night when I thought there was a better chance of finding a fight. I was always looking for a fight. I had not known I was capable of such rage. I knew I had been cheated of a future, but I felt I'd been cheated of a past, too.

The underpinnings of my life had been kicked out from under me . . . and it wasn't just the loss of Neilia and Naomi. All my life I'd been taught about our benevolent God. This is a forgiving God, a just God, a God who knows people make mistakes. This is a God who is tolerant. This is a God who gave us free will to be able to doubt. This was a loving God, a God of comfort. Well, I didn't want to hear anything about a merciful God. No words, no prayer, no sermon gave me ease. I felt God had played a horrible trick on me, and I was angry. I found no comfort in the Church. So I kept walking the dark streets to try to exhaust the rage.

Senator Mansfield was relentless. He called the hospital every day to tell me he needed me in the Senate and to keep me up to date on Steering Committee business. I remembered how monumentally important my own committee assignments seemed a few weeks earlier. Could I talk Chairman Fulbright into considering me for Foreign Relations? Would any freshman get consideration for Judiciary? What did I care now? Mansfield just kept talking. The fight between Lloyd Bentsen and Adlai Stevenson for the new slot on the Finance Committee was coming to a head, he told me, and I'd be the deciding vote on the Steering Committee. The chairman, Russell Long of Louisiana, was pushing for members from oil- and gas-producing states on his committee. The northeastern liberals thought the Finance Committee should have more representation from consumer states like Stevenson's Illinois. This was not a small-bore issue. An energy crisis was imminent. And with the right votes, Senator Long could easily bottle up any legislation he deemed detrimental to his Louisiana oil constituents. Mansfield just kept talking. He was trying so hard to engage me in something outside that hospital room, but nothing else seemed to matter. What the hell did I care about the Senate Finance Committee?

Mansfield still wouldn't quit. One night I sat on the windowsill in the hospital room, holding the phone to my ear. It was late and the boys were asleep, so I was mainly listening while the leader told me I owed it to Neilia to become one of the 1,680 men and women who had ever been sworn into the United States Senate. My wife had worked too hard for me to kick it away. I owed it to her. I owed it to my sons. Give me six months, Joe, Senator Mansfield kept saying. Give me six months. So I agreed. Six months.

☆ 6 ☆

A Start

FROM THE FIRST DAY I WALKED INTO THE SENATE, I THOUGHT of myself as an observer. I just didn't feel a sense of connection. While the rest of the freshman class had been sworn in on the floor of the United States Senate, with the vice president presiding, I hadn't been willing to leave Beau and Hunter. Frankly, I just didn't want to go to D.C. So Senator Mike Mansfield sent the secretary of the Senate up to Wilmington General Hospital to make sure I took my separate oath. The 93rd Congress was nearly a week old when I finally arrived in Washington for my first day of work as a United States senator.

One problem I would have faced accident or no was the simple question of my age. I didn't *look* like a senator. I'd run to the special Capitol elevators they held for members during votes and get the stare from an elevator operator I hadn't yet met. "Senators only, young fella." That sort of thing happened for years. I'll never forget the first time I met Henry Kissinger. The Senate was a much more formal institution in the seventies, so one day I received an embossed invitation to a Foreign Relations Committee briefing for committee members only—no staff allowed—wherein the secretary of state would be "giving his worldview." I meant to be well prepared for that briefing, and I had a few questions I wanted to put to the secretary. I showed up at the Foreign Relations Committee's regular meeting room in the Dirksen building five minutes early. Ten minutes later I was still alone in the room, so I called my office. It turns out the meeting was in the Capitol building, Room S-116. I wasn't sure where S-116 was. I literally ran to the Capitol and circled the halls at a jog, looking up at the number plates above the doors. This was before we had secure rooms in the Capitol, so they'd sometimes play music in the halls outside executive committee sessions to drown out the conversation in the meeting room. But I don't remember hearing any music in the halls. When I finally found S-116, I was really late, so I was moving fast and sweating pretty hard. And as I started through the outer door, an armed Capitol policeman grabbed me by the shoulder, spun me around, and pinned me against a wall. "Where d'ya think you're goin' buddy?"

I managed to get my Senate ID out, and he apologized in the most flowery way possible. But I was really in a lather by the time I burst through the door to the inner sanctum: I lost my grip on the door handle, causing the door to swing into a file cabinet with a loud crash. A couple of my older colleagues nearly jumped out of their seats and sat startled as I ran right up to the back of Dr. Kissinger's chair. "Uh, sorry I'm late," I tried to say. It was quite an entrance. I worked my way around to the only empty seat—which made me look like the third-ranking Democrat—but Kissinger was all but finished by the time I got settled. Mike Mansfield was acting chairman that day, and when he opened the floor for questions, I said, "Yes, Mr. Leader. I do. . . . Mr. Secretary," I started in the most senatorial tone I could muster.

Kissinger turned to Mansfield and cut me off, "Mr. Chairman, I thought no staff was allowed."

I could see one of Kissinger's deputies frantically scrawling on a piece of paper, "Biden, D-Del."

"Oh," Kissinger said, looking at the note. "I apologize, Senator Bid-den." His pronunciation wasn't even close.

"No problem," I said, "Secretary Dulles."

AVERELL HARRIMAN, THE dean of international diplomacy among the Democrats in Washington in those days, was a good friend to me in those days, but in meetings he almost always made a point to say, "Tell us what the young people think, Joe." I kept trying to tell people that just because I was young didn't mean I could speak for all young people.

But the other problem was that my colleagues all knew my story, what the newspapers liked to call my "personal tragedy." I could see that some of my new colleagues didn't know what to say to me, but others went out of their way to engage me in the business of the United States Senate and to make me feel included in its community. Senator Mansfield asked me to come by his office at least once a week to see how I was handling my Senate duties. He tried to make it seem like he did this with all the freshmen senators, but I knew better. He was taking my pulse.

Senator Hubert Humphrey would grab me on the Senate floor with his fast-talking enthusiasm and tell me I was going to have a great career. He would also stop by my office unannounced, which is a rare thing in the Senate, and sit on my couch to talk about how I was doing, how the boys were doing, how my family was doing. There were times he'd end up literally in tears because he felt so bad for me, and I'd find myself consoling him. He made it a point to include me in a Senate delegation to the Ditchley House in Oxford, England— and then personally arranged to fly my brother Jimmy over as a surprise. Humphrey told Jim to take me away on a five-day vacation.

Teddy Kennedy also made regular trips to my office in the faraway corner of Dirksen. He'd squeeze through the too-small anteroom and poke his head into my office. He wanted me to go to the Senate gym with him. I'd tell him I didn't feel like working out, but Teddy would gently explain this wasn't like a weight room. It was an old-guy gym, a place to get a massage or have a steam bath. This did not add to the appeal; I had never had a massage and wasn't sure I wanted one.

Teddy said it would be a good place to get to know some of my colleagues, most of whom I still hadn't met. "C'mon. I'm taking you to the gym." So I went. And the minute we walked through the gym door, we ran smack into three legendary senators. I knew who they were. I'd seen their pictures. I'd read about them for years. And before I could speak, Teddy was saying, "Joe, I want you to meet some of the guys." One was Jacob Javits, the New York Republican and a renowned expert on foreign policy; another was Stuart Symington, a Democrat of Missouri who had been mentioned for years as a possible presidential candidate; and the third one was—well, I really lost focus. They were standing there, two feet away from me, reaching out to shake my hand. And they were all as naked as the day they were born. I tried hard to keep eye contact, but I didn't know what the hell

I was supposed to say. They were perfectly at ease, but for me it was like one of those dreams where you look down in class and realize you aren't wearing any pants.

DESPITE THE KIND ministrations of my colleagues, I still wasn't sure I wanted to be there. Some days I just wanted to be away from everything. I was looking at houses to buy in Vermont so I could try to shake free of the accident and make a new start where nobody knew me or the boys. I had no interest in establishing personal relationships with the press, the staff, or my colleagues in Washington. My days were focused on when I could leave the Capitol and head back home. While my colleagues had lunch almost every day in one of the dining rooms open to senators, I'd eat lunch at my desk so I could call home to talk to the boys or Val or Mom.

My chief of staff, Wes Barthelmes, thought I was getting a reputation among the press and the Senate staff for being antisocial. And in Washington, Wes explained to me, reputations were fixed early and hard to escape. He told me I needed to get out to lunch, to at least make an appearance in the dining rooms. There were three to choose from: the exclusive senators-only dining room in the Capitol—members could talk freely among themselves there, Wes told me, and I could get the real inside skinny; the less formal room right across the hall—staff was allowed; and a third room for senators and staff on the first floor of the Dirksen building. Word was that the chairman of the Appropriations Committee, John McClellan, had the architects fix up the dining room in Dirksen so he wouldn't have to haul all the way over to the Capitol.

I knew Wes was right about my getting out for lunch, but it took him a few weeks to get me out of my office. When I did finally agree, I told him I wasn't ready for the senators-only room. I'd try the dining room in Dirksen.

We went down late, so the tables were already emptying, but before I could even sit down, I felt Wes tugging at my arm, steering me toward a guy in a gray suit: "There's Senator McClellan. You should say hello to him." I hadn't met McClellan yet, but before the accident he was on my list of senators I had to know. When I'd gone to see William Fulbright about serving on Foreign Relations, he'd given me one piece of advice: If I really wanted to affect foreign policy, he told me, I should go see Senator McClellan, his fellow Arkansan, who ran the Appropriations Committee. American interests and its sway in the world, Fulbright was trying to tell me, depended on how we chose to spread around our money.

"Hello, Mr. Chairman," I said. "Joe Biden." He didn't get up from his seat. I'm not sure he even looked up at me. He just said, "Oh, you're the guy from Delaware. Lost your wife and kid, huh?" He said it without a hint of sympathy, a rare and refreshing approach, but I detected too much edge in the comment.

I felt the urge to smack him across his round pink cheek, but he just kept talking: "Only one thing to do. Bury yourself in work."

I couldn't speak, but he could tell I didn't appreciate his advice. "You're mad at me, aren't you, son? But I know what you're going through." Then he told me his own story. He'd lost a wife to spinal meningitis during his first term in the House of Representatives; one son died of the same illness eight years later. He had since lost two more sons. "Work," he told me. "Work. Work. Work."

The truth is, I didn't roll up my sleeves and go to work. Freshmen weren't offered a lot of opportunities to get out front on issues in those days, and they rarely got their preferred committee assignments. The line of Foreign Relations Committee members-in-waiting was already too long. Hubert Humphrey, who had returned to the Senate from the vice presidency, got a slot there. No freshman had a chance. So I was placed on committees that affected the big industries in Delaware: Banking and Public Works. In the beginning I found it nearly impossible to sit through long hearings about the arcane workings of interest on revolving credit lines. Like my dad, I was committed to showing up every day. I was committed to being on the floor for the votes that really mattered and I was committed to knowing enough to vote the right way. I was determined to do my job and do it in a professional manner. I did what was necessary and no more. I was like the guy on the assembly line. I did my job and did it the right way, but if I saw the assembly line four rows over breaking down, I wouldn't walk across and fix it.

A better man might have handled the situation with more grace than I did. A better man would have been able to separate his personal life from his career. But Neilia's absence was like a companion that never left my side. For minutes, then hours, maybe even a day, I might forget it was there. Some days I'd feel almost . . . normal. And then I'd feel guilty for wanting to feel normal. Other times the feeling of despair, the black hole sucking at my chest, was just as powerful as the day of the accident. There were triggers I could understand, a holiday, an anniversary, her birthday; but on other days the despair would be on me for no reason—none.

My closest staff learned to read signals I wasn't conscious of sending. Even four, five, six months into the congressional term, I'd walk into the office wearing Neilia's high school ring on my little finger, and they knew I wouldn't be talking that day. I'd spend all day in my office on the phone with the boys or Val. If there was a vote called, I'd drag myself to the floor, cast my vote, and then race back to the office to call Jimmy or my mom. I didn't try real hard to hide it. I later learned that staffers from other offices were laying bets: How long would Biden last in the job?

Losing Neilia and Naomi had taken all the joy out of being a United States senator; it had taken all the joy out of life. Even on the best of days I didn't have the heart to imagine a future within or without the Senate. There was no horizon. I kept my head down and put one foot in front of the other. I literally conditioned myself like I had back at Archmere, doing wind sprints at football practice. I might have twenty to do, but I never thought of the twenty. I thought: *I gotta do one.* Then: *I gotta do one more.* Then: *I gotta do one more.* Every day in the Senate was one more, and that was triumph enough. I'd do my job, and then I'd get in the car and go home to North Star. My compulsion was taking care of Beau and Hunter, though I knew the compulsion to be with them had as much to do with healing me as with healing them.

When the boys were finally released from the hospital, Val and her husband, Bruce, moved into North Star with me. We never really talked about it, but the Biden family rule applied: If you have to ask for help, it's too late. Without my asking, Val filled in as best she could as a mother figure to Beau and Hunter. Hunter was just three; Beau was four. Beau was still in a full-body cast with a bar fastened between his knees to make it easier to carry him. My sons had had something awful done to them; something big had been taken from them. When I'd leave North Star for the drive to Washington, some mornings I could almost feel the fear in them: "Are you going, Daddy? Are you going?" They were hungry for assurances that I was *coming back.* And I meant to demonstrate to them that I would always be there, so I made it a point to get back every night.

Val usually let them stay up as late as it took for me to get home. They'd have their dessert while I ate my dinner. Then I'd take them up to their room and lie in bed with them, put my hands on them. Talk to them. We'd say our prayers together, including three Hail Marys like Grandpop Finnegan always did. And when they woke up in the morning, I was there in the house.

I also gave them the right to constant and immediate contact. Anytime they wanted to call me, they had the green light, and the rule was that I'd answer. Didn't matter if I was in the middle of a briefing with Henry Kissinger when the boys called, my staff put the call through. I had one of the early mobile phones installed in my car so the boys could reach me even when I was on the road to and from Washington. The other condition I set was just as important: "You've both got a wild card," I told them. "Anytime either of you boys want to come with Daddy to work, you don't have to give me any explanation. You want to come to work with me, fine. All you have to do is walk into my room in the morning and say, 'Wild card.' "

As Beau and Hunter settled into our new routine, I began to feel easier about being away from them and easier in the Senate. My colleagues continued to go out of their way to show me small kindnesses. There was a group of senators and their wives who had supper together once a month or so at somebody's home. (In those days Democrats and Republicans actually enjoyed each other's company.) When they started inviting me, I thought they were just being nice and didn't really want an odd number at the table. But Fritz Hollings of South Carolina and Tom Eagleton of Missouri kept at me. Fritz would grab me in the cloakroom or on the Senate floor and say, "Wednesday night, Joe . . . no excuses . . . Peatsy's expecting you." Then Peatsy Hollings would call my office to make sure I knew the time and place. I turned down a dozen invitations a week to go to dinners and parties in Washington that first year; the dinners with my colleagues became the one date I'd keep after work. I can never forget the friendship of Tom and Barbara Eagleton, Fritz and Peatsy Hollings, Ted and Ann Stevens, Bill and Dolly Saxbe, Frank and Bethune Church, and Stuart Symington, who had just lost his own wife. When I look back, I realize how lucky I was to work in a place where so many people went out of their way to watch over me.

I also started to get to know some of the old southern Democrats; the pair from Mississippi were of special interest to me. Even in 1973,

John Stennis and James O. Eastland had well over fifty years between them in the Senate. Stennis had stuck to the tough segregationist line through the fifties and into the sixties, but his heart didn't seem in it. James O. Eastland remained an unrepentant segregationist. Eastland's position on civil rights put him in a stronger political position among his constituency in Mississippi, but he always defended Stennis back home. "It's like this, Joe. Back in Mississippi, John takes care of mah conscience," he told me once, "and I take care of his politics."

My relationship with Stennis really started when I began going on rare occasions to the private Senate dining room in the Capitol. In the Senate today almost all lunches are taken up with party business. Democrats have luncheons with other Democrats to game out the issue of the day against the Republicans, or to discuss how to defend a colleague who is under heat, or to be given marching orders and hard dollar counts for the amounts of money each of us is expected to raise for the next election cycle. And Republicans do the same. As the two parties have planted their flags further and further apart, socializing across party lines has diminished. But in 1973 most of the senators took their meals at leisure in their private dining room.

There was a ritual to the meal. The two big tables—one for Democrats and one for Republicans—would start to fill in around 12:30 as each senator strolled in to take a seat. Nobody had a formally assigned chair, but everybody knew his place without a word of discussion. The southern Democrats—the South was still solidly Democratic in 1973—had to feel at home in the dining room, as in the Senate in general. As they lost their grip on the nation, the southern Democrats tightened their hold on the Senate. The Democratic Party held a comfortable 56–42 majority (there was one Independent and one Conservative) in the Senate in 1973 and controlled every lever of institutional power. Seniority ruled in the Senate, and once a man won a Senate seat in the South, it was hard to lose. The oldest and biggest of the old bulls was Eastland, chairman of the Judiciary Committee and recently elected president pro tempore of the Senate. Tradition held that the longest-serving senator in the majority have that title, and Eastland had been elected to the Senate a couple of weeks before I was born. In 1973, southern Democrats chaired a majority of the standing committees and all the most important ones. Moreover, through the Rules Committee they controlled the menu of the Senate dining room. There was the famous bean soup, but I also remember the occasional collard greens and plenty of sweet tea. When I walked into that room, the ambience of the South was unmistakable.

One of the first times I went to the dining room, I grabbed the only empty seat at the Democratic table—the chair at the head. I had just started to eat when I saw Senator Stennis standing over the table, looking for a seat. "Mr. Chairman, I'm finished," I told him as I rose to leave. "Please take my seat." And I left before I could finish eating. Stennis must have figured it out. That afternoon a Senate page delivered a sealed envelope from Stennis's office. In the envelope was an embossed note card: "Your kindness did not go unnoticed," he'd written in his own hand, "and will be remembered."

When I made my thoroughly undistinguished maiden speech on the floor of the Senate, Stennis was among my colleagues who made it a point to attend. I have almost no memory of the speech itself, but I remember the feeling I had when I rose at my desk to make it: I was stunned. That was the moment I realized that I was a senator—and I felt inadequate. How could I, Joe Biden—of Scranton, Claymont, and Mayfield—be taking my place alongside Calhoun, Clay, Webster, Harry Truman, John F. Kennedy, Lyndon Baines Johnson? I literally had goose bumps; I had the sensation of speech, but I'm not sure I knew what I was saying; I had the feeling of being outside my own body, watching. I have no memory of finishing the speech, no memory of leaving the floor. But I do remember that later that day I got another note from John Stennis, this one typewritten: "I watched you today as you took the floor. You stood tall—like a stone wall. Like Stonewall Jackson."

Jim Eastland and I got off to a less auspicious start. I got crossways with him right away—on campaign finance reform. One of the few issues I really dug into my first year was election financing. There has been constant public plaint about public office being bought by big money and big corporations. And it's a justifiable concern. Back in 1973 the liberals in the Senate were calling for reform along the lines of setting strict limits on individual and corporate campaign donations. But with another freshman, Dick Clark of Iowa, I was making the pitch for total public financing of elections, and Mansfield asked me to make a presentation about our proposal in the Democratic caucus. Freshmen rarely spoke in caucus, but I made my pitch. Once I got on a roll, I just kept going. Public confidence in the process was eroding with every election cycle, I reminded my Democratic colleagues, and the scandals surrounding the Nixon reelection campaign finances had been a new low point. Public financing was a way to win back the trust. We would never again have to worry about who our contributors were or what high crimes and misdemeanors stuck to them. It would free us all. We'd be beholden to no individual and no interest group. We'd be answerable to our true constituents only—the American people. And our proposal was simple: The government would finance every congressional election. A sitting officeholder, like those of us in the room, would get a certain amount of funding to work with, and because of the obvious advantages of incumbency, challengers would get that same amount plus an extra 10 percent. A minimal amount—a few dollars—from every tax return could easily fund federal elections, I explained. I'd done my homework; I had the math. When I finished talking and sat down, there was silence.

"Any comments?" Mansfield asked the room. Still dead silence. Nobody said a word. The senior leadership—Bob Byrd, Daniel Inouye, and Eastland—sat rock still at the front table. Eastland was chewing hard on his cigar. Later that day, in the cloakroom, Warren Magnusson literally yelled at me: "Biden, goddammit, get over here. . . . I want you to cut the crap. Shut it down. I didn't spend thirty years in the U.S. Senate to give away my seat to some sniveling little jerk who got 10 percent more money than me." But in the caucus that day, after the interminable silence, it was Eastland—and Eastland alone—who finally spoke up. "They tell me you're the youngest man in the history of America ever elected to the U.S. Senate," Eastland said, still chomping on his cigar. Actually, I was the second youngest ever elected, but it didn't seem a good time to correct him. "Y'all keep making speeches like you made today," Eastland continued, "and you gonna be the youngest one-term senator in the history of America." With that Mansfield banged the gavel: "Adjourned!"

I REMEMBER FEELING that day like I was playing high school football again and I'd just taken my first tough hit of the season. Now I had to prove I wasn't going to stay down. Game on. Let's go. I was respectful of my colleagues, but I was not intimidated. I understood how improbable it would be to push through public financing of campaigns: When a rabidly conservative southerner like Eastland and a liberal westerner like Magnusson agreed on something with that sort of vigor, I knew I wasn't going to find much support. But I didn't back off; I was determined to push this. A few weeks later I testified before the Senate Rules and Administration Subcommittee on Privileges and Elections. And I was perfectly candid. I went on the record about my experiences with the machinists union and the wealthy investors in Delaware and the sense I got that their donations to my Senate campaign came with strings attached. I told the subcommittee members I believed the system turned off people who really wanted to be involved: "The small contributor, in my opinion, feels what in the hell difference does it make whether I make the small contribution because those Democrats are the product of big labor and those Republicans are the product of big business." And I told them that we public officials were being ripped off by the system, too: "There is a great deal of pressure, in the one particular area at least, to prostitute our ideas, if not our integrity."

I believed then that real campaign finance reform is the fastest way to restore some measure of public confidence in the system. Nothing would do more to bind politicians to the average citizen than a guarantee of clean elections. Thirty-five years later I still believe that.

WHEN MY FIRST six months in the Senate had passed, I didn't even note the day. I still wasn't sure I was going to finish out my first term, but I liked that I could be focused, at least episodically, on my job. It sometimes surprised me what got my attention. I remember walking across the Senate floor to visit Mansfield's office in July 1973 when I heard that somebody was making a speech, and it brought me up short. I hadn't known what was being debated, but I heard that Jesse Helms, the conservative Republican from North Carolina, was trying to derail a Senate pay raise. Helms was a freshman like me, but he was already getting a reputation for obstructing Senate business. Mansfield was driven to distraction by Helms, partly because Jesse seemed to take such glee in scuttling the works.

Now I didn't disagree with Helms that maybe we shouldn't vote ourselves a pay raise in 1973 when most American workers were having trouble making ends meet. But Helms was talking in a way that sold the Senate short and undermined its legitimacy. He was saying my colleagues didn't *deserve* decent compensation for their public service, and I resented it. I remember thinking that maybe Jesse Helms didn't deserve a good salary, but the rest of us did. So I halted my walk toward Mansfield's office and asked to be recognized on the floor. "Mr. President, . . . it seems to me that we should flat-out tell the American people we are worth our salt. The American people would understand because they are a lot smarter than we give them credit for. . . . I do not think many of the visitors sitting up there in the public gallery or outside the Capitol feel that they want people in the U.S. Senate who are not worthy of a high salary."

In 1973 there were actually no limits on the amount of outside income a senator could receive. Some got huge checks as partners in law firms; others owned businesses. Almost everybody but me owned stock. (I'd made a pledge during a campaign event in 1972 that I'd never own a stock or a bond so I would never have a conflict of interest on a vote.) I was doing just fine, but I knew a few of my colleagues who were having a hard time maintaining households in Washington and in their home states. I thought we should give ourselves a salary that made outside income unnecessary. "If we, in fact, are going to talk about the salary of senators, why do we not really talk about it— talk about it in terms of cutting all outside income? I would love that," I said on the floor. Not a surprise, I did get some press the next day. William Loeb, the knight of the right wing, ran a front-page editorial in his *Manchester Union Leader:* "The voters of Delaware who elected this stupid, conceited jackass to the Senate should kick him in the rear to knock some sense into him, and then kick themselves for voting for such an idiot." I had the editorial framed and hung it in my Senate office. Neilia would have liked it, I thought.

As a thirty-year-old United States senator, I was something of an oddity—and for that reason I was in demand. I'd get a lot of invitations to speak. I'd find myself on stage with the legendary Supreme Court justice William O. Douglas and Jonas Salk, the hero-scientist who discovered the polio vaccine. One of my early speaking engagements was a Democratic event in Cook County, Illinois, with four other senators. Hubert Humphrey was to be the star of the show, only nobody had told me. I had been led to believe by Governor Dan Walker's staff that I was to give the keynote speech. But Walker was feuding with Mayor Richard J. Daley, and Daley had invited Humphrey to do the main talk. Daley was not just the most powerful mayor in America, he was a powerhouse in the Democratic Party. When the mayor introduced the head table, he acknowledged "Senator Hubert Humphrey . . . and the rest of the senators who came from Washington with him." That's when I realized a big keynote speech from a thirty-year-old junior senator from Delaware was not what Daley had in mind.

When I got up to speak, to try to break the ice, first thing I did was turn to Daley. "Actually, Mr. Mayor," I said, "Hubert Humphrey came out here with me. I didn't come out here with Hubert Humphrey." Daley didn't crack a smile. Then I turned back to the crowd, which was also without affect. I could tell nobody knew who the hell I was. So I told them how fortunate they were to have somebody as important as me as a speaker. Still it was silent, so I decided to take a chance. I looked back at Daley and I told the mayor, effectively, that if he wanted a political future like mine, he had better get on the stick himself.

Mayor Daley looked at me and then turned toward the audience and went "Ha!" The crowd went "Ha!" Then he went "Ha-ha-ha-ha!" and the audience went "Ha-ha-ha-ha!" Then he broke into outright laughter, and the stockyard crowd shook in unison. That was the best lesson in the power of an old-time big-city mayor I ever got.

As it turned out, I was pretty good on the political dinner circuit. I wasn't intimidated by an unruly crowd. I gave a decent speech. And I was able to help candidates raise money. So the invitations kept coming. The boys became more and more sure I would keep returning to North Star; I could be gone for a night or two on a trip, and they were okay because Val was the constant. When the director of the Democratic Congressional Campaign Committee asked me to go on the road for candidates in 1974, I said sure.

In the eight months leading up to the elections, I went to Mobile, Alabama; Boston; Johnstown, Pennsylvania; College Park, Maryland; Philadelphia (to campaign with a congressional challenger named John Murtha); Honolulu; San Antonio; Birmingham; Martinsburg, West Virginia; Syracuse, New York; New Haven, Connecticut (for a state senate candidate named Joe Lieberman); Chicago; Spokane; Salt Lake City; Scranton; Albuquerque; Bakersfield; Atlanta; St. Louis; Evansville, Indiana; Carbondale, Illinois (for Paul Simon); Harrisburg, Pennsylvania; Columbus; Detroit; Miami; Burlington, Vermont (for Patrick Leahy). Even that early there were people whispering that I was already out making a national base for my future presidential campaign. What nobody knew was that I wasn't collecting names; I was collecting sleep.

The hardest thing for me to do at home was sleep. Whenever I'd come downstairs after putting the boys to bed, my brother Jimmy or one of my old friends would be in the kitchen waiting for me. My family and friends conspired to make sure I was never alone. They'd take me out to a late movie, or just stay up until I was talked out and could no longer put off going to the bedroom that Neilia and I had shared for the few weeks we lived together at North Star. The last physical trace I had of her, her scent, was no longer present in our room. Sleep was like a phantom I was too tired to chase.

The only time I had some sense of peace, strange as it sounds, was when I was on the road. When the plane lifted off, I could feel the weight come off my shoulders. And as the plane climbed, I could finally drift off to sleep. The minute the plane touched down at home, I felt the weight again. The sensation I had was best captured in a line I knew from a sonnet by John Milton: "I waked, she fled, and day brought back my night."

Somewhere in the middle of all that running around I began to make my peace with God or with myself. Quite frankly, I just got tired of wallowing in grief. I started to think of my rage at God as an unbecoming form of egotism. What was more self-indulgent than to think God had been busying himself with my particular circumstances? There's a little cartoon I keep on my desk. In the first panel a guy just struck by lightning, charred, is shaking his fist at God: "Why me!?!" In the second panel God answers with a shrug: "Why not you?"

Why not me? Exactly. Why not me?

Bad things happen. Millions of people had it worse than me. Get up and keep moving, I kept telling myself, and be alive.

So I kept going . . . to my job . . . back home to tuck my boys in bed at night . . . on my first tentative date with a woman . . . and out on the road to campaign with people who were willing to throw themselves into the public arena. In the last days leading up to the general election, I was in California, New Jersey, and half a dozen points in between. But on Election Day 1974 I was back home at North Star for Val's birthday.

VALERIE BIDEN WAS the cornerstone that allowed me to sustain and then rebuild my family. When Neilia died, my sister was the person I trusted completely with my sons. When Hunter was released from the hospital, he stayed with Val and her husband, Bruce, so I could be with Beau. When Beau was released a few weeks later, Val and Bruce moved in with us at North Star. She quit her job as a teacher at Friends School and became the daily caretaker Beau and Hunter had lost. When Beau started school, I'd drive him in the mornings, but it was Val who picked him up every day. She did the cooking, the shopping, the laundry, and the driving. And while I was in Washington or on the road, Val was there every day. She knew and loved the boys like they were her own. Hunter was self-contained and always too proud to ask for help. While Beau was away at school that first year, Hunt could sit alone for hours, playing quietly with his toy soldiers. Beau was the opposite; he craved human contact: "Can we read, Aunt Val? Will you read to me? Can we do a puzzle?"

The point was, Val made it her business to know what they needed, together and separately—and she spent her days and nights seeing to them. I was home a lot and with Val a lot, but all our talk was about Beau and Hunt . . . and me. We talked about their school, and their friends, and how they were eating and sleeping, and how to talk about their mommy. And then Val would want to know how I was doing, and what she could do for me. She never once put her own troubles on the table, though her own troubles were not small. Even before Val and Bruce moved in with me, their marriage was pretty much over. They'd married young; she was only a few years out of the University of Delaware, and he was just back from a tour in Vietnam. They both knew they had made a mistake a few years later. There was no lack of affection, just a lack of common interests. Even for the short time Bruce lived with us at North Star, he and Val lived separate lives.

But for Val the idea of divorce was too painful to face. Divorce was no small thing in the eyes of the Church in those days. For more than a year she was tortured, but she never said a word to me. "I knew my life according to Valerie Biden is over," Val would tell me later when I asked why she'd never told me. "I had really blown it. I was going to disgrace myself, the family, the Church, all my dreams. I made a big mistake. But your life was shattered. You were bleeding from every pore, and I was trying to shore you up, to be a happy face for you and the boys."

I had begun to think of North Star as her home as much as mine. So on the way back from one trip I called Val from the airport to ask about bringing home a dinner guest. I knew she'd need some time to

get used to this one. "Look, I know you don't like him, Val, and it's
your home, but I feel really awkward. He's been so good to me. Can
I invite . . . Jack Owens . . . back for dinner?"

There was silence on the line. A few months after I got elected to
the Senate, Jack bought me out of my law firm and moved to Wilmington. Along with Jimmy, Jack was often the one waiting in the
kitchen at night to take me to the late movie. But Val and Jack steered
clear of each other. Neither of them would let go of the memories of
their disastrous blind date at Syracuse or of their epic fights during
the Senate campaign. So I figured she'd say forget it. But finally Val
was talking: "Of course, Joe. You bring anybody you want. This is
our home."

By the time Jack and Jimmy and I arrived, Val had the chicken
breasts ready to serve. It was a warm summer night, and I was looking forward to a relaxing evening, but just as we sat down, I got a call
from the Senate and so I went into the library to take it. Jimmy had a
date, so he inhaled his chicken and ran out the door. Hunt and Beau
left the table to catch lightning bugs. And all of sudden Jack and Val
were sitting across from each other at the dinner table . . . completely
alone. "The chicken was good," Jack told her.

"Save it, Jack. The chicken tasted like rubber. I'm not a cook."

"You know, Val, you really have a problem. I'm just trying to be
nice. And it just so happens—I don't know, maybe I was just hungry—but the damn chicken was good. Okay?"

"Okay." Val had finally relented. "I'm glad you liked the damn
chicken."

Then Val started laughing; then Jack started laughing. When I
came back into the dining room twenty minutes later, they were still
laughing. Jack and Val were friends. Over the next year or so their relationship slowly grew into something beyond friendship; Jack and
Val fell in love. Part of what finally drew Val to Jack was watching
him be such a good friend to me after Neilia died. Mom-mom always
said something good comes of bad if you look for it. In a strange way
Neilia's death brought Jack and Val together. Val would always remember what Neilia had said when she was trying to persuade Val to
go on the blind date at Syracuse: "I promise you, Valerie, if I could
pick any guy in the world for you, it would be Jack Owens."

Living at North Star was never easy for me after Neilia's death. It wasn't that there were too many memories there but too few—it represented all our lost dreams. The house, still spare in its furnishings, was like a reminder of the things that would never be. So I called up Bert DiClemente, an old high school friend who did real estate, and told him to be on the lookout for a new house I could buy. I wanted something big enough for two families, where each could have some privacy, because it looked like Jack and Val were headed toward marriage. Bert showed me a lot of houses, and because my schedule was so tight, he'd sometimes give me addresses of houses on the market so I could swing by on my way into or out of Wilmington.

One Saturday night in January 1975 I stopped by a place off Montchanin Road in Greenville. I was on my way to a black tie event in Philadelphia and running a little late, but Bert had said it looked promising. I couldn't even see the house from the road because there was a series of fifteen-foot-high berms of topsoil where a developer was digging roads for a new neighborhood. So I drove up the muddy drive and . . . the house looked enormous from the outside—at least three stories—but it was dark, so it was hard to be sure. I cut my headlights, jumped out of my car, and managed to climb in a first-floor window of the house. I jogged through the first floor and then up the spiral staircase. From the landing I could see two huge separate wings off the back of the house. I jogged through those. It was perfect: a wing for Val, a wing for me. By the time I finished my jog-through, my adrenaline was flowing. The place was gorgeous.

I knew I was going to be late for Philadelphia, but I had to make one more stop. I knew that on Saturday night Bert would be having dinner with his parents, so I drove to their house. For years his parents would talk about the night I came knocking at their front door in a sweat . . . wearing a tuxedo . . . in the middle of their family dinner, "Hi, Mr. and Mrs. DiClemente," I said, "I'm sorry to intrude, but, Bert, I wanna buy it."

"You're kidding me," he said, but I could see him thinking. "Ya broke in, didn't ya?"

"I wanna make an offer."

The house was a former du Pont estate, and ordinarily it would have been out of my price range, but this was the middle of a recession and an energy crisis. Nobody wanted it. The developer had bought the fifty-acre estate with plans to knock the house down and build a new subdivision, but so far all he'd done was sell off all the property and leave the house standing on a piece of property little more than an acre. I was able to sell the North Star house for what it took to buy this one and an option to buy five adjacent acres. I was ready to move on.

I FIRST NOTICED Jill Jacobs on a Friday night in March 1975. Actually, I first noticed *photographs* of Jill Jacobs in March 1975, at the airport in Wilmington. I was still commuting back and forth to Washington, usually by car, sometimes on Amtrak, and occasionally on the forty-minute flight from Washington National to the airport in Wilmington. This particular Friday, March 7, I saw in the airport terminal a newly mounted ad campaign for the New Castle County Park system; it was beauty shots of the county parks, with the same girl in a few of the photographs. She was blond and gorgeous. I couldn't imagine who was looking at trees with her in the photograph. I remember thinking to myself, *That's the kind of woman I'd like to meet.*

When I got home to North Star that night, the whole family was waiting for me in the library. They were all going out together with their dates and wanted me to go. Frank had the number of a woman he thought I could invite. "You'll like her, Joe," he said. "She doesn't like politics." But I had sort of sworn off dating, and I opted out.

The next afternoon, I'm not sure why, I decided to call the number Frankie had given me. "Um, this is Joe Biden?" The first thing the woman wanted to know was how I got her number. I explained about Frank, but I didn't waste a lot of time with small talk. "Do you think you could go out tonight?"

"No. I have a date."

I could tell this was not going to be easy. "I'm only in town for one day, see," which was sort of true. "Do you think you could break it?"

"Well, call me back in an hour and let me see," but she made no promises.

When I called back an hour later, she was free. And when I got to her door, there was the woman I'd seen in the airport photographs . . . in person. We went out to dinner and a movie in Philadelphia. Jill had accepted my invitation on a whim; it's not every day a United States senator calls. But she didn't expect to have much in common with a man of my advanced age. I was thirty-two; she was twenty-four. That was sort of refreshing; there weren't very many places I went where people wondered if I was too old. At dinner that night Jill showed no interest in politics. She didn't ask a single thing about my career, about Washington, about the famous people I'd met. I didn't want to talk about that stuff anyway. So we talked about family and mutual friends in Delaware. We talked about books and real life.

That night, for the first time since Neilia, I felt something like absolute attraction—and something like joy. And we just kept talking.

I dropped Jill off at her front door at one o'clock in the morning. As I shook her hand good night, I told her I'd like to see her again . . . like tomorrow. She said fine. And I said I'd call. Then she let herself in and, as she tells it, called her mother and said, "Mom, I think I finally met a gentleman."

We went out again on Sunday night and repeated the scene at the door. "I'd like to see you again," I said. Fine, she said. By this time I was smitten, but I knew I had to play it just right; I didn't want to appear . . . pushy. I pulled my appointment book out of my pocket and started talking fast. "Okay, next Saturday, let's see—no, I'm too busy that night. I can't do next Saturday. I can't do Friday, either. Meetings. Let me see, two weeks from Friday. No, I'm out of town the whole weekend." I looked up to see if she showed any hint of disappointment. It was hard to tell.

"Well, um, um," I said, "how about tomorrow night?"

At that point, Jill later told me, she was thinking, *Buddy, you just blew your cover.* But she agreed, and we went out the next night. She kept saying, and continued to say, that she wasn't looking for anything long-term. She'd married young, was separated, and in the process of getting a divorce. Jill liked her life as a single woman; she was looking forward to starting her first teaching job in the fall; and, most of all, she did not want to be involved with somebody in politics, let alone a United States senator. We should just think of this as fun. I woke up the next day happier than I'd been in more than two years. This was already fun. When I headed off to Washington on Tuesday morning, I couldn't stop thinking about her.

I was at the gym in the Dirksen building when I got the nerve to call her. There were phones in the gym. "Jill? Joe Biden. You know there's a lot of scrutiny about who I go out with and what I'm doing, and I have to ask you a favor. You know I really like you. And I'd like you not to go out with anybody else."

There was silence on the phone for a second. "Okay," she said. "I'm willing to try it. But I have a date to the Philadelphia Flower Show next weekend that I can't break."

She kept the date. Jill claims I never forgot that one more date because it took her years to persuade me to take her to the flower show. Maybe she's right. Maybe I was a little jealous. I sure knew wooing her was going to be difficult. But she'd said okay, and that was a start.

✴ 7 ✴

Jill

I NEVER BELIEVED THE SENATE WAS MY DESTINY, BUT IT
had been a big part of my dreams. I remember vividly the first time I
actually walked into the Senate chamber. It was a quiet morning, and
the room was virtually empty. I'd parked my car right by the Capitol
steps and walked into the building unimpeded. There were no DO
NOT ENTER signs, no barriers, no locked doors. I walked under the
arch of the Capitol, into the reception room, and then through swinging glass doors that led to the antechamber. I found myself alone in a
long, wide hallway behind the Senate chamber. I could see the teletype
machines and hear the staccato sound of the news stories issuing forth
from the AP and UPI wires. To my right—I would later learn—was
the office of the vice president, who doubled as the presiding officer
of the Senate. I continued past that door and poked my head into the
Marble Room, which smelled like leather and smoke. Senators could
sit on the big lounge chairs and read the papers—each member got to
pick one daily paper from their state to be delivered to the room. It
was almost always silent in the Marble Room except for occasional
snoring.

I continued down the hallway and through another set of doors to
my left. Nobody stopped me, and I just kept going, through another
door and out onto the Senate floor. The session must have just ended
because the lights were still on, and I realized I was alone in the room.
I was awestruck, but I kept moving, right up to the podium where I
sat down in the presiding officer's chair and scanned the entirety of

the chamber. I was mesmerized until my reverie was broken by a hand on my back. I guess a Capitol police officer had followed me in. And now I was in trouble. This was 1963, and I was a twenty-one-year-old college student.

I tried to explain: *I was down from the University of Delaware. I was visiting a college friend at Georgetown. They were all asleep, so I decided to drive over to the Capitol. Nobody had stopped me. Nobody told me I couldn't be here.*

The police officer took me to the basement of the Capitol for a little scare, but I was released after a short time. I guess it was clear what I was: a star-struck young man. The Capitol police officer took down my name and address, but I don't think he ever put it on file.

Less than ten years later I made my first entrance into that chamber as an official member of the United States Senate. And as I was entering the floor, a Capitol policeman stopped me. "Senator Biden," he said, "do you remember me?"

"No, sir," I said, looking at him. "I'm sorry, I don't."

"Well, I'm the fellow that stopped you ten years ago." He had a huge grin on his face. "I'm retiring tomorrow. But, Senator, welcome. I'm happy you're back."

AS TIME PASSED and the day of the accident receded, I found I was happy to be there, too, and fully engaged. The issues in my first term were not small; the resignation of a vice president, Nixon's impeachment, the Vietnam War, crime, busing. The fault lines that separated people on cultural issues were just beginning to show. The Supreme Court's decision striking down state laws criminalizing abortion and giving women and their doctors the right—within limits—to terminate a pregnancy hit just as I was entering the Senate. I remember vividly the first time I had to go to the floor to vote on abortion. I had just gotten off the underground subway that connects the Senate office buildings with the Capitol itself, and as I was heading toward the escalator, Abe Ribicoff grabbed me. He was a longtime Connecticut liberal, back before the right-wing Republicans had redefined "liberal" as a pejorative.

"How are you going to vote on this, Joe?"

"It's a difficult vote."

"I know that," he said, "but how are you going vote on it? What's your position?"

"Well, my position is that I personally am opposed to abortion, but I don't think I have the right to impose my view—on something I accept as a matter of faith—on the rest of society. I've thought a lot about it, and my position probably doesn't please anyone. I think the government should stay out completely."

"What's that supposed to mean?" he asked as we headed toward the Capitol corridors.

"Well, I will not vote to overturn the Court's decision. I will not vote to curtail a woman's right to choose abortion. But I will also not vote to use federal funds to fund abortion."

"That's a tough position, kid," he said on the escalator.

"Yeah, everybody will be upset with me," I told him, "except me. But I'm intellectually and morally comfortable with my position."

Even before I finished talking, he got a big grin on his face. "Can I give you a piece of advice?" he said. "Pick a side. You'll be much better off politically. Just pick a side."

Ribicoff was right, of course. It was good advice in 1973, and it's good advice today. The old bad joke—Why aren't there many politicians in the middle of the road? Because that's where the roadkill is—is still operable. I've stuck to my middle-of-the-road position on abortion for more than thirty years. I still vote against partial birth abortion and federal funding, and I'd like to find ways to make it easier for scared young mothers to choose not to have an abortion, but I will also vote against a constitutional amendment that strips a woman of her right to make her own choice. That position has earned me the distrust of some women's groups and the outright enmity of the Right to Life groups.

I'VE MADE LIFE difficult for myself by putting intellectual consistency and personal principle above expediency. I'm perfectly able to take the politically expedient way on issues that don't seem fundamental, especially when a colleague I trust needs help, but by and large I follow my own nose, and I make no apologies for being difficult to pigeonhole. The Washington press corps ushered me to town as a kind of poor Kennedy cousin: I was Irish, Catholic, young, toothsome . . . the reporters were sure I was a liberal. Senators such as Hubert Humphrey and Ed Muskie thought I'd be with them in every liberal cause. But the voters who had been paying attention in Delaware in 1972 knew I wasn't going to be an ideologue. I'd run with Democratic presidential nominee George McGovern on tax fairness and protecting the environment and ending the bloodletting in Vietnam. I didn't see the war as a moral issue but as a stupid waste of lives and money based on a faulty premise. And I made it clear that I honored the goals of Roosevelt's New Deal and Truman's Fair Deal and Johnson's Great Society, but I also made it clear that I didn't intend to be a rubber stamp on programs that no longer worked.

I'd also run away from a lot of the McGovern wing. I was skeptical about busing as a plausible solution to de facto segregation in the schools, and I would occasionally get an earful from young Democrats who didn't like my opposition to legalization of marijuana and amnesty for draft dodgers. How many people were really affected by that?

I meant to deal on issues that mattered to everyone, like national security and personal security, especially where they were related; if we were going to give money to Turkey, for example, I thought we ought to demand that the Turkish government shut down the country's huge annual export of opium to the United States. I argued that government's first responsibility was to make certain every neighborhood was safe for every citizen. Talk of attacking the underlying causes of crime was drowning out something more basic, which was public safety. I was all for tackling poverty and unemployment and gaps in education—and I still believed the justice system was obliged to protect the rights of criminal suspects and to work to rehabilitate felons—but it was equally important to lock up people when they committed violent crimes.

A couple of days before the 1972 election I was invited to a Democratic Committee meeting at a neighborhood where the limousine liberals would be out in force. There were about seventy-five people there, and the local committeewoman who was a big supporter of mine had invited a horde of press. After she got me up in front of the audience and the reporters and the cameras, she asked me to recant on some of my tougher anti-McGovern positions. Maybe she thought this was my chance to lock myself in before the votes were counted, but to me it felt more like an ambush. Everything I'd run on, I assured them, I still believed. "The problem with liberals is that they're like lemmings," I told the gathering. "Every two years they run and jump off a cliff whether they need to or not. I'm looking for solutions to the problems average people face every day—problems that are being demagogued by Nixon and ignored by liberals."

I felt most closely aligned with the old liberals in the Senate, and I admired senators such as Humphrey and Phil Hart and Mansfield and Muskie who had fought so long for social justice, racial equality, and economic fairness. But I could not follow them blindly. Humphrey was one of a handful of senators who truly took me into his confidence, and I never forgot the European trip he'd arranged for my brother Jim and me. But I think there were times I drove Hubert Humphrey around the bend.

One day in my first term Humphrey buttonholed me at my desk in the back row of the Senate chamber. He knew his time as a national candidate had passed, so he was always trying to offer me the benefit of the lessons he'd learned. He told me that if I wanted a future as a national political figure, and he thought I did, he had some advice: "You have to pick an issue that becomes yours. That's how you attract your colleagues to follow you, Joe. That's how you demonstrate your bona fides. Don't be a gadfly. . . . You should become Mr. Housing. Housing is the future. . . . You could be the leader of a whole new generation that provides decent housing in America for middle-class and lower-middle-class people and the poor." He wanted to know if I had any ideas, so I told him I did. I thought we should implement an urban homestead act that gave working people and the poor a chance to own their homes. I thought we should change the way we allocated federal money so we could mandate scattered-site public housing and quit packing all the poor into high-rises like Cabrini Green in Chicago that invariably turned into slums and chaos and didn't help anyone. I'd been to similar projects in Philadelphia and had talked to the people who had to live there; I'd visited with people in public housing in Wilmington. Their message was: It wasn't working. The first thing we should do, I told the Boss (that's what I always called Senator Humphrey), was tear down the concentrated high-rise public assistance housing.

"Whoa, whoa, no, no, no, Joe," he said. "You can't just start over."

"But, Boss, it's not working. We've got to fix it or there will be nothing left, because the middle class will abandon us, and they're the ones who provide the political support for the poor."

Humphrey put his hand on my arm. He wanted me to hear this: "Joe, do you know how hard it was to climb that mountain?" He was almost pleading. "Do you know how hard it was?"

"But, Boss"—now I was pleading, too—"we've got to acknowledge that it's not working. The public still wants to help, but they can see this isn't working anymore."

"You know if you acknowledge that the public housing program is not working, Joe, they'll eat us alive," Humphrey said. "They'll rip it apart."

I could see he was disappointed in me, and it must have been hurtful to him to see me quoted in national magazines: "We newer liberal Democrats are rejecting the theory of our more senior colleagues, which was that if you spend enough money you can solve any problem." The way I saw it, our long postwar run of surfeit was coming to an end. Great Britain, Germany, France, and Japan were becoming producer nations again. The United States was in its first economic slump in a generation; people I talked to in Delaware understood their paychecks weren't keeping up with inflation. I thought it was time to start watching the spending side of government. Good intentions had to be balanced with good finances. I told my staff that anytime they recommended I vote for a program, they had to write down how much it would cost and how we were going to pay for it. And I joined a bipartisan effort to force Congress to reauthorize federal programs every four years, so we would have to continually assess the real outcomes for real people. "Once a federal program gets started, it is very difficult to stop it or even change its emphasis, regardless of its performance in the past," I said publicly. "It is time for us to require on a regular and continuing basis that both the administrators of those programs and we legislators who adopt the programs examine their operations with care and detail."

I was finding political soul mates in newer senators such as Fritz Hollings of South Carolina and Lawton Chiles of Florida, but I'm sure the Boss cringed again; give them an opening, Humphrey believed, and the conservatives would tear down the entire structure—from the shining dome of LBJ's War on Poverty to the foundation FDR had built with the New Deal. Senators like Barry Goldwater—who had run against big government when he was the 1964 Republican presidential nominee—would be happy to wield the sledgehammer.

I was so busy making my argument that I didn't always stop to think of it as Humphrey must have. He'd been fighting for fair housing, social welfare, and racial equality since the early forties, when those causes were often lonely ones. He didn't back down when they called him a traitor to his race or soft on Communism. His idea of who he was was formed in that fight. Like most of his fellow warriors who helped change the country for the better, Humphrey was going to make sure they didn't lose an inch of the ground they'd fought so long and so hard to win. My rant was useless. The point was that Hubert Humphrey, like so many of his colleagues, was invested in these programs—personally.

THE MORE FAMILIAR I became with the Senate—the more I got to know its traditions, its rules, its parliamentary arcana—the more I realized that the series of interlocking gears that propelled even the smallest of its movements was personal interaction. I was struck by the intimacy of the well of the United States Senate—and how history is so vividly telescoped. Some of the desks date from 1819—and in 1975 the Democratic side of the aisle became even more intimate. We gained four seats in the 1974 elections, which meant four old desks had to be unbolted from the floor on the Republican side of the aisle and rebolted on the Democratic side. My sons could have roller-skated through the gaps that separated the Republican desks; ours were mashed together.

For a brief moment in my first term—before I was assigned a permanent desk—I was seated between a Democratic colleague from a southern state and one from a northern state. The desks usually passed from senator to senator by state, so I got it in my head—though I'm not sure it was ever true—that I was seated between a desk once used by the rabid states' righter and would-be secessionist John C. Calhoun and the onetime desk of Daniel Webster, the clarion of federal power and indissoluble union. In the old Senate chamber 140 years earlier, Webster and Calhoun had locked in epic oral arguments over the nature of the Constitution and the nation and the nature of the Union itself: two men debated whether our federal government was instituted "of, by and for the people" or as a simple compact between the several states. The Webster and Calhoun debates raged for years; there was almost no ground on which the two solons could find common footing. But what I always found remarkable was that when the stakes were highest, a mere handful of their fellow senators were able to bridge the ocean that separated Calhoun and Webster and hold the country together for almost thirty years more; and when their effort to keep the peace finally failed, it resulted in the slaughter of six hundred thousand men and the maiming of millions more.

Standing at that temporary desk I discovered that by simply leaning on my right foot, I could place my right hand on what I thought had been Webster's desk; then I could shift my weight to my left foot and place my left hand on what I thought had been Calhoun's desk. That was no small metaphor for me and one that explains the possibilities of being a United States senator: On rare occasions one good man or woman could be sufficient to close perilous gaps that so many others deem unbridgeable.

Not that I started off as a strong candidate to be that sort of man. If I was tough on my friends on the left, with whom I usually agreed, I was really tough on the people on the right, with whom I rarely agreed. And I really disliked the senators who were still demagoguing race.

Jesse Helms, the Republican from North Carolina, drove me crazy at first. Jesse was elected the same year I was, running against Communists, minorities, homosexuals, Martin Luther King, and anybody else who was diminishing what he saw as the God-given prerogatives of white men. The first time I saw him make a speech on the Senate floor, it really bothered me. The next time I saw Mike Mansfield, I unloaded: "I can't believe guys like Helms. He's got no heart," I said, "The guy—".

Mansfield cut me off. "Listen, Joe," he told me. "Everybody who is here has something. The people who elected them saw something good about them." Then he told me the story of Helms's adopting a nine-year-old child who had cerebral palsy. The way Mansfield heard the story, the boy had made a plea in a local newspaper for a mommy and a daddy for Christmas, and Jesse Helms and his wife had taken him in.

"Your job here is to find the good things in your colleagues—the things their state saw—and not focus on the bad."

I said I understood.

"And, Joe, never attack another man's motive, because you don't know his motive."

There was nothing difficult about taking Mansfield's advice. In the

Biden family, even as children, there had always been an assumption of good intentions. We Bidens have strong personalities, and we live close. We've been in one another's lives day in and day out for more than sixty years, so there have been plenty of bruised egos and hurt feelings in the family. But there is an article of faith that keeps us together: Never once has a member of the Biden family purposefully inflicted pain on another. We start with an assumption of goodwill toward one another. The same should hold true in the Senate family, Mansfield was reminding me. It's probably the single most important piece of advice I got in my career.

To this day if I need help on an issue I really care about, it's not always enough to bring along my political allies; sometimes I need the support of people who fundamentally disagree with me on 80 percent of the questions we decide. I never count on them to support me just because it means so much to me, but if I've shown them respect, honored my word when I gave it to them on another issue, and been careful not to question motives, I can at least expect them to hear me out.

I've learned a lot by watching my Democratic colleague from Hawaii Senator Daniel Inouye. He's a man of uncommon decency. I've never seen him demand political loyalty because of party or friendship, and I've never known him to go back on his word. We vote together on most things, and if he needs me on an issue dear to him, he's earned my support. On the rare occasions I can't be with him when he needs me, I'll explain it to him straight up: "I'm sorry, Danny, it's a matter of principle for me," I'll say. He never pushes, and he never holds a grudge. His closest relationship in the Senate is with Ted Stevens from Alaska, a Republican. Their almost forty-year friendship transcends politics and, even at this late date, confirms the power of Mansfield's advice to me.

The Mansfield method also led me to some unlikely relationships. James O. Eastland, for instance, was probably as far apart from me on civil rights as any man in the Senate, but he was also the chairman of the Judiciary Committee, a committee that handled all crime legislation, a committee on which I badly wanted to serve. I was going to need his blessing to get a seat on Judiciary, so I began to get to know him. I started by asking him questions. He was proud of his standing as the longest-serving senator and of his reputation as a keeper of the institutional flame. I think he was flattered by the deference I showed him, and his answers to my questions often surprised me.

I once asked him who was the most powerful man he'd seen in the Senate. I was curious as to whether he'd choose recently retired Richard Russell—who had served for forty years and had essentially managed Senate business from the forties through the sixties—or Russell's protégé, Lyndon Johnson. After Johnson had double-crossed Eastland and the other southerners by shoving through civil rights legislation, they never again vested so much power in a majority leader. In the early seventies, the southern chairmen—Eastland, Stennis, McClellan, Herman Talmadge, and Fulbright among others—held back the biggest portion of power for themselves. The majority leader was almost beside the point, and no single man had the power of Russell—Eastland said that when Richard Russell voted in the Senate, it was thirty-six votes. Throughout my first term the southern chairmen ruled as a bloc. If Russell Long told the other chairmen he needed them on a vote, they'd do it without question. Power in the Senate was a matter of constant curiosity for me. And when I asked Eastland who had been the most powerful man in the Senate? He didn't even hesitate: "Kerr."

Robert Kerr had been an oilman senator from Oklahoma whose name was attached to little more than a slew of tax breaks for oil producers; outside the oil patch, nobody thought much of Kerr.

"Kerr's the only man I know," Eastland said, "could move the Gulf of Mexico to Oklahoma."

I guessed Kerr had gotten favorable laws governing offshore oil drilling applied to his landlocked Oklahoma friends. Other holdovers who served with Kerr liked to tell how the oilman pol bought chits. Kerr would hop on the underground subway next to a fellow senator, slap him on the knee, and start talking: "I been meanin' tuh give you this for the past six months." And he'd pull an envelope filled with stock certificates from his breast pocket and stuff it into his colleague's breast pocket. "I knew you'd want into this deal. It's a helluva deal. Just the kind you like. So I put you in for $3,000. Just call my secretary and arrange to give her a check." As a general rule the stock certificates in the envelope were already worth ten times the $3,000 purchase price.

Another day I asked Eastland what was the most significant change he'd seen in his time in Washington. "Ahr-conditionin'," he said.

"Huh?"

"Ahr-conditionin', Joe," he said. "Useta be, we'd be on that Senate floor, and along about April the sun would start beating down and heat up that chamber to about 140 degrees. So we'd just up and go home. Then they put in ahr-conditionin'. So now we can stay in Washington all the year round . . . and really mess up the country."

At the end of my first term, Eastland gave me a spot on Judiciary; he also offered to come to Delaware for my next campaign. "I'll campaign for ya or against ya, Joe. Whichever way you think helps you the most."

I WAS STARTING to think about running for a second term, and Jill Jacobs made it possible. She gave me back my life; she made me start to think my family might be whole again. For the first time the Senate seemed fun. When I fell for Jill, I started to feel normal again, like I might be capable of running for a second term. The irony was, Jill wanted nothing to do with politics, and she sure didn't want to be married to a United States senator.

Jill was wary. I was almost ten years older and had two sons. She was just starting her own career. I think it was easier for her in the beginning of our courtship when I wasn't thinking about marriage. We both just liked having fun with somebody again, and she wanted to keep it that way. I didn't introduce Jill to the boys right away, but once I did, they hit it off, and she was happy to include them in some of our dates. But when I tried to set up a double date with Val and Jack, she kept dodging.

One night on the way to North Star, I drove Jill over to Greenville to see the new house I was buying. We had to pick our way down the driveway and through the mud. Even in the dark you could tell the outside of the house needed some work, and once I got us inside, I started to think I had made a mistake bringing Jill to see my dream house. Suddenly the place looked cavernous . . . and empty . . . and a little ridiculous. She would say later, "I couldn't imagine why you would want a home that big." Jill is a very practical woman. Where I saw a grand house with children and grandchildren, she saw a leaky roof and eighty-seven uninsulated windows. She probably anticipated better than I did that I'd spend more on my heating bill the first year than on my mortgage payments.

One of the things I loved most about Jill—aside from the simple fact that every time I saw her my heart skipped a beat—was her practicality. She was beautiful, sure, humble, and confident, and she had a rock-ribbed strength. Jill was never going to let you see her down, and she had no time for excuses. I always trusted that she'd carry her share of any burden, and with grace. But above all, Jill wasn't going to allow herself to be swept away . . . by anybody.

The first time she took me to meet her extended family, she got cold feet and told me to take Beau and Hunter to get pizza and show up later. When I got there, it felt like home. Her grandfather was sitting in the backyard among his tomato plants while children buzzed around. When the boys and I walked in, one of Jill's grandmothers grabbed me. "Honey, you know I worked for Franklin Roosevelt," she said, "in the WPA." I could see Jill didn't like that; she didn't want me winning extra converts who could apply the pressure. But Jill's world felt comfortable to me: the big family all together on Sunday; spaghetti on Christmas Eve, just like the Bidens. Her father had started as a bank teller and moved up to the presidency of a savings and loan. He worked hard all day, came home for dinner every night, and took his daughters to visit both sets of grandparents every Sunday. At Jill's Italian grandparents' house there was homemade noodles and meatballs, *pasta e fagiole,* and wedding soup; at the others' house it was roast beef, mashed potatoes, and cole slaw. They showed up at both houses every weekend they could. Her father was a reliable man, and he prized reliability in other men. He liked me because I wanted to take care of his daughter even when she made it clear she didn't need to be taken care of. Jill told her father, like she told the whole family, not to get their hopes up. This thing with the senator might not last.

But by the time the first holidays rolled around, Jill was already integrated into our lives. Even when I was stuck in Washington, she'd stop by the new house on Montchan Road—we called it The Station—to have dinner with Val and Jack and the boys. On Thanksgiving 1975 it was Jill who suggested we get away. Wes Barthelmes suggested Nantucket, so the four of us piled into a car and drove north for a long weekend. In the car on the way up, Jill helped the boys make their Christmas lists. And when Christmas rolled around that year, Jill made sure The Station was festive and happy.

Jill had odd little mannerisms that charmed me. If she'd been working in the kitchen, she almost always left a cabinet door open, and she rarely got a lid properly sealed. In that way she was exactly like Neilia. Rationally, I knew better, but there was a small part of me that wanted to believe that somehow Neilia had sent Jill to me—that these were the signs.

One morning the next year, Beau and Hunter walked into my bathroom while I was shaving, and I could tell they had something serious they wanted to talk about. Beau had just turned seven; Hunter was six. And they were having trouble getting started.

"You tell him, Hunt," Beau said to his brother.

"No. *You* tell him."

Finally Hunter spoke up: "Beau thinks we should get married."

"What do you mean, guys? Beau?"

"Well," Beau said, "we think we should marry Jill. What do you think, Dad?"

"I think that's a pretty good idea," I told them. I'll never forget how good I felt at that moment.

"But, Dad," Beau said in all earnest, "d'ya think she'll do it?"

They were observant, my sons.

I really thought she would, but the first time I asked, she said she still wasn't ready. The same problems still applied. She wasn't sure she was ready to step into being a full-time mother. There was too much at stake with the boys. And as far as politics went, well, Jill did not want to be a public person. I didn't stop asking, but the more I pushed, the more she resisted. If I pulled back, she would come forward. So we agreed to keep questions about the future in abeyance. Even then we were rarely apart. And the running joke among the staff was that I was the incredible disappearing senator. "Where the hell is he?" "I don't know where the hell he is." "D'ja check the Marble Room?" "He's not there." "Cloakroom?" "Not there." "He must be with Jill somewhere."

Jill says I must have asked her to marry me five more times, and she kept saying she needed more time. I was as patient as I knew how to be. But in 1977, as I prepared to leave on a ten-day trip to South Africa, I finally broke: "Look," I told her, "I've waited long enough. I'm not going to wait any longer. Either you decide to marry me or that's it. I'm out. I'm too much in love with you to just be friends." I told her to think about it while I was gone.

The ten days in Africa felt like forever. I had gotten through worse, but I knew that if Jill said no, it was going to hurt like hell. I had even decided to make her a deal: If she agreed to marry me, I wouldn't run for the Senate.

When I got back from Africa, Jill said she couldn't give me up. If it was marriage or end it, she was ready for marriage. I assured her I'd leave the Senate if she wanted me to. I was up for reelection in 1978, and now was the time to make a decision. We were sitting in the library at The Station one day when she said I wasn't serious about giving up the Senate. "You don't mean that."

I'd given her my word, and I was serious. I'd already let a few people in the state know they might want to be ready to run for the Senate in case I got out. But this was Jill I was talking to; I was going to have to show her I meant it. In the library that afternoon I picked up the phone and started dialing: "Okay," I told her. "I'll call Bill Frank and tell him I'm not running." Frank was the chief political reporter at the *Wilmington News-Journal,* and once I'd told him, I was finished in 1978. I could hear Frank's phone ringing on the other end. Then I heard a dial tone. Jill had her finger on the phone cradle. She'd cut off the call. "Don't do that."

She told me later why she did it: "If I denied you your dream," she said, "I would not be marrying the man I fell in love with."

⋆ 8 ⋆

Transitions

JILL AND I WERE MARRIED BY A CATHOLIC PRIEST AT THE United Nations chapel in New York City in June 1977. We hadn't told anybody but our family and closest friends; we didn't want to tempt the press. The ceremony itself was family only—but that counted nearly forty. Beau and Hunter stood with us at the altar. The way they thought of it, the four of us were getting married. Jill was thankful we had avoided a big public event, but I could see how nervous she was in the lead-up to the ceremony. On our wedding day she woke up at five in the morning in a small panic. But once we had exchanged our vows, I could feel her doubts fall away. We had a big reception lunch at the Sign of the Dove, and amid the toasts I looked at my parents and at Jill's and saw how happy they were for us.

When the reception broke up and our family headed home, the four of us started our honeymoon. Jill and I had talked about taking a bigger trip alone when we had some time, but we had decided—since all four of us were getting married—that we should include the boys on the honeymoon. We got two nice hotel rooms and let the boys pick theirs. That night we went to see *Annie* on Broadway, where Jill recognized Jackie Kennedy in the crowd at the theater. We had planned a dinner after the show, but the boys were so tired that we just grabbed a hamburger at Blimpie's and hauled them back to the hotel with us.

That night my life felt back together again. I was absolutely in love with Jill, and I knew she'd be a great mother to the boys. But I also knew she had the more difficult job. I asked her once, not long before our wedding, how she could marry me knowing how much I had adored Neilia, and she didn't even hesitate. "That's the reason I can marry you," she told me. "Anybody who can love that deeply once can do it again." That's when I realized exactly what Jill's love had done for me; it had given me permission to be me again. However deep the pain of Neilia's loss, I was lousy at building protective walls around my heart. My whole life—for good and ill—I had been driven by my passions, as if I needed to take the risk on all the big things in life to feel alive. Jill made me see that passion was still the controlling feature of my existence.

Her transition into the role as the boys' mother was virtually seamless but not without road bumps. My mom had been helping Val with Beau and Hunter for the past three years, and she had a hard time letting go. She'd call Jill almost every day in the beginning with gentle and not-so-gentle reminders. *If Beau-y's complaining about his throat, you should really call the doctor. The boys are going to need new shoes for the baseball season, you know.* What upset Jill was the undercurrent in my mom's voice, like maybe she didn't completely trust her with the boys. I knew what I had to do, and, ironically, I had learned the lesson from my mom. Jill was my wife, and my job was to support her 100 percent. I let it be known that it was time for Mom to back away; I didn't have a doubt about Jill.

I marveled at the way she let the boys come to her. I'm not sure I would have had her patience. It didn't happen right away, but I'll never forget how it felt the first time I saw her open her arms and brace herself for a running hug from Beau and Hunter. I made a point to make it home on my usual schedule, often imploring the majority leader to schedule Senate votes so I could make the five o'clock train out of Union Station. And I was pleased to have a desk in the back row of the chamber . . . for easy escapes. But Jill was the parent who showed up at the boys' grade school to serve hot dogs or work in the library. She drove them to sports and to Cub Scouts. She cooked their meals. There were plenty of nights when it was just the three of them at dinner. I'd come home, and Jill would be laughing at the earnest help our two sons had been offering at running the house. In the middle of her first week at the house, Beau had said, "Jill, aren't you ever going to do laundry?"

"What do you mean, Beau-y?" Jill said. "I usually do it once a week." She was not yet aware of the amount of laundry two young boys generate.

"You should probably do it every day," Beau gently explained.

They had secret spy adventures together, too. A few years later, when Jill thought she might be pregnant, she piled Beau and Hunt into the car and drove to Eckerd's drugstore to buy an early pregnancy test. She didn't want to be recognized at the store and have this end up in the papers, so she tied a scarf over her trademark blond hair, put on sunglasses, and instructed the boys to sit in the car while she made her clandestine purchase. The boys actually knew we were going to have a baby before I did, and Jill never forgot how excited they were that day. She told them they could pick the baby's name, and Beau and Hunter named their sister Ashley.

There was another day when they were out getting gas when the attendant said to Jill, "How much gas do you want, hon?"

"Mom," Beau said after the guy turned to his business, "if he ever calls you hon again, I'm going to go out there and say something to him."

That was the other thing that amazed me. Jill and I never talked about it alone or with the boys, but I noticed one day that they were no longer calling her *Jill.* They were calling her *Mom.* Neilia would always be *Mommy,* but Jill was *Mom.* I'm sort of used to being in charge, but in truth it was Jill and the boys who shaped the contours of our remade family. At first I wasn't even sure what to do with Neilia's pictures in the house, but Jill made that easy: When she embraced me and the boys, she embraced everything. The boys went to visit Neilia's parents in Skaneateles almost every year at Easter break and during the summer. If I was stuck on Senate or campaign business, Jill would drive the boys north. She'd call the Hunters to brag that one of the boys got an A on the test or played a good game. Jill honored our memory of Neilia, and she always said that if anything ever happened to her she'd expect me to keep her memory alive for the boys.

"How can you keep Neilia out of this?" she once said. "Neilia is in here, and it's nice feeling that she's a part of it. She left me with two beautiful children. I know this sounds strange, but sometimes I feel like she's watching over us."

Some years later a magazine fact-checker called my Senate office with a deadline crisis. A story about our family was going to press, and the fact-checker was confused. She'd read about Neilia and Naomi and the accident, but when Beau and Hunt had been asked about their "stepmom," Jill, they'd said, "Oh, no. We don't have a stepmom."

Beau and Hunter had long since made their choice: Jill was Mom.

"YOU'LL LIKE her, Joe," Frank had told me. "She doesn't like politics." Well, Jill got a baptism by fire in the 1978 Senate campaign, and it began at a big kickoff event in the summer of 1977, right after we were married. We had a picnic at a local high school for all the volunteers from the first campaign. There were thousands of Biden supporters there, and they all wanted to meet Jill. But they were also swept up in the memory of 1972, as if the mere act of gathering once again was fanning the still-glowing embers of that improbable victory five years earlier. I watched, with a pang of sympathy for my new bride, as volunteer after volunteer walked up to greet her. "I knew Neilia," they'd say. "She was such a wonderful person." And Jill absorbed it all with perfect grace. "Look, honey, I'm sorry," I said to her after the picnic broke up. "I know those people weren't thinking." She said she understood.

BY THE TIME my first term was winding down, I had finally started to think of the Senate seat as *my* seat. I was happy in it and proud of what I'd already accomplished. In 1975 I'd been given a slot on the Foreign Relations Committee, a rare position for a freshman. And I was getting to know leaders and issues, especially in Europe, but in the rest of the world as well. And I had apparently impressed the Democratic leadership enough to have landed a spot on the newly created permanent committee overseeing the U.S. intelligence agencies. The permanent committee had grown out of the Church Committee, which had been investigating the Central Intelligence Agency's extracurricular and often unlawful covert operations. The CIA had cooked up unseemly plots to destabilize foreign governments and bizarre assassination plots like the one to off Fidel Castro with an exploding cigar. The Church Committee recommended muscular congressional oversight. It proposed a truly bipartisan permanent committee with a cochairman and an equal number of senators from each party. The day after the full Senate voted the committee into existence, I walked into my office, and my friend and trusted aide, Ted

Kaufman, could tell I was in distress. "They're talking about putting me on Intelligence," I explained.

Serving on Intelligence would be like being under a constant gag order. My current colleague, Chris Dodd, called it the PacMan Committee. Committee members have to eat everything they're told in S-407, the secure room where Intelligence meets. The intelligence community tells members something that everybody knows. Members are sworn to secrecy, even after the information appears in the newspapers and everybody's already talking about it. About 80 percent of what they tell us behind closed doors shouldn't be classified in the first place.

"Look," Ted said, "if you don't want to be on it, just tell Mansfield."

I was standing in the Democratic cloakroom later that day when Senator Sam Nunn stopped by to congratulate me on my assignment to the Senate Intelligence Committee. I made a beeline across the Senate floor to the majority leader's office and told Mike Mansfield he'd done me enough favors. When I told him I didn't want to be on Intelligence, he put his arm around me and let me know I was going on that committee. This was no favor to me. He was counting on me to speak up. He was done coddling me. He told me there were some tough calls to be made on Intelligence, and I was going to have to dig in and be serious about being a United States senator.

He was right about that. One of the first big issues that came up early on was covert surveillance. With the Church Committee findings in the news, the public was outraged at the extent of illegal wiretapping by the FBI and the NSA—and rightly so. In so many cases the bureau was spying on citizens within the United States using secret warrants or no warrant at all. We could see the wave coming—the public wanted us to do away with *all* covert surveillance—and it was crashing on the Intelligence Committee. But we were still in the Cold War, and in S-407 my colleagues and I were hearing about valuable intelligence being gathered while monitoring conversations between people in the United States—citizens and noncitizens—and foreign agents in places such as Moscow and Tehran. It fell to Congress to find a way to put a stop to unconstitutional domestic eavesdropping but to preserve a legal mechanism to gather intelligence using international eavesdropping. That mechanism had to accord with our Constitution and our basic values—and still protect the nation from real harm. We had to find a way to permit intelligence services to move with speed if needed and get a court order after the fact. The solution was not obvious, nor was it simple, and the Foreign Intelligence Service Act of 1978—or FISA—was born in the struggle to balance civil rights and public safety. I'm not surprised that thirty years later, with new situations and technologies arising all the time, my colleagues and I continue to be called on to recalibrate that delicate balance.

In 1977, with the blessing of Chairman Eastland, I got my assignment to the Judiciary Committee. I wanted to start working up legislation to make our streets safer and the criminal justice system fairer. Finding a way to provide security and still protect criminal suspects' rights is one of the Constitution's founding tensions and a central government function. Circumstances on the ground were changing constantly, and I thought it was our duty in Judiciary to be constantly on guard to make sure that balance remained fair.

I'd picked up a few interesting insights in my brief time as a public defender. I pushed hard for a Speedy Trial Act because criminal charges hung over defendants far too long. But I also understood that that sentencing model was producing unintended consequences. Like so many mistakes, it started with the best of intentions, way back in the Progressive era, when rehabilitation of criminals became the great hope of the justice system. By the time I entered a courtroom as an attorney, the controlling question that determined jail time was this: How long will it take to rehabilitate a convicted criminal? Sentencing judges were expected to divine how susceptible to rehabilitation a person might be and were given wide latitude on punishment. A convicted felon who had strong family ties, a stake in the community, and an education might get probation, while a man who had few family ties, little stake in the community, and little education might draw a ten-year sentence for the same crime. And as a rule, black people got much longer sentences than white people got. So the system had created another aberration: It was discriminatory.

Criminal suspects also knew they could take chances on the street and in the courtroom. As a public defender, I found that it was not uncommon for one of my clients to reject a plea bargain. I'd say to somebody, "Okay, they got you cold, man. Got you on two burglaries, two house break-ins. The attorney general's got two clear identifications. And you left your shoe at one of the houses."

"Well, what's the deal?"

"A year in jail."

"Well, how much time can I get if I go to trial and lose?" is what they all wanted to know.

"Up to five," I'd say. "Zero to five."

"I could get zero? I think I'll take my chances."

The system wasn't working, and I thought it was time to err on the side of a new model. What might work, I thought, was a system that promoted personal accountability, consistency, and certainty. Congress could say people who committed the same federal crime, under the same circumstances, were going to go to jail for the same amount of time. We could give judges a narrower set of sentencing guidelines to work with, and felons would be required to pay the same price. We'd be judging the crime, not the person.

There were other big issues, too. Drug-related violent crime was on its way up in the seventies, so there was a need to pass tougher drug interdiction laws—and to try to get guns off the streets and put beat cops on them. Congress was appropriating adequate money to the Legal Enforcement Assistance Administration, but I knew there had to be a way to be certain that local government would use the federal funds to hire more police officers. I wasn't that far removed from county government where federal money was not always used to fund the intended purpose. But by the time I got on the Judiciary Committee, all that seemed to be crowded out by one very big, very divisive issue, one that ate up my time and energy in the Senate and out on the campaign trail. I could not walk into a grocery store or a restaurant in the northern part of Delaware without getting an earful.

I'll never forget the annual Chicken Festival in 1978, which drew big crowds in downstate Delaware. I was walking through the parking lot on the way in, stopping to shake hands with voters, when I heard a woman start yelling, "Senator Biden! Senator Biden!" She was thirty yards away and closing fast. An attractive blonde about my age, she was hurrying toward me with two little boys in tow. She had a big grin on her face, and as she got close to me, she turned to her sons and said, "Boys, I want you to meet Senator Biden. Take a very good look at him. This is the man who has ruined your life." Her tone was angry. She was talking to her sons and pointing at me. "Take a good look at him. It's because of him you're going to be bused."

"Ma'am—" I started to say. I had a lot to say about court-ordered busing. But she cut me off.

"Don't even say anything to me," she said as she turned and walked away.

The thing was, I should have been known as the guy who was trying to make sure her children *didn't* have to be bused to a different school district. But by the time my 1978 campaign started in earnest, I had attracted the ire of people on every side of the one issue that the voters in Delaware were talking about.

Busing had been a small side issue in my first campaign. I'd been a fairly vocal opponent, because while I believed deeply in the need to integrate the public schools, I thought busing was proving counterproductive. The push to use busing to better integrate black and white children in public schools began in the late 1960s. But the actual effect of busing seemed diametrically opposed to its intent. Whites were pulling their children from public schools. White flight to the suburbs increased in southern cities and northern cities alike. In Atlanta and Detroit, Louisville and Indianapolis, Richmond, Virginia, and Wilmington, Delaware, the percentage of black students in central city schools increased dramatically—the Atlanta schools had been 80 percent white, and now they were 30 percent white—while suburban districts became 80, 90, even 95 percent white. In the early seventies, federal courts began to order cross-district busing decrees to restore racial balance.

In 1974, Florida senator Ed Gurney introduced legislation mandating that children attend the public school closest to them, and essentially stripped the federal courts of the ability to use busing to remedy segregated schools. When it became clear that the Gurney amendment was going to pass, Mansfield and Hugh Scott, the Republican leader in the Senate, started to scramble. They were mindful of the fact that the floor debate was happening twenty years to the week of the heroic *Brown v. Board of Education,* in which the Supreme Court had unanimously ruled that separate schools were inherently unequal. The two leaders introduced their own amendment acknowledging that every effort should be made to ensure that schoolchildren could attend the school nearest their home but leaving the constitutionality of busing up to the courts.

In the scrum on the Senate floor, some of Mansfield's staff grabbed me. *We know you're against busing, Joe, but you're not one of those guys who wants the Court stripped of power. You respect the Court. You respect the Constitution. This is irresponsible. All we're doing is saying by definition that you don't want to do something unconstitutional here, so why don't you say it?*

Mike Mansfield was right. The courts had to be able to stop government-enforced segregation.

I voted for Mansfield-Scott, and it passed by one vote. It was a big vote that became a gigantic vote soon after, when the federal courts ordered school officials in New Castle County, Delaware, to come up with a plan to desegregate the schools—and then ordered them to make a vigorous cross-district busing scheme the centerpiece of the plan.

Busing was a liberal train wreck, and it was tearing people apart. The quality of the schools in and around Wilmington was already suffering, and they would never be the same. Teachers were going to be transferred without consultation to new school districts. In some instances they would be forced to take a pay cut. New Castle County had about two-thirds of the school-age population of the state, and now every one of those children was going to be assigned to a new school on the basis of racial balance. A large percentage of them were going to be moved to a new school—some as far as a dozen miles away—when the new school year began in September 1978. White parents were terrified that their children would be shipped into the toughest neighborhoods in Wilmington; black parents were terrified that their children would be targets of violence in the suburban schools. It also meant that a parent-teacher conference could cost them a half day of work. And what if there was an emergency? A lot of people in inner-city Wilmington didn't have cars, and there was no reliable public transportation. Nobody was happy. I kept introducing legislation to try to keep busing as a last resort, to be used only when school districts had worked actively to segregate children by race—de jure segregation. I told one reporter:

> The reason, in my opinion, why there's such a vociferous reaction to busing today in both black and white communities is that we're not using common sense. Common sense says to the average American: "The idea that you make me part of a racial percentage instead of a person in a classroom is asinine." In addition, busing also is damaging because it spends on transportation money that could be better spent on new textbooks and other educational improvements. It makes no sense to people that they can't send their child

to the school that's two blocks down the street. And what this results in is heightened racial tension. You get whites saying, "I know
why it's happening. It's those gol-darned civil rights people. It's
those damn liberals." Then, after there's turmoil, with school days
missed and teachers not showing up, it degenerates into "It's those
blacks."

MY FRIENDS AND supporters in the black community could read
through the code words of some in the antibusing lobby. I told the
same reporter:

I think my black constituency is fearful that if the nation rises up
and discards busing it will indicate something far beyond busing.
Blacks have seen what's happened in the last eight years in this
country. In the area of housing, in the area of job opportunity, and
in the area of access to higher education, blacks have been put in
the backseat again. And they know that. They're afraid that if they
really back off busing, it will be taken as a signal to all political institutions that those institutions are backing off on racial progress.

While legal challenges to the New Castle busing orders were working their way through federal appeals courts, I introduced legislation
to restrict busing. William Roth, the Republican senator from
Delaware, cosponsored the bill. We held weeks of hearings, inviting
experts in education to testify before the Judiciary Committee. For my
effort to restore a little common sense, a few of my colleagues pulled
me aside to ask how and when "the racists had gotten to me." At one
of the hearings I was accused of attempting to "propel us back to the
segregated policies of the fifties." Clarence Mitchell, a brilliant attorney who had been one of Dr. King's most important aides, seemed
truly disappointed in me. He was a man I admired, so it bothered me
when he told me I was being duped by very smart people who didn't
share my concern for real progress in the black community. And these
were my liberal friends. The truth is, I was shaken. I couldn't muster
fifty-one votes for the Biden-Roth bill, and I started to get the feeling
that busing might cost me my seat in the coming election.

Basically, I was being buffeted by every side, and with the busing
plan due to take effect two months before the election, it was hard to
talk about anything else. Ted Kaufman and I were riding the train

to Washington one day in the middle of that campaign, and we put together a strategy for a Republican nominee for my Senate seat. How would a challenger, we asked, take down Joe Biden? It wasn't complicated. Point out Joe Biden's strong commitment to civil rights and civil liberties. Point out his statements that he'd gotten into politics largely because of civil rights. Joe Biden's a card-carrying liberal, a challenger could tell people, and his campaign to minimize court-ordered busing is just a Trojan horse. Once Joe Biden was safely elected for another six years, he'll pull the rug out from under the antibusing lobby. By the time we got off the train, Ted and I had convinced ourselves I could be beaten.

Eastland and Georgia senator Herman Talmadge suggested I go home and "demagogue the shit out of the issue." But I wasn't interested in widening divides or stirring up emotions. People were angry enough. Legal challenges had postponed the implementation of the New Castle busing orders as schools opened in September, but there was no school opening anyway. Teachers went on strike to protest the busing plan. And in early October they were still on strike. People in Delaware just got more and more frustrated. There was something almost primal in voter anger as Election Day neared; all the rational talk in the world wouldn't change that. The voters would trust me to try to be fair, or they wouldn't.

I think I instinctively understood that my most important duty was to be a target. People were desperate to vent their anger, and if they could yell at a United States senator, all the better. Part of being a public servant, I came to understand in 1978, was absorbing the anger of people who don't know where to turn. If I couldn't solve the problem for them, I had to at least be an outlet.

I'll never forget going to an event in the school gymnasium in a working-class town near Wilmington. The room had tiered seating, filled to the rafters. It had to be filled to double its capacity. People were standing in the aisles; it was hot and it was tense. I noted a big police presence when I walked in. As I pushed through to the podium, I could hear people murmuring under their breath: "There he is. . . . Goddam Biden. . . . Kill the sonofabitch." And these were my voters—working-class Democrats.

Once I got up to the podium, everybody in the room wanted to know where I really stood on busing. I tried to explain what I'd been doing in the Senate and the difference between de facto (or unintentional) segregation and de jure (or government-intended) segregation. But the audience kept pushing me. What they wanted was a full-out mea culpa and a hard statement that I despised busing. And I got hot. I wanted them to be clear where I stood. Look, I told them, I was against busing to remedy de facto segregation owing to housing patterns and community comfort, but if it was intentional segregation, I'd personally pay for helicopters to move the children. There were howls in the crowd.

I stand by the statement, but it was probably the single stupidest moment I could have chosen to make it. The room was already boiling, and I hadn't helped my cause. I could sense the elected officials behind me take a few steps back. At that moment I actually felt physically threatened, so I started asking for questions from the audience and suggestions from the most vocal. I stayed up on that podium and let people yell at me until the anger was played out.

The schools in New Castle County went back in session a few weeks later and near the end of October a Supreme Court ruling permitted the busing plan to proceed. Despite my best efforts, busing took effect just a few weeks before the 1978 Election Day.

I was running ahead in our polls in the final weeks, but I was never comfortable. I think that election came down to trust. The people of Delaware believed I was trying to do the right thing and that I wasn't being partisan. By the numbers I won fairly easily—58 percent to 42—but it felt a lot closer than that. In fact, it felt more like an escape than a victory.

Many of my Democratic colleagues weren't so lucky. The conservative movement made its first big hits. Floyd Haskell lost in Colorado, Dick Clark in Iowa, William Hathaway in Maine, Tom McIntyre in New Hampshire, and Wendell Anderson in Minnesota. But the biggest surprise to me was that we'd also lost the other seat in Minnesota, the seat held by Hubert Humphrey, who had died of cancer in January 1978.

I loved Hubert Humphrey; the Boss was a singular politician. He might have won the presidency in 1968 had he not yoked himself to Lyndon Johnson's disastrous war in Vietnam. He hadn't agreed with President Johnson's policy of escalation, but as vice president, Humphrey defended his president out of a sense of duty and personal honor. He was an incredibly generous man who was often lousy at political calculation. When he arranged the surprise European vacation for my brother Jimmy and me while I was struggling through my first months in office, I remember asking him, "Boss, what about votes? We're in session next week." Humphrey told me not to worry; he'd checked the Senate calendar, and I wouldn't miss a thing. A filibuster came up the week I was away. I missed more than seventy votes, which became a very useful fact for Republicans in Delaware who wished to unseat me.

When Mike Mansfield stepped down, Humphrey asked me to support his candidacy for majority leader. I couldn't say no. And when he asked me to nominate him in the Democratic caucus, I was honored to do so. In the meantime, his chief opponent, Bob Byrd, asked for my support. When I told Chairman Byrd I was with Humphrey, he asked me if I'd support him on the second ballot in case nobody had the votes. I told him I'd still be with Humphrey. Then he asked me what if Humphrey dropped out. I told him I was pledged to Fritz Hollings next. Byrd was relentless.

Still, Byrd must have been surprised when I rose in the caucus to place Humphrey's name into nomination. Byrd's name was already in when I asked to be recognized by the chair; it was all very formal. "The senator from Delaware," said Inouye, who was presiding. "Senator Biden."

I move the nomination of Hubert Humphrey to be leader of the United States Senate, I said, and just as I was starting my speech about the particular merits of Hubert Humphrey and why he was the right man to be the leader, Humphrey himself stood to be recognized. *Joe! I love you. I love you. I can't thank you enough. . . . this is such a wonderful thing.* Then Humphrey explained that just prior to the caucus he had been speaking with Byrd. Then he said—to my shock— *And I move that we unanimously pick Bob Byrd to be our next distinguished leader.*

So Byrd was our new leader by acclamation, and I was left standing with my mouth open. Humphrey had let me hang myself. He hadn't bothered to tell me he had made a deal with Byrd. Almost everybody in the room was laughing about it; that was just the way the Boss was—heroic, generous, and self-absorbed. He hadn't given a thought to how it might affect me. There wasn't a mean bone in his body, but the Boss just could not resist hearing somebody who admired him place his name into nomination. Alas, everybody in the room also knew Bob Byrd; I hadn't done myself any favors with our new leader. John Culver grabbed me on the way out of the meeting. He was still laughing. "No good deed goes unpunished, Joe," he said.

THERE WAS ONE big campaign in which Humphrey did release me. I'd gone down to Atlanta to give a speech in 1974, and the governor of Georgia invited me to stay at his home. He was hardly a national figure, but he confided in me that he was thinking about running for president. He had seen plenty of the big Democrats who were talking about running in 1976, and he hadn't been impressed. He actually asked my advice about running a long-shot campaign. I told him he had a lot of obstacles to overcome: He was a southerner. He didn't have any experience in foreign policy. He didn't know a lot about national issues. But if he could get my sister to run his campaign, I told him jokingly, he could win.

When I got back to Washington, I asked Humphrey if he was committed to running for president in 1976, and he wasn't. In 1976, I became the first elected official outside Georgia to endorse Jimmy Carter for President. At the time I saw Carter as a necessary transitional figure in the Democratic Party, which was losing middle-class working Americans. I thought Carter could bridge gaps in the party. He was a southerner who was progressive on race. He was talking about balanced budgets. He was committed to the ideals of the War on Poverty, without being blindly for the welfare state. He was ready to negotiate arms limitations with the Soviets, and he was ready to make human rights a centerpiece of our foreign policy.

But once elected, Jimmy Carter was unable to pull it off. He couldn't overcome the orthodoxies of the Democratic Party, and he couldn't overcome himself. I started to see the troubles in the first months after his election to the presidency. Carter hadn't spent much time in Washington during the 1976 campaign, partly because he never felt welcome. The former governor had very few relationships with the Democrats in the Senate, and a lot of them had treated his candidacy as a joke. The slights, real and perceived, had helped fuel Carter's run for the Democratic nomination; he'd run against the Democratic establishment. But just before Carter's inauguration, Senate Democrats reached out to him. We invited him to speak to our caucus, and I was asked to introduce him. And as the president-elect and I stood outside in the anteroom waiting to go in together, I was struck by how nervous he appeared. He was bent uneasily forward at the waist, and his hands seemed to be shaking. He reminded me of Neilia's dad on our wedding day. His demeanor that day was understandable; it was also sad.

Carter didn't find it easy to forgive and forget, and it rippled through his staff in the White House. They trusted few people in Washington. My staff and I had as close a relationship with the Carter White House as anybody on the Hill, and we found it impossible to get them to relax. Shortly after Carter's inauguration, the Pennsylvania State Council of the AFL-CIO called my office to set up a meeting at the White House. When Johnson was president, the state council used to get a White House tour and a face-to-face meeting with the president. They asked my chief of staff, Ted Kaufman, to set up a similar meeting. They didn't need to take any of President Carter's time, they said, but a sit-down with Vice President Mondale would be nice.

So my staff called the White House staff, and the answer came back: Pennsylvania's AFL-CIO would get nothing. Carter's staff reminded us that the AFL-CIO hadn't supported Carter in the primaries. In fact, they'd thrown their weight behind Humphrey in a last-minute effort to block Carter's nomination. The Carter White House hadn't forgotten.

Carter even had a way of making me feel like he couldn't trust me, despite the fact that I'd gone way out on a limb to endorse him in the primaries against a number of my Senate colleagues. I'd also campaigned in almost thirty states for Jimmy Carter in 1976. But when I went to the White House for a meeting, I was lucky to get ten minutes. And in the meetings, I could see him roll his arm (he wore his watch with the face on the underside) tug at his cardigan sweater, and check the time.

He didn't spend much time listening to outside advice, and he was never very good at establishing relationships with people he didn't know. It got him in trouble, especially with our friends in Europe. Carter was working hard to remake U.S.–Soviet relations, but he was also alienating allies such as German chancellor Helmut Schmidt. Schmidt was not an easy guy to begin with. The first time I met Schmidt, we got off on the wrong foot. After a long trip to Bonn, I'd overslept and was late to our meeting. Schmidt came right after me. *It's no wonder the world is in such bad shape. You young people don't know anything.*

I didn't back off. "Well, Mr. Chancellor," I told him, "we can't mess up this world any more than your generation has."

Schmidt seemed to like that answer, and we got along fine after that. He had a lot to tell me that day. He was worried that Carter was sending a lot of mixed messages and that the president might be selling out his allies in Western Europe. Carter wanted an arms limitation deal with the Soviets, but he seemed intent on protecting America from long-range bombs while leaving the threat of medium-range missiles to hang over European populations. He had asked Schmidt to publicly endorse the development of the neutron bomb. Schmidt was out on a limb, and now Carter was wavering.

I had scheduled a second trip to Europe six months later, with plans to stop in and see Chancellor Schmidt, but when Senator Gary Hart asked me to speak at a Jefferson–Jackson Day dinner in Colorado, I sent Schmidt a note that I had to postpone.

The next day the German embassy called to say they really wanted me to visit Chancellor Schmidt. An hour and a half later a State Department messenger showed up with a hand-addressed envelope from Carter's secretary of state, Ed Muskie. The message was: Call me!

When I called Muskie, he explained that we had a big problem. Schmidt, who didn't like Carter, was about to meet with the Soviet premier, Leonid Brezhnev, without talking to the United States or any other allies. Muskie didn't know what side deals Schmidt was thinking of making with the Soviets, and Schmidt wouldn't talk to our ambassador. He wouldn't talk to Muskie. He wouldn't talk to Carter. But, Muskie said, he was willing to talk with me.

So I got on an airplane with Ted Kaufman and a staff member from the Senate Foreign Relations Committee, and we flew to West Germany. Schmidt chain-smoked throughout the entire meeting as he laid out his plans for his talk with Brezhnev. He promised he was not going to sell out the West. He wanted me to take the message back to the White House. But he also wanted to make it clear that he was livid at the way Carter had canceled the neutron bomb project. Carter had done so without so much as a consultation with Schmidt—and this was after he'd asked Schmidt to get out front and endorse the program. He wanted Carter to be clear and decisive in his European policy. At one point Schmidt pounded the table. "Joe, you just don't understand," he said through a haze of smoke. "Every time America sneezes, Europe catches a cold. I think presidents have to understand that words matter. They matter."

Jimmy Carter was a man of decency and a man of principle, but it wasn't enough. That's the first time I realized that on-the-job training for a president can be a dangerous thing.

THERE WAS A big transition in politics during the Carter presidency, but it wasn't in the Democratic Party. The Republican Party had become something new, and it would have a profound effect on the nation and on Congress. The Moral Majority and the National Conservative Political Action Committee were already growing forces in the GOP, targeting and torpedoing liberal Democrats. But that was the side game. The profound change was something more fundamental. And the first time I truly understood the potential depth of the change was sometime in the middle of the Carter administration. I was traveling back from an event in Rochester, New York, with a Republican Senate colleague and a Republican congressman, and we started talking about government spending and budget deficits. These were mainstream, white-shoe Republicans. I thought they felt as I did. We had to get the budgets under control and be smart about spending, but these guys were up to something altogether different. They meant to turn the clock back to a fundamentally different time. My Senate colleague explained where he thought his party had gone wrong:

> The real watershed period was Taft and Eisenhower. Taft was a guy who continued to take issue with the principles of the New Deal. But then Eisenhower came along and basically said the New Dealers had won. He made the argument for the Republican Party: "Me, too, but less. Me, too, but not as much." The Republican Party in the late forties and early fifties gave up on trying to argue about the role of government. We embraced Social Security after arguing against it for so many years. We ended up embracing Medicare after arguing against it. We became the party of fiscal responsibility—me, too, but not as much—because we reached the conclusion that we could never politically eliminate any of those programs. All we did was spend all our energy, Joe, from 1952 to today, trying to slow it up.

But now I've concluded, Joe, that you can have the deficits as an issue. I'll take it the other way. I'll be the party of deficits. You can be the party of fiscal responsibility. Because, guess what, the only way you can win in eliminating these burdensome programs on the public at large is if there's no longer any money to spend. You can have the deficits. Now you have to go out and argue about raising more taxes to provide for the potholes, the social welfare.

I started hearing it in very blunt terms in my 1978 race in Delaware. My opponent started using the example of Morris, the finicky cat who wouldn't eat cat food. He said, "I know how to get Morris the cat to eat cat food. Starve him. Starve him. Take away his food and he'll eat whatever you give him. And that's what we have to do to government." Cut revenue, cut taxes, and starve government programs out of existence: That was the new plan. And then they started attacking social welfare in the most disingenuous way. They didn't take on the welfare programs directly; they didn't talk about eliminating welfare. They just kept up a steady drumbeat about welfare cheats and how the federal government was wasting the money taken from hardworking taxpayers.

I'll give the Republicans this much: It was a mercenary message, but it resonated. And they had taken the easy way out. It required a lot less energy, intelligence, and competence to run against government than to try to make government work. But there was also a blowback effect in Congress: Respect for the institution and civility among its members began to ebb.

I mark the last days of Hubert Humphrey as the high point of bipartisan decency in my career. Hubert Humphrey died a senator, and in his last months in the Capitol, cancer was wasting him. We all watched it happen. His hair was gone; he was emaciated. He was too diminished to take part in real debate, but he'd show up to vote. He loved the Senate. "The Senate is a place filled with goodwill and good intentions," Humphrey once said, "and if the road to hell is paved with them, then it's a pretty good detour." In his last days it was like he didn't want to leave the chamber. He'd stay on the floor late into the night, and he and his friend Senator Barry Goldwater would talk about things they'd accomplished together and separately in the Senate. Politically, the two men could not have been further apart. Humphrey had been the vice presidential candidate in 1964 when

Goldwater ran as the Republican presidential nominee. And the Boss's convention speech that year was a shot across the bow of Goldwaterism. He'd listed the many programs that moderate Republicans in the Senate had voted for, following each with "but not Senator Barry Goldwater." They'd unexpectedly run into each other in an airport on the campaign trail a few weeks later and stopped for a friendly greeting. As they parted, somebody overheard Goldwater say, "Well, keep punching, Hubert."

By the end of 1977, it became increasingly clear that the Boss would not be around much longer. And on the Senate floor one day, Barry Goldwater walked across the aisle and enveloped Hubert Humphrey. Goldwater was so big and Humphrey so frail that Humphrey almost disappeared. The two men stood for a long moment, locked in a hug, and I could see that both men were crying. They made no effort to hide it.

AS THE 1980 presidential campaign got under way, I knew we Democrats were in trouble. Everything Carter touched seemed to turn to dust in his hands: the energy crisis, the recession, inflation, the Iran hostage crisis. His triumphs in the Middle East peace process paled. And even when he laid out a comprehensive policy to fix the energy crisis in 1979, he prefaced it with a long disquisition on the crisis in confidence in America. "The erosion of our confidence in the future is threatening to destroy the social and the political fabric of America," Carter said. ". . . Our people are losing that faith, not only in government itself but in the ability as citizens to serve as the ultimate rulers and shapers of our democracy." This speech became known as the "malaise speech" and fixed him in citizens' minds as a naysayer and a scold. And that perception took hold because there had always been in his manner something of the parson.

I campaigned hard for Carter in two elections, but I thought he had a dangerous penchant for moralizing. "You thump that Bible one more time," I told him once, "and you're going to lose me, too."

I wasn't the only Democrat uncomfortable with Jimmy Carter; there was a long line. In the run-up to the 1980 presidential election, a small group of Democratic political consultants came to The Station and pitched me on the idea of taking a run at the nomination. Bob Squier made the trip along with John Marttila, who'd helped Val run my Senate campaigns. The way they saw it, Carter was in trouble. Ted

Kennedy had already declared his candidacy. The consensus among these consultants was that Kennedy and Carter would bloody each other, and neither could win the general election. They said I could be the compromise candidate. There was already an organization in place in New Hampshire looking for a new face.

When they started in, I remember thinking: I have no business making a run for president. I was thirty-seven years old. I still had nights when I was brought up short by my life. I'd stop on the landing of the carved staircase at The Station and look out the back window at the two enormous wings off the back, and the size of the place just scared me. Holy God, I'd think, is this me? Have I made a mistake here? Am I flying too close to the sun? Tempting fate? And now we were talking about making a run at the White House?

But these were smart guys sitting there in my office, and I respected them, and I was flattered. We sat by the fireplace and gamed out the primaries in Iowa and New Hampshire. It wasn't impossible, my winning the nomination. This could be 1972 all over again. And then John Marttila broke the spell.

"You know, Senator," he said, "you should not run for president because tactically you can win. The questions you have to ask are why you're running for president and what will you do when you are president. You shouldn't run until you know the answers to those questions."

This Can't Hurt Us

THE DAY I OFFICIALLY ANNOUNCED MY CANDIDACY FOR
the Democratic nomination for president of the United States, June 9,
1987, the *Scranton Tribune* dedicated its front page and then some to
the story of Senator Joseph R. Biden Jr., Scranton boy made good.
There was the requisite coverage of my speech in Wilmington and of
the long ride to Washington in a train filled with family, friends, well-
wishers, and the national media. But unlike newspapers across the
country, the *Scranton Tribune* didn't spend a lot of ink on my
prospects in the early voting states—Iowa and New Hampshire—or
my national poll numbers, which offered little cheer for locals who
saw me as their favorite son. That day I was Scranton's great hope.
My old running buddies, like Charlie Roth, Larry Orr, Tommy Bell,
and Jimmy Kennedy, were quoted at length. They had shown up
unannounced at The Station the night before—the Three Wise Guys
bearing gifts: spaghetti sauce from Preno's, the best in Scranton. I was
still the same old Joe, they reassured the *Tribune* readers.

But the centerpiece of the section about me was a fuzzy photograph
dug out of the dead files by one of Grandpop Finnegan's old friends,
Tommy Phillips, the longtime political reporter for the paper. It was a
picture of a long-ago Saint Patrick's Day parade in downtown Scranton, and the focus was on that day's grand marshal, the recently retired president, Harry Truman, gliding by in a big convertible with the
top down. In the bottom of the frame, among the crowd lining the parade route, was the fuzzy figure of a school kid named Joe Biden. The

editors had drawn a bold circle around my head. This was . . . *the moment*. My old buddies from Scranton confirmed it. "Biden later told friends that the glimpse of a former president sparked his own presidential ambitions."

If I thought that at the time, or ever said it, I sure don't remember. But it was a beautiful story for Scranton: a kid from middle-class Green Ridge who has a shot (and just the kind they like—a *long* shot) at the Democratic presidential nomination. *The moment* spoke to the power of myth, and people's need of it.

In the round of newspaper and magazine features that surrounded my announcement, writers could choose from plenty of other stories about my long-standing ambition. "He would talk about being president in high school," my friend Dave Walsh told reporters. My brother-in-law told a writer from *Life* magazine about the day we first met at our newly assigned lockers on our first day of law school: "He said to me, 'I'm going to marry my girlfriend Neilia, go back to Delaware, become a criminal lawyer, and then become a U.S. senator from Delaware." Sometimes when Jack told the story, he'd say, "I don't remember if he said president, but he might have." The other one in circulation was one I knew to be true because it had happened just a few years back, in my first term in the Senate. I was talking to an elementary school class, and one of the children asked me if I wanted to be president. When I started to tell the class I was perfectly happy being a senator and had no plans to run for the White House, I could see a nun at the back of the room stand up. "You know that's not true, Joey Biden," she said as she pulled from the folds of her habit a paper I'd authored in grade school. I'd written that I wanted to be president when I grew up, she said. So I was caught red-handed, guilty of schoolboy musings. The thing was, I never thought that sort of paper separated me from other kids. Didn't a lot of twelve-year-olds write the same thing?

To me, even after more than ten years as a United States senator, the idea of my being president seemed far-fetched. I had done very little of the groundwork required. I had spoken at hundreds of college campuses, and I had never stopped long enough at any of them to take names and numbers of people who might want to sign up to work on a Biden presidential campaign. I hadn't spent extra time doing interviews with local newspaper reporters or getting to know the right people on the big-city editorial boards. I didn't stay in any town long enough to meet with the people who could raise the sort of money national campaigns devour. In short, I did not get up every day thinking about how to become president of the United States. I did not spend my career in pursuit of the Oval Office. Maybe my first run for the nomination would have worked out better if I had.

THE SAME PEOPLE who talked to me about running in 1980 came at me again about 1984, and then some. My old friend Pat Caddell, the talented young political strategist and writer who had been an important part of my 1972 race, led the charge. Nobody could divine the meaning hidden in polls like Pat could. And he had new numbers that foretold the story of 1984. Former vice president Walter Mondale was the likely Democratic nominee, but he would never beat President Ronald Reagan. Voters were hungry for a new young face with new ideas—somebody like me, Pat suggested, who wasn't tied to the tired old politics of the liberal Great Society wing of the Democratic Party. Pat and I agreed that the big force that could reinvigorate the party was the baby boom generation. If a bright new candidate could harness that boomer power, he could win the presidency and change the country. Just how the country would be changed was not so clear, but what was clear to Pat was that I could be that candidate. The campaign gurus had ideas about strategy, tactics, and, above all, a message—a message that would capture the baby boomers, the generation in waiting.

In the summer of 1983 I was trying to fashion a message to reinvigorate the Democratic Party, not so I could run for president but to push back at the ungenerous policies of the current administration. We had allowed President Reagan and the Right to control the language of the debate on civil rights, welfare, education, and tax policy. They effectively used the language of busing, "racial quotas," and "welfare cheats" to drive wedges among the varied constituencies of the Democratic Party. The Reaganauts were successfully pitting whites against blacks, management against labor, the middle class against the impoverished. Somewhere along the way Democrats had been pushed into a hunched defense of interest-group-driven tactics and lost their animating strength, which was the willingness to work together to provide our children with quality education and health care, to provide workers with their fair share of America's economic bounty, and to provide equal opportunity for all people, regardless of race, creed, or gender. I thought it was time to remind Democrats to rely again on their willingness to sacrifice a little personal comfort for the common good and to begin to recapture the national debate on social policy with the sort of language that binds people to one another. Pat, Mark Gitenstein, and I took a speech I had written on the fly, literally on the back of an envelope, for Jesse Jackson's Operation PUSH national convention that summer, and began to build on it for a speech I was scheduled to give at the New Jersey State Democratic convention in Atlantic City in September 1983, just a few months before the first primary. Most of the declared candidates were also in Atlantic City, but I appeared to be the surprise of the gathering. "It was the oratory of the younger generation that kept the delegates talking long after the results of Tuesday's nonbinding straw poll had been announced," said the *Washington Post*. "Sen. Joseph R. Biden (D-Del.) . . . brought the 1,500 delegates to their feet when he vowed that he and other younger Democrats are prepared to rededicate themselves to the values that made the Democratic Party dominant over the last 50 years."

Standing at the podium that day, as I was giving the speech, I knew it was the beginnings of a solid message. I had reiterated my long-held belief that the Democratic Party had failed

> to remember what got us this far and how we got here—moral indignation, decent instincts, a sense of shared sacrifice and mutual responsibility, and a set of national priorities that emphasized what we had in common. . . . The party that was the engine of the national interest—molding our pluralistic interest into a compelling new social contract that served the nation well for fifty years—became perceived as little more than the broker of narrow special interests. Instead of thinking of ourselves as Americans first, Democrats second, and members of interest groups third, we have begun to think in terms of special interests first and the greater interest second. . . . We have let our opponents set the agenda and define what is at stake.

I pointed out that it was time to sublimate our narrow agendas to the greater public good. We were a big and diverse political party, full of union members, civil rights activists, women's rights proponents, children and grandchildren of immigrants who had worked their way into the middle class, as well as the young and well-off children of the sixties who had been drawn to the party by the struggles over racial equality and the war in Vietnam. I meant to speak to them all, to ask something of each of them. Pat and Mark had helped me wrap the speech in a package that emphasized the fallen heroes of the previous generation—John F. Kennedy, Martin Luther King, Bobby Kennedy— and our shared opportunity to continue in their tradition.

> To my generation has now come the challenge. In the days to come we will be tested on whether we have the moral courage, the realism, the idealism, the tenacity, and the ability to sacrifice some of the current comfort to invest in the future. . . . I believe that this generation will rise to the challenge. . . . The experts believe that, like the Democratic Party itself, the less than forty-year-old voters are prepared to sell their souls for some security, real or illusory. They have misjudged us. Just because our political heroes were murdered does not mean that the dream does not still live, buried deep in our broken hearts.

I remember the feeling in the room when I delivered that line; its effect on the crowd washed back at me as a physical sensation. I could see people in the audience crying. Senator Bill Bradley, who was on the podium that day, said he was nearly brought to tears. I closed with a quote from Robert Kennedy—Pat loved RFK—pivoting off it to remind those Democrats of our legacy and our challenge:

> His words still echo, reminding us that only with our idealism, commitment, and energy can we ever hope to achieve the destiny history has laid before us. Not as blacks or as whites; not as workers or professionals; not as rich or poor; not as men or women; not even as Democrats or Republicans. But as people of God in the service of the American dream.

The crowd in Atlantic City was not the college-educated, white-collar crowd that somehow became synonymous with the term *baby boom*. This was a crowd as diverse as the generation itself and cut across generations; the convention was full of party regulars: working

men and working women, labor leaders, civil rights and women's
rights professionals. Many of them were parents of boomers. But I
could sense they were with me word for word. I could feel it in my
guts. At age sixteen or sixty, people connected with this message. It
was for everybody. I hadn't sufficiently appreciated how each person
in the audience would fill in my words with his or her own meanings,
might hear something different from what I'd intended. After all, each
person has a little something different buried in a broken heart. But in
Atlantic City on that day I could tell that people were moved to get up
and stand with me.

The gurus were thrilled, and they kept coming up to Wilmington to
push me to run. Caddell would pull from his briefcase the dot-matrix
printouts that showed the latest polling data, and then he'd make a
hard case as to why I could win this in '84, why *this* was the time. Pat
was relentless. Sitting in my library at The Station that winter, just before the filing deadline, I kept saying, "Dammit, Pat, I don't want to
do this thing." But he kept at me. Just in case, he said, sign the filing
papers to compete in the New Hampshire primary. So I signed them,
almost as a lark, but I told everyone in the room that the papers were
to remain in Val's possession. Nobody else could touch them. If I decided to run, Val could fly north to file the papers. Then Jill and I got
on a plane to take a short vacation.

I had no intention of running in 1984, and the people closest to me
knew that. But Jill and I had a serious talk on the flight down to the
islands. I wasn't worried so much about getting beat. Nobody would
expect me to win in the first place. The chances of my winning were
minuscule. But what if, unlikely as it was, I did win? I still had not
answered the big questions: *Why run? To do what?* I simply could
not visualize myself running the bureaucracy of the federal government. I didn't think I knew enough about how the government func-
tioned, and I wasn't sure I knew the people to call. Even after eleven
years in the Senate, I didn't know and trust enough of the right people. And the right people did not know and trust me. Who would I
pick to run the budget office? Who would I pick for secretary of state,
treasury, defense? I wasn't like Sam Nunn or other senators who had
personal relationships with generals. By my own standards, I wasn't
ready to be president.

By the time our plane touched down in the islands, I knew what I had to do. I called Val: "Don't file that thing," I told her. "I'm not running."

AFTER PRESIDENT REAGAN won a second term in 1984, the question of my running was back on the table. It would be a wide-open field in 1988—no incumbent and no heir apparent on the Democratic side. I was pretty sure the most formidable Democrat, New York's governor, Mario Cuomo, wasn't going to run. And when I took a look at the likely candidates—Gary Hart, Richard Gephardt, Jesse Jackson—I felt I measured up. I was just forty-two years old, but after a decade on the Senate Foreign Relations Committee and nearly that long on the Senate Select Committee on Intelligence, I knew the world and America's place in it in a way few politicians did. My education in foreign affairs wasn't just the time spent in committee hearings but in traveling the world and meeting leaders. It's important to read the reports and listen to the experts; more important is being able to read people in power. Listening closely to these leaders had been an incredible window onto the personal intimacy of diplomacy. I remember an early meeting with Prime Minister Golda Meir where she could see *my* despair at the prospects for peace and security for Israel. I found her bucking me up but also giving me an unforgettable lesson in the strength and weakness of the Israeli position: "We Jews have a secret weapon in our struggle against the Arabs," Meir told me. "We have nowhere else to go." On my first trip to China after normalization, I saw firsthand the possibility of leveraging Deng Xiaoping's very real fear of the Soviets to gain specific intelligence aid from the People's Republic of China.

I had also learned from experience that when you speak with the backing of the United States, modesty is not as important as candor. These world leaders could smell weakness, and they had radar for insincerity. Speaking frankly and showing strength was the way to gain the trust of leaders like Helmut Schmidt; and I felt I had even gained the grudging respect of the former Soviet premier Alexei Kosygin, not long before he died, when I led a delegation of senators to Moscow to talk about arms control. In the summer of 1979 the strategic arms limitations pact signed by President Jimmy Carter and Soviet president Leonid Brezhnev—SALT II—was soon to be under consideration by the Senate and losing ground. The treaty was under attack from

Cold Warrior senators like Henry "Scoop" Jackson, Barry Goldwater, and Jesse Helms, and its most outspoken defender, Foreign Relations chairman Frank Church, was battling for his political life in a tough election back in his home state of Idaho. When the public was startled by satellite pictures confirming the presence of a Soviet brigade in Cuba, Chairman Church had to take a tough public stance: no Soviet withdrawal from Cuba and no SALT II. President Carter knew his treaty was on the ropes, and he was worried that the new Democrats in the Senate might cave to pressure from the right. So the president suggested I lead a delegation of young senators on a visit to the Kremlin to get assurances that the Soviets would abide by new conditions adopted by the Senate. So I flew with five of my colleagues behind the Iron Curtain, to Moscow, for talks with Soviet leadership.

The meeting took place in an ornate meeting room in the Kremlin. After my fellow senators and I took our seats on one side of a long conference table, President Brezhnev and Premier Kosygin entered the room and sat across from us. They seemed emboldened at the sight of our delegation, which included New Jersey's new senator, Bill Bradley, then thirty-five. I was just half a year older than Bradley and was leading the discussion on our side. Brezhnev looked gray; we didn't know it, but he was already sick and dying. The Soviet president excused himself after introductions and turned the meeting over to Kosygin, the old hard-liner, to do the talking. Kosygin had already publicly thumped his chest about the Senate's delay in ratifying SALT II, and I remember how sharp his eyes were when he started talking. We were talking through translators. President Carter had dispatched the best and most experienced State Department translator to the meeting, the same one he'd used in his meetings with Brezhnev. But Kosygin was sitting directly across the table from me, and he kept his eyes on mine as he set the ground rules. *Let's get two things straight, Senator,* I remember him saying. *The first thing is I speak for the U.S.S.R. and you speak for the U.S. I talk. You talk. Nobody else.* I didn't have to tell him it wasn't hard to find a senator who would agree with that deal. *And secondly, Senator,* Kosygin went on, *you are a young man. But when I was your age my job was as important as yours.* He went on to tell me that at my age he had been given the task of keeping Leningrad supplied through the Nazi's hellish siege of the city in World War II. The point he clearly wanted to make was that I was, like the United States itself, young and untested. He was also reminding our entire delegation of the enormous price our Soviet allies had paid in World War II. Eleven million soldiers from Russia and its Soviet satellites had been killed, and 16 million civilians. About a million died in the siege of Leningrad alone. Kosygin and his countrymen had proved they could survive that kind of human devastation.

Then he said, *One more thing, Senator. Let's agree that we do not trust each other, and we have good reason not to trust each other. You Americans believe that you would never use nuclear weapons. You believe you would never use them against us first. But I hope you understand why we think you might.*

I started to interject, but he wasn't finished. *You are the only nation in the history of mankind that has ever used nuclear weapons. I am not second-guessing that, but you used them. So you have to understand we might think you might use them again.*

And, remember, you put American troops in our country to fight alongside the White Russians in 1917. We have never set foot on your territory, and we have never dropped the bomb.

Kosygin had clearly set the terms of the discussion. His points were legitimate and were stated to intimidate and obfuscate. But Kosygin's point was worth remembering. No matter how well intended our country is, we cannot expect other nations to trust us as much as we trust ourselves. The assumption of good intentions rarely extends to international diplomacy.

The meeting went on for three hours, and much of it was the long-running soliloquy from Kosygin. At one point the Soviet premier tried to engage me in a conversation about the number of American and Soviet forces in Europe. Mutual balanced force reductions was also a topic of discussion. I'd been studying the balance of both conventional forces and nuclear forces, so when he gave me a number for Soviet tanks that was laughably low, I didn't let it pass. *Mr. Kosygin*, I said, *they have an expression where I come from: Don't bullshit a bullshitter.* He seemed to like that. One of the other senators from the delegation later told me he asked the State Department translator if he'd told Kosygin straight. Apparently he'd been overly diplomatic. *Don't kid a kidder* was his translation.

Although Kosygin did most of the talking, I did manage to get an unspoken assurance from him that the Soviets would likely accede to the treaty modifications the Senate had under consideration. The Soviets wanted the treaty passed, too.

A year later Kosygin was dead, and two years after that, Brezhnev was, too. The generation of leaders formed in the bitterness of revolution and world wars, divided by hard-line ideology, was passing from the scene. As Reagan settled into his second term, it was becoming clear that the new Soviet leader, Mikhail Gorbachev, was looking for a partner to write the end to the Cold War. And there wasn't anybody lining up to run for the nomination I thought would be a better partner than me.

But in 1986 I was not pining for the White House. I didn't think that I had to change the world and that now was my time. I had decided that someday I was going to run for president of the United States of America, but I knew I couldn't string along the political operatives forever. The men and women who were with me were the best in the business, and they were hot to go. I knew if I didn't make some moves soon, they'd find other candidates who were in all the way for 1988. So now was the time to show them I was serious, to begin to lay the groundwork. There were county chairmen to meet in Iowa, mayors and city councilmen in New Hampshire. I needed to know the president of the AFL-CIO, CEOs of Fortune 500 companies, and money people across the country. The smart political people thought it would take more than $10 million just to get through the primaries. I'd never raised a million for a single campaign.

This wasn't like the early days of my first Senate race. Back then, even when I was just running around doing eight coffees a day, I could see that race all the way down to victory night, to *being* a senator, to what I would *do* as a senator. The presidential race, and being president, I could not see. But I figured I was on my own time schedule. I started the presidential exploration as a way of gathering up the raw footage I'd need to put together a reel that took me all the way to the end, all the way to the White House. And in my own head that was still years down the road.

If somebody had hooked me up to a lie detector in 1986 and asked if I was going to be a fully announced candidate for 1988, I would have said, "No." If they had asked me if I was building a base to run for president in 1992 or 1996, I would have said, "Absolutely."

I kept saying to my friend and longtime chief of staff, Ted Kaufman, as we began to build the blocks, "We're just trying this out." And I knew I was talking as much to myself as to anyone else in the room.

Jill was more skeptical than I was and more worried about the personal price we might pay in running for the nomination. She'd run into Gary Hart's wife, Lee, at a cocktail party not long after the 1984 campaign, when Hart had surprised everyone by nearly beating Walter Mondale for the Democratic nomination. Hart was the front-runner for 1988, but Lee was not exactly measuring the draperies in the White House. At the cocktail party Lee Hart had appeared in front of Jill dressed in white, like a guardian angel. "So, Joe wants to run for president?" she said to Jill in a confiding tone. "It's harder than you can ever believe."

That was the sort of thing Jill didn't forget. But I'd tell her that I didn't have to actually end up running in '88. I could go out, meet the people I'd have to know, show some appeal as a candidate, and get talked about. I could make the sort of friends I'd need in the future and meet the people who could help me raise money. "Look, let's just start down the road," I told Jill. "This can't hurt us."

THE BIG QUESTIONS Marttila had asked—*Why are you running? What will you do as president?*—still loomed, but I held them in abeyance. I had a series of more practical personal questions to ask myself: Could I be the sort of husband and father I wanted to be while running for president? And could I be the sort of senator I wanted to be while running? We Democrats had taken back the Senate in the midterm elections in 1986, and that posed immediate problems. I knew our majority leader, Bob Byrd, was not happy about having his Democratic colleagues running for president because it made his job a lot tougher. If even a handful of his members were out campaigning in Iowa and New Hampshire, Byrd had a harder time counting votes and setting the schedule. When I told him I was getting serious about seeking the nomination, he didn't exactly swoon, but I promised him I wouldn't abandon him or my job in the Senate. "Mr. Leader," I told him, "for the next couple of years if you need me for any vote you think is important, I will come back. I'll cancel whatever I'm doing and come back."

The thornier issue was the Judiciary Committee. Senator Ted Kennedy had first dibs on the chairmanship when the new Congress convened in January 1987. He called me up one day when I was in the middle of a political planning meeting at The Station. "Joe, I'd like to make you chairman of Judiciary," he told me, "but I'll need more staff." It was an old gambit in the Senate. Kennedy was also senior member of the Senate Labor Committee, so he had his choice of chairmanships. He was going to take Labor but use his seniority on Judiciary to bargain for a bigger portion of the committee staff.

"Keep it," I said. "I don't want the chairmanship."

"Joe, I'm serious."

"I am, too," I said.

Senator Kennedy nonetheless took the chair of Labor and handed me Judiciary. Even in a relatively quiet time, the Judiciary is a bear of a committee to run. The staff and budget are among the biggest in the Senate, and volumes of controversial legislation wend through the committee every Congress. As chairman I would also have to preside over the confirmation hearings of every man and woman appointed to the federal courts. I anticipated an even bigger problem because there were a lot of aging justices on the Supreme Court in January 1987: Thurgood Marshall, William J. Brennan, Lewis Powell—and if one of them decided to retire, there could be a real fight in the Senate over President Reagan's nominee.

Reagan had made it clear that he wanted to seat justices who would roll back the Warren Court's expansive vision of individual rights. The president's supporters on the right thought he'd been too timid when he nominated Sandra Day O'Connor, who turned out to be something of a centrist on abortion and affirmative action. His 1986 nomination of the staunchly conservative Antonin Scalia as associate justice had been a clear signal that the president wasn't going to make a similar mistake. If the White House got a chance to nominate another justice, they made it clear, they'd choose one who would tip the balance solidly to the right. It would mean a big fight in the Senate. I was pretty confident I could manage a contentious Supreme Court nomination and run for the presidential nomination at the same time; I just wasn't sure I could do them both well.

But things went so much better than I had expected when I first went out to campaign; wherever I traveled people seemed hungry for a candidate who believed in the basic things I did. People were so tired of the old Reagan cant that government was the enemy. When I'd tell a roomful of people that together we had the opportunity to build a political majority committed to the idea that government has an obligation to play a constructive role in improving the lives of all Americans, I could see people lean toward me. And Pat Caddell and I were right about this much: The boomer generation seemed the hungriest of all. I'm a gut politician; I know when I leave a room whether I've connected or not, and there just weren't that many misses when I started out. I started to feel that as long as I showed who I was and what I held most dear, I'd do okay. The easy part was saying what I believed. "My parents and your parents bestowed upon this generation the greatest material bounty, the broadest intellectual opportunity, and the most unlimited personal liberty ever known in the life of this planet," I'd say, and I could see people move in closer. ". . . Only through personal sacrifice, only with our idealism, our commitment, and our energy can we ever hope to fulfill the destiny that history has marked for us as a nation. We won't do it as blacks or as whites, nor as southerners or as northerners. We won't do it as rich or as poor, nor as men or as women. We won't even do it as Democrats or as Republicans, but as people of God, together, in the service of the American dream." I'd finish and people would swarm me. *Where do I sign up? How can I help?*

The truth was, it was invigorating. The speeches were key for me, both in the writing and the delivery. I'd made thousands of votes as a senator, and I could always explain a specific vote, but writing a speech was a way to sit back and think about the totality of those votes, about what animated my public service. In the beginning of 1987, I still felt like my message was a bit opaque, like audiences were hearing me through a veil. I hadn't yet boiled the speech down to words that felt absolutely authentic to me. But I was starting to find a rhythm and a cadence, and when I began to feel like I was getting traction and moving ground under my feet, I started looking at the race through the wrong prism. I looked around, judged myself against the other potential candidates for the nomination, and by the beginning of 1987 I decided I could beat them.

I had major addresses scheduled at the AFL-CIO and at major Democratic events in Florida and California. On the last day of January 1987, I flew across the country to Sacramento to give a speech to the California Democratic convention. At the close of that speech, three thousand important and influential California Democrats stood up and went crazy. I knew that day that there was almost nothing to stop me from making the run. We had put together a first-rate political team. Activists were signing on in the early states, and I was raising the sort of money I thought I'd need. I'd come back from a trip to

New Hampshire or Iowa and say to Ted Kaufman, "It's going really well out there. There's pace on the ball."

Two weeks after California I spoke to the national convention of the AFL-CIO, the most powerful labor organization in the country. The delegates in Bal Harbour, Florida, were looking for a candidate to endorse. Hart was the front-runner, but his record on labor didn't excite the leadership. Congressman Richard Gephardt had a get-tough trade policy that was supposed to protect American workers, but it seemed to me the labor bosses were skeptical of his ability to carry the country. New York governor Mario Cuomo was wringing his hands about whether or not to run. Massachusetts governor Michael Dukakis wasn't even scheduled to appear at the most important labor meeting.

I didn't give the union guys any feel-good talk about how they were going to be okay. President Reagan's trickle-down economic policies had given business interests in the country a cover for waging an outright war against union members. "The chambers of commerce understand what is at stake," I reminded them. "They are about the business of seeing to it that your say and your share in the economic bounty and prosperity of America are fundamentally changed. If you don't understand that, you're in the wrong business." Even as I told them they were going to have to wake up and make the fight with me, I could feel they were already there. When I was done, the standing ovation was so loud and so sustained that I walked off the stage with adrenaline surging through me. I'd already planned to make a stronger statement about running in 1988 to help push the fund-raising, but when I finished the speech in Bal Harbour that day, I felt that winning the nomination was a real possibility. So when reporters grabbed me after the speech, I told them flat-out that I was planning to run in 1988, but I made sure to leave myself an out: "Only if I hit a rock between now and the time of a formal announcement would anything change my mind."

A week after the speech in Sacramento, the lead political reporter at the *Los Angeles Times*, Robert Shogan, published a big take-out feature on me on the front page of the Sunday paper. I had spent time with Shogan, a tough little bantam of a guy who wasn't going to be swept away by any smooth talk. But he took my candidacy very seriously. He'd been in the audience at the Democratic convention in Sacramento, and he'd clearly seen something in me. "With such soaring rhetoric delivered to party audiences around the country over the last four years," Shogan wrote, "Biden has not only helped rekindle Democratic spirits in the midst of the Reagan era, but has also pumped life into his own presidential aspirations." He was generous in his assessment of my family, my home, my values, and my struggles with balancing being a good father, husband, senator, and potential presidential candidate.

But deep in the story came the obligatory caveats: I talked too much; I was led by emotion rather than reason; I didn't roll up my sleeves and do my work in the Senate. He summed up the big question in one fat paragraph. "Although no one questions Biden's ability to rouse an audience, this very gift has helped crystallize the most significant criticism of his performance as a senator and his potential as a President: that there is less to him than meets the eye (and the ear); that he sells the sizzle but is short on the steak; that he is more of a show horse than a workhorse."

I knew when I read that paragraph that that would be the question that rattled around the press pack for as long as I was in the race. And it would be answered by a group of people who knew next to nothing about me.

In January 1987 I could not look back and recall having had a single private meeting, a private cup of coffee, a private lunch, or a private dinner with one serious national reporter. I didn't have a personal relationship with anybody covering national politics. There was not a single big-name reporter or member of a major newspaper's editorial board I felt I could call just to chat or talk to in a serious way off the record. I just hadn't done it. I hadn't gone out of my way to avoid reporters, but I never took any time to cultivate them, either. I was intent on getting to Union Station at the end of the day to catch the train back home to Wilmington. I didn't know them, and they didn't know me. The truth was, I wasn't sure I could trust reporters.

My introduction to the big-time press had not gone well. I'd entered politics with nothing but respect for reporters; as far as I was concerned, they were doing service to the nation. But after the accident in 1972, I had been the subject of too much ghoulish attention. All of a sudden I wasn't a person—I was a good story. And the reporters just would not leave me alone. Photographers snapped my picture as I walked out of the hospital, while reporters yelled their questions at me: "Senator, how many stitches does Hunt have?"

"How many broken bones does Beau have?" "How are you *really* doing, Senator?" "How does it feel?"

Well, it felt like hell. I know they had a job to do, but they didn't seem willing to give me room to be human, to grieve. Eighteen months later, when I was having one of my bad days, a reporter walked up to me and said, "Senator, when are you going to get over this?"

My relationship with reporters was so sour early in my Senate career that I just never got comfortable with the press. There was a long-standing game between reporters and elected officials in Washington; the ground rules were well established. I understood, almost by osmosis, that I could talk to reporters without being quoted, give them information without my name attached. I could talk on background or deep background or off the record. But I didn't want anything to do with the game; I didn't feel like trading favors. In fact, somehow it seemed to me almost immoral to talk off the record. If I had something to say, I'd simply say it straight up, for attribution. I remember walking out of a closed hearing one day and feeling a longtime Capitol Hill reporter grab me at a rope line. "Senator, what was the discussion in there?

"I can't tell you that," I said.

"Look, Senator, you take care of me, and I'll take care of you."

I basically told him to take a flying leap.

My first year in the Senate, I'd get half a dozen requests a week for interviews with feature writers. I understood why I was a compelling story: the youngest senator in Washington, single father to two boys, tragic victim. I refused to talk about any of it and watched in bitterness at the speed with which the press turned me from a *tragic widower* to an *eligible bachelor*. I refused to talk about my personal life at all, and my silence only fed their hunger. My first chief of staff, Wes Barthelmes, finally took me aside and said I needed to do just one interview about Neilia and my daughter. Wes was a former reporter himself, and he knew the game. I could put my story on the record once, he assured me, and never have to talk about it again. He hand-picked a reporter. She was young and inexperienced, but Wes liked her and thought she would be fair.

So in the spring of 1974, *Washingtonian* magazine sent a young reporter named Kitty Kelley to interview me about my life in the Senate as a young father and widower. She was young and easy to talk to, and when we sat in my office and I told her about my life with Neilia and the events surrounding her death, I could see her start to fill up. I did not want my one interview about Neilia to be a sob story. I didn't see myself as a tragic figure; my life at the time wasn't so difficult. So I tried to focus on how great things had been between Neilia and me and how I was getting myself back together. When the talk was over, I was relieved to have it behind me.

Kitty Kelley's article in *Washingtonian,* "Death and the All-American Boy," made me out to be a man slightly unhinged. Kelley called my Senate office a shrine to my dead wife and reported incorrectly that I had a photograph of Neilia's tombstone mounted in my inner office. The picture was actually the seventeenth-century cemetery in Old New Castle, Delaware, just one in a series of photographs of historic sites from my home state. Kitty Kelley twisted something I'd said into an anti-Semitic joke and cut up my interview to assure that I came across as callow and brash. It was devastating. I'd been very wary of the press until then. Now I began to actively hate it.

Wes was sorry he'd vouched for Miss Kelley, but he never stopped trying to help me with reporters. That same spring he talked me into attending the Counter-Gridiron Dinner. Back in 1974 the annual Gridiron Dinner, hosted by a club of Washington reporters and almost always attended by the president, excluded women. So the Counter-Gridirons made their own dinner in a tent at Marymount College, and Wes took me there. I'd never been at an event dominated by writers and reporters, and I knew the moment I arrived I shouldn't have agreed to go. I walked in angry. At the dinner Wes came over and introduced me to somebody he really liked and admired. "Senator, I want you to meet a friend of mine, Marty Nolan." I knew Nolan's work, and it was good. He was a talented young reporter for the *Boston Globe* who was likely to be around Washington for years. Wes thought we'd get along, but I was no longer interested in even pretending to make pals in the press corps. And there stood Nolan, quite sure of himself, in his fatigue jacket.

"So you're the great Marty Nolan!" I said, and I made sure it had a little extra edge. I could see Wes look at me funny, and then he looked back at Nolan, almost apologetically. Nolan looked at Wes like I wasn't even there and said, "Who let him out of his cage?"

Wes had been like a big brother to me; he understood why I acted the way I did around reporters. But my anger made his effort to convince them that I was a decent guy that much harder. Almost every other elected official in Washington worked the press. Not me. All I was to reporters was a tallish young guy asking questions at hearings, running by them in the Senate hallways, or making speeches. The most they knew about me was that I was in a hurry to get on the train and go home to Wilmington. Wes tried to explain the basic problem to me one day after I'd spoken at an event in town: I was a cipher to them. He told me that David Broder, the top political reporter at the *Washington Post* and a onetime colleague and longtime friend of his, had said something I'd better be aware of. As Wes explained it to me, after my speech he had asked Broder's opinion, and Broder said he hadn't seen anyone move a crowd like that since Robert Kennedy. Broder's only question, according to Wes, was whether I was a Robert Kennedy or an Elmer Gantry. That stung, but at the time I didn't think I had to prove my sincerity to any reporter, no matter how important he was.

By 1987, David Broder was the leader of the pack, and we'd never had a substantive discussion about anything. My anger had faded, but I was still wary and hadn't made any friends in the national press. The reporters who had covered the Senate closely and knew my work on SALT II or on steering the comprehensive crime bill of 1984 through the Senate did not cover political campaigns. The Big Feet, as the major national political reporters were known, just didn't know the Senate. They'd asked me, What had I ever done on foreign policy? What had I done in criminal law? I knew intuitively that I'd never really escaped the reputation I'd gotten in my first term. Any reporter who didn't take the time to sit down and talk to the senators who knew me best was going to know only what everybody else knew or *thought* they knew: Biden was the guy who wasn't sure he wanted to be a senator. Biden was the guy who wasn't willing to stay in his seat for Budget Committee hearings. Biden was the guy who wasn't willing to roll up his sleeves and do the hard work. I believed I'd long since put that behind me with my colleagues in the Senate, but it was an indictment that political reporters were still prosecuting. Was I a show horse or a work horse?

One bright, cold day early in 1987, I was sitting in a plane in St. Louis, awaiting takeoff, with the only reporter then traveling with the nascent Biden for President campaign: Paul Taylor, a big-foot-in-training at the *Washington Post*. I was in the window seat, staring out at the sunlight bouncing off the silvery wing; the plane was quiet and nearly empty. Taylor was in the aisle seat, leaning across the middle seat, talking to me. "Can you handle the white-hot heat of this campaign?" he asked. There was nothing menacing about the way he said it, but I remember hearing that phrase "white-hot heat" as I watched the bright light of a full sun bounce off the wing. I thought later that Taylor had just meant this as a friendly heads-up, but I knew what he was saying. My political advisors had warned me that the press would be turning over every rock in my past. The character question was all the rage that year, and that was fine by me. These were reporters who'd ascended to the top of their field. They were smart and, I believed, diligent. So I trusted that when they took a long, hard look at my life, they'd conclude I was an honest, honorable, stand-up guy. There were good reporters in Delaware who had been covering me for fifteen years, and they judged me solid. *Yeah*, I told Taylor, *I could handle that.* I wasn't sure my record in the Senate was sufficient to convince voters I could be president; I wasn't sure if voters would accept that a forty-four-year-old man could be qualified to run the country. But if they want to judge me on my integrity, I thought at the time, I welcome that scrutiny. If they want to judge me on my character, I win.

I think it's fair to say I was naïve.

EVEN BEFORE LEE HART had issued her dire warning, Jill was sensitive to the demands of a presidential campaign. Now as it got more real, her instinct was to warn me off. She'd remind me of how perfect our life was now. Beau was about to graduate from Archmere, and Hunt was just a year behind. Ashley was just starting elementary school. They were all happy and comfortable, and they saw me plenty. I didn't miss games, plays, birthdays, or big events. And they'd long since figured out how to be children of a public figure. But even as Jill suggested that our children's lives would surely change if I got in, I convinced myself I could run for the nomination and still be the kind of father I needed to be.

Never underestimate the ability of the human mind to rationalize. I actually told myself that because the children were so young, it would be easier to run in 1988 than four or eight years down the road. In eight years it would be harder to shield Ashley from the worst things people were saying about her father. In eight years Beau and Hunt would be starting their careers, and people might say this guy is where he is today because of his father. I managed to convince myself that 1988 was the right time for the Biden family.

THERE WERE DAYS when I felt like my head was in a vise, and I sometimes had pain shooting down the back of my neck. I'd never in my life had any real physical troubles beyond childhood asthma or a separated shoulder. But in February and March 1987, as I rolled around to California, Florida, Alabama, Iowa, and New Hampshire, my traveling aide always carried a jumbo-size bottle of Tylenol. I was popping six, eight, ten Tylenols a day. I'd ask for two or three every four hours, and sometimes I'd say out loud to whoever was with me that these headaches seemed strange. I'd never had anything like them before. My family, my friends, and my staff—almost to a person— kept telling me this was understandable. *I was trying to be a husband, a father, a senator, and a presidential candidate. I was under a lot of pressure. The headaches were probably caused by stress.* The more people said it, the angrier I got. This was like an attack on my self-image. I was the guy who always handled the pressure. Stress had never bothered me. I'd gone through worse. They had to be wrong.

And then something happened that made me wonder if maybe they were right.

I had a full day scheduled in New Hampshire on March 23, 1987: a foreign policy speech at the Rotary Club luncheon in Nashua, an endorsement from a former mayor, a press conference announcing my state steering committee, and a speech on constitutional issues at a law school. Now that I was an all-but-officially-announced candidate, there was even a little press coverage. The local reporters were there, and a Boston station was sending a crew. Taylor was traveling with me. And a new CBS show called *West 57th Street* was preparing a long profile of me, so there was a lavalier microphone pinned to my lapel.

The anchor of the day was the foreign policy speech at the Rotary Club. I was going there to explain that President Reagan's Strategic Defense Initiative—the Star Wars dream of mounting a shield in the sky to protect us from nuclear weapons—was likely to destabilize our relationship with the Soviets. President Reagan was being counseled that he could unilaterally reinterpret the Anti-Ballistic Missile Treaty that Nixon and Brezhnev had signed in 1972. If Reagan did that, it would call into question our willingness to honor our treaties. It was an important thing to say, and I was glad for the press that my campaign had gathered up.

But even as I got to the country club luncheon for the big speech of the day, the schedule was starting to unravel. I'd just found out that Byrd might be calling a cloture vote on contra aid that day, and I'd promised him that I'd get back for votes if he asked. While the Rotarian made his introduction of me, my staff was already trying to arrange flights back to D.C. And my head hurt like hell. As soon as I stood up to take the podium, a pain shot up the back of my neck. I tried to do a couple of jokes, but I could tell from the look on people's faces that I was flat. Then I started to get dizzy. "Hey, folks," I said jokingly. "I've got a problem. I'll be right back. . . . Don't worry. It's not the food." And while the baffled audience watched, I walked off the dais and went downstairs to a locker room.

I groped my way over to one of the hard wooden benches and sat down, but it didn't help much. I tried lying down, but being on my back just made the spinning worse. My head felt like it was going to explode. By now the pain was so intense, I became nauseated. I got up and started wretching. God knows what the CBS sound person was thinking—I'd forgotten to take off his microphone. The next thing I knew, Bert DiClemente, who was traveling with me that day, was standing over me and asking what was the matter.

"Just give me a minute, Bert."

"Maybe some air, Joe," Bert said. He sounded worried.

Bert opened the locker room door and helped me outside so I could lie down on a little stone retaining wall. The sting of cold made me feel better. I picked up some snow and started rubbing it on my face. "Look," Bert said, "I'm going to get you out of here." But I was sure I could at least get through the speech. The speech should be news. And what would the press say if I couldn't answer the bell?

After about ten minutes one of the Rotarians came outside and asked me if I was okay. I assured him I'd be right there. I got up, still a little woozy, walked upstairs, and made the speech. It was like being in eighth grade again and trying to face down the stutter. There were times in the middle of the speech when I thought I might faint. I felt like I was out of my own body. And as I fought to read the words on the page and render them out loud, I was thinking: Have these people who know me so well been right? Or was there something *really* wrong with me?

Anyway, there was no time for doctors. I slogged through the speech, climbed down off the podium, popped some more Tylenol, did a press conference to announce my New Hampshire steering committee, and flew back to Washington to make the Senate vote. Then I took another flight back to New Hampshire to do the law school speech. The Tylenol dulled the pain, but it never went away that day.

Within the week a national poll came out that showed Gary Hart as the leading contender for the Democratic nomination. He was at 42 percent; I was at 1 percent. The *Washington Post* published a story that I was shirking my duties as chairman of Judiciary. Another publication headlined a brief item about me: "Is Joe Biden More Than Just a Speech?" Then, at a small campaign event in Claremont, New Hampshire, I lost it. I shouldn't have been there in the first place. I felt like hell. My headache was worse than ever that day, and I was also coming down with the flu. And in the question-and-answer session that followed my speech, it sounded to me as if one of my own *supporters* doubted my intelligence. The way I heard it, this fellow was basically saying I wasn't too bright. I could feel the heat rise again on the back of my neck; it was like being a freshman in high school again, when the guys made fun of my stutter. My reaction was visceral, and my staff probably cringed when they saw my chin come out. "I have a much higher IQ than you do, I suspect," I told him. And then I was off, talking about my college degrees and awards, my place in my law school class. I didn't feel any better afterward; what I'd said was a quick and stupid rant that I wished I'd never said. Worse than that, without realizing it I'd exaggerated my academic record. Thank God, I thought as I left the event, there weren't many people in the room to see my outburst.

Maybe Tom Donilon understood I'd need some cover one day. He was one of the smartest guys on my political team, and he thought it was time for me to make the effort to get to know some of the big-feet-to-be in the national press. He set up an off-the-record dinner with several good young reporters from the newsweeklies and the major newspapers. I went to dinner at a small restaurant in Georgetown, and I made a hash of the meeting. Maybe I was tight; it was the week that Gary Hart was fighting for his political life amid charges that he'd been caught having an extramarital affair. In fact, Paul Taylor had just publicly asked Senator Hart if he had "ever committed adultery." And the first thing these writers wanted to know from me was about a story that Taylor had told them. On one of our earlier trips I had tried to explain to Taylor why I hadn't been an outspoken Vietnam War protestor in school and how far away from that I was. *I was in law school. I was married. I was wearing sport coats,* I'd told him. *I can remember walking out of law school and walking down to Genessee Street to go to the Varsity Pizza Shop for lunch. I was with a couple of law school buddies. We walked by the Administration Building and we looked up and there were people hanging out of the windows—out of the chancellor's office—with SDS banners. They were taking over the building. And we looked up and said, "Look at those assholes." That's how far apart from the antiwar movement I was.* Apparently Taylor had been retailing the story in the press pack, and the folks at dinner that night were trying to figure this out. Was I a sixties protestor or not? I tried to explain that I never saw the war as a great moral issue. To me it hadn't been the defining moral issue the way civil rights had been. To me the war had just been a tragic mistake based on a faulty premise. I tried to explain that I saw the Vietnam War in terms of stupidity, not morality.

We barely got off the Vietnam War topic. I told them how I'd stood up to Nixon and Ford as a senator during the war, but they just didn't seem willing to reconcile my current call to arms with my lack of moral outrage about the Vietnam War. I could see the wheels spinning. These reporters all appeared to be five or ten years younger than me, in the age group of people who had been driven to demonstrate against the war by the draft. They'd been old enough to remember Bobby Kennedy's antiwar campaign of 1968, but not much before that. As I thought about it later, I realized that when these college-educated reporters heard me invoke Bobby Kennedy in speeches, they probably thought first of the passionate pleadings of Kennedy's antiwar rhetoric. I hadn't quite figured out how to explain that when I spoke about the generation of people who could reinvigorate the mission of the Democratic Party, I thought of the forty-year-old labor leader who had lost an eye while serving in Vietnam as much as I thought of the campus protestors or Peace Corps volunteers. I was trying to say one thing. They were hearing something else. When the dinner broke up that night, all I really knew was that I hadn't done a thing to convince these smart young reporters that I was more than a show horse.

But those were just a few bad hours in a campaign that was actually working. I didn't really care about the national polls. What mattered to me was what was happening in front of my own eyes in Iowa and New Hampshire. And even before Gary Hart dropped out of the race in May 1987, I already believed we had a chance to win both states. I could feel it in the crowds out there. I had crossed the threshold of being able to persuade Iowa and New Hampshire to vote for me. There were sufficient numbers who believed that I not only was honest and decent but that I was smart, I had some answers, and I could handle being president.

But I still understood I had to convince the Big Feet that I had depth. And so I told everybody in the campaign to back off the hard sell of Joe Biden as the candidate of passion and the candidate who could win. I wanted to take some time to prepare a series of speeches that showed the framework of ideas on which a Biden presidency could be built. I prepared separate speeches on the economy, on the fight against child poverty, and on foreign policy. A few of the political gurus were skeptical, but I wanted to do this for me as much as for the national press. Things had happened too fast for my comfort; if I was really running for 1988 and not just to prepare for a race down the road, I had some catching up to do. I'd been dealing as a United States senator on issues of war and peace, international relations, crime and punishment, civil rights, civil liberties, women's issues, and tax fairness for almost fifteen years. But I had never really stopped working long enough to take a breath and think about the biggest question that Marttila had posed. *What did I mean to do as president?* The University Series would be the beginning of laying out the answer to that question.

I made the University Series speeches in late May and early June, in the weeks leading up to my official announcement. They were, for the most part, fairly well received by audiences and well covered by the national media. But the foreign policy speech, which I delivered to a full and rapt house at Harvard's Kennedy School, got panned by the *Washington Post*. The *Post*'s op-ed page took two separate shots at me. David Broder acknowledged in his column that he hadn't attended my speech at Harvard, but that didn't stop him from taking me behind the woodshed. "The Harvard speech suggests that Biden is a long way from refining his experiences into a clear set of standards—or even a position consistent enough to maintain for the course of one speech," wrote the Leader of the Pack. "Give him an E for Effort. But ask him to keep working on the assignment. . . . Biden's speech demonstrated more of the temptation to fuzz the issue than to give a straight answer."

Broder's piece hadn't bothered me on the substance; I'd done homework on the Foreign Relations and Intelligence committees that he would never hear about. But it really bothered me that nobody in the foreign policy establishment stood up to defend my knowledge base on the subject, my years of experience in international affairs, or my basic instincts and intelligence. Averill Harriman and Jake Javits, who both knew my talents, had died. Henry Kissinger was a Republican. I didn't feel close enough to anybody in the establishment to call them up and ask the favor of a legitimate defense. My formal announcement was less than a week away, and I knew that there was probably nothing I could say to convince the Big Feet that I was more than a show horse.

The closer the announcement got, the more I was on edge. I had to fight off the campaign pros who didn't understand why they had to schedule the announcement around Beau's graduation from Archmere and Jill's and Ashley's birthday celebrations. The campaign was eating into my family's life. The Station had become an informal Biden for President office. There was always somebody there—sometimes people we were just getting to know. One morning just before the announcement, Jill and I retreated upstairs after one in a series of meetings. We were getting changed for the first public event of the day, and Jill was sitting at her makeup table. Sunlight was slanting through the window into our bedroom; it was a near perfect morning. I was thinking about how good our life was at that moment, and I was about to do something that would change everything. Up to now there had been an out for us, but I knew once I made the official announcement, there was no turning back.

"I don't want to do this," I said to Jill.

She turned to me and didn't even hesitate: "You have to do this now. You have too many people's lives on hold." Jill, who had been so wary, had come to appreciate the sacrifices other people were making on our behalf. One staff member was a Massachusetts political operative who had blown his relationship with his own governor, Michael Dukakis, who was also in the race. Another woman had left

Senator John Kerry's office, and John wasn't happy about it. People on my campaign staff had turned down other candidates, left jobs, or left behind family in Boston or Washington to move to Wilmington. Jill didn't have to say any of that. I knew what she meant. It was too late to change my mind.

"Too many people," she said.

✳ 10 ✳

Intellectual Combat

THE DAY I ANNOUNCED MY CANDIDACY FOR THE DEMOCRATIC
presidential nomination, fewer than one in five voters could recognize
me by name. I didn't need pollsters to tell me that—though they were
always happy to offer. I'd felt it firsthand, like in Cleveland the year
before when a local television reporter caught a glimpse of me from
across the room at a crowded fund-raiser. He came rushing over with
his cameraman in tow: "Commissioner!" He obviously thought I was
Peter V. Ueberroth, the ubiquitous former head of the Los Angeles
Olympics and then commissioner of Major League Baseball. "What
brings you to Cleveland?"

"Drug testing," I said, ". . . for reporters."

The TV crew didn't stick around for a follow-up.

I was painfully aware that outside Delaware the overwhelming majority could not name me as a senator and knew nothing of my career.
I was a blank slate. From the day I became an officially announced
candidate for the nomination, I figured I'd have about half a year to
show myself to Americans in a way that filled in that blank slate. If
they got to know me, I thought I had a shot to win.

The first big chance was going to be at the Wortham Center in
Houston on the first day of July. Public Television had scheduled a na-
tionally televised debate hosted by William F. Buckley, and all the
Democratic candidates were going to be there. PBS was promising 10
million viewers, comparison shoppers who'd be getting a first impression of all the candidates. With Gary Hart out of the race, the field

was set: Governor Michael Dukakis of Massachusetts, Governor Bruce Babbitt of Arizona, Missouri congressman Richard Gephardt, the civil rights leader Reverend Jesse Jackson, and three senators: Paul Simon of Illinois, Al Gore of Tennessee, and me. It was an unfortunate number; the press had taken to calling us the Seven Dwarfs.

The Houston event presented an opportunity for a wide audience to take the measure of us all, and I knew how important that was. I'd never forgotten the televised debate between Senator John F. Kennedy and Vice President Richard Nixon in the 1960 campaign. On substance, the debate had been a draw. But Kennedy had looked tanned and hale, and Nixon was pale and haggard. The vice president had come straight to the studio from a long run of campaigning. Compared to Kennedy, who had come off the campaign trail to prepare and rest for the debate, Nixon looked like something the cat dragged in.

So I asked my schedulers to set aside two full days of debate prep at a hotel in Chicago. I'd get off the road and do the homework in Chicago, fly straight to Houston the morning of the debate, get some exercise, get some rest, and be fresh that night. If this was going to be the nation's first look at Joe Biden, I was going to be at my best.

I might have asked for more time, but there was a round of fundraisers already set up in California—and they couldn't be rescheduled. The campaign always needed more money. And so on Friday, June 26, Jill and I boarded a flight with our traveling aides Tommy Vallely and Ruth Berry, and headed to Los Angeles to shake the money trees. While we were in the air, the White House was making an announcement that would alter my life in ways I'd never dream. As soon as we touched down, one of our local campaign workers grabbed Vallely. "Senator needs to call the office immediately," he told Tommy, but I heard the news: "Justice Powell has resigned."

This was a bad turn for the country and bad timing for me. I was already dubious about running for president and chairing the Judiciary Committee; I didn't see how I could plan and execute a confirmation hearing on a potential Supreme Court nominee and campaign at the same time. That it was Lewis Powell resigning made it worse. Powell was a Richard Nixon appointee; at the time of his confirmation he was expected to be business friendly and tough on law and order. But in recent years the courtly Virginian had been the deciding vote on a number of controversial 5–4 decisions on abortion, affirma-,tive action, and separation of church and state. Justice Powell was essentially the finger in the dam holding back the Supreme Court from ratifying the conservative social agenda of President Ronald Reagan.

Much of Reagan's agenda lacked popular and legislative support, so the Court was his best chance to fulfill the Reagan Revolution. "The appointment of two justices to the Supreme Court could do more to advance the social agenda—school prayer, anti-pornography, antibusing, right-to-life, and (ending) quotas in employment—than anything Congress can accomplish in twenty years," White House communications director Patrick Buchanan had written in 1986. The Reagan White House had already put Antonin Scalia on the Court, so if the country was to take the White House at its word, Powell's resignation represented an opportunity for the president to tip the balance for a generation or more.

"Get Mark," I told Vallely.

By the time I got to Mark Gitenstein, my chief counsel at the Judiciary Committee, he'd already talked to John Bolton at Reagan's Justice Department. Bolton, who would go on to be the controversial and unconfirmed ambassador to the United Nations under George W. Bush, had a strong feeling that the new nominee would be the darling of the conservative movement, Federal Court of Appeals judge Robert Bork. Mark told me the White House was already waving a copy of a quote I'd given the *Philadelphia Inquirer* a year earlier. He read me the quote: "Say the administration sends up Bork, and after our investigation, he looks a lot like Scalia. . . . I'd have to vote for him." I remembered the quote. I'd simply been trying to say that I wouldn't let the liberal interest groups tell me how to vote; I'd make my decision based on my own investigation. "I said 'after an investigation,' " I reminded him. "Besides, this is different."

Scalia had replaced another conservative; unlike his ascension to the Supreme Court, Judge Bork's *would* change the ideological balance. The president was free to try to shift the political makeup of the Court, but I believed the Senate held the power to block the attempt if it so chose.

Gitenstein set up a conference call for me with constitutional scholars and legal experts, liberal and conservative both, who were familiar with Judge Bork's record. He was no Lewis Powell, they all agreed. He was very conservative, they said, and contemptuous of many of the Warren Court's landmark decisions involving privacy rights and criminal suspect rights, and more recent Burger Court decisions on abortion and affirmative action. Bork, they told me, had said in numerous forums that he would not be shy about overturning earlier decisions.

By the time I got off the phone with the experts that day, I had grave doubts about Judge Bork. But one thing I knew for sure: An ideologically driven nominee who was chosen for his willingness to overturn settled precedent would invite a divisive and unnecessary fight. I released a statement that I hoped would head off that kind of bloodbath:

> Justice Powell has been the decisive vote in a host of decisions in the past fifteen years relating to civil rights and civil liberties. The scales of justice should not be tipped by ideological biases. I will resist any efforts by this Administration to do indirectly what it has failed to do directly in the Congress—and that is impose an ideological agenda upon our jurisprudence. In light of the special role played with such distinction by Lewis Powell as the deciding vote on so many cases of tremendous importance, I will examine with special care any nominee who is predisposed to undo long-established protections that have become part of the social fabric that binds us as a nation.

Article II, Section II of the Constitution gives the president the power to select Supreme Court justices, "by and with the Advice and Consent of the Senate." I thought it was time to offer some advice, and I put a call in to Reagan's chief of staff, Howard Baker, to see if I could head off a Bork nomination. Baker had been a colleague in the Senate. He was a moderate Republican from Tennessee who had the respect of members on both sides of the aisle. The president had brought Baker into the White House to right a listing ship. The Iran-contra investigation—which revealed how the Reagan administration had defied Congress and federal law by funding the contras in Nicaragua and traded arms for hostages in Iran to help raise the cash—and ethics scandals swirling around Attorney General Ed Meese and others in the administration had badly wounded the White House. The midterm elections the year before had looked like a rebuke to the president. Democrats took back the Senate, and we now held a comfortable ten-person margin. Many of the new Democrats were from southern states that the Republicans had come to count on. There was talk that the seventy-five-year-old Reagan was losing his political fastball.

Howard Baker had unerring political radar, and he had to know the administration was in no shape to make a tough battle. In my experience he'd never been a man to go looking for a political fight. He agreed to meet with me before any decision was made on the nominee.

I settled into the first day of debate prep in Chicago figuring I'd bought a couple of days anyway, and I was looking forward to some downtime to prepare for the Houston debate. I'd shed the guru's explicit generational call-to-arms message; it was too narrow, and it didn't speak to the sort of president I wanted to be. I wasn't confused about what I meant to say on trade or energy policy, education, the environment, the Middle East peace process, or the new realities for dealing with the Soviet Union. But I was still searching for the simple, direct, and concise language that connected public policy to my deepest personal beliefs. I was hungry for time to think, and two full days of debate prep with senior staff and policy people had to help. But much of the staff was bickering about message or their own place in the campaign. Worse than that, somebody had invited a businessman I didn't really know and was trying to get me to sign off on this stranger taking over management of the campaign. So debate prep was off to a wobbly start. And I was still patching my continuing headaches with Tylenol; I was probably taking ten a day now. I told Ted Kaufman that I thought it might be time to wipe the slate of political gurus—just fire them all and start fresh. Then Howard Baker called me back about the Supreme Court nomination: "Joe, this thing's moving pretty fast," he said. "You'd better get down here."

"Howard, I thought we were going to talk first."

"We are," he said, "but we'd better do it this afternoon."

I continued debate prep on a flight to D.C., but I can't say I was much focused on trade policy or education reform. When we landed at Washington National Airport, we were met by a police escort and hustled all the way into Majority Leader Robert Byrd's office just off the Senate floor in the Capitol. Byrd, Baker, and Attorney General Meese were waiting for me. I almost felt sorry for the attorney general; MEESE IS A PIG signs and T-shirts were popping up all over the country. Even under the pressure of the embarrassing revelations about his unseemly and possibly illegal role in a scandal involving a

New York company that had received no-bid contracts from the Department of Defense, Meese was a jolly and unthreatening presence. But I knew Meese still had the president's ear, and I knew he was pushing Bork. Bork was the intellectual knight errant of a movement intent on rolling back the Warren Court's expansive reading of criminal suspect rights, individual liberties, and the reach of FDR's New Deal economic policies. Meese was the movement's highest-ranking government official. The attorney general had been giving speeches about what he called the "jurisprudence of original intention," which essentially allowed state legislatures to pick and choose which of the constitutional guarantees in the Bill of Rights they would offer their citizens. Meese was not playing small ball.

Under Byrd's big chandelier, Baker and Meese presented us with a list of potential Supreme Court nominees, and they read the names off one-by-one to get reactions from both Byrd and me. When they got to Bork, I suggested he might be a tough sell to the Democratic Senate. When Baker asked Byrd if he, too, had problems with Bork, Byrd said he wouldn't block a Bork nomination. It sounded to me like Byrd was essentially offering to support Bork.

"If you go ahead with Bork," I interrupted, "it's going to be a long, hot summer."

Broder must have gotten the story that Byrd had left me hanging. "Biden is really under the gun," he wrote in the *Washington Post* the next morning, "facing a test he cannot afford to lose. . . . If Biden sets out to defeat the president's choice, he had better line up his votes. . . . To have a Democratic Senate confirm a Supreme Court justice he had vowed to defeat would leave Biden hanging out to dry. That's a fight the president will enjoy." As I flew to Houston for the PBS debate, I held out some hope that Howard Baker wouldn't go along with Ed Meese.

I knew something was up when I came off the jetway in Houston where a horde of reporters and cameras were waiting for me. *What about Bork? What about Bork? What about Bork?* Reagan had announced Bork while I was in the air. *Are you going to oppose him? Do you have the votes?* I had never been inside a press pack that big or that buzzed, and if I had any doubts, the noise in that scrum reinforced for me how big this nomination was not just for politics but for the future of the nation. All I could do was promise to give Judge

Bork a full and fair hearing. But I also made it clear that given what I already knew, the judge was unlikely to win my support.

I'd given up on rest and relaxation, but now I had to chuck most of the last-minute debate prep. The debate that night was a blur to me. I had other things on my mind, like how the Reagan group was trying to shift focus from Bork's record to me. And they had plenty of help. George Will, the conservative columnist, was already carrying water for the White House, holding up the *Philadelphia Inquirer* quote as evidence that I was acting in bad faith. "Six months ago, Biden . . . was given the chairmanship of the Judiciary Committee, an example of history handing a man sufficient rope with which to hang himself," Will wrote. "Now Biden, the incredible shrinking presidential candidate, has somersaulted over his flamboyantly advertised principles. . . . Either Biden has changed his tune because groups were jerking his leash or, worse, to prepare for an act of preemptive capitulation."

BY THE TIME I got back to Washington, things were hot. Senator Ted Kennedy, the second ranking Democrat on the Judiciary Committee, had already made a statement on the floor of the Senate: "Robert Bork's America is a land in which women would be forced into back-alley abortions, blacks would sit at segregated lunch counters, rogue police could break down citizens' doors, schoolchildren could not be taught about evolution." The liberal interest groups were promising a similar frontal assault on Bork; some of their spokespeople were already frothing at the mouth. The New York State director of the NAACP had threatened to take down Democratic senator Patrick Moynihan if he didn't stand up against Bork. And George Will was right about one thing: The groups were trying to yank my leash.

Even before Bork was nominated, the director of the Federation of Women Lawyers had warned that Joe Biden had better focus on the nomination and "exercise the kind of leadership we expect from the Chairman of the Senate Judiciary Committee. . . . If he can't, he'd be wise to think carefully about resigning the chairmanship."

The whole fight was getting personal. If the liberal groups were attacking me, I could only imagine what they'd do to Bork. I could see it very quickly devolving to name-calling; Bork would be painted as a racist, a sexist, and a tool of the rich and powerful. Even if those things were true, it was the worst strategy I could imagine and one I wanted no part of. I told Bork as much when he paid a visit to my office a few weeks after his nomination was announced. I'd done enough research into his avowed views of the Constitution by then to be almost certain I'd oppose his nomination. I didn't see how he could talk his way around the extreme positions he'd taken in so many published articles and speeches. Among other things, he'd refused to recognize a general right to privacy. But in our first and only private meeting, I assured Judge Bork that he'd get a fair hearing in the Judiciary Committee and that I'd give him ample opportunity to make his case. I'd already told the head of the major civil rights coalition that there would be no filibuster. We wouldn't rely on Senate rules and tactics. The judge would get an up or down vote from the full Senate. And I gave the judge my word: "I will engage in no personal attacks."

A few hours later I met with leaders of the various liberal interest groups. The first thing I made clear at the meeting was that anything I said was for their ears only. I told them I knew as well as they did that Bork's nomination was of historic importance, and I assured them that, notwithstanding the sniping from some of the very people in the room, I'd devote my time and energy to the hearings. I had serious doubts about Bork, I told them, but just by way of advice I suggested that they cool their jets or they were going to blow the chance to stop him before the nomination process lifted off. The groups didn't have the votes to stop Bork if they were going to play to the liberal base. If there was an argument to be made against Bork in the Senate, it would have to be made to Republicans and Democrats in the political center. If we tried to make this a referendum on abortion rights, for example, we'd lose. "Look, I want to make something else clear. . . . I'll decide what the strategy is for those of us who have concerns about Bork. . . . If I lead this fight, it will not be a single issue campaign." I told them I was not going to engage them in a discussion about tactics. I was going to run the nomination my way. Everybody in the room seemed agreeable.

Minutes after I left the meeting, the *New York Times* was calling my staff to confirm that I'd promised the groups I'd "lead the fight" against Bork. I hadn't, but I didn't want it to look like I was saying privately that I was against Bork and publicly that I was still going to wait and see. I knew enough about Bork to know it would be nearly impossible for him to convince me that he was right for the Court. So we didn't dispute the story. When the report ran the next day, the *Times* again noted my statement in the *Philadelphia Inquirer* a year earlier. The impression—and one the White House was eager to exploit— was that I'd been threatened by the groups and buckled under pressure. So now it looked like I was doing their bidding. And I got hammered for it. One centrist columnist called me "the patsy of liberal pressure groups." The White House was peddling the story that I was going after Bork as a cynical tactic to win support in the Democratic presidential primaries. Marlin Fitzwater, the president's spokesman, said his boss found it "regrettable" that I had "chosen to politicize the hearings in this kind of partisan fashion." And it worked. The next day the *Washington Post* editorialized: "How can [Bork] possibly get a fair hearing from Sen. Biden, who has already cast himself in the role of a prosecutor instead of a juror in the Judiciary Committee?" A few weeks later Senator Al Gore of Tennessee, who was also running for the Democratic nomination, started using a line from the *Post*'s editorial. Gore was withholding judgment, and he accused me of taking a page right out of Lewis Carroll's *Alice in Wonderland*: "Sentence first, verdict afterwards."

Welcome, I told myself, to the dark intersection where presidential politics meets a controversial Supreme Court nomination. I had gotten there first, and I didn't have much friendly company. The Republicans in and around the White House had clawed to power largely by making personal attacks stick, unfounded or no. And they were staying with that playbook with me. In the two weeks since Lewis Powell resigned, I'd been cast as a waffler, a tool of the liberal interest groups, an unprincipled opportunist, and a man wholly unfit to stand up to the gargantuan intellect of Judge Robert Bork or to the political skill of the Reagan White House. As a headline writer at the *Washington Post* put it: "The Senator Is Overmatched." I was pretty sure I wasn't overmatched, but I'd certainly been outmaneuvered politically. The White House had orchestrated the early press on Bork brilliantly, and we had a lot of catching up to do.

The politics of Bork in the early Democratic primaries were pretty clear. As they got to know more about the judge, Democrats in Iowa and New Hampshire were breaking against him in big numbers. Lowell Junkins, the honorary chair of my campaign in Iowa, and David Wilhelm, who was running Iowa for me, saw a big upside in a dramatic public fight with Bork. Junkins had just finished a long run as the majority leader of the Iowa State Senate, so he knew his politics. He flew up to Washington to make the case that I should come out hard against Bork, and soon. "Gephardt, Dukakis, even Babbitt are going to come out against Bork at the NAACP convention. Everybody's asking, 'Where's Biden?' " I told him now was not the time. This was bigger than politics. I was coming off the road to prepare for Bork. The presidential thing would sort itself.

The truth was, I had settled on a strategy for defeating Bork within a week or so of his nomination. The first thing I had to do was reset the table on the nomination process, which in the recent past had focused almost solely on character and qualifications. Robert Bork was a bona fide scholar. He'd been solicitor general of the United States, acting attorney general of the United States, esteemed professor of law at Yale University, and a judge on the District of Columbia Circuit of the United States Court of Appeals. The way to stop Bork, as I saw it, was on the question of his outside-the-mainstream judicial philosophy—or ideology—and that was a long shot, too. There was no modern-day precedent for that kind of fight in the Senate. Ever since I had been in the Senate, and back to when I was in law school, the basic understanding was that as long as a Supreme Court nominee had the intellectual capacity, a breadth of experience in constitutional law, and a reasonable judicial temperament and had committed no crimes of moral turpitude, the Senate was bound to confirm a nominee. Ideology was the third rail of Supreme Court nominations. The president should have his choice. Scalia, the most conservative justice to be nominated in decades, sailed through the Senate in 1986, 98–0. Even Senator Ted Kennedy, who was hammering Bork, had not voted against Scalia.

But I knew that the tough fights over Supreme Court nominations of the sixties had skirted questions of ideology by *attacking* a nominee's character. Abe Fortas (financial improprieties), G. Harrold Carswell (competence), and Clement Haynsworth (judicial ethics) were rejected for personal shortcomings, but the clear and unspoken reason was ideology. Personal attacks had merely given the opposition cover in each case.

I thought it was time to take up ideology in the open and avoid personal attacks. I intended to argue to my colleagues that if the president wanted to nominate based on Bork's stated constitutional philosophy, the Senate was bound to investigate the meanings and potential implications of that philosophy. I set my staff to researching the long history of the confirmation process to undergird that argument. And I wasn't surprised at what they found. When I rose at my desk on the Senate floor on July 23, 1987, I laid out the long and principled history of taking political ideology into account when considering a Supreme Court justice. I cited precedents in history going back to George Washington's failed appointment of John Rutledge in 1795 and the vicious fights over Andrew Jackson's attempts to seat justices who would help him rout the Second Bank of the United States. When Franklin Delano Roosevelt tried to force Congress to increase the number of justices in a bald attempt to override an unfriendly Court, the Senate had slapped him down. I told my colleagues:

> The last nominee to be rejected on exclusively political or philosophical grounds was John J. Parker, a Herbert Hoover nominee [in 1930]. And in Judge Parker's case, debate focused as much on the net impact of adding a conservative to the Court as on the opinions of the nominee himself. Parker's scholarly credentials were beyond reproach. But Republicans, disturbed by the conservative direction that Court had taken under [Chief Justice William Howard] Taft, began to organize opposition. Their case rested on three contentions . . . First, that Parker was unfriendly to labor; second, that he was opposed to voting rights and political participation for blacks; and third, that his appointment was dictated by political considerations.
>
> Parker's opinions on the court of appeals drew attention to his stand on labor activism. He had upheld a "yellow dog" contract that set as a condition of employment a worker's pledge never to join a union.
>
> But the case for the opposition was put most eloquently by Senator [William E.] Borah, of Idaho: "[Our justices] pass upon what we do. Therefore, it is exceedingly important that we pass upon these matters."
>
> And Senator [George] Norris of Nebraska added, in stirring words that we would do well to remember today: "When we are passing on a judge . . . we ought not only know whether he is a good lawyer, not only whether he is honest—and I admit that this

nominee possesses both of these qualifications—but we ought to know how he approaches these great questions of human liberty."

Parker was denied a seat on the Court by a vote of 41 to 39.

The seat that Parker lost was taken by a man, I noted, who provided the deciding vote in a 1937 opinion that cleared the way for President Roosevelt's New Deal. That vote allowed the president, Congress, and state governments to write the new social contract this nation has honored ever since. With Parker on the bench, the Supreme Court would likely have blocked, just for example, Social Security.

Later in the speech I reminded some of my colleagues of their own place in the history of "advice and consent." The ranking Republican on Judiciary, Strom Thurmond, had himself invoked ideology in the confirmation process of Justice Thurgood Marshall, the first African American to sit on the bench. "Senator Thurmond emphasized the importance of balance: 'This means that it will require two additional conservative justices in order to change the tenor of future Supreme Court decisions.' "

Thurmond, I noted, had expressed similar sentiments the next year when lame-duck president Lyndon Johnson nominated Abe Fortas to replace Earl Warren as chief. " 'It is my contention,' he said to the Chamber, 'that the Supreme Court has assumed such a powerful role as a policymaker in the Government that the Senate must necessarily be concerned with the views of the prospective justices—of Chief Justices—as they relate to broad issues confronting the American people, and the role of the Court in dealing with these issues.' "

In the Fortas fight, I told my colleagues, one senator had cited arguments made by a young attorney named William H. Rehnquist, the current chief justice of the Supreme Court. "As early as 1959," I explained, "Mr. Rehnquist had called in the *Harvard Law Record* for restoring the Senate practice 'of thoroughly informing itself on the judicial philosophy of a Supreme Court nominee before voting to confirm him.' "

The nut of the thing was this, I said on the floor that day: "We are once again confronted with a popular president's determined attempt to bend the Supreme Court to his political ends. No one should dispute his right to try. But no one should dispute the Senate's duty to respond."

There have not been many moments in my thirty-four years in the Senate when I believed I had helped change the course of that institution, but as I came to the end of that speech, I had that feeling. "As we prepare to disagree about the substance of the debate, let no one contest the terms of the debate—let no one deny our right and our duty to consider questions of substance in casting our votes. For the founders themselves intended no less."

After the speech Senator Arlen Specter grabbed me to tell me he'd never before heard a convincing case for using ideology as a measure of a Supreme Court nominee. Specter was a moderate Republican from Pennsylvania who would be a key swing vote on Judiciary. Specter's reaction was the first glimmer that I might have some success setting the ground rules of the hearings. When two newly elected southern Democrats weighed in on my side of the argument, I was pretty sure I'd picked up traction where it mattered—in the United States Senate.

The speech on the floor spoke to the Senate's constitutional prerogatives only; I'd mentioned Judge Bork only in passing and only to note his nomination. But while we were working on laying down that constitutional marker, the committee staff was also preparing briefing books full of Robert H. Bork's judicial opinions and his scholarly articles. After years in academia and as a judge, he had left behind an enormous paper trail that led straight to his core beliefs and judicial philosophy. He hadn't been shy about staking out his positions. I started poring over the books as we began a series of meetings with really smart constitutional scholars, liberal and conservative, who were helping me parse Bork's opinions, academic and judicial. I wasn't spending any time gaming out how the Bork fight would affect my presidential chances, but the more I knew about the judge, the more strongly I felt that it was necessary to keep him off the Court.

The exercise of learning about Robert Bork's judicial and constitutional philosophy allowed me time to revisit my own beliefs about the fundamental underpinnings of American democracy. Judge Bork and I held very different views of the scope and meaning of the United States Constitution, I discovered, and I remember when it became absolutely clear to me. I was sitting out on my side porch at The Station talking to a few scholars and legal thinkers when Duke University Law School professor Chris Schroeder said something that caught my attention. Schroeder had read everything on Bork, and he'd been fascinated by his arguments. Schroeder didn't think Bork went as far as the radicals in the Chicago School who believed the 1930s Court had been right in striking down Roosevelt's New Deal legislation and keeping government almost wholly out of the free market—"He believes, as long as Congress acts within its sphere, it can resist the market"—but Bork did share the Chicago School's basic conception of the Constitution and a judge's narrow role in interpreting the laws of the land. According to Bork's line of thinking, the only tool that judges have to work with in determining "what the law is" is the intentions of the legislators who wrote the law.

I asked Schroeder about Bork's views: "Every legislative act is simply a contract or deal made by the people's representatives at one particular point in time and, like a business contract, must be read literally?"

"Correct."

"So according to Bork, the Constitution and the Civil Rights Law of 1965 are no different from, say, a public works bill? They have no animating spirit?"

It was more fundamental than that, Schroeder told me. "Individual choice is protected because human ends and aspirations are held to be essentially subjective and arbitrary matters. To quote Bork, 'There is no principled way to prefer any claimed human value to any other.' " In Bork's view, Schroeder explained, a judge had no business making subjective choices about which human values deserved protection from majority rule.

"Where do notions of condemning prejudice or extolling human dignity fit in?" I asked.

"They don't, unless they are incorporated in a specific reference in a statute or the Constitution, and if they don't, the rights simply cannot be enforced by the courts. Discriminatory prejudices, animus toward immigrants, tolerance for dissenting views, compassion for victims of poverty, all stand on a par as arbitrary."

Then Schroeder quoted from an article Bork had written in the *Indiana Law Review* in which the judge asserted there was no solid legal basis to favor the right of a husband and wife to use contraception over the right of an electric utility to be free to pollute. "An observer must be able to say," Schroeder said, continuing with Bork's train of thought, "whether or not the judge's result follows fairly from premises given by an authority, an external source, and is not merely a question of taste and opinion."

"So," I said to Schroeder, "to Bork and his friends there are just two choices for a judge when he decides a case: external sources, which are the literal words of a statute or the Constitution, on the one hand, and his prejudices on the other. He should only choose the former."

Schroeder continued my thought by way of answer: "And all external sources are ultimately compressed into exactly one type. Wills, contracts, statutes, and constitutions are basically the same."

I was already deep into my Bork reading by the time I had this conversation with the law professor, but the conversation highlighted the heart of my discomfort with Robert Bork's judicial philosophy. "Bork's Constitution," I said out loud, "is essentially a contract to be narrowly construed—nothing more, nothing less. It has no spirit; it is not a reflection of the hopes and aspirations of the American people."

Robert Bork was a man of capacious and sharp intelligence, but I was starting to think he had been trapped by his own intellectual gamesmanship. I didn't believe, like many of the liberal interest groups did, that Bork was a one-man crusade intent on stifling individual rights and liberties. I thought that Bork's philosophy of a judge's limited role was so much a product of an intellectually consistent and absolute academic construct that it led him to odd and mechanized positions that would, in practice, roll back rights and liberties. For example, I knew Bork contributed to Planned Parenthood. I came to believe that Bork was probably pro-choice personally, but he was intellectually honest in saying, in effect, *I will vote for a pro-choice candidate to vote for legislation allowing women to have abortions. But I cannot find that explicit right in the Constitution, so in my role as judge, I cannot protect that right just because I personally find it worthy of protection.*

At some of our sessions at The Station, conservative legal scholar Philip Kurland laid out the logic and reasoning that girded Bork's argument. Kurland had respect for Bork's views and could elaborate on them based on interactions he'd had with the judge. Part of what Bork argued remains a legitimate concern: If you let nine individuals appointed for life set the bar, then what stops them from simply making up fundamental rights on their own? Bork was dubious that there were fundamental rights that trumped the right of the public through their elected officials to determine the value set of the country—unless that right was specifically written into the Constitution.

It's a legitimate academic argument, but the man Bork was replacing, Lewis Powell, had made the point that in almost two hundred years the Court had never gone very far beyond the public and had rarely outrun the trust of the country. We should have faith in the Court, Powell had said. I actually thought Robert Bork was a man of integrity and sound judgment, and I found it sad that he did not have more faith in his own best instincts. Part of judging is bringing to bear individual wisdom, intellect, and compassion. Even Felix Frankfurter, whose jurisprudence bowed almost without fail to the will of the political majority, had said: "To believe that this judicial exercise of judgment could be avoided . . . is to suggest that the most important aspect of constitutional adjudication is a function for inanimate machines and not for judges."

Frankfurter, like almost all justices who have served the Court and like most of the framers themselves, believed there were fundamental rights that deserved the protection of courts whether or not they were specifically enumerated in the Constitution. And that was where I parted ways irreconcilably with Judge Bork. I, too, believe there are natural rights that predate any written political or legal documents; we have these rights merely because we're children of God. "We hold these truths to be self-evident," the authors of our Declaration of Independence wrote, "that all men are created equal, that they are endowed by their Creator with certain unalienable Rights, that among these are Life, Liberty and the pursuit of Happiness. That to secure these rights, Governments are instituted among Men, deriving their just powers from the consent of the governed." To me that was the central glowing idea that lights the path of our democracy and defines the relationship between individual citizens and government. If there were no Constitution, I believed, human beings would still have a right to marry whom they want. We would still have the right to see our biological offspring, the right to speech, and the right to practice a religion. Judge Bork, however, thought we have our rights because the Constitution relinquishes them to us—and jealously. As a judge he would not recognize fundamental human rights beyond what was spelled out in the Constitution.

It was an argument that went back to the framing. James Madison, who was the closest thing there is to a father of the Constitution, meant it to be expansive of individual rights and liberties. And he worried that the Bill of Rights might actually narrow liberty, that if the framers listed certain rights by name, those not named would be left beyond the possession of citizens. The Ninth Amendment was meant to answer to that: "The enumeration in the Constitution, of certain rights, shall not be construed to deny or disparage others retained by the people."

When the Supreme Court first laid out its constitutional arguments about a fundamental right of privacy in a case called *Griswold v. Connecticut* in 1965, Justice Arthur Goldberg wrote, "To hold that a right so basic and fundamental and so deep-rooted in our society as the right of privacy in marriage may be infringed because that right is not guaranteed in so many words by the first eight amendments to the Constitution is to ignore the Ninth Amendment and to give it no effect whatsoever. . . . The Ninth Amendment shows a belief of the Constitution's authors that fundamental rights exist that are not expressly enumerated in the first eight amendments and an intent that the list of rights included there not be deemed exhaustive."

But Goldberg's was exactly the sort of judicial reasoning that worried Bork. To Bork the Ninth Amendment was vague and tempting language that lured judges to places they ought not go. He had suggested that the Ninth Amendment was about as helpful a guide to judges as a water blot on a page and should therefore be disregarded.

WITHIN A FEW weeks of the nomination the White House released "Materials on Judge Bork," a paper that cast Bork as a moderate in line with Justice Lewis Powell. The paper actually obfuscated Bork's most controversial views. If that was the White House strategy, I thought, it was going to be running counter to the nominee's instincts. I didn't think Bork himself was going to go into the hearings and shave his beliefs. He had well-reasoned views that he had forcefully articulated, and I thought he would be pretty damn honest in defending them. Bork would say later he viewed service on the Court as an "intellectual feast." To me the upcoming hearings were going to be intellectual combat.

By early August I was beginning to believe that if Bork engaged in a debate about fundamental rights, he could be kept off the Court—and the country would be better for it. But there wasn't much room for error. There would be plenty of other senators ready to fight the nomination, but as chairman I knew to be ready to meet Bork head-on and forthrightly. I was determined to be prepared.

I cut huge blocks out of the campaign schedule—two and three days at a time—to meet with legal experts and continue my reading on Bork. I had set the hearings to begin September 15, and that meant six weeks of preparation, two or three more weeks of hearings, and then possibly a tough fight on the Senate floor. I would be managing that vote. The people running Biden for President operations in Iowa and New Hampshire were understandably panicky. Michael Dukakis was the governor of Massachusetts, and his hometown media market included neighboring New Hampshire. He was practically a native son there, and the people on my staff from Massachusetts talked about the Dukakis ground campaign like it had all the precision and resources of the Prussian army. They were rolling through Iowa counties locking down votes block by block, while I fiddled with Bork. Richard Gephardt had practically moved to Iowa, and he had the lead in the early polls. If I gave up the rest of the summer, my advisors counseled, and let Gephardt get too far out front, I'd never catch up. Now was the time for me to be in people's living rooms and dens, sewing up support among state legislators, local mayors, town council members, and regular voters. Junkins and Wilhelm were both saying August was the time for me to be in Iowa closing the deal with the caucus voters. So I asked my wife to go there for me.

Jill was working part-time as an English tutor for children in a psychiatric hospital, so she had much of the summer off, but this was a big leap for her. Up to now Jill was going along with my dream. She had never had any great desire to be in the White House—the thought of it worried her. I had always told her she wouldn't have to do anything she didn't want to, and I knew she wanted no part of going out on the road to campaign on her own. But now I was asking her to do just that. And she agreed.

So as I sat down in our side porch at The Station and burrowed into the briefing books on Bork, and had meetings with staff and legal experts, Jill went to campaign in Iowa. She'd go for three or four days at a time, and when she got back, she'd be exhausted. Ashley was six, and whenever Jill came off the road, our daughter was happy to see her mom and hungry for her time and attention. After three days of Dad making his only reliable dish—*pa-sghetti*, Ashley called it—she'd be starved for Mom's cooking as well. Jill would tell me how she dreamed she could come back from a trip to Iowa, get a hotel room where nobody would bother her, and sleep for a day so she could recharge for Ashley and the boys. But when Jill was home, I could see how diligent she was about her follow-up notes to the people she'd met in Iowa. And even tired she'd already be taking in the plans for the next trip out.

She had traveling aides she liked, and once they were on the ground in Iowa, our friend Bruce Koepple would drive them from stop to stop in his van. Jill went to diners and cafés and people's homes, and everywhere she went people were absolutely understanding about why I couldn't be there. The Bork hearings were consequential, they all agreed; they didn't want me to take any shortcuts on preparing. Jill found the rolling hills and the farmland of Iowa completely captivating, and the people were so engaged and so serious about picking the right person for president that they were easy to talk to. They were also friendly; people would leave homemade cookies in her motel room.

When Jill was at home, she couldn't wait to tell me the size of the crowds they drew in Cedar Rapids and Des Moines and Sioux City. Jill was not easily swept up in the excitement of politics, but she was invested in a way I hadn't really anticipated. "Joe," she started to tell me, "I really believe we're going to win Iowa."

The second week in August I flew to San Francisco to address the American Bar Association. The ABA would rate Bork on qualifications, as they did all Supreme Court nominees, and I wanted to make the case to them that they should consider Bork's judicial philosophy as well as his résumé. I made the same argument I'd made on the Senate floor, but then I appended to it some basic facts about Bork's record. First, that he had testified before the Judiciary Committee in 1981 that there were "dozens of cases" in which the Court had misapplied or misinterpreted the Constitution. And some of those cases, he said, might warrant reconsideration. When I listed some of the decisions Bork had deemed constitutionally suspect, there were gasps in the audience of attorneys.

One. *Griswold v. Connecticut*, 1965. The Court struck down a state law making it a crime for a doctor to advise married couples about the use of birth control.

Judge Bork has described it as an "unprincipled decision" and stated that there is nothing in the Constitution to distinguish the desire of a husband and wife to be free "to have sexual relations without fear of unwanted children" and the desire of an electric utility to be free of a smoke-pollution ordinance.

Two. *Skinner v. Oklahoma,* 1942.

The Court struck down a law authorizing the involuntary sterilization of criminals.

Judge Bork has said that Skinner was "as improper and as intellectually empty as Griswold."

Three. *Shelley v. Kraemer,* in 1948.

The Court held that the Fourteenth Amendment forbids state courts from enforcing racially restrictive covenants.

Judge Bork has written that he "doubted" that it was possible to find a "neutral principle" which would "support" such a decision by the Supreme Court.

Four. *Baker v. Carr,* in 1962, and five, *Reynolds v. Sims,* in 1964.

The Court adopted the one-man-one-vote principle. Judge Bork concluded that "on no reputable theory of constitutional adjudication was there an excuse for the doctrine of one-man-one-vote 'imposed' by the Warren Court. . . ."

The right of married couples to buy contraceptives, one-man-one-vote, the Voting Rights Act—is it true, as Judge Bork suggests, that the Constitution does not protect them?

Racially restrictive covenants, the sterilization of criminals . . . Is it true, as Judge Bork has written, that the Constitution does not forbid them?

We cannot be certain that these are among the dozens of precedents that Judge Bork might vote to overturn. But we can be certain that if judge Bork has meant what he's written for the past thirty years—and that had he been Justice Bork during the past thirty years and his view prevailed—America would be a fundamentally different place than it is today. We would live in a very different America than we do now.

It was the first substantive speech I'd made about Robert H. Bork, and when it was over, the crowd of button-down lawyers came out of their seats and erupted in a long ovation.

I was followed by former Chief Justice Warren Burger: "I don't think in more than fifty years since I was in law school there has ever been a nomination of a man or woman any better qualified than Judge Bork. . . . I don't really know what the problem is."

When the ABA evaluated Robert Bork at the time of his nomination to the federal circuit court in 1981, their Standing Committee on the Federal Judiciary had given Bork the highest rating, unanimously finding him "exceptionally well qualified." This time the ABA's raters would offer a split decision. Ten found him "well qualified," one voted "not opposed," but four members found him "not qualified" on the basis of his judicial temperament. I was pretty sure they found Bork too far outside the ideological mainstream.

I was mindful that talking to a roomful of practicing lawyers about Bork's odd legal views was a lot easier than talking to the larger public. I knew when the time came to engage Bork, I had to persuade conservative Democrats on the Judiciary Committee like Dennis DeConcini of Ariziona and Howell Heflin, and the moderate Republican Specter. If I could convince them to vote Bork out of committee with a negative recommendation, the nominee would never get fifty-one senators to vote for his confirmation. But I also believed I had to make the case in a way that brought along the average American. I was sure Americans would be against the Bork nomination if they understood his views, but my job was to boil my argument down to simple and direct language. And I wanted it to be an argument that every American— black and white, rich and poor, Republican and Democrat—could rally around.

A funny thing happened on the way to finding that argument; it opened me up to new ways of thinking about my own long-held political beliefs. At base, my argument with·Bork was about the role of government itself. Bork and his adherents thought it should get out of the way and let society and the markets operate as they pleased. I thought government was obligated to be active in helping its citizens. I thought government should serve people. The conservatives could sneer about "social engineering" if they wanted, but I thought most people believed as I did that government should embody our best hopes and lend a hand to people who were struggling.

That same month a professional TV pundit who liked to hang around campaigns sent over a tape of an ad featuring the British

Labour Party leader who was running against Margaret Thatcher's conservatives. The ad was riveting; I couldn't take my eyes off Neil Kinnock as he spoke:

> Why am I the first Kinnock in a thousand generations to be able to get to university? Why is Glenys the first woman in her family in a thousand generations to be able to get to university? Is it because all our predecessors were thick? Did they lack talent? Those people who could sing, and play, and recite, and write poetry, those people who could make wonderful, beautiful things with their hands? Those people who could dream dreams, see visions? Why didn't they get it? Was it because they were weak? Those people who could work eight hours underground and then come up and play football? Weak? Those women who could survive eleven child-bearings? Were they weak? Anybody really think that they didn't get what we have because they didn't have the talent, or the strength, or the endurance, or the commitment? Of course not. It was because there was no platform upon which they could stand.

That was my argument at its heart. It was so simple. That's what the Democratic Party should be doing for all citizens, providing "a platform upon which they could stand." People weren't asking for a free handout from government or a promise of fabulous outcomes. They just wanted a little support to help raise them higher. I watched the Kinnock ad once, and I never forgot it—partly because it rhymed with my own family experience. Uncle Boo-Boo never let my father forget that I had been the first *Biden* to go to college. I had ancestors from the coal mining town of Scranton.

And on the few trips I made to Iowa and New Hampshire that August, I started quoting from the ad in my stump, always with a nod to Neil Kinnock. I could see people connect to that message. They were tired of the old Reagan Right saw of blaming the poor, branding welfare moms as cheats, and telling American workers they were on their own when their jobs went overseas. The Republican message was that it was their own fault that they didn't have the right skills. Most Americans just wanted somebody who was *for* them. And Kinnock's platform spoke to that.

Nowhere did I sense the power that message had on an audience more than at the Iowa State Fair debate on August 23. I had spent

Joe Biden Sr. as a young man. Photo by Bachrach

Jean Finnegan as a young woman.

Grandpa Finnegan with
Joe and Val.

Val, Joe, and Jimmy at
Val's First Communion.

Neilia and Joe at Joe's thirtieth birthday, immediately after the 1972 election. © Corbis

Beau, Val, and Hunter after Val moved in to help care for them.

Beau, Hunter, Joe, and Jill soon after Joe and Jill met. © Steven Goldblatt

Joe and Jill soon after they met.

Joe and Jill.

Joe with Ashley.

Val with Joe at a
campaign event.

Hunter, Ashley, and Beau. © Bradford L. Glazner

Joe, Hunter, Frankie, and Beau.

Jean and Joe Biden Sr. at home in 1999.

The Biden clan at Jean Biden's eightieth birthday.

The Bidens gathered for Thanksgiving in Nantucket, November 2006.

two full days in Bethany Beach, Delaware, doing Bork prep and then, at the last minute, got on a charter plane with two members of the judiciary staff and a pile of briefing books for the flight to Iowa. All the way to Des Moines we talked Bork: the Ninth Amendment, the Fourteenth Amendment, the right to privacy line of cases from *Griswold* to *Eisenstadt* to *Roe,* Bork's view on precedent, and former Justice John Marshall Harlan III's view of fundamental rights. On the flight to Des Moines we didn't stop talking about Bork substance. I confess to a certain amount of arrogance in not taking some time to get ready for the State Fair debate. This was beyond my thinking it would sort itself out. This was about my believing I could talk my way through the most important campaign event of the summer. There was no political event that summer bigger than the Iowa State Fair debate, and I spent almost no time planning for it. When the plane touched down in Des Moines, I hadn't prepared an open or a close.

David Wilhelm met us at the plane, and on the way over to the fairgrounds he wanted to know about my close. I said I didn't have one. The good news, he told me, was that I'd drawn the right to close last among the seven candidates. But I still had to come up with something. "Why don't you use the platform stuff?" David said in the van that day. "It's working great."

When we got to the fairgrounds, the debate organizers put each of us candidates in a separate holding pen, and I had about twenty minutes to write out something for an open and close. But before I could get started, I got an urgent summons from Jesse Jackson. So I went over to see Jesse, who was just trying to help me. Each of the candidates would get to ask one question of another candidate. Reverend Jackson had drawn me, and he wanted to tip me to the question. I said he didn't have to do that, but Jesse said he was tired of how mean the little guy, Dukakis, was getting. There had been too much bickering among friends. He was trying to inject a little decency in the proceedings. By the time I got back to my holding pen, we were being called to the stage, so I found myself sitting in front of an audience with a sheet of paper folded into threes, trying to write down a close.

The debate went fine, and when I got to my close, I just did Kinnock's platform thing. But it was a limited time, so I rushed: "I started thinking, as I came over here . . . why is it that Joe Biden is the first in his family ever to go to university . . ." I ran through the piece whole, from memory. *The family of coal miners. Were they not smart? . . .*

Were they weak? . . . No . . . they didn't have a platform upon which
to stand. The power of the sentiment was hard to miss. There was
dead silence as I spoke, and I remember looking down at a lady in the
front row who was, despite her best efforts, in tears.

When we left the stage, one of my staff members grabbed me and
said, "You know you didn't mention Kinnock?" I hadn't found a
place to stop and slip in the standard attribution. There was a big
pack of reporters who had climbed up on the stage to talk to candidates and their proxies.

All I had to do was gather the reporters and say, *Hey, folks, I want*
to make it clear, on the record, that was a bit I end my stump speeches
with, and I should have credited Kinnock. I didn't say, "as Kinnock
said." I should have. I always do. It's his language.

I wish I had.

In the few weeks leading up to the hearings I made the rounds to
the editorial boards: *Time,* the *Washington Post,* and the *New York*
Times, among others. Bork had been to most of them first, and he'd
clearly been persuasive. It seemed to me like there were a lot of people on the boards who were clearly unswayed by my argument about
ideology as fair game in the confirmation process. But I'd go back to
old John Rutledge and make the case for judicial philosophy as a
proper criterion for judging a Supreme Court nominee. I'd talk about
Bork's views on fundamental rights, *stare decisis,* the lifeless contract
that was the judge's Constitution. I loved to tell the editors about
Bork's view of the Ninth Amendment: "When the meaning of a provision . . . is unknown," Bork had said, "the judge has in effect nothing more than a water blot on the document before him . . . and his
proper course is to ignore it."

I wasn't convinced that the editorial boards were going to back me
in print, but I hoped we could at least stop them from endorsing Bork
before the hearings. And by now I was fully prepared for intellectual
combat with the judge. The last weeks before the hearings started felt
like the end of the preseason, just before the first football game of the
year. I couldn't guarantee a win, but I was prepared. I was in shape. I
had been catching the ball. I knew my pass patterns, and I knew the
plays that would work best.

By Labor Day I was convinced I had the play that would take us
down the field. We had polling that suggested Bork was vulnerable if
we highlighted his personal insensitivities on race and gender. But I

disagreed. This didn't have to get personal; this could be simply about what kind of judge Bork would be. I remember when I became certain. It was one of those hot late-August days in Wilmington when we were trying to boil down legalese to words that resonated with ordinary people. A friend and longtime staffer, Vince D'Anna, was there to help keep the conversations with law professors and constitutional scholars from becoming overly heady and abstract. One day Vince and I got to talking about the holding in *Griswold* that Bork had criticized so fiercely. "Could you imagine what would happen," I said to Vince, "if I went down to Girardo's restaurant and told a group of married couples there after a softball game that I was taking away their right to use birth control?"

"They'd go nuts."

"We should make this about privacy," I said. We'd never even have to bring up abortion. The key was *Griswold*. I suggested to Professor Kurland that it was time to do a little test at the local shopping mall. "I tell you what I'll do," I said. "We'll go up there, and I will ask the first three or four people who walk up, 'Do you think a man and woman in the privacy of their own bedroom have a right to make a decision about whether they have a child, use birth control, or what kind of sex they engage in? What do you think?' "

This was not an exercise in which Professor Kurland wished to engage. Asking people their thoughts about sex at a shopping mall on a hot summer day smacked of a bad television gag to the conservative scholar. But we did it anyway. I think Kurland was relieved that we didn't have to seek anybody out. People who knew me would walk up and say, "Hey, Joe," and I'd ask them if they thought married couples had the right to use contraception. They looked at me like I was crazy. "Of course!" And when I asked why, none of them said the right to privacy. They all said, "The Constitution."

✳ 11 ✳

You Have to Win This

THE WEEK AFTER LABOR DAY, FALL WAS BEGINNING TO TAKE the edge off a hot summer. The nation was heading back to business and turning its attention to the Robert Bork confirmation hearings. And for me it was like that old feeling of the doors swinging open; everything was lining up. I was leading the Democratic field in fundraising. Ted Kaufman was telling me we were raising more money outside our home state than the other six candidates *combined*. The Biden for President pollsters had new numbers, too. The middle class in Iowa was breaking for me already. If I did well on Bork, Caddell and Marttila were saying, I might just win the first two states. Even Jill was telling me we were going to win Iowa . . . and New Hampshire, too. And when I got on the road for some quick campaign tours, I started to see what she was seeing. At an event at a private home in New Hampshire near the end of August, the crowd that showed up was so big it spilled out into the yard. So I went out on a porch balcony to give my stump speech. In the middle of the talk it started to mist, and I told them I'd stop, but they said no. And nobody left. They stood in the drizzle and listened, rapt, when I explained to them about this ad I'd seen by Neil Kinnock and the "platform" the Democratic Party could provide the American people. It rained and nobody left. This was new territory for me. These people were *in*.

New York Times reporter Robin Toner was with me in New Hampshire on that trip, and even she grudgingly noted my appeal on the trail. "When he connects with his audience, as he did in Keene, he can moisten eyes and set heads to nodding. 'The American people have not become heartless,' he said, after a long paean to the Democratic Party and its commitment to equality of opportunity, improvising on a speech by Neil Kinnock, the British Labor leader. 'If I'm wrong, I'm in deep trouble.' An older woman called out, 'You're not wrong!' "

But that was deep in the story; Toner had led her piece with a less flattering notion. "The Biden campaign," she wrote on August 31, "has been sputtering." According to the pundits, Michael Dukakis had New Hampshire sewn up. But I never believed his most stirring line—"good jobs at good wages"—was going to be good enough. I thought I was breaking through. When a woman called out in New Hampshire, "It's good to hear a real Democrat talking again," it felt like one of those special days in the 1972 Senate campaign when it was a closely held Biden family secret: We could win this thing. Iowa and New Hampshire were doable.

And I knew my audience was about to get a lot bigger than the curious voters of Keene, New Hampshire, or Sioux City, Iowa. The Bork confirmation hearings were going to be televised live, and indications were that the country would be paying attention. While most agreed on the high stakes of the Bork nomination, only a quarter of the American people had already made up their mind about Bork—and they were evenly split on the question. More than two of every three Americans had not yet decided about Bork. They were anxious to get a good look at President Reagan's new Supreme Court nominee.

And according to the public opinion polls, I had already won the prehearing battles. Sixty percent of the country believed the Senate should take into account Bork's positions on constitutional issues. Seventy percent trusted the Senate more than the president to make "the right decision" on a Supreme Court nomination; only 23 percent had more faith in the president's judgment. The hearings were scheduled to start on Tuesday, September 15, and I was ready.

TOM DONILON HAD been fielding calls from the *New York Times* about my close at the Iowa State Fair debate, so I knew the story was coming, but I didn't think it was worth big worry. I was in Washington the Saturday morning before the hearings for the christening of my brother Jimmy's daughter, Caroline Nicole, when the piece ran . . .

front page, *New York Times,* written with some real bite by a talented young reporter, Maureen Dowd. Biden "lifted Mr. Kinnock's closing speech with phrases, gestures and lyrical Welsh syntax intact for his own closing speech at a debate at the Iowa State Fair on Aug. 23— without crediting Mr. Kinnock," Maureen wrote. She quoted from my close. She quoted from Kinnock. They matched up perfectly, and she wrote it like I had tried to pull a fast one. "Biden began his remarks by saying the ideas had come to him spontaneously on the way to the debate. 'I started thinking as I was coming over here, why is it that Joe Biden is the first in his family ever to go to a university?' " I don't remember Maureen Dowd being at the Iowa State Fair, and I don't remember her ever being out on the road with me, but she'd clearly done some reporting in the weeks since the fair. Deep in the story Dowd noted that I had credited Kinnock at various campaign appearances in August. Maybe she'd talked to her fellow reporter Robin Toner. And she did give Donilon a chance to explain. "To the degree it wasn't attributed, it was an oversight or inadvertent," said Mr. Donilon.

But nowhere in the story did she mention that she'd received a copy of a videotape with my State Fair close and a copy of the Kinnock ad from Dukakis's campaign. Nor did she report that the Dukakis campaign had also peddled the tape to the *Des Moines Register* and NBC News. The *Register* ran a next-day story acknowledging that another campaign had been sending around the "attack video." NBC News was different. Its correspondent Ken Bode did a double screen, one with me, one with Kinnock. Watching that on the national news that night made my stomach hurt. This looked terrible—and it couldn't have come at a worse time.

So I found myself at home on Sunday afternoon, two days before the Bork hearings, doing phone interviews with reporters who were working this Kinnock story. I told them about seeing the ad, how I'd always credited Kinnock, and how the state fair was just an oversight. I hadn't prepared well, and I hadn't even realized I'd forgotten to cite Kinnock until I was done. "I'm quite frankly confused by the whole thing," I said. "Even if I didn't [cite Kinnock], I do not understand what the big deal is. I guess I'm beginning to understand."

Later that day the *San Jose Mercury News* was calling. They wanted a response to new allegations. Hadn't I used a Bobby Kennedy quote without attribution in a speech in California, and a Hubert Humphrey line in another? I'd never tried to hide those quotes, but now I was finding out that one of my speechwriters had inserted an RFK line into the speech in California without telling me. People from the Hart campaign had brought it up then. *Newsweek* correspondent Howard Fineman would refer to the hubbub a few days later as somewhere between a traffic ticket and a minor misdemeanor, but I knew what was happening. There was a hint of blood in the water, and it was mine. These reporters who kept calling, none of whom had any personal experience of me, were starting to see the emergence of *a pattern . . . a character flaw*. Until then I hadn't seen it coming, or I thought I could handle it. But the alarm bells went off for Jill right away. They were questioning the one thing she saw as my greatest strength—and something I would never be able to defend with words alone. "Of all the things to attack you on," she said, almost in tears. "Your integrity?"

AS I GAVELED the Bork hearings to order on Tuesday morning in the historic Russell Senate Caucus Room, most of the major papers had picked up Dowd's Kinnock story and the *Mercury News* business also. This was the fourth day of stories questioning the honesty and integrity of Joe Biden, so I found myself fighting two battles: one with the Reagan White House over Bork and the other to defend my good name. The *New York Times* columnist William Safire had already called me "Plagiarizing Joe." Safire was leading the editorial legions who were in support of Judge Bork, and I was fair game. I felt like I was at the edge of an abyss. The White House was playing hardball politics, but I had left myself wide open. I couldn't even say it was a cheap shot. And if I let the hits on me affect the way I ran the Bork hearings, my colleagues on the Judiciary Committee would see it. The full Senate would see it. The entire watching public would see it.

I had held my opening statement to the end of the first session, but I wasn't sure I'd be able to keep my head from spinning out all the ugly political and personal implications of the developing stories. But as my colleagues made their opening statements, I was pleased to hear the swing votes on the committee—DeConcini, Heflin, and Specter— make it clear that they had trouble with positions Bork had taken in various essays and decisions he'd authored. They weren't ready to cede the Bork nomination to the president. And the Bork supporters had their back up from the start. When the Republican senator from Wyoming, Alan Simpson, started his opening peroration, he turned and spoke directly to the Democrats whom he thought were gunning for Robert H. Bork. "Who among us here on the panel—we in the U.S. Senate—are designated the 'official score keepers' of our fellow humans? Who does or does not judge, when we put aside the mistakes, the utterances, the errors of our earlier lives, and who in this room has not felt the rush of embarrassment or pain or a feeling of plain stupidity about a phrase previously uttered or an act long ago committed? Who can pass that test? . . . It seems to be an unpleasant reality that a Supreme Court nominee has every single constitutional protection until he or she walks into this room. And once in this room, unlike a defendant in a court of law, the nominee is not guaranteed any single right."

When Senator Simpson finished his speech, I held up the committee gavel and spoke to the nominee, who was just twenty feet away, facing the panel: "Judge Bork, I guarantee you this little mallet is going to assure you every single right to make your views known, as long as it takes, on any grounds you wish to make them. That is a guarantee, so you do have rights in this room, and I will assure you they will be protected."

Weeks before, I had privately assured Bork that he would have as long as he needed to explain his views and that he could call any witnesses he desired, so I was simply reiterating that point. Then, turning to my own opening statement, I had an odd sense of relief. This was game time. I meant to be clear and direct, beginning with the story of the Constitution and the possibilities embedded within it. "America is the promised land, because each generation bequeathed to its children a promise, a promise that they might not come to enjoy but which they fully expected their offspring to fulfill. So the words 'all men are created equal' took a life of its own, ultimately destined to end slavery and enfranchise women. And the words 'equal protection' and 'due process' inevitably led to the end of the words 'separate but equal,' ensuring that the walls of segregation would crumble, whether at the lunch counter or in the voting booth."

I was speaking to Judge Bork, but I was also speaking to the large audience of citizens tuning into the hearings.

Let's make no mistake about it, the unique importance of this nomination is in part because of the moment in history in which it comes, for I believe that a greater question transcends the issue of this nomination. And that question is: Will we retreat from our tradition of progress, or will we move forward, continuing to expand and envelop the rights of individuals in a changing world which is bound to have an impact upon those individuals' sense of who they are and what they can do? Will these ennobling human rights and human dignity which is a legacy of the past two centuries continue to mark the journey of our people?

So, Judge, . . . this nomination is more—with all due respect, Judge, and I am sure you would agree—than about you. In passing on this nomination to the Supreme Court, we must also pass judgment on whether or not your particular philosophy is an appropriate one at this time in our history.

You are no ordinary nominee, Judge, to your great credit. Over more than a quarter of a century you have been recognized as a leading—perhaps the leading—proponent of a provocative constitutional philosophy. . . . You have been a man of significant standing in the academic community, and thus, in a special way, a vote to confirm you requires, in my view, an endorsement of your basic philosophic views as they relate to the Constitution. And thus the Senate, in exercising its constitutional role of advice and consent, has not only the right, in my opinion, but the duty to weigh the philosophy of the nominee as it reaches its own independent decision, a view that I think you share, but I will ask you about that in this question and answer period. . . .

My role as chairman of the Senate Judiciary Committee in my view is not to persuade but to attempt to ensure that the critical issues involved in this nomination are laid squarely before my colleagues and the American people.

As I made clear when Senator Baker contacted me and when Attorney General Meese came to see me prior to your selection, as I told them privately, Judge, that as a matter of principle I continue to be deeply troubled by many of the things you have written. I would have been less than honest then or now to pretend otherwise.

Judge, assuming you meant what you have written, our differences are not personal. They relate to basic questions of principle. I will question you in several areas to determine what our differences mean in terms of real cases with real people, with real winners and losers.

I talked briefly about the instances in the recent past in which the Supreme Court had heroically stepped in to ensure civil rights, voting rights, basic rights of privacy in marital and family relations, and the freedom of expression, both political and artistic.

From much of what I have read, and I honestly believe, Judge, I've read everything that you have written . . . we appear to disagree about whether the Supreme Court was right or wrong in many of these cases. While there is plenty of room for debate about these issues, each of us must take a stand on whether or not we believe the Court was wrong in these most critical decisions of our time. . . .

I believe all Americans are born with certain inalienable rights. As a child of God, I believe my rights are not derived from the Constitution. My rights are not derived from any government. My rights are not denied by any majority. My rights are because I exist. They were given to me and each of my fellow citizens by our creator, and they represent the essence of human dignity. . . .

You have a very precise, as I read it, viewing of how to read the Constitution. You have suggested equally forthrightly that we should examine in reviewing your nomination—when you said, and I am quoting you: "You look for a track record, and that means you read any article, any opinions they have written. There is no reason to be upset about that," end of quote.

I agree with you that there is a consistent thread that runs through your writings. You said just two years ago that you, quote, "finally worked out a philosophy which is expressed pretty well in that 1971 *Indiana Law Review Journal* piece," end of quote. And your most definitive writing to date has been, as I can read it, that piece.

Later you added, "My views have remained about the same."

In the end, whatever my reaction or anyone else's reaction to your record, the process of confirmation is best served if we hear each other out and use this unique opportunity to educate ourselves and the American people about your record and what it may mean for the Supreme Court and for the future of this country that we both love so much.

At various points in my statement Judge Bork nodded assent. He betrayed absolutely no fear of a little intellectual jousting with me, and it was clear he wasn't going to back down. In his opening statement directly following mine, he again invited the discussion of his judicial philosophy. He said,

> How should a judge go about finding the law? The only legitimate way, in my opinion, is by attempting to discern what those who made the law intended. . . . Where the words are general, as is the case with some of the most profound protections of our liberties— in the Bill of Rights and in the Civil War Amendments—the task is far more complex. It is to find the principle or value that was intended to be protected and see that it is protected. As I wrote in an opinion for our court, the judge's responsibility "is to discern how the framers' values, defined in the context of the world they knew, apply in the world we know."
>
> If a judge abandons intentions as his guide, there is no law available to him, and he begins to legislate a social agenda for the American people. That goes well beyond his powers.

Judge Bork obviously believed himself to be correct. My job, I thought, was to simply draw him out, let him tip the balance from self-confidence to arrogance. If he wanted to be condescending to me, I'd let him. My first question was straightforward: "In 1981, in testimony before the Congress, you said, 'There are dozens of cases' where the Supreme Court made a wrong decision. This January, in remarks to the Federalist Society, you implied that you would have no problem in overruling decisions based on a philosophy or rationale that you rejected. And in an interview with the *District Lawyer* magazine in 1985, you were asked if you could identify cases that you think should be reconsidered. You said, 'Yes, I can, but I won't.' Would you be willing for this committee to identify the 'dozens of cases' that you think should be reconsidered?"

"Mr. Chairman, to do that I'm afraid I would have to go out and start back through the casebooks again to pick out the ones. I don't know how many should be reconsidered. I can discuss with you the grounds upon—the way in which I would reconsider them. . . . There is in fact a recognition on my part that *stare decisis,* or the theory of precedent, is important. And in fact I would say to you anybody who believes in original intention as the means of interpreting the Constitution has to have a theory of precedent, because this nation has grown in ways that do not comport with the intentions of the people who wrote the Constitution. . . . I cite to you the legal tender cases. Scholarship suggests—these are extreme examples, admittedly—scholarship suggests that the framers intended to prohibit paper money. Any judge who today thought he would go back to the original intent really ought to be accompanied by a guardian rather than be sitting on a bench."

Judge Bork, it was clear, had come to talk. In fact, it was clear he believed he was able enough to talk himself right onto the Supreme Court. Any jitters I had were gone; concentration was not going to be a problem. I just had to find the right opening . . . and then he paused.

"Well, let's talk about another case," I interjected. "Now let's talk about the *Griswold* case. Now, while you were living in Connecticut, that state had a law that made—I know you know this, but for the record—that made it a crime for anyone, even a married couple, to use birth control. And you have indicated you thought that law was 'nutty,' to use your word, and I quite agree. Nevertheless, Connecticut, under that 'nutty' law, prosecuted and convicted a doctor, and the case finally reached the Supreme Court. The Court said that the law violated a married couple's constitutional right to privacy. You criticized this opinion in numerous articles and speeches, beginning in 1971 and as recently as July 26 of this year. In your 1971 article 'Neutral Principles and Some First Amendment Problems,' you said that the right of married couples to have sexual relations without fear of unwanted children is no more worthy of constitutional protection by the courts than the right of public utilities to be free of pollution control laws.

"You argued that the utility company's right or gratification, I think you referred to it, to make money and the married couple's right or gratification to have sexual relations without fear of unwanted children, as 'the cases are identical.' Now, I'm trying to understand this. It appears to me that you're saying that government has as much right to control a married couple's decision about choosing to have a child or not as that government has a right to control the public utility's right to pollute the air. Am I misstating your rationale?"

"With due respect, Mr. Chairman, I think you are. I was making the point that where the Constitution does not speak—there is no provision in the Constitution that applies to the case—then a judge may not say, 'I place a higher value upon a marital relationship than I do upon an economic freedom.' Only if the Constitution gives him some reasoning. Once a judge begins to say economic rights are more important than marital rights or vice versa, and if there is nothing in the Constitution, the judge is enforcing his own moral values, which I have objected to."

Bork went on to explain that his objection was to the way in which Justice William Douglas "derived" the right to marital privacy.

"Then I think I do understand it," I told Judge Bork. "That the economic gratification of a utility company is as worthy of as much protection as the sexual gratification of a married couple, because neither is mentioned in the Constitution." But I asked him to help me be clearer about his reasoning. "If it were a constitutional right," I continued, "if the Constitution said, anywhere in it, in your view, that a married couple's right to engage in the decision of having a child or not having a child was a constitutionally protected right of privacy, then you would rule that that right exists. You wouldn't leave it to a legislative body no matter what they did."

"Yes," Judge Bork said. "That's right."

"But you argue, as I understand it, that no right exists."

"No, Senator," Bork said. He wanted to be clearer. "I argued that the way this unstructured, undefined right to privacy that Justice Douglas elaborated, that the way he did it did not prove its existence."

"You have been a professor now for years and years," I said. "You are one of the most well read and scholarly people to come before this committee. In all your short life, have you come up with any other way to protect a married couple, under the Constitution, against an action by a government telling them what they can or cannot do about birth control in the bedroom? Is there any constitutional right anywhere in the Constitution?"

"I have never engaged in that exercise," Bork said.

Ninety-nine out of a hundred law professors and constitutional scholars must be fascinated by this colloquy, I was thinking. And ninety-nine out of a hundred average citizens must have been thinking: *Bork can't come up with a good reason to stop the government from intruding in my bedroom?* I wanted to make sure it registered.

"Does a state legislative body, or any legislative body, have a right to pass a law telling a married couple or anyone else that behind a married—let's stick with a married couple for a minute—behind their bedroom door, telling them they can or cannot use birth control? Does the majority have the right to tell a couple that they can't use birth control?"

"There's always a rationality standard in the law, Senator, and I don't know what rationale the state would offer or what challenge the married couple would make. I have never decided that case. If it ever comes before me, I will have to decide it."

When we reconvened the next morning, I thought Bork was already in trouble. I'd even gotten some good press in the *New York Times* from the uber-Big Foot, R. W. "Johnny" Apple: "For the lay audience—which includes many of the senators and most of the television viewers—Mr. Biden's sweeping invocations of human rights antedating the Constitution were far easier to grasp than Judge Bork's insistent examinations of the purported legal derivations of such rights."

Senators Specter, Heflin, and DeConcini all had tough questions for Bork about the Ninth Amendment, women's rights, and minority rights. Heflin went a little far afield in the hearings, referring to questionable reports that Bork was or had been an "agnostic" and asking about his physical appearance: "Would you like to give us an explanation relative to the beard?" But Heflin, a former chief justice of the Alabama State Supreme Court, was well versed in constitutional law yet folksy enough to keep a clear focus on issues that mattered to his constituents in Alabama—to wit, the right of privacy.

In the middle of the testimony that morning, two members of my staff pulled me out of the hearing. There was a new story bubbling now about problems I'd had back at law school in Syracuse. The acting dean at Syracuse, who had coincidentally been a partner in a Cleveland firm Bork once worked at, apparently told people at a dinner party that there was a big black mark in my law school records. Reporters chased it down, and they were calling the campaign for comment. Now, in the addition to everything else, I had to answer for my screwup in Legal Methods twenty-two years earlier.

Even before my announcement, I had requested a copy of my files from Archmere, the University of Delaware, and Syracuse Law School, but I'd never taken the time to look at them and I wasn't sure where in my house those files had ended up. My instinct was to go home that night, find the records, and release them to the press. I made an academic mistake, nothing that went to my integrity or honesty. It would all be in the records. It seemed easy enough to answer.

Except that I was beginning to understand nothing was going to be that simple. In the middle of the presidential campaign, in the middle of a contentious fight with the White House, reason was not the standard operating procedure. There were members of the national political press who were already patting themselves on the back for saving the nation from Gary Hart. Was I their next civic duty? One good bit of news was that Maureen Dowd wasn't calling about my law school records. E. J. Dionne was chasing the Syracuse story for the *Times*. E.J. was a serious and hardworking reporter; I knew he'd try to be fair. If he read the file, he'd understand. E.J. was one of the few reporters with whom I'd had long one-on-one talks in the past six months of campaigning. He knew me. And then I remembered E.J. saying to me in one of those talks, "Everything's always come easy to you, hasn't it?" At the time I thought, *How the hell does he think that?*

But the more I reflected on it, the more E.J.'s innocent aside started to gnaw at me. Here was E. J. Dionne, a guy without a lot of advantages who worked like hell to become a Rhodes scholar. He was the kind of guy who knew he couldn't afford to shirk on homework. He was the kind of guy who took school more seriously than I ever did. And he sees me out there on the campaign doing what I think leaders should do, making things *appear* easy. I get off a plane and make a speech that people seem to like, and people shake my hand and tell me I'm great, and E.J. sees that the political stuff really does come naturally to me. And what do guys like E.J. think about guys like me? They think we cut corners. I started to worry that E.J. believed I cut corners at Syracuse.

When I got back to the hearing that day, I asked for a brief recess to have a private meeting with my colleagues on Judiciary. We borrowed the conference room of a senator with an office near the Russell Caucus Room, and I chaired the meeting from the head of the table. They all knew, I told them, that I was taking a lot of heat in the press, but it was about to get a lot worse. I didn't want my troubles to damage the Supreme Court nomination process. I offered to step aside as chairman.

There was silence, and for a moment, in the space of that quiet, I felt lost. For the first time I wondered if I'd lost the confidence of my colleagues on the committee. The ranking Republican spoke first. "Absolutely not," Senator Strom Thurmond said. "You're my chairman. You're my chairman."

"This is ridiculous," Ted Kennedy said. "You don't need to step aside."

"Well, listen," I told them, "at least let me explain—"

"You don't have to explain anything," Alan Simpson said, cutting me off. "We know you."

Nobody wanted me to step down, and when we went back into session, I was proud to be presiding over the committee. All but one of my Judiciary colleagues offered personal words of support that day. And many of them, from both sides of the aisle, made public statements of support. That was probably the most personally gratifying hour I had ever had in the United States Senate, and I started to believe I could still handle the hearings—and defeat Bork.

But while the hearings continued, E.J. was on the phone to my communications director, Larry Rasky, saying he'd gotten the confirmation he needed. He was going with the Syracuse story the next day. Could I comment? I wasn't ready to make a statement; I hadn't even seen the file. What did he want me to do, bail on the hearings to explain myself? By then there were other queries. Reporters were asking if I'd really been part of a group who objected to the treatment of a black high school teammate who could not get served in a Wilmington restaurant . . . and if I'd really supported an effort to desegregate a downtown movie theater. The *Philadelphia Inquirer* was making the case that I had lied when I told a couple of reporters that the toughest speech I ever gave was simply welcoming parents and friends at my high school graduation. The *Inquirer* reporter was out to prove that I had claimed, falsely, that I gave the "commencement address." The *Inquirer* even called Father Justin Diny, who was still the headmaster at Archmere. He had to go back and check the program from 1961 and said that I had not given the commencement address. I could explain it. I did what I said: As class president I welcomed the guests. But would these reporters listen?

While things swirled that afternoon, Bob Osgood, a friend and former classmate from Syracuse, flew to campus to retrieve my law school file. When I finally sat down in my private Senate office to read it that evening after the confirmation hearing ended, the consensus among the political gurus was that it was mea culpa time. I was reading back through the records: the technical writing paper—there was the attribution; my letter to the dean; the outcome of the faculty meeting. It was all right there. This was an academic mistake. I hadn't been trying to cheat.

John Marttila said it didn't matter. CBS had already aired a report. The newspapers would all have their versions of the "plagiarism" story tomorrow. Now was not the time to litigate the issue. If we did that, the press would be on the story for days. "Just say you did it and ask for forgiveness," John said. "Say, 'Look, it was a big mistake. It was a long time ago. I was young. I'm sorry I did this.' "

"But I didn't do it," I said. "Not what they're saying."

"Well, it looks like you did," somebody said. And then I heard another voice say to Bob Osgood, "Well, what is it?"

Osgood turned to me: "Look, Joe, in an absolutely technical sense, you only cited the law review article once, after the last paragraph. You should have made the same footnote after each of the other paragraphs you referenced. Technically, they can say you plagiarized."

"But it was an academic mistake. I wasn't trying to hide it. If I was trying to hide it, why would I cite this article that no one else in the class found? I was the only one in the class who found the article. *I didn't cheat.*"

I thumbed through my law school file reading the letters from the faculty, including one from Dean Robert W. Miller that accompanied my application to the Delaware State Bar. It was written two months after I graduated: "Mr. Biden is a gentleman of high moral character. His records reflect nothing whatsoever of a derogatory nature, and there is nothing to indicate the slightest question about his integrity."

"I didn't cheat," I said again.

Marttila's job was to do the politics, to manage the story. He was trying to help. "Look, you can't let this thing hang out there," he told me. "You can't let this thing go on. Just say you did it."

We called a press conference for the next morning to answer any questions the reporters wanted to put to me. E.J.'s story in the *New York Times* that morning fairly screamed that I had been accused of plagiarism in law school, and I started my day in a roomful of very interested reporters. The central question was: Is Joe Biden going to fold his tents and leave the race for the Democratic presidential nomination? I'd made a "stupid mistake" twenty-two years earlier, I told the gathered press. "I was wrong," I said, "but I did not intentionally move to mislead anybody. And I didn't. To this day I didn't." I was not going to give them the story they really wanted that day. "I'm in the race to stay," I said. "I'm in the race to win."

The *Times* headline the next day was "Biden Admits Plagiarism in School but Says It Was Not 'Malevolent.' " There was a separate story about the law school business in which members of the faculty were quoted. Buried in the piece was the recollection of Robert Anderson, who had been in the faculty meeting where my case came up. He said the question of my mistake had been such small potatoes he hadn't even remembered it. "It is not an uncommon occurrence for a freshman to get screwed up on the acknowledgments he should have used," Anderson had told the *Times* reporter. My old professor also passed me a little advice through another classmate that week: "Tell Joe that the next time he quotes from the Bible he should cite God."

The biggest Big Foot of the *Times* entered the conversation, too. "One of the most serious problems for Mr. Biden is that the disclosures about him have seemed to confirm his critics' complaints," R. W. Apple wrote. "Just as Mr. Hart's relationship with Miss Rice appeared to lend weight to reports that he was a longtime womanizer, so the news that Mr. Biden appropriated whole sections of a law review article and of other politicians' speeches, without giving credit, seemed to many to substantiate assessments that he was shallow and insubstantial—'plastic,' in the lingo of the campaign." I don't remember a single editorialist coming to my defense. I was becoming a caricature, and there was no one in the press I could call to ask for help.

In the middle of my personal hurricane, the proceedings in the Russell Caucus Room became the calm eye of the storm. I couldn't wait to get back to the Bork hearings, because the focus they demanded kept my mind off the worst of the reports. Bork had settled down a bit after the first day, but he had already revealed enough of his governing philosophy of judging to raise red flags among Reagan Democrats. According to public opinion polls after the first week of hearings, the percentage of white southerners opposing Bork had grown from 25 percent to 41 percent. "I better have a hell of a good reason to vote for Bork," a southern senator told reporters.

I was on the train back to Wilmington early that first week when a conductor friend grabbed me to say he had been fascinated by the hearings. "I didn't know there were people who didn't think you had a right to . . . you know." That's when I knew we had gotten through the permafrost. Average people knew what was at stake, and not so many wanted Judge Bork to go to the Supreme Court. I thought we had a good chance to beat the Reagan White House the right way— on the merits.

By Sunday night *Newsweek* had a new story. Howard Fineman had seen a C-SPAN tape of the event in Claremont, New Hampshire, back in April when I had blown my top. And it didn't look good. What did I have to say about that? the press was asking. There were reporters camped out near my house. Helicopters occasionally hovered overhead. The Station had become The Alamo. Beau was a freshman at Penn, just a few weeks into his first semester, and he had to watch the television news piped into his dining hall, questioning his father's integrity. A reporter had grabbed Val's teenage daughter and asked her if "her uncle had ever lied to her."

And it was my fault. When I stopped trying to explain to everybody and thought it through, the blame fell totally on me. Maybe the reporters traveling with me had seen me credit Kinnock over and over, but it was Joe Biden who forgot to credit Kinnock at the State Fair debate. I had been immature and skipped class and blown the Legal Methods paper. I was the one who thought it was good enough to just get by in law school. I lost my temper in New Hampshire. What I'd said about my academic achievements was just faulty memory or lack of knowledge. I hadn't remembered where I finished in my law school class. I hadn't cared. But to say "Wanna compare IQs?" was so stupid. All of it was my fault, and I didn't want to compound the mistakes. That was the truly dark portent Apple had alluded to in his think piece a few days earlier: Biden's trouble could usher Bork onto the Court. "The danger . . . is that Mr. Biden will be seen as an unfit evaluator of Mr. Bork's suitability." He even quoted an unnamed "Asian diplomat" who called me a guy who "cheated in school" and then took a drive-by shot at Ted Kennedy's academic record. If I let the story drag on so long that it compromised my ability to help stop Bork, that would be a mistake I'd have trouble living with.

I called a family meeting on Tuesday night, exactly a week into the hearings, to talk through options. We gathered in my living room at The Station—Jill and the boys, Val, Jack, Jimmy, Frank, and my parents. I had a hard time sitting still, so I kept pacing the room. My family was ranged on the big couch, and as the night went on, my political team and closest staff came in and hovered on the periphery to offer advice. Pat Caddell was on the phone from California, arguing that we could salvage the presidential campaign. We'd have to go immediately to Iowa and New Hampshire, Pat was telling everybody who would get on the phone with him. We'd have to demonstrate to all the reporters in the frenzy that we still had support. We can weather this, Pat kept saying.

My colleague Arlen Specter, a Republican, was trying to get through to me, too. I knew he wanted me to stay in. "This is not what you think it is," he'd been saying to me. "It seems awful now, but no one thinks you're dishonest. No one. They can't make that case. They can't make this stick."

Mark Gitenstein, my chief counsel on Judiciary, didn't want to see me quit, but he worried that I'd have to spend too much time in Iowa, away from the hearings. "If we win Bork, it will be in spite of us," he said. "If we lose now, it's going to be because of us."

Ted Kaufman, who was almost like family, was protective. "There's only one way to stop the sharks and that's pull out," Ted said. But he knew how hard it was going to be for me to walk away, to be *driven* away. We both knew it would feel like a concession that the pack had revealed some deep character flaw in me. "We can catch up after the Bork fight," Ted said. "Come back to these things later."

Larry Rasky was in the kitchen, on and off the phone with E. J. Dionne, who wanted an exclusive on the big story. Was Biden out?

I was torn; it really came down to family. The gurus and friends could talk, but this was a family decision. Beau and Hunter were both so angry that night; the whole thing was a cheap attack, they kept saying, and we couldn't let it stand. "All the stuff they said, Dad— there's nothing real." That's what Beau said in front of the group, but when my sons got me alone, I could see they weren't just angry, they were worried for me—for us. In the middle of that long evening I had wandered out of the living room and found Beau and Hunt standing together in the tiny hallway leading to our library. I tried to cheer them up. "Don't worry about this, guys," I said.

"But, Dad, if you leave, you'll never be the same," Beau said.

"The only thing that's important is your honor," Hunt said. "That's what you've always taught us. Your honor."

They weren't talking about my presidential prospects or my place in the Senate. They were talking about something much deeper. If I quit the race, I was conceding that the Johnny Apples were right. My sons were afraid I might walk away from public life, fold up my tents, and call it a career.

"You'll change, Dad," Beau said. "You'll never be the same."

I walked back into the living room and got a final vote from everybody, but I noticed my mom hadn't spoken. "What do you think, Mom?"

"I think it's time to get out."

I asked Mark and Bob Cunningham to work on a withdrawal statement, just in case. Then I went upstairs with Jill, just the two of us. Once we were alone, the question we asked was simple. Could we save my presidential campaign *and* stop Bork? And which was the most important?

My daughter's ride to school came at about the same time we were loading into our cars to head for Washington the next morning. Jill, Ted, and I were in the lead car with Chris Schroeder. We had a Bork briefing to do. The rest of the staff was piling into other cars. There were dozens of reporters, photographers, and TV camera people camped outside our front door. I could hear the news helicopter overhead. My head hurt.

Mark Gitenstein told me later he had caught a glimpse of six-year-old Ashley coming out of the house to catch her ride to school. She looked straight ahead, like she refused to be bothered by the commotion. Her face was pure determination, like none of this could possibly bother her. She looked like a smaller version of her mother.

Jill was right at my arm when we walked through the door leading from the anteroom to the regular Judiciary Committee hearing room, where I was going to make my statement. There must have been two dozen TV cameras waiting for me and more reporters than I'd remembered at any of my other campaign events. "Hello, everybody. You know my wife, Jill." For the first time in my career in the Senate I wasn't sure I could perform with the grace the day required. This was no time for self-pity, I kept telling myself, no time for rancor. "Although it's awfully clear to me what choice I have to make, I have to tell you honestly, I do it with incredible reluctance—and it makes me angry. I'm angry with myself for having been put in this position . . ."

No. That wasn't right. I was looking at a sea of press, but I remember trying to focus on individual reporters in the crowd, to remind myself that they were just people doing a job. Nobody had been after

Joe Biden. Things happen. Still, it didn't make it easier for me. I had never quit anything in my life. I'd stayed in and got beat, but I'd never backed down from a fight in my life. I'd never quit. But I had to do it right.

". . . for having *put myself* in the position of having to make this choice. And I am no less frustrated at the environment of presidential politics that makes it so difficult to let the American people measure the whole Joe Biden and not just misstatements that I have made. But, folks, be that as it may, I have concluded that I will stop being a candidate for president of the United States."

Looking out and seeing so many members of my staff in tears was worse than I'd expected. I knew better than to speak much longer or to take any more questions. "I appreciate your consideration. I appreciate your being here. And lest I say something that might be somewhat sarcastic, I should go to the Bork hearings."

I took Jill by the arm and went back through the door leading to the anteroom and then down a little interior hallway, through a door, and then toward the Russell Building and the Caucus Room, where I would preside over the continuing hearings on Judge Bork. We didn't have time to do postmortems. Jill was still at my side, and Ted was there, too. My legs felt heavy as we walked, and I was surprised by a sensation of physical pain. Quitting hurt. As we neared the back door of the Caucus Room, I heard Ted say, "Just go in there and do your best." Jill must have heard Ted, too, because I felt her grab my arm and turn me toward her. She locked her eyes right into mine and then said something that sounded like profanity. Jill didn't often use profanity, but she wanted my full attention. She wanted me to understand that doing my best wasn't good enough now. "You have to win this thing!"

As I settled back into my chair and took over the hearings, Ted Kennedy passed me a note reminding me that there was life after a presidential campaign. I looked up and saw Jill enter through the far door and stand with her back against the wall. She didn't like to make appearances in these hearings, but she was there. Alan Simpson must have seen her come in. Simpson was a staunch defender of Bork, and he could not have been pleased with me. But Simpson looked down the committee dais at me, caught my eye, and pointed at Jill. "Nothing else matters, man. Nothing else matters."

When I looked again at Jill, she blew me a kiss, and I could see her mouth the words across the crowded hearing room: "I love you."

Jill understood what I needed more than I did, and she meant to show me something else that mattered. She stayed with me through that day, and when the hearings concluded, we took the train back to Wilmington together. In the car ride from the Amtrak station to our house, Jill suggested we stop and have dinner out.

I didn't have much of an appetite. The day had drained me, and I didn't want to be seen. "I really don't want to be out in public tonight," I told her.

Jill said she was too tired to cook. She rephrased the question. In fact, it wasn't a question anymore: "We're going out to dinner tonight."

So I grudgingly agreed, and we drove to a favorite place of ours, Ristorante Attilio's. Jill and I were sort of regulars at Attilio's, so our presence was never a big deal, but I worried that this night would be different. People in Wilmington hadn't seen me since I'd become a butt of jokes on *Letterman* and the *Tonight Show* or the subject of withering punditry on the Sunday news shows. Would I be their joke, too? Or, worse, would I be pitied? It was late when we got there, and it was hard to find a parking space. When we walked in, the bar and the dining room were full, and people were lined up waiting for tables. The minute we got inside I started to hear murmurs. Then it was more like a rumble. I could hear people say, "There's Senator Biden. There's Senator Biden." This, I thought, was exactly what I meant to avoid. And all of a sudden one guy in the dining room started clapping. Then there was a smattering, and then it seemed like everybody at Attilio's was on their feet, giving me a standing ovation.

* 12 *

The Kind of Man
I Wanted to Be

FROM THE TIME I GOT UP TO HEAD BACK TO THE CAPITOL the next morning, back to the chairmanship, back to the hearings, back to life in front of the public, I was determined to show the world I was not a quitter. No matter how long it took me, I was going to demonstrate that the mistakes that had forced me from the presidential race did not, *would not,* define me. My sons had worried that I'd be diminished if I withdrew from the campaign, and it was my duty as a father to show them that I would not let that happen. My own father had always said the measure of a man wasn't how many times or how hard he got knocked down, but how fast he got back up. I made a pledge to myself that I would get up and emerge from this debacle better for having gone through it. I would live up to the expectations I had for myself. I would be the kind of man I wanted to be.

And now it felt like everything was riding on my performance in the Bork hearings. When Jill had said, "You've got to win this thing," she had in mind that this was the first step in restoring my reputation. But Jill was also angry, and she also wanted to take some starch out of the Reagan administration.

She was convinced the White House had played a part in taking me down. I never believed the president's team was out to destroy me, but from the time the Kinnock story broke, Reagan's office of political affairs was stirring the pot; so was the White House's conservative friend William Safire. The *New York Times* columnist thought better of continuing his early tactic of out-and-out name-calling—he dropped his new sobriquet for me, "Plagiarizing Joe Biden"—but he kept up his attacks on my handling of the Bork hearings. Safire accused me of anti-intellectualism and demagoguery for my *Griswold* questioning, and then suggested I had allowed Bork to be "savaged by the A.C.L.U., A.F.L.-C.I.O., N.A.A.C.P., NOW powerhouse operating out of a Democratic 'war room' in the Senate chamber." His rhetorical growl reached crescendo in the charge that I had led a "personal vilification and public lynching" of Judge Bork.

Safire sounded desperate, and I could see why he would be. Reagan had made a public declaration that the Bork confirmation was his number one domestic priority, and five days into the hearings, as Judge Bork finished his thirty hours of testimony, the Reagan team had to understand that their support in the Senate was slipping away. After three weeks of hearings the Judiciary Committee met to take its vote on the nomination of Robert Bork. The Russell Senate Caucus Room was packed with press that day, along with an odd sprinkling of Hollywood celebrities, which only added to the buzz in the room. Press assistants for Alabama senator Howell Heflin, who had yet to publicly declare himself for or against, were standing at the edges of the room, ready to pass out copies of his prepared remarks. I knew what was coming. The ranking Republican on the committee, Strom Thurmond, would be voting for Bork that day, but he wasn't exactly offering a spirited defense of Reagan's nominee. When the White House had enlisted the help of Senator Thurmond to persuade the committee to report the Bork nomination to the floor with no recommendation instead of a negative one, Thurmond had demurred. He was still angry that the White House hadn't nominated Billy Wilkins, a respected judge from Thurmond's home state of South Carolina. "I think Judge Bork was candid and straightforward in his testimony before this committee. And this is definitely to his credit," Thurmond said in his tepid statement of support before the vote.

Senators Specter, Byrd, DeConcini, and Heflin, the swing votes that Bork needed to win, made public their reasons for voting against. When it came time for me to make the final statement, it was clear that Bork had won just five of the fourteen senators on the panel. This had to be a humiliating moment for a man who had had his share of humiliations since his name had been put in nomination. His opponents on the far left had taken some cheap shots, but Bork had to have been hurt by the actions of his chief benefactor. The judge had reportedly gone to the White House within days of finishing his own testimony before the committee and pleaded for help. "I've been trying to win this on my own," Bork told the Reagan political deputies. "I need the president. Unless there is a personal presidential effort, I am going to lose. I may lose anyway, but I can't win without the president." Ronald Reagan had apparently been unwilling to expend any of his shrinking political capital on a personal defense of his nominee. "We also have to be worried about the president on this," one of Reagan's political operatives had told Bork. "If this thing doesn't go, he is going to take a pretty big hit on it."

As I began my statement in the Caucus Room the day of the vote, it was apparent to everybody in attendance that Robert Bork had been abandoned by the White House political team. "This is an individual we're speaking of," I told the gathering that day, "a man of honor, integrity, and intellect. But notwithstanding the fact, I must tell you honestly, I feel sorry for him sitting home at this moment, watching this nomination go down, feeling—because we've all been there at one point in our lives—the personal loss he must feel at this moment. With all due respect, this is not about Judge Bork. It's about the Constitution. And I have never had any doubts at all, once the issues were framed, and you, my colleagues, addressed them and the American people saw them, there'd be no doubt about where the public would come down and where my colleagues would come down."

Reagan, Safire, and others started in again with overheated and offensive rhetoric about the "lynching" of Judge Bork. But I was gratified by the conduct of the Senate Judiciary Committee and by the reaction of less partisan editorialists who recognized the care the committee had used in exercising its constitutional responsibilities. The *Los Angeles Times* editorialized that the Bork hearings were "an extraordinary lesson; it was a celebration of Republican democracy at its best." Anthony Lewis, who had long covered the Supreme Court for the *New York Times,* wrote of the hearings: "They have instructed all of us on the Court and the Constitution. They have confounded the cynical view that everyone in Washington has base political motives."

"The struggle over the Robert Bork nomination will be remembered as one of the great events of American history—not for the way it is about to end but for the reasons why," the *St. Petersburg Times* declared a few days after the committee vote. "What the Senate majority has done is to say that the Supreme Court was correct when it declared that privacy is a fundamental right inherently protected by the Constitution. It has reaffirmed freedom of speech and equal protection of the laws as rights that belong to all Americans. It believes in access to the courts. It has chosen the concept of a living Constitution over the sterile philosophy of 'originalism.' "

The full Senate vote wasn't even close. Bork's nomination was rejected 58–42. The day of the vote, my staff was elated. Their dedication had been monumental. Dozens of men and women had worked for four months, twelve and fifteen hours a day, on this nomination; I had had to send one of them home when it looked like the grind was threatening his marriage. And on the day that Judge Bork was finally turned down by the full Senate, all that sacrifice had been redeemed. When I walked into my office, they had champagne on ice, but I could not let them open it. "There's nothing here to celebrate. There's a guy sitting at home whose whole life has been directed toward being on the Supreme Court," I reminded the staff. "Imagine how he feels when that last vote's been tallied, when he's realized he lost."

A few weeks after the final vote on Bork, and after President Reagan's next nominee withdrew in a scandal involving marijuana use, I got an invitation to the White House to meet with the president and his chief of staff, Howard Baker. The president probably wanted to be sure he didn't lose a third choice, and I assumed he wanted to get my read on which potential nominees could make it through the confirmation process. When I got to the White House, Baker took me into the Oval Office, and the president got up from his desk to greet me. Ronald Reagan was always a sunny and affable guy; he had a way of making everybody he greeted feel that he was genuinely happy to see them. No matter what had happened, I never knew Ronald Reagan to show any hard feelings to somebody in front of him. "Hi, Joe," the president said. He was coming at me with his head cocked slightly to the right and his right hand extend, "Congratulations on Bork."

"No, Mr. President," I said. "There's no cause for congratulations. I feel bad for Judge Bork. He was a good man."

"Ah," Reagan said, still apparently happy to see me. "He wasn't all that much."

He wasn't all that much. The president's judgment about Judge Bork was so by-your-leave firm and final, and said with such ease and conviction, that it shook me. I had heard that Reagan was angry that

Bork had complained about the president's inability to push his nomination through the Senate, but it surprised me how easily Reagan dismissed the judge. Reagan was on to other things now, such as preparing to host Soviet leader Mikhail Gorbachev in Washington. The men would be signing the first treaty ever to *reduce* the number of nuclear weapons. Reagan didn't take time for regret. He was on to his historic Intermediate-Range Nuclear Forces (INF) Treaty and a new Supreme Court nominee. Bork was old news; his epitaph was written in stone.

"Who do you want, Joe?" Reagan asked.

"Mr. President, that's not my job," I told him. And I told him the story of a president asking a similar question of Senator Borah of Idaho more than fifty years earlier. The president had handed Borah a list of possible nominees to get his preference. Borah took a look at the list, turned it upside down, and handed it to the president, saying, "Now you've got it right."

But I think President Reagan, Baker, and I all wanted to avoid another fight. "I'm happy to give you an honest appraisal of the prospects for potential nominees," I told the president. "And no one knows the Senate better than Howard, Mr. President. He can tell you if I'm being accurate."

Reagan began to work down his list. "Wade McCree?"

"Former solicitor general?" I said. "I think he'd go through the Senate like a hot knife through butter."

"Posner?" Reagan asked.

"Seventh Circuit?" I said. "I think he'd have the same problem Bork did."

"David Souter?"

"Supreme Court, New Hampshire?"

"Right."

"I don't know enough about him to tell you, Mr. President."

The fifth name on Reagan's list was Anthony Kennedy, a federal judge on the Ninth Circuit, in California.

"Based on what I know, he's a mainstream conservative," I told the president. "He would probably pass."

"So that means you're for him?" the president said.

"No. Based on what I know, he'd pass the Senate. I might vote for him, but I don't know enough."

"Right," the president pressed. "You're for him."

I turned to my former colleague from Tennessee. "Tell him, Howard," I said.

I'd recently been in meetings on foreign policy issues in which the president hadn't seemed engaged, but I could see a glint in Reagan's eyes this day.

"Joe," he said as I got up to leave, "have you got a few more minutes?"

"Of course, Mr. President."

He took me by the arm and led me over to a door to the president's private study. He opened the door, and standing inside was Judge Kennedy. "Tony," the president said, "Joe says he's for you!"

I tried to explain to Judge Kennedy and to President Reagan that that's not exactly what I'd said, but Reagan wasn't one to get mired in messy details. He was a guy who operated in the essence of the thing. I had to hand it to Reagan—he did have a deft touch. I sort of enjoyed the well-rehearsed theater of the meeting. And the president was not without his charms. He had a way of making people want to help him do well.

Compared to Bork, Judge Anthony Kennedy sailed through the Senate. And in the almost twenty years he's been on the bench, I've never regretted trading Kennedy for Bork. By the end of January 1988, Kennedy was through the Judiciary Committee and on his way to the Supreme Court. And I could turn my attentions elsewhere.

After being such a rock in the worst of times back in September, Jill was having a hard time. She'd say it felt like getting kicked in the stomach. When she thought about the frenzy, the reporters staked out by our home, the helicopters overhead, she considered the whole thing menacing and so sad. She was glad it was over, but somehow the day-to-day things got harder. I had been forced back into the world as soon as I announced my withdrawal from the presidential campaign, but Jill had found it easier to retreat to the solace of home. All of a sudden she didn't like going to the grocery store. Everybody who saw her, she told me, felt they had to say something about my problems. People would come up to her and she could see *they* were self-conscious, like they were required to offer condolences. She just wanted normal, and nothing was normal.

Jill was the only person who knew—she was the only person I'd let see—how devastated I was. In public I was fine; at home when the children were in bed and it was just the two of us, I could sink into despondency. Jill and I would sit and talk late at night, after the day was done. Jill might be soaking in the bath, and I'd pull up a stool.

"It's hard to smile," she said one night.

"I know," I said. "Things will get better."

REAGAN'S APPRAISAL OF Bork—*He wasn't all that much*—had been a valuable reminder: A person's epitaph was written when his or her last battle was fought. As long as I was still in the game, I had a shot to win back my good name. I had even gotten some sympathetic press from David Broder, who had called Val when my campaign was exploding. Val told me later that he'd asked her to talk about me on background, off the record. "Nobody knows enough about your brother," Val remembered him telling her. "I'm going to ask you to tell me about him, about what makes him tick." Val was never at ease talking to reporters, but she finally agreed to talk to Broder. And he actually wrote some nice things about me in his eulogy of my campaign:

> The focus has been too narrow to do justice to the man. He is im-
> pulsive, but not all his instincts are self-serving or self-aggrandizing.
> His sister Valerie tells touching and convincing stories of his gen-
> erosity and protectiveness as an older brother. And last summer, I
> saw him walk away from a large number of clamoring fans at a
> Chicago meeting (many were political activists any presidential
> candidate would love to recruit) and closet himself for close to an
> hour with a stranger in pain. The man had almost broken down
> while telling Biden he had just learned he had a fatal disease—
> AIDS. He could deal with the threat to his life, but not with the
> prospect that his treatment might leave his family financially bank-
> rupt. "What kind of a society is this?" he asked in his pain. That
> much I overheard. The rest was between Biden and this man, but
> when I saw the man later in the meeting, he seemed calmer. Biden
> had found a way to help him, if only by listening. And he did it out
> of a generous impulse. That compassion, too, deserves to be noted
> about the latest departed candidate.

I agreed to sit for a long interview with Broder around Christmas time. On New Year's Day 1988 he wrote a long piece based on our talk, graciously noting my seriousness on the issues and my role as a Senate expert in foreign affairs. He followed the next week with an opinion piece:

> In the view of this longtime skeptic, Biden has grown up tremendously in the four months since he withdrew from the presidential race amid a swirl of controversy. He has begun impressively by running the Judiciary Committee hearings on the Supreme Court nominations of Judges Robert H. Bork and Anthony Kennedy with skill, tact and fairness that earned bipartisan praise. . . . As gifted as he is at 45, I think the Democrats will find him far better presidential material at 49 or 53 or 57 or 61. And meantime, Delaware and the nation have a senator who is providing no small service by taking on some of the most important challenges we face.

I was anxious about getting back on the road to talk to the public but started accepting invitations to speak in early February. I scheduled speeches in Scranton, the University of Rochester, Rochester Institute of Technology, and Yale the second week in February. Most of the talk would be about my role managing the Senate ratification of the INF treaty, but I knew the political questions were coming. The Iowa caucus was coming up fast; the New Hampshire primary was the following week. And the organizer at RIT said I should be prepared to answer questions "about the presidential campaign and your candidacy as well." I was leery, but determined to show people I wasn't going to walk away from public service.

My only nagging problems were physical. The headaches didn't ease up after the campaign ended; I still had to keep the big bottle of Tylenol at the ready. And one day I was working on a shoulder press machine at the Senate gym when I felt a pain shoot through my neck. On the train back to Wilmington that night, the pain came back, only worse, in my neck and my head. My right side went numb, and my legs were suddenly heavy. A heart attack, I wondered, at forty-five? By the time the train pulled into Wilmington, I was able to walk. I didn't want to worry Jill, but I gingerly told her that maybe I'd pulled a muscle or something. So she made arrangements for me to see a doctor, who concluded I had probably pinched a nerve lifting weights. I went to a pain clinic where they gave me a neck brace and some exercises to help get me back to the Senate debate on the ratification of the recently signed INF Treaty and to make the trips to Scranton, Rochester, and Yale.

February 9, 1988, I was in Scranton, Pennsylvania, giving a foreign policy speech. There was a lot to talk about. The INF Treaty was under consideration in the Senate, where most of my colleagues wanted a quick ratification. I was for the treaty also, but there was real concern about the Reagan administration's willingness to stick to the letter and spirit of the accord. The administration had unilaterally reinterpreted the fifteen-year-old Antiballistic Missile (ABM) Treaty to allow development and testing of the Star Wars technology, the expensive and dubious protective umbrella in the heavens. A number of us in the Senate thought this was in violation of the plain meaning of the ABM Treaty—and something of an embarrassment to the United States in the international community. Senators Sam Nunn and Robert Byrd were threatening a delay on the INF unless the administration gave assurances they wouldn't monkey around with this one after the fact also.

Nunn and Byrd asked that the testimony administration officials gave to the Senate concerning the meaning of the treaty be binding on the White House. Secretary of State George Shultz basically said forget it. So I made a compromise proposal I hoped would avert a long legal wrangle between the Senate and the administration but would secure the Senate's constitutional prerogatives. I asked that the Senate attach to the new treaty—by majority vote—a statement that bound the executive branch to the meaning it testified to in asking for Senate ratification. The statement would "establish that, as required by the Constitution, the INF Treaty will be interpreted in accordance with the text of the treaty and the understanding shared by the executive and the Senate at the time of ratification," I said that day. "Any change in that interpretation would require the consent of the Senate."

But while I gave my speech at the University of Scranton that evening, the American people were not exactly focused on treaty ratification. Much of the country was tuned to the special election coverage of that night's voting at the Iowa caucus. The network anchors were reporting the results from Des Moines, with the gilt dome of the Iowa State Capitol over their shoulders. Representative Dick Gephardt had won Iowa, with Senator Paul Simon second and Governor

Michael Dukakis third. Hard to know where I would have finished in the voting had I stayed in, but one thing I knew: I would have been getting up the next morning like everybody else to make the flight from Iowa to New Hampshire for the last week of campaigning before that primary. And I would have been wondering, along with Dukakis and Jackson, Gephardt and Simon, Babbitt and Gore and Hart, who had reentered the race, which of us was going to be a politically viable presidential candidate at the end of that week. Instead, I was going to Rochester, New York, to give a speech to what I figured would be a quiet smattering of students and professors.

But when I walked into the hall at the University of Rochester, the reception was overwhelming. There were hundreds of people there, and they stood clapping and cheering when I walked in. My speech was a little less than forty minutes long, just a quick tour of my views on American foreign policy, but the crowd wouldn't let me out of the room. They just kept asking questions—about the INF Treaty, the Iran-contra scandal, Bork—and they would not let me go. I talked to them about my presidential race and the plagiarism charges. I hadn't really been in front of a civilian audience this big in months, and I wasn't sure how friendly they'd be. But this was well beyond my expectations. They were so warm and so happy to see me. It was healing. In fact, I found it impossible to walk away from the crowd. I just kept taking questions—half an hour, an hour, an hour and a half. My traveling companion, Bob Cunningham, gently tried to get me off the stage, but there were still hands up in the audience, so I wasn't going anywhere. Finally, in desperation, Bob had the organizers turn off the public address system. But more students and professors grabbed me as I was leaving the podium—some of the kids were literally hugging me—and Bob stood there with my topcoat and briefcase trying to get me out the door.

It was nearly eleven o'clock when I finally got into my hotel room in Rochester, and I was so sky-high from the reception I'd gotten that I knew it would be hours before I fell asleep. But God, it felt great. Nobody in that room thought I was a plagiarizer, a liar, a cheat. I was going to be able to turn this around, I thought as I sat down on the edge of my bed and noticed a little cardboard cutout in the shape of a pizza hanging from the television knob. There was a phone number to call for delivery, and I remember thinking, Hmmm, I'm going to be up for a while. Do I want to order?

I woke up on the floor, fully clothed, at the foot of the bed. I was able to focus on a door and tried to remember where exactly I was. *What town am I in? Is this a hotel? What was I doing on the floor?* I remembered back to the pizza tag, then to the sharp stick in the back of my neck and something like lightning flashing inside my head, a powerful electrical surge—and then a rip of pain like I'd never felt before. I could still feel the waves of dull ache from that first blast of pain. My neck was stiff, too, so it was hard to turn my head. I rolled over and saw red numbers. The alarm clock read 4:10—had to be the middle of the night; there was no sunlight in the windows. I'd been unconscious for five hours.

The effort to crawl up onto the bed was almost beyond me; my legs felt like dead weights. I didn't even try to get undressed or get under the covers. I just tucked into a fetal position and pulled the bedspread around me. I was so cold, I tucked myself into a tighter ball. Still I was freezing. My flight back to Wilmington, I remembered, was scheduled for seven that morning, so I knew it wouldn't be long before Bob came to get me. I lay there, not really able to sleep, watching minutes melt off the alarm clock. Bob will be here soon, I thought to myself. I've got to get home. If I can just make it home . . .

I don't remember much about the flight home, but when my Senate aide and old high school football teammate, Tommy Lewis, picked us up at the airport, he knew something was very wrong. I'd asked Bob to carry my briefcase; Tommy had never seen that. Bob and Tom suggested a visit to the doctor, but I told them I wanted to go home to my own bed. I'd be fine if I could just get back home.

They barely got me upstairs to my bed and then watched in horror as I curled up again into a fetal ball. Within the hour Jill came into the room; somebody must have called her at school and told her she should get home. I could see her standing over me, and she looked worried. I was so gray, she didn't even stop to ask me what I wanted to do. The next thing I knew, we were on the way to Saint Francis Hospital. The doctors there suggested this was something more than a pinched nerve. As the medical staff prepped me for a spinal tap, doctors explained to Jill that I wasn't likely to be released any time soon. So Jill went home to get Ashley settled with a babysitter and to alert Hunter. I was still in a hallway, but the doctors were now arranging to get me into a room.

The results from my spinal tap came back as Jill was returning to the hospital. About the time my wife was walking through the front doors of Saint Francis, I looked up and noticed a Catholic priest at my bedside. When Jill turned the corner to my hallway, she noticed a nurse sitting outside my room writing on charts at a little table. As Jill neared the room, she stopped to talk to the nurse: "Hi, I'm Jill Biden."

"Oh, hi, Mrs. Biden," the nurse said. "Don't go in now. They're giving him last rites."

Jill entered the room and tried to put an end to the ceremony, but not long afterward the doctors came in to explain why they'd sent for the priest. The results of the spinal tap were not good: There was blood in my spinal fluid, which meant I had an artery somewhere in my head that was already leaking blood. They wanted to do more tests in a hurry and told us to gather the family. Mom and Dad, Val, Jack, Jim, and Frank all came to the hospital. My assistant, Norma Long, and her husband, Leo, drove to Philadelphia in the beginnings of a snow squall to get Beau; nobody could find Hunter, who had apparently gone to his girlfriend's house after school.

After a computed tomography, or CT, scan and an angiogram, the doctor who explained the results of the combined tests looked worried. I had an aneurysm lying just below the base of my brain.

I wasn't sure exactly what *aneurysm* meant, but doctors have a direct and simple analogy for explaining the malady. They told me to think of my artery as an inner tube inflated inside an old bicycle tire. When a spot on the inner tube thins, it weakens and begins to bulge. Air can begin to leak out, or it can burst. Mine had already leaked, and that's what had knocked me out in Rochester the night before. It might have accounted for the episode in Nashua nearly a year before. I was lucky to be alive. But if the aneurysm bled again, I probably wouldn't survive. The size of the worst bulge and the leak meant that a fatal rebleed could be imminent. Surgery to shore up the spot where I'd bled was the best chance I had of survival, but the procedure I'd need was delicate and dangerous.

My brother Jim began making calls all over the world to find neurosurgeons who had experience with this operation and could be available fast. My best chance, Jim discovered, was to get to Walter Reed Army Medical Center, outside Washington, D.C. Not only was it nearby, but the chief of neurosurgery there was one of the most experienced and accomplished practitioners of the relatively new procedure required to save me. Weather conditions made a medevac helicopter flight too dangerous. I had no idea what time it was, but I found myself on a gurney, my test results strapped to my chest, being wheeled out the doors of Saint Francis toward a waiting ambulance. As the firemen pushed me outside, I felt the sting of the cold, wet snow on my face. The snowflakes slanting hard against the glowing lights of the ambulance made a scene like an Impressionist painting, and I could sense and feel—more than I could see—Jill next to me. The crew loading me in was obviously nervous, and I could feel the *bang-bang-bang* of the wheels of the gurney when they put me into the back of the ambulance. Jill tried to calm them with a joke. "You know, Joe, you always screw everything up," she said to me, but loud enough for everybody to hear. "We were supposed be going to a spa for Valentine's Day. . . . And another thing: I hate this snow. If you die, I'm moving to North Carolina. They have a nice, long spring there."

The tension seemed to ease as the crew successfully strapped me into the back of the ambulance, which was manned by my friends in the local volunteer fire department, and we made our way with a police escort to Walter Reed. Jill along with a doctor and nurse team from Saint Francis were sitting on benches in the back of the ambulance with me. The medical personnel did not seem easy with the situation. If the aneurysm burst, there wasn't a thing they could do for me out on the open road. We rode on for about half an hour, talking in fits and starts, as the ambulance driver picked his way through the snowstorm until suddenly we noticed we weren't moving anymore. The snow was coming down harder now, and we weren't going anywhere. We were stopped at the state line where Delaware State Police officers were turning us over to the Maryland State Police. But there was some confusion about where we were going. Beau had been riding in the lead car with the Delaware police, and when he got into the official lead car from Maryland, the escort asked *him* for directions. So we sat while they tried to map out the quickest way to Walter Reed—for about five minutes. "Why are we stopped?" Jill kept saying. "Why are we stopped?" Finally she started banging on the partition that separated us from the driver's cab. "What's the matter?!"

"The Maryland State Police aren't sure where to go" came the answer.

"Move!" Jill yelled.

"We can't."

"Dammit," she said. "Move this ambulance!"

The next thing I knew, we were moving again.

At Walter Reed, Dr. Eugene George scheduled a more detailed angiogram so he could see all the major blood vessels inside my cranium. The repeat angiogram gave him a better look at the aneurysm below the left side of my brain, but it also showed a smaller one on the right side. After looking at the angiogram, Dr. George wanted to move the surgery on the left-side aneurysm to that same day. Even so, my brother demanded a second opinion, which was fine with Dr. George. When he heard that Jim had located the vascular neurosurgeon at the University of Virginia, Dr. Neal Kassell, who happened to be in town for a conference, George said he'd be happy to have him consult. They'd trained under the same instructor. Later that morning, Jill gave the doctor the okay to do the surgery.

The microsurgical craniotomy Dr. George was about to perform on me was delicate and fairly extensive. George would have to open up my head, lift my brain slightly, and travel through the thin space containing the cerebrospinal fluid between my skull and my brain—all just to *get to* the aneurysm lying deep beneath the base of the brain. Once there, he would carefully expose and dissect all the small arteries until he found the tiny berrylike aneurysm surrounded by a small clot. After gently dissecting the aneurysm, the neurosurgeon would then place a tiny metal spring clip to occlude the neck of the aneurysm permanently, while being careful to allow for normal blood flow through the adjacent artery. Dr. George explained that the second, smaller, aneurysm was unlikely to burst anytime soon, so he would leave that for another operation weeks later. When he finished explaining the procedure, I asked George about chances in the first surgery.

"Mortality," he said, "or morbidity?"

"*Morbidity*?" I said. I wasn't sure what that was.

As I heard it, my chances of surviving the surgery were certainly better than fifty-fifty. But the chances of waking up with serious deficits to my mental faculties were more significant. Dr. George had to skirt by a lot of the brain to get to the aneurysm. Any incidental damage could leave me seriously impaired. The most likely incidence of morbidity for this sort of procedure, Dr. George explained, was loss of speech. I think I laughed out loud when he said that. "I kind of wish that had happened last summer," I said, but I don't think the doctor heard me.

Dr. George said what he was about to do was going to be difficult, but he had done many of these before *and* he was going to be assisted by a world-class surgeon. But he recommended that I speak to my family—it might be my last chance.

Maybe I should have been frightened at this point, but I felt calm. In fact, I felt becalmed, like I was floating gently in the wide-open sea. It surprised me, but I had no real fear of dying. I'd long since accepted the fact that life's guarantees don't include a fair shake. And there was literally nothing I could do to save myself. My family and closest friends were in the next room pulling for me. My brother Jim had delivered me to the best medical team available. Those doctors had identified the problem, and they knew what had to be done to fix it. My life was in somebody else's very able hands.

Jill was so strong. She hadn't shown a hint of panic through the entire ordeal, and I had absolute faith that Jim and Val would look after her and the children if I died. And I also knew I could count on Val's husband, Jack, who had been so supportive of his wife's involvement in my life and my campaigns over the years. But I had an overwhelming sense of sadness. Ashley was only six years old, not much older than Beau and Hunter had been when we lost Neilia and Naomi. Jill would have to tell my daughter I wasn't coming home again. Beau and Hunter might be losing a second parent. Hunter wasn't even out of high school yet.

Jill went out to get the boys so I could talk to them alone; George hadn't given me much time, but I figured this talk with my sons was the most important five minutes of my life. If this was the last time I was going to speak to them, I had to do it right. If this was to be the last image of their father, I wanted it to be one they could honor. Two days earlier, restoring my reputation to the world seemed vital to me. But now everything felt different. The rest of the world could have their doubts about my integrity and my character; the thousands of Washington, D.C., epitaphs—good and ill—be damned. Now was for the people who meant the most to me. They were the one true thing that mattered in my life.

My sons were trying to be upbeat when they came to my bedside. *You're great young men*, I told them, *and I'm so proud of you. So I know you'll live up to your obligations. I know you'll take great care of your mother and your sister.*

Don't say that, Dad, Beau said. *You're not going anywhere.*

Look, I'm probably going to be fine, guys, but in the event something happens, you know what I expect of you. You take care of each other. You take care of your sister. You take care of your mom. I know you'll do it.

I tried to crack a joke. *By the way, on my tombstone, I don't want any senator and all that stuff. I want it to read: son, brother, husband, father . . . athlete.* They laughed. I could imagine my brothers' responses when the boys relayed this information. "Athlete!?" they'd exclaim. "Oh, God. Delusional to the end."

There was only one last thing to say to my sons: *I love you guys.* Then I kissed them good-bye for now. When it was over, I felt at peace. No matter what happened, I knew my sons would be fine. And I had lived up to my own expectations. In the moment that mattered most to me, I had been the kind of man I wanted to be.

Then I was on another gurney, being wheeled down a corridor to an operating theater. The doors of the operating room swung open, and I went through feet first, as Jill let go my hand and stayed behind. The room was cavernous, and the lights bounced off the high sheen of silver—seemed like everything in the room was chrome; it was like being on a shelf inside a giant freezer. There were people everywhere, all in scrubs and moving silently with mordant purpose. They were moving wires, shifting trays, lifting material that glinted like pieces of polished steel. No one was saying a thing, which worried me. These people seemed tight. As the anesthesiologist, Dr. Hart, was about to put the mask on my face, I recalled the story I'd heard about President Reagan going into surgery after he'd been shot in 1981. Would all the Republicans in the room please raise their hands, he'd requested, to take the edge off the nervous operating room professionals. Now I understood how that line might have been less a joke and more an effort at self-preservation. I started to say, "Would all the Democrats in the room please—" But was I talking? Was the mask already on? I think I could feel it press down around my mouth, could hear the faint echo of my own breath, as a bright flash of white light blinded me.

✳ 13 ✳

Time Will Tell

THE NEXT SENSATION I HAD WAS WAKING . . . OR DREAMING of waking. I thought at first I might still be in the O.R. I could make out a bank of machines, which must have been six feet high, all along a wall. Then I saw a clock with a second hand sweeping slowly past numbers, and I remembered with a start the word the doctor had used: *morbidity*. Was I whole, I thought? Was I able to process? The big hand near the 12, the little one on the 4. Four o'clock . . . but wait—in the afternoon? In the morning? I didn't care. I could tell time. Then I stared at the ceiling and counted the tiles above my head, calculating the total number by multiplication. I could cipher. I moved my feet. I picked up my hand and touched my finger to my nose. I stared at the machines at the foot of my bed, the waves, the bar graphs, the numbers—none of them still. That had to be good, I figured, but I wasn't sure if I was truly conscious.

Then I sensed someone leaning over me and felt the warmth of breath on my face and a press of lips on my forehead. "Joe?" I heard her say.

"Jilly, is that you?"

"It's me. I'm here."

"Am I alive?"

Jill hadn't been so sure when she first walked around the little curtain in the recovery room with Beau and Hunter, seven hours after the surgery began. Dr. George had been very pleased when he'd reported back to my family that I'd come through, so Jill wasn't entirely prepared for the instant she saw me amid a tangle of wires and tubes. Her knees, she told me later, almost buckled. A line of staples ran down my shaved, swollen, and disfigured skull. My head looked like a misshapen baseball that had just had its cover nearly knocked off. She was shocked by how small I looked in the bed. But I was still there, and I was talking.

"You're alive," she said.

The way Jill saw it, I'd been saved. Her anguish at watching my honesty questioned and my presidential campaign disintegrate was almost gone by the time she pronounced me alive. What if I hadn't been forced to leave the campaign, she thought? I would have been running across New Hampshire, from Nashua to Manchester to Concord to Bristol, when the aneurysm started to bleed. Would I have stopped long enough for treatment? Would I have tried to push through the pain? She knew me pretty well. "You wouldn't be alive," she told me later. "Things happen for a reason."

For the next ten days I was a patient at Walter Reed, and in the beginning, after the elation of survival wore off, I wasn't sure I had what it took to keep going. The worst of the pain was gone and never really returned, but the early days of recovery were unremittingly difficult. There were at least three and sometimes four monitors hooked up to me at all times, and in my few waking hours the only way to fill the time was to lie and stare at the graphs measuring my systems. I wasn't even sure what I was looking at—blood flow, oxygen flow, heartbeat, blood pressure? All I could do was stare at the screens, trying to make meaning out of the glowing movement of graphs and lines, knowing that if one of those lines or bar graphs went flat, I was probably a goner. And I remember times in the darkness when I felt like I didn't have the strength to keep those lines and graphs in the air. This was hard labor. There was a time, I believe, when I almost quit the fight. The graph slowed, and I didn't have the energy to breathe it back up . . . until I felt a nurse lean over me. It seemed like Pearl Nelson was always there. She was about my age, with that taut, sinewy rail-thin strength of Appalachia; nobody quit on Pearl if she could help it. And I could feel her mouth over my nose, forcing her own air into my lungs.

The nurses at Walter Reed were the embodiment of absolute comfort and unquestioning love; they brushed my teeth, washed me, were familiar with me in ways I could never have imagined allowing another human being to be—and in a way that never shamed me. When my neck was bothering me and I couldn't get comfortable, Pearl worked through pillows until she found one that worked. I suspected she got it outside the regular Army requisitioning process.

A few days later, about the time Michael Dukakis was winning the New Hampshire primary by a record margin, I was moved out of the ICU to a regular room. The doctors who were in and out of my room were all happy with the work they'd done and seemed pleased with my recovery. Ten days after the surgery I was released from Walter Reed with the understanding that I'd be back when I was strong enough—maybe five or six weeks—to have the second aneurysm surgically repaired. I was wheeled out of the hospital under an overhang that darkened the driveway; it reminded me of leaving meetings at the State Department. Jimmy was waiting in his car to drive me home. At the door I got up out of the wheelchair and faced the press, and I could see surprise in the faces of the reporters who were there. I was emaciated and a little unsteady on my pins. I had a Delaware Blue Hens baseball cap to cover the row of staples planted across my skull. My staff had already released a statement that I'd need the second surgery, so the reporters wanted to know how I felt about that and what my chances were. Dr. George and others on my floor had taken a lot of time to educate me about my condition and my prognosis. I was getting better, sure, but there were a lot of unknowns in neurosurgery patients. My instinct, as always, was to make light of my predicament. I told the reporters that I thought the second surgery would be a piece of cake, which apparently set off a bit of a firestorm in the neurosurgery community. Dr. George was not happy the next time I saw him. He'd gotten calls from colleagues who wanted to know why on earth he'd told his very high profile patient that the next surgery would be easy. There was nothing easy about it, he'd always told me, and I didn't doubt him. In fact, I'd been reminded of that on the car ride home. Jim was driving, and we were talking about our children. I started to ask him about his youngest daughter, my two-year-old niece, whose christening I'd attended the day the Kinnock story broke. I started to ask, "How's—" And I could not bring to mind her *name*. I felt the cold stab of panic. Would I ever be the same again? Even the doctors couldn't say for sure. Time will tell, they'd say. Time will tell.

While I worried about my mental comeback, my physical recovery was a point of personal pride. I was determined to get back up faster than anybody expected, and I really felt okay in the first few weeks. Jill would catch me on the staircase. "The doctors said you're not supposed to take the stairs yet, Joe," she'd remind me. I'd nod, but I was so sure I was making a remarkable recovery, so intent on proving my health, that I took chances. Things were going so well that by the beginning of March the doctors gave me permission to take a quick trip to a friend's condo on the water at Bethany Beach. I wasn't used to being cooped up in my house for so long, and I needed a change of scenery, so Jill and I drove down alone. The first night we were there I was lounging on the floor in front of the fireplace. I turned my head to look at the ocean and felt something rattle in my skull. Then the room started spinning, and I couldn't control it. I was too dizzy to get up. I called to Jill in the next room, and she telephoned Dr. George, who reassured me: "Senator," he said, "that's normal."

"But why'd it happen?"

"We don't know why, but I'm telling you it happens. It will go away, but healing is a process."

"Could it happen again?" I wanted to know.

He couldn't be sure, but what had just happened to me wasn't uncommon.

When we got back home, I treated my brain like a delicate egg. I was terrified to turn my head on the pillow. Whenever I got up, I'd keep my neck straight, making sure not to rattle my noggin again. Then one morning I couldn't get up at all. I had pains in my chest and my abdomen that were so excruciating I could not raise myself off the pillow. This was pain of an order I'd never felt before, even in the bleed. Every time I breathed in, it felt like a paring knife was slicing through my insides. I managed to double myself into a ball and took small, shallow breaths to take the edge off the sharpest pain. But I still could not raise myself out of bed even when I started talking to myself out loud: "Get up! Dammit, Joe, get up!" Jill called a doctor we knew nearby, the same one who had diagnosed my aneurysm as a pinched nerve. He asked me what I'd eaten for breakfast. When I told him scrambled eggs, he diagnosed a gas bubble. I wanted so badly for him to be right. The idea of being incapacitated again for days or weeks was almost too much to bear. But my neighborhood doctor was wrong again.

A few hours later I was carted out the front door on a stretcher and taken to my local hospital, where doctors discovered a blood clot lodged in my lung. They weren't quite sure where it had first formed, but it wasn't uncommon, the medical staff assured me again, given that I had spent so much time in bed. But the doctors were worried that I might have other clots, especially in my legs, that could break free and do serious damage.

I was taken back to Walter Reed, where I spent ten days under the care of surgeons and blood-clotting specialists. The surgeons installed some more hardware in me. They put a little filter in through my jugular vein and down into my mid-thorax, where they attached it to the sides of an artery. Once planted in my artery, the titanium filter opened up into something that looked like a badminton birdie; it would catch any wayward clots from my legs before they could reach my lungs or my heart.

But the doctors were also worried about the possibility of clotting in one of the veins above my heart. The hematologists and neurosurgeons together were worried that another big clot could break free, travel into my lungs, and cause a massive pulmonary embolus, killing me instantly. They suggested an additional anticlotting drug to help cleanse my arteries and break down the worst of the clotting. If I took the drug, they told me, they could more or less guarantee the clots would be sufficiently eroded that even if one did break free, I would survive. If they didn't administer the drug and something big was loosed in my bloodstream, I would likely die.

I was in the hospital another week and a half, and every day it seemed like a new hematologist or surgeon looked in on me. President Reagan even sent his own doctor to check on me. One of them, I remember, patted me on the arm. "Lucky man," he said. What about this was "lucky" I wasn't sure. It kind of reminded me of E.J. saying, "Everything comes easy to you, doesn't it?"

I would have felt luckier if it weren't for the tests. Seemed like somebody was taking blood from me every few hours. The worst was the angiograms, when they'd have to stick me in a tender part of my groin. I think I had eight or nine, and every one was more dreadful than the last. In the meantime, I also got an interesting education in embolisms and aneurysms. More than sixty thousand people a year die of embolisms in the United States. The lead hematologist on my case had been at a medical school in North Carolina, which turned out to be ground zero for embolisms and strokes. Stroke Alley, I think he called it. He explained to me that elderly snowbirds from the Northeast driving back and forth to Florida often got into trouble in North Carolina. Ten or twelve hours in a car without stopping to stretch did them in.

While I was recovering, the doctors started going through my family history, and it turned out that one of my grandfathers had been killed by a blood clot and one of my grandmothers had died in a way that strongly suggested an aneurysm. A little more than one in ten Americans has the sort of aneurysm I had, but the defect generally went undetected. After my full recovery was assured, I was let in on a dark joke heard around the neurosurgery wing back in those days: *When do you know somebody has an aneurysm? On the autopsy table.* When I asked why they didn't screen for aneurysms, the doctors explained that the only way to test in 1988 was an angiogram, and more people would die as a result of the test than would die from a burst aneurysm. Ninety percent of those who have it die from something else. Even with all the information in hand, I still wasn't sure whether or not I'd been lucky.

The reporters were again waiting in the Walter Reed parking garage when I was finally discharged from the hospital. But I was grateful just to be getting out. "I've asked you all to come today," I told them, "because I've decided to announce that I am reentering the race for president." At least they laughed.

Patience had never been my strength, but somewhere in that second hospital stay I had started to think about the virtue of being in less of a hurry. If I had taken it easier and done what the doctors advised, I might have avoided the second stay. The presidency, for instance, could wait; there would be another time if I really wanted it. The restoration of my reputation would be a long process. Time would tell.

When I got back home, Jill and the staff made the decision to keep me completely isolated. There would be no work, no phone calls, no nothing. President Reagan had called twice. Jill was grateful to the president, but she made no exceptions to her rule; she would not let me take the call. Jill and the staff brooked no argument from me. The world kept spinning without my help, Jill assured me.

And it did. Jesse Jackson won the presidential primary in my home state of Delaware and turned the contest into a real race, but Michael Dukakis outlasted him to win the Democratic nomination. When

Senator Al Gore dropped out of the race, he was generous in his praise of the other candidates who had run. "From Joe Biden I learned the importance of grace under pressure," he said in his withdrawal speech. "When his campaign was unraveling around him, I saw him conduct the Bork hearings with absolute fairness and honor. Joe Biden put the country ahead of his own political struggles and honored us all as Democrats and as Americans."

The Dukakis crew started making noise that spring about bringing back John Sasso, the campaign manager whom the Massachusetts governor had fired for making and sending out the "attack video" that began the demise of my campaign. Apparently the Dukakis team was making calls to my friends to see how I might feel about that, but nobody told me at the time.

And Justice Robert H. Bork had resigned from the federal appeals court and was on the road giving speeches about how he'd been mishandled by the Judiciary Committee. Part of the problem, Bork would reportedly tell his audiences, was that the senators on the panel were not intelligent enough to understand the complexities of his judicial philosophy. His views on the right to privacy, for instance, had been misconstrued. "It was impossible to straighten that out," he was quoted as saying, adding sarcastically, "even with so powerful an intellect as Joe Biden."

The good news for Bork was that he was able to cash in on being denied a seat on the Supreme Court. A hefty book advance, five-figure speaking fees, and a little work in the field of law, the *Los Angeles Times* noted, "was likely to earn Bork as much this year as perhaps a decade on the court."

But I didn't know any of this. Jill kept me in my splendid isolation so I could get strong enough for the next surgery. I'd get up and move around, have my daily walks, but most of what I did was sleep. I didn't even have the concentration to read. I did have a lot of time to think, and a lot of time to think about the next surgery. The first surgery had been so bang-bang that I didn't have much time to think about it. But I had plenty of time to think about the second one. My chances of survival, as I recall, were about nine in ten. But the issue of morbidity still pertained; there was a possibility of paralysis, of loss of speech, of short-term memory loss. And even if I came through the operation 100 percent, I was in for another long recovery. The truth was, as Jill noticed, I got angrier and angrier as the date for the second surgery approached.

When they wheeled me into Dr. George's operating theater again in May 1988, I entered with an abiding faith in my surgeon's abilities, but I wasn't leaving anything to chance. I'd been given special permission to carry a set of rosary beads into surgery. George deemed the second surgery a success, but because the doctors needed to monitor my blood complications, I was in the hospital for almost all of May, with no guarantee as to when I could go home and little to do. My focus was, as much as anything, on the physical world. I'd sit on my bed and stare out the window, watching a radio tower rising day by day on the horizon. Ten feet, then twenty, then thirty, then fifty—by the time it's done, I told myself, I'm going to be out of here. Jill was keeping me up to date on the progress of our kitchen floor. We were having bright white Mexican tiles put in the kitchen at The Station. For some reason I couldn't wait to see those tiles.

Since I'd first gone down in February, our friends and neighbors around Delaware had been dropping off food and offering help. Jill was teaching full-time that year, running back and forth to Walter Reed at nights or on the weekends, so she needed the support. When I was in the hospital that May, one of our favorite sub shops in Delaware would send me fresh sandwiches three or four days a week. They'd make them and drive them to Washington, and even when I couldn't eat them, the nurses did.

When I left the hospital this time, I felt pretty strong but more self-conscious than the first time. I was so thin that it bothered me to look in the mirror, and, worse than that, during the second surgery the doctors had stretched a scalp nerve that affected muscle control in my forehead, so the right side of my forehead was immobile. My right eyelid drooped. Being seen in public was not what I desired, so when Jill suggested a night at the ballet, I agreed to go but only if we entered our box after the lights were down. I dreaded the moment when the lights came up after the show. I asked the doctor when this problem with my dead face would clear up, and he couldn't be sure if the damage was permanent or not. The best he could offer was a prognosis that seemed to hang over my every waking minute: Only time will tell.

All I could do was accept it.

I was weak, my forehead was half paralyzed, and I still had trouble concentrating. My attention span was minimal, and I tired very easily. So I waited. I followed doctors' orders and Jill's, stayed away from work and phones, and for the first time in my life I really rested. I used the archery set that Jimmy gave me when I got strong enough, or I drove over to Kennett Square to sit out in the sun and eat lunch, or I hit golf balls at a driving range. Six weeks after the second surgery, the muscles in my forehead and cheek finally came to life again. But I still didn't get out much.

There were so few Biden sightings around Delaware that my office started getting calls from newspaper reporters saying they'd heard from solid sources that the senator was a vegetable. Some remembered the line from Ben Bradlee, the famous editor of the *Washington Post:* "Biden'll never be the same," he'd said when he heard about my first surgery. So reporters demanded to talk to me, or they were going to write the story. But my staff still kept me off the phones. Jill still wouldn't let President Reagan's calls through.

The only Washington friend who broke the rule was Ted Kennedy, who called up Norma Long at my Wilmington office one day and asked for somebody to pick him up at the train station. He had taken Amtrak up from Washington and was determined to visit me at home. He wouldn't take no for an answer. Jill was hosting a luncheon for some girlfriends when Senator Kennedy came walking into the house. He was carrying an etching of a big Irish stag he'd had framed. "To my Irish Chairman," he'd written on it. Teddy had brought his bathing suit.

I found out later that Kennedy and his staff had taken up the slack on the Judiciary Committee for me, and although it's rare in the Senate, they had generously deferred to the wishes of my staff members while I was gone. This gesture of friendship made me feel less guilty about my seven-month absence. The day Kennedy showed up at The Station, I was never so happy to see a colleague. But he didn't want to talk business. He just wanted me to know that I was missed and that my colleagues were looking forward to my return.

By the end of August I felt like myself again. My energy and ability to concentrate were completely restored. The doctors looked me over and gave me the okay to return when Congress reconvened after Labor Day. My first public appearance was at the end of August at the annual Sussex County Jamboree in Delaware, where I stood and listened to seven hundred old friends chant, "Joe! Joe! Joe!" All I wanted to do was assure them that I was back to serve them in the Senate to the best of my abilities. "The good news is that I can do anything I did before," I assured the crowds. "The bad news is that I can't do anything better."

I had had a lot of time to think about my past and my future, and I wanted to be in the Senate for years to come. For good or ill, I was a public man. I was a lucky man, to be sure. This was, I said that day, "my second chance in life. . . . I'm alive. I'm well. My family is happy. I do something I love."

A couple days later, sitting in my kitchen with Jimmy, I got an interesting call. Michael Dukakis, the Democratic presidential nominee, was on the line. He had to speak to me. Jimmy told me not to take the call, but I did. Election Day was just two months away, and Vice President George Bush was starting to pull away in the polls. The last time Dukakis had called he wanted me to intercede with a union president who was dragging his feet on endorsing him. Now he wanted another favor: "Joe, I need your help."

He wanted to bring John Sasso back to help run his campaign. He said he wanted to know what I'd say publicly about the guy he had fired after he shot the first torpedo at my campaign.

"What will John say about me, Governor?" I asked him.

"What do you mean?" Dukakis asked. He had no interest in making amends with me. He just wanted to smooth the politics of bringing Sasso back onto his campaign team.

"Joe," he said, "John has had a terrible year."

I had a funny feeling after I hung up the phone; there was no lingering anger at all, for any of it. I realized I didn't actually hold a grudge against John Sasso. Why spend the time? The bottom line was that I hoped he could help Dukakis beat Vice President Bush.

Dukakis announced the return of his friend John Sasso a few hours later. Apparently they'd already scheduled the press conference before they called me. "I'm very pleased that John is rejoining the campaign," Dukakis told the assembled press. "He's paid the price—a year is a long time." The governor said Sasso had made a terrible mistake but "there was nothing illegal about what John did," and he told the reporters that he had talked to me about restoring Sasso. According to Dukakis, Joe Biden "could not have been more gracious."

Sasso made his own statement: "What I did back in September was an error in judgment. I am sorry it hurt Senator Biden and his family.

The fact is, Senator Biden is a man of strong character. He has proven that both in his personal life and in his professional life. If the incident last September left the impression to the contrary, I believe strongly that impression is wrong. . . . On other occasions he certainly had quoted and given attribution to Neil Kinnock, and I do not believe in any way he intended to mislead the American people."

On Wednesday, September 7, 1988, I got on the Amtrak train in Wilmington for my customary ride to Washington; Jill, the kids, my parents, and my siblings traveled with me. It was the first time in seven months I'd been on that train, and the workers at the station had put up signs and balloons. My engineer friend saluted me with an extended toot of the whistle.

In Washington I was walking through a parking lot toward my office when I heard a shout. I looked up and saw my colleague Daniel Patrick Moynihan bouncing toward me. "You're back," he said as he threw his long arms around me. "You're back." I was actually surprised at the strength of his embrace. From the first day I walked into the Senate after Neilia's death I had received genuine and warm support from my colleagues, but the spontaneity and generosity of the response on my return after seven months moved me.

My staff hosted a surprise party, and senators from both parties dropped by to look in on me all day long. I chaired a Foreign Relations subcommittee hearing that day, with my entire family and a large gathering of reporters in tow. My family was there, I joked to reporters, "to make sure I enunciate the questions and understand the answers. . . . I'm back. It's over. Let's go back to work." But there was nothing normal about the day—seemed like every corner I turned there was another reception in my honor.

Near the end of the day on the Senate floor, my colleagues unanimously passed a resolution welcoming me back, then stood and gave me a standing ovation. I sat at my desk, with my family watching from the gallery above, and listened to tributes from my friends in the Senate. One of the nicest came from the Republican leader, Bob Dole, who knew what it was like to deal with health problems. He'd been wounded so badly as a twenty-year-old soldier in Italy in 1944 that he had lost the practical use of both arms. He'd overcome that adversity to rise to the top of the Senate and would win his party's presidential nomination in 1996. "To the surprise of no one who knows Joe

Biden's spirit and tenacity," Dole offered, "he triumphed." Coming from Bob Dole, that meant a lot to me.

I was asked to talk a lot that day, but the only time I got choked up was after the tributes on the floor of the Senate. The Senate had been like a second home to me for more than fifteen years, and it felt good to be home. I remember looking around the Senate chamber and seeing so many men and women I'd come to respect and admire. A few of them, like Bob Byrd, Daniel Inouye, Ted Stevens, Arlen Specter, and Pete Domenici, are still there twenty years later. But so many—such as Daniel Patrick Moynihan, Fritz Hollings, Wendell Ford, Nancy Kassebaum, Alan Simpson, and Bob Dole—are gone now, and the Senate is lesser for their absence. These were people of breadth and character and experience who knew there was more to Senate business than mere partisan politics; they had reached out across party lines to make great friendships and important alliances. They cultivated those relationships not out of political expediency but because they understood how crucial the bonds of personal relations are in a democracy as jangled and diverse as ours. Back in 1988 I had faith that no matter how fractious the issue, the passions of the day could not undo the esteem these senators held for one another.

"Friends make a difference," I told the men and women who served in that chamber with me that day. "Having a place where you want to be makes a difference, and knowing that you will be welcomed back to that place you want to be makes an even bigger difference. If I say more, the Irish in me may creep out, and I'll become too sentimental."

On the way out of one of the buffet-strewn receptions in my honor that day, my Senate friend Alan Simpson joked about the momentous changes that had taken place in the Senate in my seven months away—"We never had shrimp before Joe left"—but I was happy to find the rhythm and constancy of the place were intact. There was something different that day, however, and it was my own internal rhythms. For years Wendell Ford and Fritz Hollings would say to me, "You gotta slow down," but now I could finally feel the wisdom of that advice. My sense of urgency was not so acute. The last year had taught me one big lesson: The only things that are truly urgent are matters of life and death.

I was no less committed or passionate, but I no longer felt I had to win *every* moment to succeed. I could miss a Judiciary Committee hearing and the crime bill would not be lost. I could miss a Democratic caucus meeting, a staff meeting, or a political event and still do my job well. Most important I understood that a single moment of failure—even one so public and wounding as the end of my presidential campaign—could not determine my epitaph. I had faith in the ultimate fairness and reason of the American people, and I had faith that I could rebuild my reputation.

Only time would tell . . . and I had time.

✳ 14 ✳

Engage

MY YOUNGER SON, HUNTER, RARELY ASKED ME FOR FAVORS, so I was sort of surprised when he brought up the idea of my speaking at Georgetown. Whenever Beau had asked me to speak at Penn, I made an effort do it. In fact, over the years I'd probably done a dozen public forums for Beau, but I couldn't recall having done a single talk for Hunter. So when he asked me, I couldn't say no. The president of Georgetown wanted me to give a talk at Hunter's Jesuit Volunteer Corps retreat about how my faith and my religion informed my public policy views. It was a topic I had always shied away from because it makes me a little uncomfortable to carry religion into the arena of politics, but writing that speech turned out to be one of the most enlightening exercises of my political life.

I've made more than twelve thousand votes in the Senate and there are plenty of political handicappers who, like baseball statisticians, could parse the votes, run the numbers, and make a profile of my career. In fact, the statisticians on both sides like to take all one hundred senators and line us up on the slippery sliding scale of liberal to conservative. But those ratings never meant much to me or to the people in Delaware who elected me. And because my presidential campaign was so brief and tangled, I had never really had time to sit and think about the overarching ethic that connected all those votes. I was like a pointillist painter who had been so busy making each dot, he hadn't taken the time to stand back and look at the picture emerging on the canvas. So the topic of the Georgetown speech forced the issue, and as I was entering my second-chance life it seemed like a good time to take stock.

What came clear to me as I wrote the speech was very simple: The central lesson I received from the Catholic Church, my Catholic school education, and my own parents had always been the governing force in my political career. To wit, the greatest sins on this earth are committed by people of standing and means who abuse their power. That was a message constantly reinforced in Sunday sermons, in school, and at home. Jesus didn't spend time with the Pharisees. Jesus hung out with the prostitutes, with the lepers, with the bad guys. That's what I remembered about my faith. In my own house the lessons about the abuse of power were constant, big and small—from the Nazi party in Germany to the father on our street in Mayfield who chastised his children with a belt. "It takes a small man to hit a small child," my dad used to say. My father never once raised his hand to any of his children. I remember Mom and Dad talking in our living room about a friend of theirs slapping his wife across the face. My father, who was not given to temper tantrums, was pacing the floor, enraged.

With power and privilege, I was taught, comes a responsibility to treat others with respect and fairness. Generosity is not simply a virtue; it's a Commandment. And when we see people abusing power, it is our duty to intercede on behalf of their victims. As I worked on that Georgetown speech, I saw that the lessons I had learned growing up had *always* been the guiding principles of my career in politics, and that the issues that captured my attention had always all related to the abuse of power. From civil rights and voting rights to my interest in putting police on the streets to protect people from violent criminals in their own neighborhoods, to stopping banks from redlining practices that made it nearly impossible for people living in black neighborhoods to get loans, to pushing for federal guidelines that made criminal sentencing more fair and uniform, to fighting violence against children, to the disgust I felt at watching Richard Nixon and J. Edgar Hoover abuse their high offices (I was one of the few senators who voted against naming the FBI building after Hoover), to the fight against the drug cartels of the 1980s, there was a single common thread. As I looked back on my career, it was obvious that what had always animated me was the belief that we should stand up to those who abused power, whether it was political, economic, or physical.

So as I look back again today, it comes as no surprise that in the next several years after that Georgetown speech, the two big issues that drew my attention were both flagrant abuses of power. One was a systematic genocide loosed by a venal, power-hungry European demagogue; the other was something here at home, an inexcusable abuse of power that had insidiously wormed its way into our American life and institutions. And we as a country didn't seem to have the stomach to face our dirty little secret.

SINCE THE MID-SEVENTIES I'd been working on crime issues in the Judiciary Committee, and since the mid-eighties I had been the Democrats' point man in the Senate on crime legislation. While I have always been a defender of robust civil liberties for the accused, I have worked hard to give police the tools to fight crime—more cops on the street, better equipment, sentencing guidelines that put people away for committing violent crimes. There have been times when my Democratic colleagues have thought I've gone too far over to the side of the police in law-and-order issues, but I have always felt that public safety and security is the first duty of government. A government must ensure safe homes, streets, schools, and public places before it can fulfill any other promises. So I was constantly watching the crime statistics for anomalies and new problems, for example the jump in violence that accompanied the crack epidemic that ravaged the inner cities in the 1980s.

While looking at Bureau of Justice crime statistics in 1990, I was struck by a particular number. The violent crimes perpetrated against men had fallen greatly in the previous ten years; the number of violent crimes against young women trended up. My initial hunch was that because of the women's movement, more women were willing to come forward and report rapes or domestic violence. But as I looked into it, there was much more than that going on. In fact, I quickly came to see that violence against women was a cultural expectation shared by men, women, and children. I remember reading shocking statistics from a survey of middle-school children done in Rhode Island. If a man takes a woman out on a date and spends $10 on her, one question asked, does he have the right to force sex on her? A quarter of the boys said he did, which stunned me. But the bigger surprise was that a fifth of the girls agreed. This was a big problem, and it was deeply ingrained in our society. I later learned that one in ten

American males believed it was okay for a husband to hit his wife if she didn't obey him. That meant millions of women were at risk of being beaten in their own homes.

I knew from experience that it wasn't just uneducated thugs who thought this way. I had never forgotten a scene back in 1981 when the Judiciary Committee was rushing to get a big new crime bill out of committee for a vote on the floor. The clock was running out on the session of Congress and I was pushing this to get this bill out the door. We had the votes to report the entire package favorably to the floor. The committee was meeting in a small room just off the Senate floor; Chairman Thurmond called for a committee vote, unless there were any objections. Alabama senator Jeremiah Denton objected, and loudly. Denton was angry about a provision I wanted in the bill that made marital rape a crime indistinguishable from any other rape. "Damn it, when you get married," he said that day, "you kind of expect you're going to get a little sex."

In 1990 I assigned one of my staff on Judiciary full-time to the problem of violence against women. The staffer, Victoria Nourse, and I wrote preliminary legislation called the Violence Against Women Act of 1990, and in June we began hearings. By the time we concluded our hearings at the end of that year I was convinced that this might be the most important piece of legislation I had ever introduced and among the most difficult to turn into law. I also understood that the problem was much deeper than the Bureau of Justice statistics could tell. The first panel at the Judiciary Committee's hearing on "Legislation to Reduce the Growing Problem of Violent Crime Against Women" included a model whose face had been slashed by men hired by her landlord and a married mother in Iowa who had been abducted and raped by a complete stranger. These women made clear that their victimization had continued as their cases wended through the courts. Marla Hanson, a New York fashion model whose face had been slashed, told the committee about the letters from friends and strangers she began receiving while she was in the hospital recovering from the attack. "There seemed to be an underlying element of blame, even anger," she testified, "coming in comments like: 'Well, what were you doing in a bar at twelve o'clock at night in the first place?' Or: 'I told you something like this would happen if you moved to New York.' "

Her ordeal continued, according to her committee testimony, at the trial of her attackers: "One defense attorney in his opening statement to the jury began by saying, 'Let me tell you about a woman named Marla Hanson who was after every man in the city who had a woman, who preyed on men and their relationship with women.' When the prosecutor objected, the judge remarked, 'even though we may live in the twentieth century, some people still have a feeling that it's improper, low even, to make a pass at another woman's man, and the point counsel is making, I think, is that someone who would do that is a person who is utterly selfish and self-interested, and therefore, at least in part, that person should not be believed and it's as simple as that. . . . I can't say that it's an inappropriate attack because it deals with what she should be prepared to do in her own self-interest. I will allow it.'

"Throughout the trial," Ms. Hanson continued, "it was insinuated that I was a prostitute of sorts and that I had loose morals. I was asked about intimate details about my sex life. . . . The viciousness of the trial made me wonder if I was in America."

The Iowa woman had good things to say about how she was treated by medical staff and police in the immediate aftermath of the rape, and although she was not subject to the same sort of humiliations at her trial, she was still stunned by the way she had become, quite literally, a body of evidence. "I quickly learned that the crime that had been committed against my body and my person was a crime against the state. It was no longer a crime against me, and that was frustrating; that was very frustrating to me. I became just a witness for the State of Iowa and a case number. That is all I was, and it was frustrating. . . . I was just a person that the State of Iowa needed to convict this man."

The woman from Iowa was accompanied at the hearings by her friend and lawyer, a man whose condescension toward her highlighted the problem women face: "I don't think there's anybody there to take their hands and thoroughly brief them ahead of time, let them know what the system might expect of them," he testified. "I think they feel had after developments occur in the system. In Iowa recently, in the Quad Cities in Davenport, [there was] a notorious arrest of a fifteen-year-old victim who filed a complaint against a male assailant, and then when she refused to testify, the judge jailed the victim for contempt. Well, there is a logic to that, but for one who is a victim it is hard to figure out. . . . After they realize what the system is all about and that this right of confrontation means you get dragged out in the arena, they feel bruised again."

I'll never forget the testimony of a college student who said she was violated in her dorm room by a boyfriend of one of her own friends. After the attack she took a scalding hot shower, and while she sat on her bed sobbing, the residential advisor came in and heard her story.

"You were raped," the RA exclaimed.

"No, I wasn't," the victim said. "I knew him."

Other witnesses testified that victims of acquaintance rape often blamed themselves and that those feelings are reinforced by their female friends. A college senior who cofounded an antirape organization on the University of Pennsylvania campus, where my son Beau was still in school, was frank about the problem she and her friends faced:

> For me the reality of acquaintance rape hit home midway through my first year at Penn when a friend of mine was raped in a fraternity. She fit the stereotype. She was eighteen, at college. She was trying really hard to fit in and make friends, and she had also drunk more than she could handle that night. As her friends, we also fit the stereotype. We asked why she went upstairs. We did not want to believe that these guys that we went to class with and who we knew could be rapists. We did not tell her it was not her fault and we really did not say anything at all, because we did not know what to say. . . . [The victim] has been permanently scarred. She says now that we do not know what she was like before and we only know the girl of after the rape. She has left Penn.

This was the sort of testimony the Senate—and ninety-eight of a hundred were men in 1990—needed to hear, but the early hearings were sparsely attended by the members of the Judiciary Committee. I felt like a voice in the wilderness, and I was a bit surprised at the resistance I met from the inside-the-Beltway women's groups.

I knew these groups didn't entirely trust me because I wasn't pure on the issue of abortion. I supported a woman's right to have an abortion, but I was still against federal funding of the procedure. They probably would have been more comfortable if Howard Metzenbaum or Paul Simon had been spearheading the legislation. "Oh, Victoria, you're a nice little girl, but you work for Joe Biden," a Washington women's group member said to my lead staffer on the Violence Against Women Act. "Why should we believe you?"

But there were other things beyond the groups' long-held suspicions of me. I got the sense that the inside-the-Beltway women's advocacy groups were worried that the VAWA would be a distraction from their main issues. And there was also a certain amount of personal pride I sensed among women I knew well. The first discussion I had with Jill about the legislation was an eye-opener. She was getting ready to go to school one morning when I turned to her and explained how excited and proud I was about the act we were writing. I was half-expecting—and surely hoping—that my wife would give me a big hug and tell me how proud she was of me. But after a long silence she said, "Why are you doing that? We don't need protection."

I didn't fully understand what bothered her until we had another discussion months later. Jill was working on her first master's degree in 1991, taking night courses at West Chester University. So when I'd arrive home after a day in the Senate she'd be waiting in the driveway with the car running. Once she knew I was in the house with our daughter, she'd head for school, and I'd set to making my "pasghetti" for Ashley. But on this particular night I wanted to make sure my wife knew about the reports I'd been hearing, so I rapped on the window of her car. "Jill, did you hear about that rapist?" I asked. There were reports of a rapist on her campus. "Why don't you park in front of the Old Main Building, where there are lights?"

"There's no parking there," she reminded me.

"Just park there, and we'll pay the damn ticket," I said, but I could tell she was angry. As she started to drive away I was literally hanging on to the car. "Dammit, Jill, slow up. Promise me you'll park out front," I yelled. "What's the matter with you?"

"What's the matter with me?" she said. "I really resent it. I know you're right, but as a man you don't have to do that, and I resent it." Why should a woman have to park in a no-parking zone in front of the main building where it is well lighted just to be able to go safely to school? She was right. It wasn't fair, but it was the case.

What I learned in the continuing hearings made it clear to me why there was a deep well of resentment among women. For much of the history of the nation they had been deemed second-class citizens and even property. We had testimony from experts that the earliest rape laws were written to protect, for instance, a father's property. A daughter, once raped, was damaged goods, making it more difficult to marry her off. The victim would likely remain a burden to her father.

In 1868, experts testified, the Supreme Court had denied a wife the right to sue her husband for assault and battery. State courts in the 1800s ruled that men had the legal right to beat their wives. The experts pointed out that the *Encyclopaedia Britannica,* as recently as 1958, defined rape as "the crime committed by a man in obtaining unlawful carnal knowledge of a woman without her consent by fear, force or fraud. A husband cannot commit rape upon his wife unless she is legally separated from him." Just twenty years ago, the committee was reminded, rapists routinely went free if the victim couldn't prove that she had risked her life fighting back with the "utmost resistance."

We heard contemporaneous stories of judicial insensitivity or incompetence, such as a story about a judge who suggested that a rape victim had invited the attack by wearing a crocheted miniskirt. There was an idiot doctor at one of the hearings who testified that there is a sexual trigger in a man's mind, and when a woman hits that trigger, the man can't be held responsible. The stupidity was infuriating.

By the time we reported the crime bill out of committee, Victoria Nourse and I had written comprehensive legislation that attacked deficiencies in protecting women and their basic rights in schools, homes, police precincts, and courts of law—and made it the federal government's business to help. The legislation was aimed at the prevention of violent crime against women, and better training and resources for the people who deal with the aftermath—police, hospital workers, and victims' advocates. It even called for training and sensitizing judges to the problems that female victims of crime faced in the system. A hotline would make reporting domestic abuse easier, and states would be forced to honor restraining orders from other states. But to me the most important part of the bill was Title III, which recognized that in some cases violence against women was a violation of civil rights—a hate crime.

We decided that the VAWA would have to have a civil rights component, and that was Title III, which permitted women to seek civil damages against their attackers in a federal court and gave them a purchase of power in the system. If women couldn't get satisfaction in state criminal court, the federal courts would be open to them.

Acknowledging that a woman's right to be safe from a gender-based attack was a "civil right," I believed, was critically important in changing the American consciousness. When a right reaches the status and categorization of a "civil right," it means the nation has arrived at a consensus that is nonnegotiable. Violence against women would no longer be written off as "she was asking for it" (rape), "sexual miscommunication" (date rape), or "a family matter" (domestic abuse). Once our criminal justice system—at the local, state, and federal levels—recognized these as serious and inexcusable crimes, women could stop blaming themselves.

But I remained a lonely voice in the Senate. The VAWA never made it to the floor for a vote in 1990, or in 1991 after I reintroduced it. And at the beginning of 1991, Chief Justice William H. Rehnquist tried to gut the bill before it could get to a vote. In his 1991 year-end report on the federal judiciary, Rehnquist made an unusual assault on legislation pending in Congress, specifically attacking Title III of the Violence Against Women Act. "The bill's definition of a new crime is so open-ended," he wrote, "and the new private right of action so sweeping that the legislation could involve the federal courts in a whole host of domestic relations disputes."

He followed his report with newspaper editorials about the "caseload crisis" in the federal courts. Rehnquist had built a career on keeping the federal courts clear of issues he thought best left to the states—such as, for instance, domestic violence. Domestic violence, as Rehnquist saw it, was a family problem best left to state courts.

And now he was trying to torpedo the Violence Against Women Act with the argument that it would burden the federal courts. When Rehnquist made the case in a speech to the American Bar Association in February 1992, my staff and I sat around a conference table lamenting the fate of the VAWA. None of us appreciated Rehnquist's sticking his nose in congressional business, and I was especially offended at suggestions made by his minions that women would use the civil rights remedy as leverage in divorce proceedings. Worse than that, I knew that if Rehnquist's argument won over the ABA and the ABA came out against the bill, it would die without a vote.

In the middle of Rehnquist's campaign, I testified before the House Judiciary Committee's Crime and Criminal Justice Subcommittee, which was considering my VAWA legislation. Victoria had prepared a statement for me, but I tossed it away. I explained to the House members:

The civil rights provision of the bill is a hate crimes law. That means an element of proving whether or not there has been a civil rights violation—if this bill were passed—is that the crime has to be motivated by hate. You cannot establish a cause of action under this bill by saying that "I am a woman; I have a bruise; ergo I have a civil rights claim," as the Chief Justice would lead you to believe. . . . Critics said that Title III would encourage women to raise false claims to extort more alimony in divorce cases, a claim made by the Chief Justice that is not only wrong but verges on the offensive to the extent that it suggests that women have a greater propensity to file false claims than men do. It is outrageous.

The bulk of our bill deals with matters relating to federal law enforcement—from providing dollars to achieve better lighting in areas of high crime straight through to providing that a stay-away order issued in one state should be enforced in all states. "Now we have got a Chief Justice who, I respectfully suggest, does not know what he is talking about when he criticizes this legislation. Now, the Chief Justice and others have suggested that the bill may burden the federal courts unnecessarily. Let me tell you something. We have, under Title XVIII of the U.S. Code, provisions making it a federal crime if you move across a state line with falsely made dentures— dentures. We cover a myriad, a host of crimes—for example, if you take a cow across a state line, if you rustle a cow, it is a federal crime. And I hear the outrageous assertion from some on the bench that we should tolerate a system in which a state court in Pennsylvania tells a man who has battered, or is likely to batter, his wife, "You must stay away," but when that woman crosses the state line into Delaware, that order has no effect whatsoever—is unenforceable. This notion that what is ordered in the state court in Pennsylvania should be enforceable in Delaware is, I don't think, any radical expansion. If we can take care of cows, maybe the vaulted chambers of the Supreme Court could understand it may make sense to worry about women.

MY INTEREST IN the breakup of the former Yugoslavia started with a very persistent monk. He showed up at my office with a K Street lobbyist to help translate for him, but his English was pretty good, so he spoke just fine for himself. He was wearing the traditional robes, and he was earnest and compelling. The monk was Croatian and a

Roman Catholic. He had a story he wanted to share with me about what was happening in his home country of Yugoslavia.

People from all over the world literally petition to see me, and then tell me about some awful thing happening in some remote corner that nobody is paying attention to and say that America has to get in there and help. When they come to my office pleading, America is always the great hope—as well we should be. People from all over the world rely on America. More to the point, they rely on our belief in the fundamental principles of freedom and equality and common decency. They rely on our belief that we can and should help make the world a safer place. And they rely on our belief that there are compelling moral reasons to act that go beyond naked national self-interest. Sometimes we succeed, sometimes we fail, but the point is, people all over the world see us trying. That's why the monk, for instance, wouldn't stop asking for a meeting. One member of my foreign relations staff, Jamie Rubin, said he thought there was something there. We ought to talk to the guy.

He wanted to tell me about these terrible things the ethnic Serbs were doing at the Catholic shrine in Medjugorje, in southern Bosnia. The Medjugorje shrine might be considered the Lourdes of Bosnia, and the Orthodox Catholic Serbs were not only denying access to the Croats, they were desecrating the shrine. He was afraid the Serbs were going to destroy the shrine altogether . . . he knew of Catholics in Bosnia and Croatia who were being killed by Serbs . . . he knew Milosevic was whipping the Serbs into a frenzy. He was also forceful, appealing to me as a Catholic. I was such a supporter of Israel, he reminded me, and these were Catholics who were being killed here, so why didn't I pay as much attention? By the time the monk came to see me in 1991, I knew the situation in Yugoslavia was deteriorating, but he focused my attention. I was the chair of the Subcommittee on European Affairs of the Senate Foreign Relations Committee; Yugoslavia was part of my portfolio, so I started hearings on the breakup. Other Yugoslavs came in with stories to tell: Orthodox Serbs, Croats, Muslims from Bosnia, and Albanian Muslims from Kosovo. None of it sounded good. The country was splitting apart, and our deputy secretary of state, Lawrence Eagleburger, who knew the region better than anybody, was warning that a breakup would be a bloodbath.

From 1945 to 1980, Josip Broz Tito had ruled Yugoslavia; through personality, will, and an efficient secret police, the wily old Communist had held together an ethnically and religiously mixed federation. The Orthodox Serbs dominated Serbia and Montenegro; Croatia was mainly Roman Catholic; Kosovo was overwhelmingly Albanian Muslim. In the middle was Bosnia and Herzegovina, which had the greatest mix of all. Bosnia's population was 44 percent Muslim, 31 percent Serb, and 17 percent Croatian. It had taken a certain genius to keep this multiethnic federation together—and that certain genius was Tito's.

I started to understand how he did it back in 1979, on a trip to represent the United States at the state funeral of Edvard Kardelj, Tito's intellectual mentor. I flew over with Averell Harriman and his wife, Pamela. Harriman was one of the stalwart internationalists of the midcentury and, even then, a walking piece of history—an architect of the Marshall Plan and the ambassador to the Soviet Union for FDR. He had been at Roosevelt's side every day at Yalta in 1945 while the president, Churchill, and Stalin reckoned a postwar Europe. Harriman had met Tito during the war, and he'd spent more than thirty years trying to pull the marshal toward the West, even while the Soviets were trying to reel him in. (As it was, Tito insisted on independence from East and West alike, but happily accepted military and economic enticements from both.) So after the funeral in Zagreb, Harriman requested a private meeting with Tito, but the marshal made it clear that he was meeting with no one for fear of offending everyone. Harriman wasn't used to taking no for an answer, and he refused to leave the country until he got the answer he wanted. Tito finally agreed to meet for lunch, but not in Zagreb, where somebody might find us out. He wanted us to meet him at his villa in Split, down in Croatia, overlooking the Adriatic. So we flew to Split, over a piece of Bosnia and Herzegovina, with Harriman talking at me the whole time. He was a classic old-school internationalist. We should engage Yugoslavia, he said. This is not a place to isolate.

That entire trip was a strange kind of awakening for me, with Harriman as my own personal tutor. He was a continental figure and a man worth emulating. It wasn't just his elegant style in dress or his courtly manner. He had inherited a great deal of money, but he put his shoulder to the wheel, first in business and then in a long career in public service as an ambassador, a Cabinet member, and the governor of New York. He also had a habit of adopting people, and when I got to the Senate as a thirty-year-old kid, he adopted me. All through my first term he invited me to his dinner parties, where he was literally educating me. And he took great pains. He invited the Very Important People to these dinners and he liked to get me to speak. But I was hesitant to say what I thought; his guests could be daunting to a foreign policy novice. One night we sat down in his parlor to have a talk before the meal, and Governor Harriman was in his chair and I was on one end of the couch. Henry Kissinger was across from me, Ted Kennedy sat at my left, and sitting next to Kennedy was Paul Warnke, the biggest name in arms control at the time and a leading voice for slowing the arms race between the United States and the Soviet Union. In the middle of a discussion about arms control, Harriman turned to me and said, "Well, Joe, what do you think?" As I started to talk, I leaned over and—I guess I was nervous—picked up the first thing I saw, this spherical object that was on the coffee table. I was fondling it and moving it in my hands as I talked. When I looked over at Kissinger, I could tell he was alarmed. Everybody was squirming. *What the hell was I saying that was so awful?* The butler saved the day by coming in and calling dinner. Everybody jumped out of their seats and sprinted to the table. As the other accomplices ran, Ted Kennedy put his hand ever so gently on my arm and whispered, "Joe, put that down."

I started to worry that I had been playing around with a Fabergé egg, which was probably worth more than my house. But I was too embarrassed to ask our host.

But Harriman didn't give up on my education. As we flew toward Split for our meeting with Tito, Harriman was teaching me two lessons. One, never accept received wisdom about a foreign country or a foreign leader when you can go and see for yourself. Tito might be a "Communist," but not all Communists were the same. And two, Harriman wanted me to see the benefits of constant engagement, even with avowed enemies. Don't trust, he'd say, but engage. Be tough, but engage. By keeping up relations with leaders like Tito, we could nudge them toward change.

Harriman played the long game. If Tito was ever forced to choose between the Soviets and the United States, Harriman wanted the marshal to know the score. Harriman believed deeply in the ideals and ideas of America and the West, and he thought that the more familiar our adversaries were with the strength of those ideals and the power of those ideas, the more they'd be persuaded toward friendly relations with the United States—and the more successfully we could affect their internal policies. Even in the Cold War, our nation's best weapon was ideas. The governor had taken the measure of the Soviet system, he explained to me, and he saw that its collapse was inevitable. He said I should get to know Yugoslavia because it was an area that we could bring into the twenty-first century as an ally. He had been working long and hard toward that goal, but he was an old man now, and it might be left to another generation to finish the job of making a friendly pro-Western Yugoslavia.

I was already starting to like Yugoslavia; it wasn't what I'd anticipated. I had expected Communist gray and dull, with trailers and institutional postwar architecture—all the appeal of a concrete sidewalk stood on end—and the dark pall of acrid smoke from burning coal. And it wasn't any of those things. Zagreb was bright and clear with Habsburg-era buildings that had gleaming white colonnades and soft yellow stucco and brick. People drove decent cars and wore clothes with real color. The thing that most intrigued me about the Balkans was the beauty of the land itself. I saw it all from the air on the flight to Split, and it was breathtaking: rushing water, beautiful glades, and giant conifers—like the Rocky Mountains with character.

When we got to Split on the Adriatic coast, I got the sense that people were doing okay. They were driving decent cars there, too; television aerials sprouted from roofs. There was a feeling of life that you didn't get in other places behind the Iron Curtain. In Moscow the police state was a constant presence, like a weight on my shoulders. In the American sector of Berlin I always felt like the city was under siege. Nothing about Yugoslavia was what I expected. There were ski slopes, and people skied. I hadn't thought much about the recreational pursuits of Communists. This notion of Communism being this great monolith and the same in every country was just not true. There was room for individual expression in Split; there was openness; there was capitalism within the system. People ran restaurants and stores as private enterprises. There was this subterranean entrepreneurship. What Tito demanded in return was that everybody be on the same page in terms of Yugoslavia's policy of nonalignment.

Tito's home on the Adriatic was a modest place for a leader's palace. If it were sitting on a lake in Maryland, it would be a nice $2 million property. In fact, as we drove down the driveway toward the house I was reminded of Lake Skaneateles, where Neilia grew up.

Tito himself greeted us at the door, led us into a room overlooking the sea, and sat us all at a small table. At one end of the table was Harriman, at the other end of the table was Tito—and Tito had the view. That surprised me. I guess he liked to let his visitors know where they stood. I sat alone on one side of the table while our ambassador, Larry Eagleburger, and his Yugoslav counterpart sat on the other. It's a good thing the table wasn't any bigger because Tito and Harriman were each pushing ninety and both men were hard of hearing—so they hollered at each other across eight feet. Tito reminded me of my old colleague Strom Thurmond. He had more hair than Strom, but dyed like Strom, sort of red, and he was small compared to Harriman. But he was a tough, wiry little guy with a raspy voice, like his vocal cords were made of leather.

Eagleburger spoke Serbo-Croatian, so he was translating. The issue was the future of Yugoslavia relative to the Soviet Union, but the two old lions reminisced about how Yugoslavia became nonaligned. It was like watching a ping-pong match going back and forth. I'd been a senator for a full term and had some real foreign policy experience: I knew the latest intelligence, and I'd gone toe-to-toe with Kosygin. In fact, I had wondered if maybe Harriman's views and experiences were no longer relevant to what was going on in 1979. But to be in that room with those two men, whose generation was passing from the scene, was remarkable. Here were the last two living men who remembered Yalta—at least they talked about Yalta and how Europe broke down after World War II and how the Soviets grabbed East Germany, Hungary, Czechoslovakia, Romania, Bulgaria, and Poland. Harriman was still angry about Poland. Roosevelt and Stalin had both agreed to keep their hands off Poland, but even before Roosevelt died, Stalin broke his word. I felt like I was on the set of the old Sunday TV program I used to watch with my father when I was a kid, *You Are There*—the great battles, the great men, the great events of World War II. I mean they talked about Joe Stalin—*Joe,* their old acquaintance. Every time Tito said the name, it was *"StAAAlin!"* and I could see the veins in his neck bulge. I couldn't understand what he was saying, but I damn sure knew how he felt about Stalin and the Soviets. I got the impression that he felt about Stalin the way he did about Hitler. He hated Stalin. He talked about leading the partisans during World War II, up in the mountains, and how they'd held off the Germans, and he sure as hell wasn't going to let the Soviets take the country he'd fought for. Even after his rapprochement with Khrushchev, Tito bristled at the idea that Yugoslavia was a Soviet satellite.

At one point Harriman turned to me and said, "Tell him what the young people think, Senator." And me without my Fabergé egg. I talked about the importance of the mutual balanced force reduction talks, about pulling back conventional forces as well as nuclear weapons, about minimizing the possibility that a dumb mistake would trigger something catastrophic, how it would make the world safer—and make Yugoslavia safer. Tito didn't seem much interested. He said nothing.

On the flight home Harriman and I discussed Tito's political savvy, how he'd used his personal will and his personal story to bind his federation. He'd fought off Hitler. He'd kept Yugoslavia out of the orbit of the Soviet Union, unlike almost everyone else in Eastern Europe. And it was precisely the narrative of defying the great powers that he used to keep Yugoslavia whole. Anti-Soviet sentiment was widespread among all the ethnic groups in Yugoslavia; it was the glue. But Tito also made sure everybody in Yugoslavia got a piece of the pie. He recognized Muslims as citizens equal in stature to the Orthodox Serbs and Catholic Croats. He brought in the Albanian Muslims in Kosovo, giving them some measure of autonomy. Bosnia and Herzegovina was a multiethnic society where people in cities such as Sarajevo lived in mixed neighborhoods, went to the same schools, and intermarried. What they shared, other than each other's lives, was fierce pride in the independence of their country and their leader. But in 1979 we all knew that Tito wouldn't last forever. And even the old lion Harriman wondered on that plane ride home what would happen to Yugoslavia after Tito. Were the Soviets going to get what they had never been able to achieve before? Was the ethnically and religiously diverse Yugoslavia going to hold together? That was the $64,000 question in 1979. Tito did die the next year, but there was an extension of his way, starting with a rotating presidency. The Croats, the Bosnians, the Kosovars, the Slovenes, the Serbs—everybody got a piece of the action. But as Tito's economic model started to falter, nationality politics began to take hold.

By the time the Soviet Union collapsed, the multiethnic world of Yugoslavia was unraveling, and that was what the monk who came to my office had witnessed at Medjugorje. In 1991 the Bush administration policy was to keep Yugoslavia together at all costs. That was fine with the rising Serbian leader, a former Communist party apparatchik named Slobodan Milosevic. Milosevic was all for a unified Yugoslavia, as long as the Serbs controlled it. When Kosovo, Slovenia, Croatia, and Bosnia and Herzegovina started making separate noises about independence, Milosevic ended the presidential rotation, took the job for himself, and began calling the Serbs to arms. Over and over he rehearsed a story of centuries of betrayal, neglect, and victimization of the Orthodox Serbs. Now, when they were finally set to take power in Yugoslavia, Milosevic warned, the Muslims and the Croats were pulling away, robbing them of a destiny six hundred years in the making.

On the six hundredth anniversary of the Battle of Kosovo Pole (Blackbird's Field) near Pristina—where the Serbs claim they were abandoned by all of Europe and slaughtered while trying to hold back the Ottoman Turks from moving into the West—Milosevic reminded them of this betrayal and how it "follows the Serbian people like an evil fate through the whole of its history." He bewailed Tito's treatment of the Serbs as mere equals to the Muslims and the Croats. It was time, he said, for the Serbs to seize their new destiny, to "remove disunity."

When I held Senate hearings on the Yugoslav problem in 1991, most of my colleagues thought I was being alarmist. There were small skirmishes breaking out back and forth among the Croats, Serbs, and Muslims, but most folks in the U.S. government insisted this was nothing to get worked up about. Slovenia managed to slip out with its independence. Croatia, with support from its old allies, the Germans, declared independence, and in seven months of war that left ten thousand dead, it fought Milosevic to a rough stalemate, although ethnic Serbs held onto the Krajina region and part of eastern Croatia. The situation seemed manageable, though by September 1991 the United Nations was sufficiently concerned that it instituted an arms embargo in all of Yugoslavia. Leaders in Bosnia and Herzegovina decided to play by the international rules. After consulting with the United Nations and the European Community, the Bosnians held a referendum in March 1992 and voted overwhelmingly to secede from Yugoslavia. Many of the Bosnian Serbs, led by a churlish demagogue named Radovan Karadzic, boycotted the vote—because they hadn't sufficient numbers to change the outcome—and set up their own rump state within Bosnia. In early April 1992, when the international community officially recognized the independence of Bosnia and Herzegovina, Milosevic and Karadzic decided it was time to scrub Bosnia of the Croats and, especially, the Muslims.

The U.N. weapons embargo made it easy, having frozen into place a huge arms advantage for the Serbs. Eighty percent of the Yugoslav National Army (JNA) officer corps was Serb; the JNA controlled all the heavy weapons at the time of the embargo. In just a few months, the Serbs had taken control of nearly 70 percent of the Bosnian territory—and their campaign was ripping through the countryside.

We began getting isolated reports that spring, but it wasn't until August 1992 that the details of the Serbian blitz in Bosnia came clear. Brcko, Gorazde, Srebrenica and Sarajevo had been surrounded by tanks and artillery and were shelled constantly. All across Bosnia, regular JNA soldiers, Bosnian Serb paramilitary troops, and Chetniks simply sliced their way through small towns, rousting every villager, separating Muslim from Serb and then the men from the women and children, leaving the elderly and infirm to burn when they torched their homes. The educated and political Muslim men were killed first. The paramilitary troops who called themselves the White Eagles were especially fearsome. From the reports we received, they took real pleasure in torturing their Muslim captives. They forced Muslim men to chew up and swallow pictures of Tito, carved Orthodox crosses in their chests, cut off their fingers, noses, and ears, gouged out their eyes, pulled off their skin with pliers, and castrated them. They killed with automatic weapons, knives, and their bare hands. One Bosnian Serb who tried to help a Muslim neighbor and friend was pummeled to death. They killed husbands in front of wives, fathers in front of sons and daughters, and children in front of their parents. They shot one little girl as she hid behind her grandmother and forced a man to watch his twelve-year-old daughter being gang-raped. Karadzic would later refer to the program as "ethnic shifting"; others called it "ethnic cleansing." I would call it the beginning of genocide.

The captives who survived the first wave of murder were shipped off to concentration camps. Some were able to flee into the forests, such as a man who explained his escape in a letter to President George H. W. Bush: "I think we were lucky that we went through all this in the first days of the Serbian occupation, while the Serbian killing machinery was not so well developed yet." The development happened fast, probably because it had been well planned. Makeshift concentration camps sprang up in little motels and cafés. Many were "rape camps." A twenty-one-year-old Serbian soldier described to an American journalist how one commander encouraged Serb soldiers to take women from the Sonja Café prison seven miles north of Sarajevo. "You can do with the women what you like. You can take them away from here—we don't have enough food for them anyway—and don't bring them back." The soldier said he himself raped eight women and killed them all.

At the bigger concentration camps, the machinery of death shuddered up to speed in the first weeks. At Omarska, a middle-aged Serbian woman kept meticulous shift schedules, time sheets, and payroll records for the guard crew. They ran three regular guard teams on twelve-hour shifts: One shift boss was a former policeman, another a waiter in the nearby Hotel Europa. Each shift ran scores of Muslim captives through one of two torture chambers, "the White House" and "the Red House." A few internees straggled back bloody and beaten from the White House, where guards flayed one man until his fellow inmates could see tendon and bone. Nobody wanted to be near the victim because his open wounds began to reek. And those were the lucky ones; no internee ever returned from the Red House.

Prisoners were often detailed to destroy corpses of their friends and neighbors. At the Luka camp in Brcko, one witness stated, he was in a work party that dumped frozen corpses into a meat-processing machine and then loaded the grounds onto trucks to dump into the Sava River. Wednesdays and Saturdays were particularly bad for the female prisoners at Luka. Between two and six on those afternoons, a Serb woman named Monika, who was fond of beating men in the genitals, selected eight or ten women for presentation to the camp commander. He would select his girl and escort her upstairs—leaving the rest to be split among fifteen or twenty guards. When one girl resisted, Monika stabbed her with a broken bottle and waited while the girl bled to death. The terror of rape was worse at Foca. When they heard the song "Mars Nu Drina" (March on the Drina, a fighting song banned by Tito) from the loudspeaker of the mosque, they knew the gang rapes were beginning. One estimate had twenty thousand women raped. Some were gang-raped by as many as twenty-eight soldiers.

By August 1992, all of this, including the most vicious and inhumane detail, was known to the Bush administration, the State Department, Congress, and the United Nations. The Brits and the French, whose alliance with the Serbs went back generations, maintained in the face of all evidence that the situation in Yugoslavia was a civil war and there were atrocities on both sides. (CIA estimates said the Serb aggressors committed 90 percent of the atrocities.) The Bush administration called it a European problem. As Bush's secretary of state, James Baker, famously said, "We don't have a dog in that fight." Colin Powell, then chairman of the Joint Chiefs of Staff, was telling Bush the problem in Yugoslavia had the whiff of a new Vietnam and he wasn't going to risk a new stink on the U.S. military, rightfully proud new victors in the Gulf War. When the United Nations shipped its peacekeeping troops into Bosnia, the Bush administration refused to send American soldiers. British, French, and Dutch troops made up most of the U.N. force. The administration also insisted on calling the Serb aggression a civil war, the result of ancient and intractable ethnic and religious conflicts. Dick Cheney, then secretary of defense, was detailed to the news and chat shows: "It's tragic, but the Balkans have been a hotbed of conflict . . . for centuries." I was having some really harsh exchanges with Deputy Secretary of State Eagleburger. I kept calling him. "You know this area, Larry," I'd say. "You know what's happening. How can you not tell the secretary of state? How can you not tell the president? *Larry, goddammit, you know better.*" But he wasn't budging. Publicly, he stuck to the administration line—or maybe it was his own line—that this was a civil war and a European problem, and we had no business getting involved: "The tragedy is not something that can be settled from outside, and it's about damn well time that everybody understood that. Until Bosnians, Serbs, and Croats decide to stop killing each other, there is nothing the outside world can do about it."

The United Nations agreed on calling for "all means necessary" to get food, supplies, and medical aid into Bosnia and to work toward a negotiated peace. European leaders tasked a British diplomat, Lord David Owen, and Jimmy Carter's secretary of state, Cyrus Vance, to work out a settlement. Milosevic seemed to have the ear of the two diplomats. *This is a civil war, a civil war, a civil war. The West doesn't want to get messed up in this. Let me handle it for you.* The Vance-

Owen plan quickly became cutting up Bosnia into ethnically containable cantons; it even divided the multiethnic capital of Sarajevo. The Vance-Owen plan would have handed over most of the land the Serbs had seized in Bosnia to the Bosnian Serbs, essentially rewarding the aggressors. And almost everybody in Washington seemed to think this was a perfectly reasonable plan.

15

Effort Pays

I WAS A PRETTY ACTIVE AND FAIRLY FORCEFUL CHAIRMAN of the Senate Judiciary in the early nineties, so I think most of my colleagues at least pretended to be interested in my Violence Against Women Act. But I noticed that as the amount of press surrounding the hearings grew, more and more committee members wanted to be seen at the proceedings. I could feel a little groundswell of support out in the communities, and I was getting invitations to speak to the leaders of the fight against this sort of abuse. And that was an education for me. One of the first places I spoke was in Providence, Rhode Island, to a group of women who ran shelters and rape crisis centers around the state. Many of the battered women shelters that my staff or I visited were held together with baling wire and noble intentions. Their second best source of revenue was bake sales. And these were the people who looked into the pleading eyes of women every day and night; they could tell me about the extent and depth of the brutality some women face. I had a hunch that if America could see what they saw and hear what they heard, we could get the support for the Violence Against Women Act.

So we brought them into the legislative fight. The women on my staff would tell me how these battered women's groups and the women who staffed the shelters and rape crisis centers were shocked that somebody wanted to hear what they had to say. They knew America's dirty little secret, but nobody had asked them to tell it. Not long after my small tussle with Chief Justice Rehnquist, my staff went to work on an ambitious report that not only revealed the truth about violence against women but gave it the power of narrative.

Using the contacts they'd made at shelters and rape crisis centers around the country, my staff and I collected data for a report called *Violence Against Women: A Week in the Life of America.* "This nation will be powerless to change the course of violence against women unless and until its citizens fully realize the devastation this violence yields," I wrote in the introduction to the report, which we released in October 1992. "Today we release a report that graphically portrays the human tragedy of a single "Week in the Life of Violence Against Women." We found that at least twenty-one thousand crimes against women were reported every week. At least 1.1 million assaults, aggravated assaults, murders, and rapes against women were committed in the home and reported to police in 1991; unreported crimes were likely more than three times that total. Women, we found, were six times more likely than men to be the victim of a violent crime committed by an intimate. One out of every six sexual assaults in a week is committed by a member of the victim's family.

The twenty-page timeline of narratives culled from a week's worth of business at police stations, battered women's shelters, and rape crisis centers was horrifying. If we had included all we knew in the timeline, it would have run two thousand pages. If we could have included unreported crimes, it would have been seven thousand pages. But twenty pages was enough to make the point. It included a woman whose boyfriend broke her right arm with a hammer, a woman whose father had beaten her in the head with a pipe three inches in diameter, a fifteen-year-old girl who was stabbed by her ex-boyfriend on the day he was released from jail, a woman whose husband broke their dog's legs just to terrorize her, a college student raped by her academic advisor, one raped by her neighbor, another by her boss, another by a taxi driver, and even a woman raped by her clergyman. There was a woman sexually assaulted by her ex-boyfriend and his brother, and a seventeen-year-old girl raped by her grandfather. And all that before Tuesday was done. The timeline included credible reports of women assaulted by guns, knives, and axes, and numerous reports of husbands raping their wives or ex-wives with their children as witnesses. There were women who straggled into shelters or hospitals with broken jaws, eyes swollen shut, teeth knocked out, and one with a fractured knee cap. And there was a forty-one-year-old woman raped by three men who refused to report the rape to police because she thought the one she knew would kill her if she did.

The victims and the perpetrators cut across race, religion, and socioeconomic class—and this in a country that in 1992 had three times as many animal shelters as battered women's shelters. But in October 1992 the legislation still languished. With the George H. W. Bush–Bill Clinton presidential election about to happen, it was impossible to get floor time unless there was assurance that a bill would not be subject to extended debate. The good news was that Bill Clinton was promising to sign the Violence Against Women Act if Congress ever passed it.

IN SARAJEVO THE multiethnic Bosnian government also got some hope from the election of Bill Clinton, who had talked tough in his campaign to unseat George Bush, but Lord Owen was trying to tamp down those hopes. "Don't, don't, don't live under this dream that the West is going to come in and sort this problem out," he said. "Don't dream dreams." While the Bosnian government waited for Clinton's inauguration in January 1993, the torture camps, death camps, and rape camps rolled on. Thousands of people a day were fleeing their homes in Bosnia. Not a single European country was willing to extend itself to do something about the continuing slaughter of Muslims and Croats.

The truth is, in 1992 it was up to the United States to lead. As long as there is one good actor in the world, every other nation can play at the margins. Every other nation can act out of realpolitik and the basic decency in the world won't collapse. But when every country is acting with nothing but self-interest in mind, it's a much more dangerous world. It was up to the United States to stand up to the abuses of power where we saw them. To me, "Don't dream dreams" was not an option.

On the floor of the Senate I called the Serbs out as the villains and started talking about a plan called "lift and strike," insisting first that the United Nations lift the weapons embargo so that the Bosnians and their government could defend themselves. The U.N. weapons embargo in Yugoslavia was a perversion of international intent. Bosnia was a sovereign state, recognized by the United Nations, the European Community, and the United States. According to the U.N. charter, the Bosnian government had a right to defend itself. The Serbs not only began the war with all the resources of the Yugoslav army, they had retained their covert connections with Russian arms suppliers; the Serb monopoly on heavy weapons within Bosnia had produced some of the most monstrous atrocities in modern warfare. For that reason I called for NATO air strikes to knock out the Serb artillery and tanks that ringed Bosnia's besieged cities.

I also declared that it was time the world recognize Milosevic for what he was: a war criminal and a mass murderer. It was time to stop him. I called for a return to our nation's first principles. What was our first principle if not stopping genocide?

In March 1993 I asked the full Senate Foreign Relations Committee to join me in helping to end the incipient genocide by demanding tough sanctions against the Serbs and supporting "lift and strike." The full committee decided not to act. I felt like a lonely voice, but I wasn't going to give up.

Around this time the ambassador from Belgrade, Milosevic's man, showed up at my office. He was a well-tailored, obsequious fellow—so respectful, so reasoned. He didn't push, but he suggested that maybe I had it all wrong. *The Muslims in Bosnia will make an Islamic state,* he told me. *Look, we Serbs are the good guys. I've been an admirer of the United States. We patterned ourselves after you. We are more Western, like you.* The upshot was that Milosevic wanted me to go to Belgrade to talk to him one-on-one. Slobodan thought he could put the Serbian situation in a more generous light. I took him up on the offer . . . but not right away.

Before I agreed, I talked to John Ritch, who was running my European Affairs subcommittee, and another staffer, Jamie Rubin. We talked about Hitler and wondered how people in my position could have been seen meeting with the Führer in the mid-1930s. I also checked with our embassy in Belgrade, where they knew something about Milosevic. They warned me that he liked to get pictures of himself with visiting dignitaries to put on state TV, which he and his wife controlled. He would make it seem like I was his great new friend, coming to praise his excellence. There were obviously risks to taking the trip, but if I was going to insist that the entire world get tough with the Serbs, I'd better be sure—so I decided to go see for myself what was happening in the Balkans.

I had one condition, which I conveyed to Milosevic: I said I wouldn't meet with him publicly. No press. No cameras. He said that was no problem. Whatever you need, Senator, he told me. He just wanted a chance to make his case. There was none of the old Eastern European Communist bluster I'd seen in Hungary and other places behind the Iron Curtain. This guy was as smooth as glass. There was a second condition I didn't relay to Milosovic: I promised myself I would not break bread with a mass murderer.

We flew to Europe in a U.S. government plane. It's one of the privileges of having been a U.S. senator for more than twenty years. When I asked my chairman on Foreign Relations, Claiborne Pell, to request a plane so I could check out the situation in Bosnia, there were no questions asked. The privilege comes with a responsibility I take seriously. If I'm using fuel paid for with your tax dollars, I'd better be doing something useful. I went with Ritch, Rubin, and Ted Kaufman, and a military attaché. The plan, aside from seeing Milosevic, was to get as close to the action as I could, to see what was happening on the ground. After a quick stop in Stuttgart to get a briefing from our military leaders in Western Europe, we landed in Zagreb, Croatia, on April 7, 1993—exactly one year after Milosevic and Karadzic began their genocidal campaign.

From Zagreb we took a two-hour helicopter ride, escorted by the United Nation Protection Forces (UNPROFOR), into the Bosnian town of Tuzla, a refugee camp. Flying over Bosnia toward Tuzla I was struck again by the beauty of the landscape, but there was something sinister happening below. How many Muslims and Croats cowered in the forests, waiting for the White Eagles to descend?

Tuzla was overrun with refugees from the city of Srebrenica. The Serbs' heavy artillery had pounded Sarajevo and Srebrenica constantly for months. And the Serbs were regularly turning back or plundering U.N. relief trucks filled with food and medicine. Officials in Tuzla said they'd taken in about sixty thousand refugees. They figured on more as the weather warmed and the Serbian fighters returned en masse. If Srebrenica fell, Tuzla might get another fifty thousand. While we were in Tuzla, we actually saw these giant dump trucks with "U.N." written on the sides, so full of refugees that parents were standing with arms extended, hanging their kids over the side. Later that day we went to a school that was set up as a refugee motel and met a family who had just made it out with soldiers following them all the way. They wanted to tell us their story through the interpreter, but the husband kept getting choked up. Finally the interpreter calmed him down enough to get the story: "We walked all the way to Tuzla over the mountains. And my mother, who was seventy-eight, couldn't make it. She said, 'Leave me. I can't go any farther.' The last time I looked back, she was sitting on a rock freezing to death. But if we stopped we all would have been killed—me, my wife, my children."

The aid workers were doing their best to deal with the stream of broken people, but our UNPROFOR escorts were cynical. More Muslim sob stories, they suggested. Everybody had them. The Serbs, Muslims, and Croats were all a disaster. How could anybody fix this?

Our schedule was to meet Milosevic in Belgrade the next evening, and I was eager to tell him what I thought. When we arrived, we had to kill time in a local hotel, so I flipped on the television and watched the state-controlled news. Milosevic's TV commentators were baldly asserting that Bosnian Muslims were massacring Serbs, killing Serbian babies, and hanging them on hooks like they'd hang chickens. This was the big public relations campaign in Belgrade, and it tracked with one of the State Department reports we'd read. Young Muslim internees had been forced by heavily armed Serb television reporters to confess on camera to killing Serbian babies. They threatened to kill parents, wives, and siblings if the men refused to perform for the camera.

I hadn't truly understood how evil Milosevic was or how successful until my first meeting in Belgrade. Our embassy had set up the meeting; it was with a group of dissidents. They were intellectuals, poets, and writers, led by Vuc Draskovic, head of the Serbian Renewal Party. They hated Milosevic, but they were still Serb nationalists, and even they were retailing the stories about Muslims in Bosnia hanging dead Serbian babies on hooks. They were feeding on state-controlled television and had a full belly. They never once made the argument that Milosevic was a bad guy because he was killing Muslims. He was a bad guy because he was denying his own people, the Serbs, freedom of speech. He was denying them their rights. I expected dissidents to say, 'Hey, look, this guy is waging a war on innocent people. Genocide is going on." Either they didn't know what was going on, or they didn't care. There was room for only one set of victims in Belgrade, and that was the Serbs. The Serbs had an overwhelming sense of being put upon by history. Their argument ran like this: We are the noble people, the Serbs, who did so much for Europe and the world and were always persecuted. We were always the losers. Why didn't we, the best educated, the largest population, the tribe who stopped the march of Islam into Europe and saved the Habsburg empire, why didn't we have a place of honor in Europe? Milosevic had understood the power of the Serbs' victim mentality. He fed it back to them in a constant self-fulfilling loop, and he used it to climb to power.

I heard Bill Clinton talk once after he left office about the tragic human weakness: All hatred is about the Other, he'd said, and most of it is irrational. That's what I concluded studying Milosevic. The twentieth-century tragedies that related to genocide started with very smart people who preyed on those prejudices for purposes of power. Milosevic impressed me as being very, very antiseptic about it. He saw that the threat of the Soviets could no longer keep Yugoslavia together, and he concluded that he could grab power for the Serbs with a raw appeal to xenophobic nationalism in the extreme. As the time for our meeting approached, I thought I knew all I needed to know about Slobodan Milosevic. But I didn't know the half of it.

A little after eight at night we pulled up in front of Milosevic's presidential palace—the sort of building I love. It was a three-story mansion with yellowed stucco and white Doric columns. In the darkness I could make out six or eight guards in long leather jackets; most of them were smoking while standing watch in front. They were big guys, like mob enforcers, but security wasn't that tight. Milosevic apparently felt little threat from anybody, so the guards just nodded us through as we walked up the outer stairs toward the building. Even inside I kept an eye out for cameras. The big formal hall was deserted, lit with the dim charm of a mortuary and so quiet we could hear the soft fall of our own footsteps. We followed a red carpet up a giant marble staircase, across a landing, and then up another set of marble steps. Milosevic was waiting in his office at the top of the stairs. He was about my age, conservative in dress, round-faced and doughy, like a cherubic, self-satisfied banker at the coasting end of a long and lucrative career. His dark silk suit set off his white hair, which swept back off his enormous forehead. He came at me with his hand extended; he seemed very happy to see us. When I refused to shake his hand, he nodded calmly, unperturbed.

Come, Senator, sit. Let's talk. He sat us down at his conference table, and he talked. *You know, you've got us all wrong, Senator.* His English was good; he'd spent time working in banks in Western Europe. Eagleburger had known him and thought he was somebody we could work with when he first came to power. *This is not about the Serbs making trouble. This is about the Muslims and the Croats persecuting Serbs.* He took down maps of old Yugoslavia and arrayed them on the conference table between us. He wanted to show me where the Serbs were being attacked. I told him the whole world knew who was doing the attacking, and it was up to him to stop it. He had to stop giving weapons, fuel, and food to the Serbian forces in Bosnia, and he and Karadzic, the Bosnian Serb leader, had to sign on to the Vance-Owen Peace Plan. He was still calm. And he lied to my face. *First of all, Senator, we are not giving any aid to the Bosnian Serbs. They are an independent fighting force. And second, Karadzic is his own man, and I have no real relation to him. I can suggest, maybe, but I cannot control a man like Karadzic.*

Then he started in with the map again, so I started pointing out things I knew. How about Sarajevo? A shell blew up twenty-two innocent people waiting in a breadline. Snipers took out innocent children in the streets. How about Omarska? Women and girls raped. Taunted by men saying now they'd have to produce Serbian babies. How about Luka? Electric shock torture. Mass killings. Literally hundreds of dead bodies thrown in the river. There were mass graves, and we already knew about them. He denied every charge one by one, with an excuse for each, without ever raising his voice. *The Muslims were shelling their own people and blaming Serbs. There is no genocide going on. There is no displacement going on. There is no ethnic cleansing. If anyone is being cleansed, it's the Serbs.* He went back to the map and continued to make his points. Milosevic was nothing like his ambassador; he wasn't pleading with me, he was just telling me. *Look here. This was a Serbian area, and the Serbs were run out. Look at Croatia. They couldn't be independent. The referendum was rigged. The people who got cheated were the Serbs. You have to understand what they're doing to Serbs all over Yugoslavia. The Muslims and the Croats are murdering Serbian babies. They're expelling Serbs. We're just fighting back. And, yeah, there may have been some counter-atrocities, but this is just tit for tat. I'm trying to hold the place together.*

I brought up Srebrenica, a largely Muslim town that was trying like hell to hold off the Serb soldiers who were firing on civilian neighborhoods from artillery pieces that ringed the town, who were plundering the humanitarian relief convoys. *No. No. The U.N. had proved that in the recent bombing of Srebrenica villages, the Serbs were not responsible.* Then he tried to tell me that all sides in Bosnia have artillery and tanks, including the Muslims. It reminded me of that old Lenny Bruce joke: "What do you do when your wife comes home and finds you in bed with another woman? Deny it!" But this wasn't funny. I could feel the blood rise in my face.

"Mr. Milosevic," I said, "you are the only person in the world who would say such a thing."

Milosevic could tell I had just about had it with his lies, and at one point he looked up from the maps and said, without any emotion, "What do you think of me?"

"I think you're a damn war criminal and you should be tried as one," I said. I was looking right in Milosevic's eyes, and his expression didn't change. There was not the slightest twitch in his face. It was like I'd just told him he was a wonderful guy.

So I got right back to business. A few minutes later, I asked him for an escort to Srebrenica so I could see for myself what was happening. He thought that would be a splendid idea, but, alas, even he couldn't get into a war zone. It wasn't safe. In that case, I told him, what he'd best do is let U.N. forces into the war zones and turn over the heavy weapons or have them destroyed by NATO air strikes.

Believe me, Senator, I'd love to help, but I can only do this in Bosnia if the Bosnian Serbs agree.

Then, without warning, he asked me if I wanted to speak to Karadzic. Now my chin was really out. "Yeah. I do."

"I think he's in town," Milosevic said, and he reached back, picked up the phone, and started speaking Serbo-Croatian.

After he hung up, we continued our talk for several minutes, when all of a sudden the front door of the palace slammed open, echoing through the marble foyer below. We all looked up from the maps, silent, and listened to the hurried footsteps in the entryway. They padded up the red carpet, *bam-bam-bam,* and across the landing and then up the next flight at a gallop, **bam-bam-bam.** The door to the office burst open, and there stood Radovan Karadzic, breathing hard, with his great swoop of Vegas magician hair setting off his florid face. He hurried over to take the seat at Milosevic's right and tried to spit out a hello. I felt like saying, Somebody get this guy a glass of water. I thought he might have a heart attack. "Uhhh, Mr. President, . . .

Uhhh, I'm sorry . . . uhhh . . . I'm late. . . . Uhhh, I came as fast as I could."

I turned to Milosevic. "No control, huh?"

It was the only time I saw Milosevic's expression change. He looked daggers at Karadzic, the porcine, blow-dried chucklehead, as Karadzic introduced himself to me. "Senator, it's an honor to meet you. I know of you. Thank you for giving me a chance to explain my position."

"Oh, it's interesting to meet you, Doctor," I said.

Milosevic returned to the maps, and Karadzic joined his boss in insisting that the Serbs were the aggrieved party. How could Serbs in Bosnia live with the Muslims? Karadzic said. They were animals, killing Serbs in the cradle, and no friends to Western interests.

After more than two hours of this talk, I was really hot, and I began to push hard. First, I told them they had to back off Srebrenica and let the U.N. forces in. Second, they had to make sure they made a cease-fire stick while they worked out a peace plan. Karadzic demurred. His Bosnian Serb assembly had flatly ruled out foreign troops on Bosnian Serb soil. I made it plain that there was a new American president and that the U.S. attitude was hardening. The Serbs would wind up with strangling economic sanctions, with a fully-armed Bosnian force to knock them back, with NATO air strikes raining on their heads. I explained that the United States hadn't ruled out using force. And I suggested they study the Gulf War if they wanted to know about the American fighting force.

All they wanted to do was go back to the maps and carve up Bosnia, taking the best for themselves. It was all so simple, Milosevic kept saying. We could solve all this over drinks and dinner tonight. Still, he didn't act offended that I refused his offers of food and drink. (We would all be starving by the time we got back to the hotel around midnight.) Slobodan just kept talking: The Serb provinces in Bosnia had to be contiguous, he said, and he saw no reason to compromise. Moreover, Milosevic and Karadzic made it clear that they simply weren't worried about outside military intervention.

By the time we left the meeting, after three hours, I knew all I needed to know about Milosevic. He'd lied to me without compunction in the face of all the evidence. I trusted him as far as I could throw a piano. But he was good. Jamie Rubin later said he was like a mob boss. No matter the accusation you laid out, he kept his calm. The guy was smart. He was tough. And he wasn't going to make a lot of mistakes. He might be a no-good son of a bitch, but he knew what he was doing. And he wouldn't stop until the West stopped him.

A COLONEL IN the foreign legion was the lead officer on our plane to Sarajevo. The first day we couldn't make it in—bad weather and sniper fire. But the colonel let us on the flight the next day. She didn't care one way or another if a U.S. senator was allowed on a dangerous flight. "So we lose an American," I heard her say. "What the f**k do I care?" As we made our approach to the airport, I looked down and saw these big homes nearby. These 3,500-square-foot houses with picture windows and bright red-tiled roofs had been blown to hell; they were just cavities. Serb snipers sat in what was left of those homes and took potshots at the airport. The Serb artillery commanders were worried about accidentally shooting down U.N. aircraft, so they liked to shut down the airport with sniper fire before they started shelling Sarajevans. That was the cause of our one-day delay. The French Special Forces on the plane with us sat on their helmets all the way into Sarajevo. They didn't want to get shot in the rear end, or worse.

The airport was controlled by UNPROFOR, mainly French and British. The French troops hadn't even been given the machinery to dig decent bunkers, so we met Bosnian president Alija Izetbegovic and his deputy, Haris Silajdzic, at a makeshift bunker in an airport lounge. There were sandbags up to our eyeballs, and the windows shook from the percussion of shells hitting in the distance. The two Bosnian leaders were on their way out of town to beg for aid and money, but they waited for me because they hoped I would carry their message to the new president, Bill Clinton. Silajdzic had testified at Senate hearings and I respected him, but this was my first meeting with Izetbegovic. He was a weathered little guy with a rough hide. He looked to be in his early seventies, beset but resolved. He thanked me for coming and then explained the situation. The U.N. forces in the country were incapable of protecting Bosnia; even with the U.N. on the ground, Sarajevo was on the verge of collapse. He thought they might hold on through midsummer. What he wanted was to get UN-PROFOR out. Their presence made it impossible to convince the international community to allow for lift and strike because the UNPROFOR soldiers might get caught in the fight. He didn't understand the logic of putting the safety of a "protection force" over the safety of the people they were sent to protect. He wanted international monitors on the Bosnian border to keep Milosevic's men and weapons out of his country. And by the way, he said, he didn't need American ground troops or anybody else's. There were plenty of Bosnian soldiers who could defend their country if they had weapons. It hardly seemed unreasonable. I told him I'd do what I could.

We had to have an armed escort to get through "snipers' alley" and into downtown Sarajevo. I remembered the city from the television coverage of the winter Olympics a few years earlier. It didn't look so charming. Sarajevo sits in a valley, surrounded by mountains, and the Serbs had set their big guns on the high ground overlooking the city. For a full year now Sarajevo's population had been shelled and sniped at and denied water, food, medicine, electricity, and gas. In fact, the scene was what World War II must have looked like—pockmarked buildings, floors knocked off. It looked like Dresden with graffiti. The main streets of Sarajevo were all no-man's-land. The meetings in Sarajevo were with some of the most remarkable people I've met in all my years in the Senate. In the Presidency Building we sat down with the popularly elected government officials; they were Serbs, Croats, and Muslims. The meeting included the ethnic Serb member of the Bosnian presidency, Nikola Pejanovic, and an ethnic Croat deputy foreign minister, Branimar Huterer. We met in a big room with fifteen or twenty people who all wanted to keep their thing alive. They told us about the neighborhood in Sarajevo where Karadzic himself lived for years, cadging free baklava off his Muslim friends and neighbors. (An old acquaintance of Karadzic later described the neighborhood to an American reporter: "Funerals, weddings, birthdays, we never counted how many Muslims there were, how many Serbs, how many Croats. The only important thing was to be together, to have fun, to drink a little. It had been like that for so many years, I never suspected it could change.") They were all afraid that violence and want were turning people against one another. There were marauders in the streets and a black market for every necessity. But they thought they could withstand the siege for a little longer if help was on the way. They explained to us that the Bosnian force fighting for Bosnian independence wasn't all Muslim. The Bosnian army, like its government, was Muslim, Croat, and Serb. In fact, ethnic Serbs still made up 28 percent of the Bosnian army. The world needed to know that.

The other meeting was with editors of the independent newspaper *Oslobodjenie* (Freedom) at the paper's building . . . or what was left of it. The building had been five or six stories, maybe eight. It was hard to tell because the top floors had been blown off. The offices and the presses were all two stories below ground level now. The staff was there day and night, sleeping in beds they'd set up in the basement. They were all sure the city could hold on—and now, with a new American president who had talked so tough during the campaign, they were sure they could hold on. I gave them an interview and hoped I gave them some cause for hope. I went on record saying Milosevic was a war criminal, that the world was beginning to understand that, and that we'd put a stop to him.

Our final briefings in Sarajevo were from UNPROFOR commanders. It was a surreal performance. They showed us compelling evidence that equipment and personnel from the Yugoslav National Army were directly involved in the attacks on Srebrenica, that artillery units in Serbia have fired across the border, and that JNA artillery units have, in recent days, relocated to Bosnian territory to participate in the destruction of Srebrenica. JNA artillerymen in Bratunac, inside Bosnia, were shelling civilians and defenders of Srebrenica. They acknowledged that the JNA and not the Bosnian Serbs were directly responsible for the collapse of eastern Bosnia. And the JNA was under the direction of Milosevic.

In Sarajevo there were more than six hundred Serbian artillery positions around the city. They noted, with no sense of irony or alarm, that the Serb forces were exceptionally well armed but seriously lacking in manpower, while Bosnian government forces were awash in manpower but seriously lacking in firepower. There were Bosnian units fighting with little ammunition and obsolete small arms. They also acknowledged that the Serbs probably ceded control of the airport to the U.N. because if the Bosnian government were to gain even partial control over the airport, the siege of Sarajevo would effectively be broken. The pure strategic stupidity at UNPROFOR was sickening. What was worse was the attitude.

A captain started giving me a hard time about NATO air strikes. It was just too dangerous, too risky to the UNPROFOR troops. "Don't worry about NATO, Senator," he said. "NATO shouldn't be involved here." Finally, I couldn't take it anymore: "Son, just exactly where would you have NATO involved? You don't have to go down on the

Senate floor and argue for a $100-billion-a-year appropriation for NATO. If NATO doesn't have a role here, what is NATO's role? We might as well disband it, send it home, and save our money. Where is NATO's role? This is exactly where NATO should be!"

The problem was that although the UNPROFOR officers had plenty of facts on the ground, they believed what they wanted to believe. It was like they were sitting around the airport watching Milosevic's television station. They speculated that maybe the Bosnian Muslims were arranging for their own people to be shelled to win international support. (Almost none of this speculation ever proved true.) The airport was down again by the time we were ready to leave, so the Brit commander escorted us out in an armored personnel carrier. Wearing flak jackets and blue helmets, we drove through the mountains to Kiseljak to catch a helicopter to Split. On the drive up, the Brit was particularly pernicious, like a stock character in a Noël Coward play, a lethal mix of self-importance and willful ignorance. "They're all bad," he kept saying. "They're all bad." It was the Bush argument. All sides are equal. There are atrocities on every side. Don't get involved. They've been killing each other for centuries. By then I was tired of arguing with people who chose to close their eyes—and happy to get on a helicopter and get away from the UNPROFORs.

On the way out, when we flew over the mountains, the pilot hugged them pretty tight, and I still remember the softness of the landscape. These weren't jagged peaks like the Alps but rolling mountains with rounded knobs like the Appalachians. And I could see a minaret at the top of a peak and on the next a Greek Orthodox cross and on the next a Roman Catholic church. From the air they were so close together, less than half a mile away. In a strange way it gave me hope—that maybe the Bosnians would be able to maintain the world they'd made for themselves. I really thought I could convince President Clinton that Bosnia could be saved—and should be saved.

We were already in flight on our way to Germany when we got a surprise call from Naples, from Admiral Mike Boorda, the commander-in-chief of the Allied Forces Southern Command. He had taken the liberty of changing our flight plans. Could we have dinner with him? We rerouted to Italy and had a hair-raising late-night drive through the streets to try to keep to our schedule. Boorda's residence was up high, overlooking the city. He had set a table for us and invited Brigadier General James L. Jones. They wanted to brief me on the military options in the Balkans. Boorda went out on a limb for me or, more particularly, for his country. The admiral would later commit suicide after accusations of wearing combat medals he didn't earn, which was a blow to the country. In the Balkans, the admiral was truly heroic. Bosnia was a crucible for me in a lot of ways—and one was how it changed my mind about the military. I came to the Senate trying to stop the Vietnam War. Like a lot of my generation, we thought military, we thought *Dr. Strangelove*—Slim Pickens riding an atomic bomb or generals using helicopters to go to lunch at the Rive Gauche. That was the image. But if you asked me today to go back and pick out the twenty brightest, most informed individuals I've worked with in government, twelve of them would be military— Admiral Bobby Joe Inman and General Wesley Clark among them, along with the two guys in the room with us that night, General Jones and Admiral Boorda.

Boorda pointedly told us that not all of the president's top officers thought there was nothing we should—or could—do about Bosnia. He was quite open about Powell, saying he thought his boss was wrong to say nothing could be done in Bosnia without hundreds of thousands of troops on the ground. Boorda thought air strikes could shut down the Serb aggression and could end the sieges in Sarajevo and Srebrenica. "But, Admiral," I said, "everybody tells me air power won't work." He just looked at us. Then he said, "Come with me."

The admiral told us he had satellite photos of Serb positions all over Bosnia. He had radio intercepts of JNA generals talking to the Serbs in Croatia or the Serbs in Bosnia, saying, "Go get 'em." Boorda confirmed that it was Milosevic's JNA and not the Bosnian Serbs running the show. It was driving him nuts. He insisted with a few spotters on the ground they could take out the Serbs' heavy artillery. They'd try to hide it behind schools and mosques, but if a guy on the ground could get a laser on the guns, we could take them out. American air power had awesome capabilities, he said. And we weren't even trying.

"Look, Senator, for example, if you wanted me to, I could drop a fifth of bourbon that would land in front of any Serb general's tent in Srebrenica. That's how accurate we could be. . . . I think we should do something. We could use air strikes. We could interdict in the Adriatic. We should be engaged. The Joint Chiefs doesn't want to hear this. I've got a number of admirals above me here. I've got the Joint

Chiefs. I can't be making policy. But, Senator, you're right." That was the last piece of the puzzle for me. There was genocide going on, and we had the capacity to stop it without putting in large numbers of ground troops. We knew who the bad guys were—and where they were. We had the military power to stop it. I had to convince the president.

Within days of our return I went over to the State Department to brief the new secretary of state, Warren Christopher. We met at his office at Foggy Bottom; he used the small office, which fit with his personal modesty. He worked night and day, but he wanted every visitor to understand that he was there to serve the president's interests, not his own. Warren Christopher carried himself with the polished Zen of a corporate lawyer. He was placid and inscrutable on the one hand. He'd shake change out of your pockets on the other. Still, I had great respect for him and I knew he was open. So I was direct. This is genocide. We can stop it. Lift and strike.

He pushed back pretty hard, using every argument a good lawyer would. *First, even if we want to, air strikes are not our call. It's NATO's overall. Second, arming the Bosnians would only cause more killing. Third, this is a civil war.* But the argument he really leaned on was the problem of getting the support of the nation. He was never confrontational; he was a trained diplomat after all. *Well, Senator, will the president be able to get the support of Congress? . . . He'll need bipartisan support, right? Will he be able to get the support of the American people? . . . Will they support attacking the Serbs?*

"Mr. Secretary, I have great respect for you," I said. "You may know a lot more than me on foreign policy, but I know politics pretty well. The American people will support this if they know what's happening. We have to inform them."

The secretary of state's position was that I might be right, but the president really couldn't do much unless the United Nations and Europe led. He didn't want me getting out front. I told him I was going down to tell the president myself, and he really didn't want to hear that. In fact, he tried to talk me out of it. When I did get a chance to talk to President Clinton, Christopher made it a point to be there.

The White House—just a hundred days into Bill Clinton's first term—was feeling a bit besieged in April 1993; the president had been elected with only 43 percent of the vote. His honeymoon had been a rainout. By three to one, according to some polls, Americans trusted

Colin Powell more than Bill Clinton on foreign affairs. People were already attacking the president's wife. And he hadn't really absorbed the first lesson of being president. It's almost impossible for a president to set an agenda and follow it day by day. He's got to react to something new every day and take the waves as they come. But Clinton was the most talented politician I've ever seen, the quickest study, and one of the best informed. He took the job seriously. Moreover, I believed he had good instincts. I believed if I laid it out for him, he'd go for lift and strike, so I did. Right away the president and Christopher said Powell was telling them it would take hundreds of thousands of American soldiers on the ground in the Balkans.

"Mr. President, Mr. Secretary," I said, "it's a matter of honor. I don't want him in trouble, but I'm telling you what Admiral Boorda and others told me. Just do me one favor. If you don't believe me, do me one favor. Don't go through the chain of command. Boorda can't say anything to you directly, Mr. President, but if you pick up the phone and call Admiral Boorda, he'll tell you what we can do. . . . Mr. President, this is unconscionable. There are tens of thousands of people dying. There are mass graves. There are rape camps. Srebrenica is about to fall. Sarajevo is about to fall."

Clinton was not comfortable implementing lift and strike unilaterally, but he said he would ask Secretary of State Christopher to go to Europe right away to get the Brits and the French to sign on to the plan. I could tell President Clinton wasn't yet sure enough of himself to get too far ahead of our European allies.

It took a while for me to figure out Bill Clinton, but I vividly remember a conversation I had with him in the midst of the Balkan crisis. We were walking from the Oval Office to the press room, where he was about to make a statement. As we neared the press room, Clinton stopped, turned around, put both his hands on my chest, and said, "Joe, what year was the Battle of Kosovo Pole?"

I jokingly said, "What the hell difference does it make, Mr. President?"

"It makes a lot of difference to me," he said, and I could tell he wasn't kidding. "What year was the Battle of Kosovo Pole?"

I've seen seven presidents up close, and one thing I've come to understand is that a president usually gets about 70 percent of the information he needs to make a decision. Ultimately, the president has got to fill in the remainder with his own judgment and wisdom. It requires extraordinary confidence. I think Clinton always believed his command of issues, his knowledge, had helped carry him to the Oval Office. And I think in the beginning of his presidency he worried about what he *didn't* know. He didn't have much experience in foreign policy, so he trusted his instincts less. He was always asking for more information, sometimes too much information. There would always be something new to consider.

"Mr. President, you know what your problem is?"

Clinton had a quick temper, especially when he was feeling unsure. Now he was talking through clenched teeth: "*No, what's my problem?*"

"You suffer from the Rhodes scholar disease."

"What the hell do you mean by Rhodes scholar disease?"

"Mr. President, you're so accustomed to having facts at your disposal, you don't trust your instincts. Trust your instincts on this, Mr. President. Trust your instincts."

He just stared at me: "*What . . . year . . . was . . . the Battle . . . of Kosovo Pole?*"

"1389, Mr. President."

Talk of air strikes to halt Serb aggression and lifting the arms embargo against the Muslims in Bosnia met a lot of resistance in Washington. And one of the loudest voices against was John McCain, a former Navy pilot who had been a prisoner of war during the Vietnam conflict. Senator McCain kept saying there wasn't a single military expert he'd heard from who thought air strikes alone could do the job, and he worried about committing ground troops. "I will not place the lives of young Americans, men and women, at risk without having a plan that has every possibility of succeeding, a way in, a way to beneficially affect the situation, and a way out, and we do not have that," he said. It was the last week in April. A day later he invoked the most forbidding ghost among America's foreign policy failures. "It has a hauntingly familiar ring to me. It was the same rationale we used to start the bombing of North Vietnam. That's the way we got our fist into a tar baby that took us many years to get out of and twenty years to recover from."

While the Clinton foreign policy team was willing to keep the "lift and strike" option open, they weren't willing to twist arms to get the Europeans on board. So Secretary Christopher's trip to Europe was a disaster. The next time I saw Christopher, he was testifying before the full Foreign Relations Committee, just back from his trip to Europe where the Brits and the French had kicked him in the teeth. Lift and strike was a nonstarter. European leaders preferred the easy way, which was essentially to do nothing but talk. Clinton had got the word straight from British prime minister John Major. Lifting the arms embargo was too dangerous. They weren't willing to risk the safety of their troops on the ground. The U.N. called for making cities like Sarajevo and Srebrenica "safe havens" under UNPROFOR protection—but only after demanding that the Bosnian army holding out in those cities give up their weapons. The day Christopher showed up at our committee, I had just read that foreign ministers meeting in Brussels asserted that the United States lacked standing to call for lift and strike because we had no troops on the ground in Bosnia. And nobody in the administration was kicking back. I told him during his testimony,

> Let me put it plainly, Mr. Secretary. You are required to speak diplomatically; I am not. I cannot even begin to express to you my contempt for a European policy that is now asking us to participate in what amounts to a codification of the Serbian victory. . . . What you have encountered is a discouraging mosaic of indifference, timidity, self-delusion, and hypocrisy. . . . After they held our coats on Kuwait and Somalia, they are asking us to put in a few thousand troops on the ground in order to have the right to speak and in order to help implement their new idea of "safe havens" for the Bosnians. . . . Let's not mince words. European policy is based on cultural and religious indifference, if not bigotry. And I think it's fair to say that this would be an entirely different situation if the Muslims were doing what the Serbs have done, if this was Muslim aggression instead of Serbian aggression.

The same day Clinton disappointed me by echoing the old Bush administration sentiment: "We can't act alone. We should not act alone. . . . We want to try to confine that conflict so it doesn't spread into other places and involve other countries, like Albania, Greece, and Turkey, which could have the impact of undermining peace in Europe and the growth and stability of democracies there. . . . The United States cannot go in there and get involved in a civil war."

As more and more disheartening news rolled in, I could not get out of my head a meeting I'd been in with the Bosnian foreign minister Haris Silajdzic. When Silajdzic had come to visit Washington that spring, just a few weeks after my trip to the Balkans, I called a meeting of key senators in the executive meeting room of the Foreign Relations Committee. I wanted them to hear Silajdzic behind closed doors, without forcing him to be on the record. I invited Ted Stevens, John McCain, and John Warner, among others.

We all sat at the conference table, and I made the case for lifting the arms embargo unilaterally if we had to. The European powers, I was pretty sure, would follow. When Silajdzic started to talk, Senator Stevens broke in. Stevens is famously brusque, and he said to Silajdzic without a hint of sympathy: "Look, the reason why we don't want to lift the arms embargo is more people will die. We'd just be spreading weapons through the area." I looked over at Silajdzic, who was an elegant man, so polite, so quiet. "Senator," he said to Ted Stevens, "please do me the honor of allowing me to choose how my wife and children and I are going to die. Because we will die. At least allow me the honor of defending myself and my family." There was dead silence. It was one of the most dramatic moments in my career in the Senate and one of the most human. And it didn't budge anybody.

I WAS FINALLY getting the help I needed on the Violence Against Women Act, and it wasn't just the four new female senators who were sworn in at the beginning of 1993. Orrin Hatch, the Republican senator from Utah, was more and more a supporter of the legislation. He'd been diligently sitting through those hearings since 1990, and he was clearly persuaded by what he heard. I lent Victoria Nourse to Senator Hatch to help him run a field hearing in his home state. "The true human cost of this violence to the victims, to their children, and to society as a whole are immeasurable," Senator Hatch said in opening his hearing in Salt Lake City. Victoria told me later that Hatch had actually been moved to tears while listening to some of his constituents testify to the pain and humiliation they'd suffered. "This is very meaningful to us on the Senate Judiciary Committee, and I know Senator Biden, the chairman, and I, as ranking member will do all within our power to try and pass legislation that will help in these areas," Senator Hatch told the first panel. "Your testimony here today is extremely important, because I think it will add the incentives to do even a better job than what we have done in the past, which I think is pretty pathetic—what we've done has been pretty pathetic—and I think we'd better do more in this area. Each of you has made a tremendous impression on me."

The Judiciary Committee had produced, as Justice David Souter would later write, "a mountain of data" supporting the need for the Violence Against Women Act. Not only had we proved the size and scope of the problem, but we had shown the deleterious effects on the national economy. But passage still required some key senators to step forward and voice loud support, and Senator Hatch turned out to be a crucial voice.

In November 1993, a year after Clinton's election, I finally saw an opportunity to get the Violence Against Women Act through the Senate. There was by now a lot of support for the bill; seemed like half the senators were cosponsors. But the legislation wasn't ever going to make it through as an orphan because the Senate was only acting on big bills. I knew the crime bill we'd voted out of Judiciary had strong bipartisan support in the Senate that year. We were granting money for one hundred thousand new street cops, for the construction of new prisons, and to extend the threat of the death penalty. So I added the Violence Against Women Act to the bill. And then my Republican colleague from Texas, Phil Gramm, caviled: "Why do we want this kind of thing in this bill?"

But the ranking Republican backed me. "Now, Phil," Orrin Hatch told his fellow Republican senator, "Joe's worked very hard on this. And we've got to remember he cares about this. You just be quiet. It's a good bill."

Phil "Barbed-wire" Gramm wasn't much for granting favors, but he was always straight with me. Just a year earlier, right before the Bush-Clinton election, Gramm had importuned me to move the floor vote on five Texans appointed to the federal bench. He didn't expect me to do it. These were judges appointed by the first President George Bush. We'd had hearings and reported the nominations out of the committee, so as chairman of Judiciary I could have blocked a vote on the floor of the Senate and waited in hopes that Clinton would be elected and fill the seats with Democrats. But my view was that we shouldn't be playing politics with the lower courts, so I let the nominations out for confirmation. After they'd passed, I saw Gramm walking toward me on the floor of the Senate. "You know," he started in his Texas drawl. "you're the sweetest guy in the Senate, Joe. You're really a decent guy."

"Well, thank you, Phil."

"I really appreciate what you did for me," he said. "I'd never have done it for you, though." We both laughed, and I actually admired his candor. I could handle that, because I always knew where Phil Gramm stood. He wasn't one to fly under false colors or make promises he wouldn't keep.

I knew Gramm was somebody I could do business with, and that's how I got the VAWA funded. As the crime bill was moving to a vote and it became clear to Gramm that he wasn't going to peel off the VAWA, he offered me a deal: "I'll back off if you commit that the only money that can be spent on this crime bill is money saved by reducing the size of the federal work force."

"I tell you what," I said, "I'll take that deal if you agree I can set up a trust fund and that the paychecks for these people being laid off get put into this trust fund that will continue to pay for the programs." The trust fund could only be used for funding programs of the crime bill, and no new taxes would have to be raised. On the floor of the Senate we made the deal and shook on it. I think Gramm thought he'd pulled a fast one on me. Barbed-wire Phil was sure the Clinton administration would not have the discipline to reduce the size of the federal government. I was sure they would. And I was right. With Al Gore in the lead, the administration reduced the size of the federal government by nearly three hundred thousand people, down to the size it had been during John Kennedy's presidency. The crime bill passed the Senate with a funding mechanism in place. The Violence Against Women Act was in for full funding of $1.8 billion.

The House passed a version of the bill, but in conference they threatened to strip out the Title III "civil rights" provision. I simply refused. Title III, I told them, was non-negotiable. The Title III provision was staying in.

AS THE WEST negotiated on, Milosevic didn't fail to receive the message that the price of his aggression was small. Through the previous summer, Serbs had fired nearly four thousand shells into Sarajevo in a single sixteen-hour period. The Sarajevans were cracking; men were running into the empty streets begging for a quick death. The Serbs felt sufficiently confident to taunt the world. In December 1993, Serb general Ratko Mladic warned that if Western military forces entered the fight, they would "leave their bones" in Bosnia. He also threatened to spread terror where he wished. "If the West bombs me, I'll bomb London," he said. "There are Serbs in London. There are Serbs in Washington."

The taunts changed nothing. From my earliest days in the Senate I had a standard joke I used at political events: "You folks are lucky to have me here. I'm one of the most powerful men in the United States." It was good for laughs, but it didn't feel funny these days. Where Bosnia was concerned, being one of one hundred senators wasn't good enough. I kept trying to bring my colleagues on board, quite frankly, to shame the administration into acting. I got help from Senators Bob Dole and Jesse Helms, among others. But this was another pretty lonely crusade for me.

There was another moment I'll never forget in the Senate Foreign Relations room, in another closed-door meeting. I was still arguing that we could do something even without American ground troops. I was a broken record by then. Arm the Bosnians and let them fight, I'd say. The Air Force generals said we could take out every bridge across the Drina River. Milosevic wouldn't be able to get fuel, ammo, or guns across to the Serbs ransacking Bosnia. We could take out armor and artillery all over Bosnia. We knew where they were. We had the satellite pictures.

A Senate colleague who had served in the armed forces kept saying, *That's a bunch of bullshit, Joe. In order for this air power to work, you've got to have people on the ground. We have to put spotters on the ground to make sure we hit the tank behind the school and not the school. We need somebody to lay a laser on the tank and shoot it up to this high-tech capability we have. This isn't going to be bloodless; Americans might die.* My argument was that casualties would be minimal. We weren't trying to win a ground war here, I said. We were trying to take out the capacity of the Serbs to *make* war against an unarmed people. We could have blown up the railroads used to ship all the Jews to the concentration camps in World War II. How many lives might that have saved? Air strikes on the Serbs might just stop unfolding genocide. At one point, my colleague asked me point-blank: *Joe, can you guarantee to me no American will be killed?*

That was a moment I'll never forget—my college history lessons and my career colliding. It was a physical sensation. I could feel it in my throat, could feel in my heart, could feel it down in my stomach. I think I understood, for the first time, why United States senators could sit around that same conference table and decide it wasn't worth trying to stop Hitler in 1935. I could never understand how they could sit there knowing what they knew about the German military buildup and not act. But I had the benefit of hindsight. If we'd acted in 1935, it probably would have cost one thousand American lives, and in 1937, maybe five thousand. But what would those senators have proved? How do you prove a negative? Could they have proved they'd stopped World War II? Could they have asserted it had saved 6 million Jews, gypsies, and other "undesirables" from the Nazi death camps? Who would believe it?

There is never a time when a president can act to stop a tragedy from occurring without being held politically accountable one way or the other. If he does it and fails, he's wrong. If he does it and succeeds, he was never right because it didn't happen. If we go in and stop an act of genocide, we can't prove what we stopped. And American lives are at stake.

That calculation obviously tormented the Clinton administration. Vice President Al Gore was pushing the president hard to take action, but without much success. When the Serbs shelled sixty-eight Sarajevans to death at a marketplace in February 1994, Clinton condemned the "murder of innocents," but we *did* nothing. By then the administration had publicly ruled out any American military intervention. When Serb shells killed seventy-one people in Tuzla and other U.N.-designated "safe areas," we still did nothing. When I visited the Balkans again in June 1994, Sarajevo was in worse shape.

I had gone to Europe for the fiftieth anniversary of D-day, and Senator Bob Dole and I decided to take a side trip to the Balkans. Dole had been one of the few strong supporters of lift and strike. I learned later that the surgeon who put Dole back together after he was so badly injured in World War II was an Armenian whose family had deep memories of the genocidal campaign the Turks had waged against them. When Senator Dole and I arrived in Sarajevo, the cityscape was apocalyptic. We saw blankets and sheets strung across the narrower streets in the old parts of the city. When I remarked later that it was, to me, an unusual way of drying laundry, I was told that it was the best way they knew to keep the Muslim and Croatian children out of the sights of the Serb snipers. The gunmen were in the hills above the town, taking potshots at children. It was an act of pure terrorism, designed to get the Muslims to flee their homes. When we got to a hospital later that day, we weren't sure what we'd see.

A neurosurgeon at the hospital escorted us through the ward—a cavernous place with big rooms, twelve-foot ceilings, and tiled walls. The doctor steered us toward an antiseptic room with a steel bed. Lying under starched white linens was a raven-haired girl who must have been about fifteen. As I moved to the side of her bed, I noticed that her eyes didn't follow me; she turned toward voices. Dole stayed at the end of her bed, watching, while the surgeon explained that the girl's optic nerve had been severed by a bullet fired by a Serb sniper. I put my hand on the girl's arm and gave her a pat as the doctor talked. Dole was planted at the end of the bed. He was clearly moved; I have come to believe that Bob Dole was one of the most emotional men I ever served with, but he was never comfortable showing it. "Elizabeth," he said to his traveling aide, motioning her to give the girl something. "Candy. Candy." I thought I heard his voice crack. "Teddy bear."

It was bad enough the snipers were killing and maiming so many innocents in the street, but the Serbs were actually *targeting* children. This was happening in full view of the entire world. I mean, it was on television. And nobody was acting to stop it.

This was the first big test of collective security in post–Cold War Europe, and it was a shameful display. For this new generation of leaders, collective security meant arranging to blame one another for inaction so that everyone had an excuse. They weren't standing together; they were hiding together.

THE GOOD NEWS was that after almost a year's worth of wrangling, President Clinton finally signed a version of the crime bill that included the fully-funded Violence Against Women Act with the Title III civil rights provisions intact. The VAWA was a small part of a sweeping $30 billion anticrime legislation that had come to be known as the Biden-Hatch crime bill. At the ceremony on the White House lawn, the president graciously mentioned my efforts in passing the entire crime package, but I was most gratified knowing the Violence Against Women Act had finally become law. "Let us roll up our sleeves to roll back this awful tide of violence and reduce crime in this country,"

President Clinton said as he signed the package. "We have the tools now. Let us get about the business of using them."

GIVEN THE FECKLESS performance of the United Nations in Bosnia, it was no surprise that the Bosnian Serbs violated U.N. resolutions with impunity. Emboldened, Milosevic, Karadzic, and their generals overran the safe zone of Srebrenica in July 1995—and it was my saddest day in the Senate. From the beginning of the Serb invasion, the Bosnian government's military had maintained their presence in Srebrenica, as in other safe areas, fighting the onslaught of Serb tanks and heavy artillery. But they'd agreed to hand over their weapons in return for a guarantee of U.N. protection. That was the deal: End the fighting in exchange for protection of the city. But when General Ratko Mladic attacked, the United Nations did not live up to its end of the bargain. The lightly armed six-hundred-man U.N. protection force was unable to withstand the Bosnian Serb onslaught. The Dutch blue helmets called in NATO air strikes, but the United Nations concluded it was too dangerous. By the time the United Nations approved NATO air strikes, it was too late. The safe area of Srebrenica proved to be safe for Serbian aggression only. Mladic was all over the television news that day, humiliating the U.N. commanders on the ground. I saw the sickening sight of Dutch U.N. forces standing helpless, watching trucks being loaded with Muslim men and boys, headed to certain death. Seven thousand unarmed Muslims were killed in Srebrenica. The U.N. forces just stood there and watched it happen. I thought about the many times I'd been told that the Bosnians were not able to defend themselves against the Serb juggernaut. Well, of course they couldn't defend themselves. *They had no weapons.* The United Nations had seen to that. The United Nations had defaulted on its honor. It had disgraced itself. And I felt like I had personally failed the Bosnians; whatever I'd done, it hadn't been enough.

I went back to the well of the Senate to go on the record.

Many of my colleagues have commented on my passion on this issue. . . . But I do not apologize. . . . In the twenty-three years I have been here, there is not another issue that has more upset me, angered me, frustrated me, and occasionally made me feel a sense of shame about what the West, what the democratic powers of the world, are allowing to happen. . . . I am tired of all of this, and I am sure you are tired of hearing me over the last couple of years repeat these arguments. . . . There is no more time, Madam President. Time does not work for these people. Time is not on their side. They will all be dead by the time the West decides to do anything at all about this problem. I do not apologize for the passion. I do not even apologize for the time, but I do apologize to the people of Bosnia. I do apologize to the women in those rape camps. I do apologize to the men in concentration camps. I do apologize. For we are not to blame, but we have stood by—we, the world—and watched in the twilight moments of the twentieth century, something that no one thought would ever happen again in Europe. It is happening now.

Two weeks later the Serbs overran the safe area of Zepa. Clinton was reportedly walking around the White House, lashing out at his staff. "We have to do something about this. I'm getting creamed!" The next day, nearly three years after I'd first called for the plan, the Senate voted to unilaterally lift the arms embargo on Bosnia. The House followed the next week. NATO began its air campaign in earnest. We started lobbing Tomahawk missiles into Serb positions. Milosevic finally folded and came to the negotiating table.

By the end of November 1995, the Dayton Peace Agreement was in place. Milosevic and Karadzic had agreed to withdraw their military forces from Bosnia and Herzegovina and to recognize and respect the sovereignty of the independent state of Bosnia and Herzegovina. The Muslims, Croats, and Serbs all agreed to a cessation of the killing and violence. Refugees were guaranteed safe return to their homes and property or just compensation for what had been destroyed. And all sides agreed to "cooperate fully with all entities, including those authorized by the United Nations Security Council, in implementing the peace settlement and investigating and prosecuting war crimes and other violations of international humanitarian law."

The carnage was over, but there was still a bitter taste in my mouth. Two hundred thousand Bosnians had been killed in the previous three years, and 2 million more had been run from their homes, their lives ripped apart. And the men who led the rampage were not being held to account. Karadzic and General Mladic had not been brought to justice; even more distasteful, Milosevic was still in charge of the Federal Republic of Yugoslavia.

Two years later the warring parties in Bosnia and Herzegovina were separated, more than three hundred thousand troops demilitarized, and five thousand heavy weapons systems destroyed. But I was still agitating for a final accounting. "Dayton cannot be fully implemented until war criminals are apprehended and brought to the international tribunal at the Hague to stand trial," I said in a speech near the two-year anniversary of the accord. "It is absolutely necessary that SFOR [Stabilization Force in Bosnia and Herzegovina], under our command, take every opportunity to apprehend *all* indicted war criminals of *all* nationalities remaining at large, beginning with the biggest violators . . ."

The cost of leaving Milosevic in charge of the Federal Republic of Yugoslavia was dear. Milosevic didn't dare menace Bosnia and Herzegovina with the world watching and a strong international force on the ground. He wasn't so cautious in neighboring Kosovo, another largely Muslim state that tried to break from Milosevic's grip. By 1999 we were watching a replay of Milosevic-led ethnic cleansing there, too. The Kosovo Liberation Army (KLA) was making smaller reprisals against the Serbs.

And there was only one man in the world truly powerful enough to put a stop to Milosevic—the president of the United States. More than seven years into his presidency, Bill Clinton had gained much confidence in foreign affairs. Both Vice President Al Gore and now-Secretary of State Madeleine Albright had been powerful advocates for going after Milosevic in Bosnia, and now they were for strong military action to get him out of Kosovo. But the decision rested with Clinton, and he had a lot of complications. With the exception of Bob Dole, John McCain, and a few others, the Republican members of Congress were waging such a vicious campaign against Clinton that they were loath to go along with anything the president called for, including a robust military response to Milosevic's aggression in Kosovo.

When I pressed Clinton to begin air strikes against Serb military positions in Kosovo—and against Milosevic's hometown of Belgrade if we had to—he was worried about public response at home and abroad. There were fears voiced that taking action in Kosovo could spread the conflict into Albania, Macedonia, Greece, and Turkey. The alarmists weren't sure where it might end. The French president, Jacques Chirac, was dragging his feet while Kosovars were killed by the thousands and fled their homes by the tens of thousands. I kept saying to go ahead and strike, that public opinion all over Europe was running against Milosevic. The European powers would be with us. But it was easy for me to say; it was Clinton who had to take the heat.

And he did. In March 1999 I introduced a resolution in the Senate authorizing the president to use any means necessary to stop Milosevic's ethnic cleansing in Kosovo. The resolution passed with nearly unanimous Democratic support, plus the votes of about fifteen Republicans. The House of Representatives failed four times to pass a similar resolution. With Clinton resolved to act, NATO began bombing Serb targets at the beginning of the spring of 1999. Air strikes took out Serbian heavy artillery in Kosovo and targets in the capital city of Belgrade, such as the television and radio facilities spewing Milosevic's propaganda and the electric power grid that Milosevic needed to operate his command and control center. A few weeks after the air strikes began, I made a trip to the region to be briefed by military leaders there, including General Wesley Clark, whose leadership in saving Kosovo was so meaningful. There was real discussion about not just using the threat of deploying ground troops but actually deploying our troops. I'd seen enough of Milosevic to know we had to be willing to use every option we had to shut him down. General Clark, with Clinton's backing, was ready to act.

I landed back in the United States after a twelve-hour flight from Macedonia and drove straight home. I hadn't seen Jill in nearly a week and was looking forward to waking up next to her in the morning. It was late when I got home, so I took a quick shower, brushed my teeth, and climbed quietly into bed, trying not to disturb Jill. But apparently she was already awake. "Welcome home," she said. It was so dark, I couldn't quite make out her face. Then, without really hesitating, she asked me: "Are you sure you're right? Because if you're wrong, a lot of boys are going to die."

"C'mon, Jill, that's unfair," I said.

"No, it's not," she said. "Not if you're the one convincing the president to do this."

I had been pounding on Clinton relentlessly for years about Milosevic—not just in private meetings but on the floor of the Senate and in the media, too—and for that moment in the dark I had to admit to myself that, in truth, I wasn't *100 percent* certain I was right. I was pretty damn sure. But I had to admit to myself I could see why Clinton had been cautious. The final decision about the American action was his and his alone, and the president and the people of the Balkans would ultimately have to live with the consequences.

From the first days of the bombing campaign, the criticism of Clinton by the Republicans in Congress and by the faint hearts in Europe was withering. There were mistakes, like the accidental bombing of the Chinese embassy in Belgrade; civilians in the war zone died. But through the seventy-eight-day campaign, Clinton never wavered in public. I got worried about his resolve only once.

Clinton was taking a five-day working vacation at a private resort and nature preserve in Florida, and late one night he called my house. *I'm looking out my room at an armadillo,* Clinton told me by way of hello. *You believe that?*

He went on to tell me about his golf game that day. He said he'd shot a 77. I believed him about the armadillo, but I told him I was dubious about his golf score. Then he got to the point: *What would you say to my halting the bombing?*

We were nearly ten weeks into the bombing, and Clinton was getting a lot of pressure to stop the air strikes in the hopes that Milosevic would come to the negotiating table. I didn't think we wanted Milosevic to show up and start attaching conditions to a peace plan. He'd been indicted for war crimes, and I didn't want him to wriggle free again. I thought we should go for pushing him into total surrender.

I wouldn't do that, Mr. President.

What would you say if I did halt it? he asked.

I'd call a press conference and say you reneged on a promise, I said. I'm sure by now Clinton was sick of hearing this from me, but we were so close to making Milosevic cry uncle that I wasn't going to sugarcoat anything. *Don't yield, boss. He'll capitulate.*

I have no idea if my advice had any effect on the president, but Clinton did not halt the bombings. He kept the pressure on Milosevic, and it paid off. Less than two weeks after the late-night call from Florida, I was in one of a series of meetings the president called to brief congressional leaders on the progress in Kosovo. Secretary of Defense William Cohen, National Security Advisor Sandy Berger, Secretary of State Madeleine Albright—who had been a strong voice for action in the Balkans—the Joint Chiefs of Staff, and key members of Congress were all meeting in a second-floor room of the White House. And in the middle of the meeting the president walked in and announced that Milosevic had surrendered without a single demand. Milosevic was giving up on Kosovo; he was pulling out.

I was gathering up my briefcase after that meeting when one of Clinton's staffers grabbed me and asked if I could stick around for a quick talk with the president. He ushered me into the Yellow Room, where Clinton was standing at a window looking out at the ellipse.

Congratulations, Mr. President, I told him. *You got your sea legs. You did it. You saved thousands of lives. Only you.*

But he wasn't ready to accept congratulations.

You've been unfair to me, he said.

I started to explain, but he cut me off. *I was a governor. You've been doing this your whole adult life.*

Mr. President, I told him. *You deserve credit. You did it.*

A few weeks after Milosevic folded up his tents, I made a visit to Kosovo. I went to Blackbird's Field, near Pristina, where Slobodan Milosevic had initiated his campaign to wipe out most of the Muslim population of the former Yugoslavia. It was a big open plain that dwarfed a small obelisk. Six hundred years, I thought, and still fighting over religion and ethnicity. Lives and treasure had been wasted for no good reason. Whether the Croats, Serbs, and Muslims in the Balkans could really secure peace remained to be seen, but I felt like the world—with the United States in the lead—had given them the breathing room to try.

Later on that trip we drove to the permanent base that the United States military was constructing on an eight-hundred-acre tract in south central Kosovo. Camp Bondsteel was just then rising as a strong statement of U.S. intentions—it was a big, powerful, shiny village of a base that was meant to last. It said we were here to stay and to secure the peace.

When we pulled up to the front gate, our Kosovar driver stared in awe at the construction. "That's America," he said, pointing at the enormous construction project.

But my gaze was drawn to the four American soldiers standing at the gate. As I recall it, there stood a white female captain, a black female NCO, a Hispanic female NCO, and a white male colonel. I got our driver's attention and pointed to the four soldiers in the road.

Effort Pays ★ 289

"No," I told him, "that's America. When you can learn to live together like we do, then you will be like America."

Almost a decade later two of the most murderous Serbs—Radovan Karadzic and General Ratko Mladic—are still at large. The Serbian and Bosnian governments have been unable to apprehend them and turn them over to The Hague where they have been indicted for war crimes. But Slobodan Milosevic was turned over to the international court where he went on trial in February 2002 for war crimes, crimes against humanity, and genocide. He managed to drag the trial out for more than four years, and he was still on trial in March 2006 when he died of a heart attack, alone, in a jail cell.

* 16 *

New Opportunities

THINGS RARELY WORK OUT ACCORDING TO PLAN. THAT'S what I was thinking as I dragged more than three hundred feet of garden hose up the hill along my driveway on a hot day in June 2001. Our sons had set up their own households by now, and Ashley was in college, so Jill and I had sold The Station and bought some land, and I designed a house from the ground up. We called it the Lake House. It took more than two years to get it built, so Jill, Ashley, and I bounced around to rental houses in the meantime. We moved in just in time for Christmas 1998. But even after a few years on the property, there was still landscaping to be done. I'd planted these beautiful Leland Cypress trees; they were big, fast-growing trees in need of a lot of water—and, of course, right after I planted, Wilmington fell into a scorching drought. I wasn't about to let these things brown and die, so there I was hoisting this hose up my driveway, sweating in the heat, when Ashley came running up the hill behind me. "Dad," she yelled, "the president's on the phone."

In my three decades in the Senate, I'd rarely known the routine of a presidential call to vary. A White House assistant places the call, asks if I'm available to talk to the president, and says he will be calling in, say, five minutes. My job was to stand by the phone and await the call.

"Okay, Ashley," I told her, "tell them I'll be there in a minute."

But Ashley was insistent. "Daddy! The president!"

"Honey, I know. Tell them I'll be there in a minute."

"Daddy, *the* president is on *the* phone! I've spoken to enough of them to know."

Her tone was: Do whatever you like, you jerk, but I know a president when I hear one. So I went trotting down the hill, laughing at Ashley, and picked up the receiver. It was indeed the president himself. "I apologize for keeping you waiting, Mr. President. I was just watering some trees. Placing your own calls these days, huh?"

"Yeah. Effective, idn't it?" He paused for comic effect. "Hope you're not watering too *liberally.*"

"Well, I appreciate the call, Mr. President. What can I do for you?"

"How'd I do?" said President George W. Bush.

I knew just what he was talking about.

THE FIRST TIME I'd really spoken to George W. Bush was just after he'd secured the Republican nomination in 2000 when we were seated together at the annual Chamber of Commerce event in Wilmington. He made a point of telling me that as governor of Texas he'd worked with the Democrats in the legislature. And if he got elected, he thought the two of us could work together. I told him that if he did get elected, I'd look forward to working with him.

In the first months after he took office, George W. Bush reached out to the ranking Democrat of almost every Senate committee, but not to me. I didn't take it personally. I was the lead Democrat on the Foreign Relations Committee, and Bush wasn't much engaged in foreign policy. He was like most of the other governors I'd seen take office. Carter, Reagan, and Clinton had all been shy about taking on big issues in foreign policy unless and until forced by circumstances. Bush seemed even more uncertain.

And it worried me that he had put in place a team that was essentially at war over foreign affairs. On one side was Secretary of State Colin Powell, an old-school Republican internationalist who seemed to want to engage in the world. On the other side were the neo-isolationists like Vice President Dick Cheney and Donald Rumsfeld. The Rumsfeld clique was talking about pulling out of the Balkans, walking away from the international global warming pact called the Kyoto Treaty, and canceling President Clinton's signature on the international treaty that set up the new International Criminal Court for prosecuting individuals for genocide and other war crimes. They were so intent on going ahead with Reagan's Star Wars missile defense shield that they were willing to pull out of earlier arms control treaties to get there—inviting, in my view, another arms race. The missile defense system seemed to be the perfect metaphor for the neo-isolationist policy. Let's arm the heavens, they were saying, and protect the United States of America, the rest of the world be damned.

They seemed intent on sending their "United States interests first and foremost" message, no matter how damaging it might be to our ongoing peace efforts in the Middle East, for instance. One of Secretary Rumsfeld's early plans was for pulling 860 American troops out of the Multinational Force and Observers cadre that had been in the Sinai since 1982. The MFO was put in place by the Camp David Accords, at the behest of both Israel and Egypt, and had served as a cooling mechanism for the region for nearly twenty years. Secretary of State Powell did not share Rumsfeld's enthusiasm for the U.S. pullout, so the administration was sending mixed signals. The Israelis, the Palestinians, and the Arabs I was talking to were starting to wonder if the United States still cared to be engaged in the peace process.

The rest of the world was trying to figure out what exactly would be the guiding principles of the Bush foreign policy, and they were hard to divine. A San Andreas–like fault ran right down the center of the Bush foreign policy team, with Secretary Powell and his team at the State Department on one side and Cheney, Rumsfeld, and the civilians at the Defense Department on the other. I'd watched with concern during the transition and confirmation process as Cheney and Rumsfeld tried to put their neo-isolationist compatriots into key positions in the State Department to spy on Powell. Powell had to be pretty forceful to keep Rumsfeld's allies off his State Department team. This sort of infighting did not portend an administration that spoke with one voice. And the president didn't seem interested in putting his finger on the scale to favor either side. I knew where I wanted the president to come down: If Bush went with Rumsfeld and the neo-isolationists over Powell, the United States, I said at the time, could end up in deep trouble.

In June 2001 news reports had Secretary of State Powell frozen out of key policy decisions, and I was already beginning to talk in public about the danger of the White House's San Andreas fault—and the greater danger of the Cheney-Rumsfeld policies. And I was suddenly speaking as the chairman of the Senate Foreign Relations Committee. By then, Vermont senator James Jeffords had left the Republican

Party, and his defection had given Democrats a one-vote majority in the Senate. (Apparently, the White House had leaned too heavily on the diplomatic skills of Vice President Cheney. When the White House heard that Jeffords was thinking about switching parties, Cheney was shipped over to Capitol Hill to talk him out of it. Jeffords emerged from his meeting with Cheney as a *former* Republican.) I had just taken back the chairmanship of the Senate Foreign Relations Committee when the call came. I was about to walk out onto a football field to give a high school commencement speech when my cell phone rang. It was the president, who said he wanted me to meet with him at the White House the following Monday morning. When I asked him what the meeting was about, he told me he wanted me to "brief him on Europe." Now, I knew the president had a lot of smart people on his staff who knew a lot about Europe, so I figured this was his way of reaching out across the aisle. He'd lost his majority in the Senate, and he understood he might need some Democrats.

Mr. President, I said, *I'm always honored to be at the White House. But you don't need to do this for me. I know I'm on the tickler file— Call Biden. I appreciate your call, Mr. President. Anytime you ever need me, I will be available. But there's no need to do this.*

But Bush insisted. So I said, *Mr. President, may I ask you why?*

And he explained he was preparing for his first trip to Europe— and not just his first trip as president but *ever*. Now, I still didn't think he really wanted my advice, but I agreed to meet him at the White House the following Monday.

The meeting was scheduled for something like twenty after the hour, and I was struck by the time—who schedules to the ten minutes? Even Jimmy Carter, who habitually looked at his watch throughout any meeting I had with him, didn't schedule every ten minutes. I figured the Bush staff would have me in and out of the Oval Office in about eight. As I was being ushered in, Secretary of State Powell was leaving. Bush yelled across the room to remind Powell to be prepared for their upcoming European trip. "Colin!" the president said with a cackle. "Remember to pack clean underwear."

"See what I have to put up with, Mr. Chairman?" Powell joked as he passed by me.

As the secretary left the office, the president motioned me to a chair across from his own, which sat in front of the fireplace. We were accompanied by White House staff; must have been ten or fifteen people in the room, led by Condoleezza Rice, the president's national security advisor and close confidante. His congressional liaison was at the meeting, as I remember, and so was Alberto Gonzalez, the White House counsel.

Mr. President, I said, *it's an honor to be here.*

Thanks for being here, Mr. Chairman. As I remember it now, Bush wore his self-confidence rather lightly that day. He'd just signed into law his first big initiative, the Bush tax cuts, so he had a bit more swagger than I'd seen in him back in Wilmington before the election. But there was a sort of half-ironic macho drawl to his tone and a manner that took the edge off the formality of the office. Actually, I felt pretty comfortable in his presence that day.

What can I do for you, Mr. President?

Brief me on Europe, he said.

Mr. President, is this for real?

The staff in the room all put their heads down to look at their papers, but President Bush laughed. *Yeah. This is for real.*

Mr. President, I said, *you've got some really good people in here. They know as much or more about Europe than I do.*

But Bush insisted again. For starters, the president solicited my opinion on what would constitute a successful first trip to Europe, and I told him I thought he needed to walk away with headlines in Europe saying "Bush Engaged in Europe."

What do you mean by that?

Mr. President, I said, *no one knows what your foreign policy is. You've got two different policies. Let me give you an example. You know how you were engaged in the tax cut. What did you do, Mr. President? You were fully engaged. No one had any doubt that that was your policy. You were on the phone working for this. With all due respect, Mr. President, I think it was the biggest mistake made in a long, long time, but it was you, Mr. President. You did it. You were engaged. People knew where you stood. People are looking for your foreign policy, and they're getting different signals.*

I remember seeing National Security Advisor Rice out of the corner of my eye, and her body language indicated that she took issue with my analysis. Rice might have wanted to cut me off, but the president encouraged me to keep talking.

On the one hand, I said, *the secretary of defense keeps talking about being overextended in Bosnia and Kosovo and the Middle East, and the secretary of state is saying other things. Nobody knows what the policy is, and they don't know that you have any policy. Mr. President, I think the most important thing is to say "Bush Engaged in Europe."*

He asked my advice on how to get that headline, and I told him one thing he could do was call for the expansion of NATO.

Who? he asked.

I don't think it matters which country you call for. The mere fact that you call for the expansion of NATO means you consider the United States to be the main European power.

The president seemed to like the idea. I am convinced the president had already heard that particular idea from his own advisors and that it was already on his trip agenda, but I thought it was good personal politics on his part not to say that he already knew that—to let me wonder whether I'd swayed him in some way. Then he did something I found even more interesting. He asked me for my opinion on some of the world leaders he was dealing with, and not just those on his schedule for the European trip.

Why is your friend Kim Dae-jung so upset? he asked.

You mean the guy who won the Nobel Peace Prize? Guy who brought democracy to South Korea? He's not my friend. I admire him, but he's not my friend.

President Bush leaned over and re-created the scene he'd had with the president of South Korea in the Oval Office a few months earlier, patting me on the knee as he spoke. *All I said to him was I just don't trust that little Commie* (meaning the North Korean leader, Kim Jong-Il) *up there.*

I reached over and patted the president's knee. *Mr. President, you know what he was thinking when you were patting his knee. He was thinking, "I look just like that little Commie up there." Mr. President, if I'm not mistaken, just before you were speaking with him, Secretary Powell was out talking about how you were going to continue the Clinton policy of engagement with North Korea and support South Korea's Sunshine Policy. Then, Mr. President, in walks Kim Dae-jung, and you apparently unceremoniously tell him, "Okay, this Sunshine Policy is a failure. We're out." Mr. President, you obviously embarrassed him. It put him in a tough spot at home. I think that's the reason he's upset.*

I had been in the Oval Office a long time, but nobody was moving to push me out. Bush hadn't looked at his watch, like Carter always did, or referred to three-by-five note cards, like Reagan often did. Instead, he asked me about the German chancellor: *How about Schroeder? What's he so upset about?*

Mr. President, let me ask you a question. How about you're being picked up in a limo to go see Chancellor Schroeder and you get into his office and sit down, and Dr. Rice says, "Mr. President, before you go into the chancellor's office, there's something you should know. He made a speech this morning nationwide comparing the Nazi skinheads to the Christian Coalition." Mr. President, the chancellor walked in here, and it appears that he hadn't been forewarned that we were pulling out of Kyoto. You announced that five minutes before he walked into your office. Mr. President, the chancellor relies on the Greens. His coalition in the Bundestag includes the Green Party. You announce, apparently without his knowing it, that we're out of the treaty. Mr. President, that's embarrassing. That's why he's upset.

Bush wasn't in the least defensive; he seemed genuinely interested. And I started to get some appreciation for the particular talents of George W. Bush; they were not small. He didn't know much about foreign policy, but he was already a pretty good gut politician. He had all these other policy people to talk to, but he wanted to talk with another politician who had sat down with these leaders, who maybe had a read on the personalities and the motivations. George W. Bush trusts his ability to deal one-on-one, but first he wants to know about the other person's wants and needs, personally and politically. That's what he wanted to hear from me. And he was very direct in questioning me: What's my problem with these leaders? he wanted to know.

I've since had a discussion with former president Bill Clinton at his house in Chappaqua about George W. Bush, and I told Clinton that Bush was a lot more intelligent than people think he is. I don't know about his cognitive capability, I told Clinton, but I think he's a lot smarter about people and where he sits with them than anybody thinks he is. And Clinton told me he thought Bush has a remarkably high emotional IQ. Bill Clinton even allowed that if his opponent in 1992 had been George W. instead of George H. W. Bush, he might not have won the presidency.

Anyway, walking out of my first meeting with Bush, I believed this president was more intelligent than people understood and surprisingly willing to take the time to listen to other people. And I also came away believing his foreign policy ideas had not yet been settled. I really believed Secretary Powell could pull President Bush over to the old Republican internationalist side and away from the neo-isolationist side. The truth is, a week later, when I went running down my driveway to take the president's call, I was already beginning to think that Bush really did want to work across party lines—and that I could be a small voice nudging the president toward Secretary Powell's internationalist policy initiatives.

How'd I do? the president asked me on the phone that day.

In the week since I'd seen him in the Oval Office, Bush had done well in Europe. The president had pledged to keep U.S. troops among the peacekeeping forces in Bosnia and Kosovo. "We went into the Balkans together," he'd said, "and we will come out together. Our goal must be to hasten the arrival of that day when we can all come out together." He'd made a strong statement on the expansion of NATO. "I believe in membership," the president had said, "for all of Europe's democracies that seek it and are ready to share the responsibilities that NATO brings." He'd extended his scheduled meeting with Russian president Vladimir Putin by almost a full hour, and the two men walked out promising big things. "We have a great moment during our tenures to cast aside the suspicion and doubts that used to plague our nations," Bush said. "After our meeting today, I'm convinced Russia can be a strong partner and friend—more so than people could imagine." Bush hadn't let Putin off the hook on human rights violations and repressive characteristics reemerging in Russia, but he focused on where they could find common ground. The president had even gone out of his way to reassure Putin that he had nothing to fear from the enlargement of NATO, which would not include Russia. "When a president of a great power says that he wants to see Russia as a partner and maybe even as an ally," Putin said, "this is worth so much to us."

"It was clear to all of us," a European Union's commissioner told reporters in the aftermath of the Bush trip, "that we were dealing with a president and an administration who are internationalist in outlook, open to dialogue, and ready to develop, not discard, America's relationship with Europe."

There was only one way to sum up the president's trip: Bush Engaged in Europe.

How'd I do? the president asked me.

I think you did pretty well, Mr. President.

Yeah. I got the headline, he said. *At a future time I'll brief you on the trip.*

In spite of the president's phone call, I remained a vocal critic of the Bush administration's foreign policy priorities through that summer because I didn't trust most of the people he had around him. The civilians in the Department of Defense were unlike any I'd ever seen. They seemed to think our nation was so powerful that we could simply impose our will on the rest of the world with almost no ill consequence. It seemed to me that Rumsfeld and his chief deputy at Defense, Paul Wolfowitz, were so totally in thrall to that conservative think-tank-generated ideology that they were steering the president down a dangerous path. And they were so intent on overturning President Clinton's foreign policy initiatives that they were losing sight of the bigger goal, which was keeping America safe at home and engaged in doing good in the world.

The Bush administration's first budget was a sobering document because it seemed to reflect the Cheney-Rumsfeld-Wolfowitz view of the world. The administration had said they were willing to walk away from the decades-old ABM Treaty in order to unilaterally develop and deploy the missile defense system, and now they were putting real money behind it. They were willing to put tens of billions of dollars into the Maginot line in the sky that could quite likely set off another arms race, while *cutting* funding for a program to help Russia destroy its nuclear, chemical, and biological weapons before they got into the hands of terrorists. To remind the administration of the strong bipartisan support for safeguarding the country and our allies against "loose nukes," chemical and biological attacks, I chaired hearings in the Foreign Relations Committee to investigate the very real threats I thought the administration was ignoring to fund Star Wars. When those hearings wrapped, I prepared a speech called "U.S. Foreign Policy in the 21st Century: Defining Our Interests in a Changing World." The purpose was to suggest that if we wanted to ensure our national security, it was time to rethink our priorities and to think about what the United States—as the only superpower left standing—owed to the international community. The first time I made the speech was at the National Press Club in Washington, D.C., on September 10, 2001.

At the end of the Cold War, when the wall came down, we found ourselves on the brink of extraordinary changes [I said that warm end-of-summer night]. From that day on, we inherited a profound obligation of leadership, and an even more profound obligation to get it right in the Middle East, in the Balkans, in Europe, and in Asia, in our hemispheres, in our commitments, our treaties, and in our defense policy—missile or otherwise. Now, the spotlight remains on us and is brighter than ever. We're at a pivotal moment when American values and principles have taken center stage like no other time in our history and in the global theater. How we perform on that stage is as much about our honor, our decency, our pride as it is about our strategic policy. So before we start raising the starting gun that will begin a new arms race in the world, before we dip into the Social Security trust fund to satisfy the administration's almost theological allegiance to missile defense at the expense of more earth-bound military and international treaties, before we watch China build up its nuclear arsenal and see an arms race in Asia and in the subcontinent, before we squander the best opportunity we've had in a generation to modernize our conventional nuclear forces, let's look at the real threats we face at home and abroad. Let's reengage and rethink and meet our obligations with a strength and resolve that befits our place in the new world. . . . I don't believe our national interests can be furthered, let alone achieved, in splendid indifference to the rest of the world's views of our policies. Our interests are furthered when we meet our international obligations and we keep our treaties. . . .

We can't forget or simply disregard the responsibilities that flow from our ideals. . . . Are we a nation of our word or not? Do we keep our treaties or don't we? Are we willing to lead the hard way, because leadership isn't easy and requires us convincing others? Diplomacy isn't easy. Multilateral policy initiatives aren't easy. Or are we willing to end four decades of arms control agreements and go it alone—a kind of bully nation, sometimes a little wrongheaded but ready to make unilateral decisions in what we perceive to be our self-interest, and to hell with our treaties, our commitments, and the world? . . . Even the Joint Chiefs of Staff say that a strategic nuclear attack is less likely than a regional conflict, a major theater of war, terrorist attacks at home or abroad, or any

other number of real issues. We have diverted all that money to address the least likely threat, while the real threat comes to this country in the hold of a ship, the belly of a plane, or smuggled into a city
in the middle of the night in a vial in a backpack.

I MADE IT back home to Wilmington late that night, so I got on the
8:35 train and—like any other day—made my regular commute to
my office in the Capitol the next morning, September 11. My schedule was fairly light that day: a morning meeting with the Delaware car
and truck dealers and hearings on the president's nominee to head the
Office of National Drug Control Policy. I got on the train alone, like
I always did, and a little more than half an hour into the ride there
was a buzz in the car about a plane crashing into a building in New
York. Nobody knew quite what to make of it. Then Jill called. She
was at school, she told me, but nobody was in class. Everybody was
in the lounge watching the television news coverage, and it looked
bad. An airliner had crashed into one of the World Trade Center towers. Then, in mid-sentence, she said, "Oh my God. Oh my God. Oh
my God."

"Jill, what is it?"

"Another plane . . . the other tower."

By the time I got off the train at Union Station in Washington, the
third plane had hit the Pentagon, and I could see a brown haze of
smoke hanging in the otherwise crystal-clear sky beyond the Capitol
dome. All flights were grounded; Washington and New York City
were locked down. The military was scrambling fighter jets. And yet
there was an eerie stillness on Capitol Hill—like a moment of pro-
longed equipoise between inhalation and exhalation. There were a lot
of people milling in the park between Union Station and the Capitol,
and one of my staff members explained that they were evacuating the
House and Senate office buildings and the Capitol because a fourth
hijacked plane was apparently en route to Washington.

I grabbed one of my colleagues nearby and asked why we went out
of session. "They said it was too dangerous," he said.

"C'mon," I said. "The public should turn on their televisions and
see that their government is still there. I'm going into the Capitol."

I got all the way to the steps before a uniformed Capitol police officer came running up behind me. "Senator Biden! Senator Biden!
You have to evacuate the area. Incoming plane! Incoming plane!"

"Damn it, I want to go in."

"You can't go in. You have to evacuate. Evacuate!"

There must have been a dozen other staff members milling around the steps, and the police herded us all back to the middle of the park. I was standing there when a staffer for a Republican senator came walking up to me and started telling me this was why we needed Missile Defense.

"National Missile Defense?" I said. "What are you talking about?"

I felt like I spent the next few hours trying to calm people down. Ashley called me from Wilmington in an understandable panic: "Daddy, where are you?"

"I'm standing in the park across from the Capitol."

"Daddy, they say a plane's coming. Get out of there."

"Honey, I promise you," I said, looking at the clear sky. If the other plane was coming, we'd see it. "This is the safest place to be."

"Daddy, no. They said on television you're still up there and others are still up there."

"Honey, I promise you. This is the safest place for me to be."

Within a half hour of Ashley's call the fourth plane went down in a field in Pennsylvania, and both towers had collapsed. Nobody knew how many people were still in the buildings when they went down—news reports suggested there might be as many as ten thousand people dead in New York City. A section of the Pentagon had collapsed, and there were fatalities there, too. Nobody knew who was behind these attacks or if more were coming. The television newscasters were already talking as if we were a nation at war.

The Capitol police brought me and other congressional leaders into a briefing in a building on the north side of the Senate office buildings. Not that they could tell us much, but they were getting word from Vice President Cheney, who was in the command center at the White House, that it might be best to fly key congressional officers to the safe cave in West Virginia. The president pro-tem of the Senate, Bob Byrd, refused to be taken off the Hill—and West Virginia was his home state.

I called the Senate Democratic leader, Tom Daschle. "Tom, look, don't go," I suggested. "Stay here. Stay here."

"Joe, I don't want to," he told me, "but I don't want to embarrass the rest of the leaders. Everybody else is going. If I don't, I look like I'm grandstanding. Byrd's not going. I gotta go." Daschle was right;

this was no time for even the appearance of partisanship. But I still thought we should get back in session. Along with Philadelphia congressman Bob Brady, I started agitating to go back into the Capitol and show the country we were still doing business. But around noon we both gave up; it was clear there would be no return to session that day. Congressman Brady decided to drive back home for the night and come back the next day, and he offered to drop me in Wilmington. He even had room for my brother, Jim, who was in Washington and had come over to the Hill to find me.

As we walked to the parking lot, an ABC News reporter, Linda Douglass, grabbed me at a rope line outside the building where we were briefed. She was anxious—like everybody else—to know anything we'd learned in the briefings. Even though there wasn't a lot of hard information I could offer, Congressman Brady thought it would be a good thing for me to go on television to reassure people. Other than a very brief statement from President Bush, there had been near total silence from federal officials. So I went on the air and explained that the United States government was going to be back in business soon, that we weren't going to let the terrorists force us to fundamentally change our civil liberties, and that—despite the tragedy—we remained strong. Douglass suggested other senators were talking about America being on a "war footing" or "at war," but I thought we should keep our perspective until we knew more. "What I don't want everybody to think is this is some worldwide conspiracy where there's tens of thousands of people that are part of the army that attacked us. This is a group of people very well organized, obviously relatively well funded. And we have to figure out how their network is run. We have to penetrate it. But this is now, we can't . . . just say we're going to focus only on this kind of incident and not on chemical, not on biological, not on pathogen, not on anthrax. This is in a sense the most god-awful wake-up call we've ever had in terms of how we have to redirect our resources."

"At the Pentagon," Peter Jennings said to me from his studio in New York, "people are already saying this is so sophisticated, this has to be Osama bin Laden. Maybe so, but is the United States too focused on one man?"

"The tendency in these circumstances is to be too focused on one man, one idea, one prospect," I answered. "I think that we should be calm. Those of us who hold high public office just calm down a little bit, collect our thoughts, collect the information in a methodical way, analyze what we know happened and what we can derive from that. I think it's much too early for us to make those kinds of judgments. The first thing is what the president is doing. He called for calm. He's getting in the airplane. He's coming back to Washington, D.C., and I applaud him for that. And we should be back up and running as quickly as we can. This cannot be dealt with overnight. It's an incredible tragedy. But it's a new threat of the twenty-first century, and we will find a way to do it. This nation is too big, too strong, too united, too much a power in terms of our cohesion and our values to let this break us apart. And it won't happen. It won't happen."

After I finished the interview, Jimmy and I piled into a van with Brady and his staff, and we headed north to Wilmington. We were nearing Baltimore when my cell phone rang. President Bush was on the line. *I just watched you on television,* he told me, *and I'm really proud of you. You made us all proud. You were saying the right things.*

Thank you Mr. President for calling, I said. *Mr. President, may I ask where you are?*

I'm on Air Force One, heading to an undisclosed location in the Midwest.

When I asked him when he was heading to Washington, he said the intelligence community told him he shouldn't.

Mr. President, you've got much, much better access to intelligence, I told him, *but you know that if there's even a small percentage of a possibility of something happening, they will tell you not to come home.*

I recalled at the time a story about the leader of the French resistance, Charles de Gaulle, near the close of World War II. When France was liberated, there was a celebratory parade down the Champs-Elysées in Paris—dignitaries, generals, and officers—led by de Gaulle himself. As they walked toward the Hôtel de Ville, shots rang out from overhead, and everyone hit the ground except de Gaulle. He continued to walk ramrod straight.

With that one defiant action he lifted France off its knees.

Mr. President, I said, *come back to Washington.*

I hung up the phone, and there was silence in the van until Jimmy spoke up. "Whatever staffer suggested he call *you* just got fired."

The president spent the day doing a hopscotch around the country in Air Force One, unseen by the American public. He taped a brief statement, which the White House press operation handed to news organizations early that afternoon, and didn't arrive back at the White House until 7:00 that night. George W. Bush didn't make a real speech or show himself to the nation until almost 9:00 P.M.—a full twelve hours after the first attack. As it turned out, the congressional leaders even beat him back to Washington. And I sort of felt bad that I was sitting in Wilmington, watching them sing "God Bless America" on the steps of the Capitol building and promising to be back in session the next day.

I'd spent the afternoon watching news coverage, and I'd been heartened by the response of my fellow Americans. I'll never forget all the people in the blood lines that snaked through New York City streets. Everybody seemed to want to do his part even if the nation's leaders were AWOL. By the time I headed back to the Capitol the next morning, I was convinced the American people would hold up their end of the bargain when it came to facing this new challenge. Whatever sacrifice the president asked, they would make. But given what I'd seen on September 11, I was less sure that President Bush could provide the wisdom and judgment this new reality demanded.

In my twenty-eight years in the Senate, I'd never seen a single day change the stakes for the country as drastically as 9/11 had. The way I saw it, this wasn't just about meeting the challenge of terrorism; it was about taking advantage of an incredible opportunity to fundamentally improve our internal security and solidify our relations around the world. I can't remember another moment in those twenty-eight years when the sympathies of the overwhelming majority of the international community were so openly avowed. The French newspaper *Le Monde* carried an editorial headlined "We Are All Americans." For the first time in the fifty-year history of NATO our European allies invoked Article 5, which said when one of us is attacked, we are all under attack. I really thought this was the moment we could drive a stake through the heart of the Cheney-Rumsfeld unilateralism. Terror was an international phenomenon with an international solution. President Bush's task was to summon the American people to the fight and to appeal to the rest of the world to make it their fight, too. More would be demanded of this president in this term than in any single administration I'd seen in twenty-eight years. I can't say I had much confidence that George W. Bush was up to the job, but I was determined to keep my doubts to myself. My job was to do all I could to help the president succeed.

I had no doubt that there was a serious threat to our security, but this was a different kind of struggle—one that couldn't be won by military strength alone. There were public officials comparing it to Pearl Harbor, asserting baldly that the country would never be the same. People were nervous enough—I heard it in their voices and saw it in their eyes—and I thought it was important for those of us in positions of authority to be calm and hard-eyed about what had happened and what we had to do about it. At the time I was truly confident that my own children and grandchildren would look back at 2001 from an unchanged America. They'd see it—like my parents' generation saw the Depression and World War II—as another chapter and another challenge met. The threat existed, it was real, but we'd deal with it and move on, and the national ideals would not be fundamentally diminished. A generation down the road, I was sure, America would be as open, as united, and as strong as it was in 2001. So I spent a lot of time preaching calm and perspective to my own constituents in Delaware, especially in the schools. One of the most important talks I made was eight days after the attacks, at the University of Delaware, where the kids were understandably jittery. I told them how I was living proof that these moments of crisis pass if we keep our heads. I told them how I had sat in the lounge at their school nearly forty years before, surrounded by my hushed schoolmates, as we listened to President Kennedy, who was sitting in the Oval Office with ominous-looking maps behind him and telling us that the Russians might very well have put nuclear-tipped warheads in Cuba. "And we looked at the maps," I told them, "and I can remember calculating: Can those missiles reach Delaware? Not figuratively—literally. And knowing that if they did, we would all be annihilated—not a hundred of us, not five thousand of us, but tens of thousands and millions of us." But here I was—here we were—still standing.

I told those students the same thing I told everybody in those first days after 9/11:

> You are going to hear from experts on terrorism. . . . Put it in perspective. Don't let yourself get carried away. What happened was horrible. Some have called September 11 a "second day of infamy." Some are telling you that it will change our way of life. I'm here to

tell you it will not—cannot, must not—change our way of life. It is the beginning of the end of the way of life for international terrorist organizations—not ours. I'm telling you, we're not talking about a Soviet army of millions of people; we're not talking about the Japanese empire; we're not talking about fifty or a hundred or two hundred thousand people. We're talking about tens and hundreds of people for whom we can suck the oxygen out of the air that they breathe if we change a couple things, but not our way of life. There is one parallel between that day of infamy when the Japanese attacked Pearl Harbor and these madmen, these deranged people, who have attacked innocent civilians. Admiral Yamamoto was prescient that day of the Pearl Harbor attack. Do you know what he said to his fellow officers in Japan? He said, "We have sown the seeds of our own destruction. We have awakened a sleeping giant. We have filled it with terrible resolve." That is what happened here. A sleeping giant has been awakened, and the American people and the civilized world have been filled with a terrible resolve.

I told the students about the calls I had from officials of Pakistan, which stood ready to help in the fight against terror. The Chinese, the Russians, and even Iran had signaled their willingness to be our ally in this particular struggle.

The world has come to realize this is a battle between nationhood and chaos. They are not uniting with us out of a newfound zeal for democracy or human rights. It's born out of self-interest. Self-interest we should—and to his great credit the president has begun—to take advantage of.

But my central message to the students was that they had the stuff to win this new struggle. (I was explicit in saying we were not engaged in war.)

If I get asked one more time on *Larry King* or *Meet the Press* or *CNN Town Meeting*, I think I'm going to strangle the person who asks me the question, because every single generation in this country that's been faced with a serious challenge has risen to the occasion. The only difference is you're a hell of a lot smarter than we were. That's the only difference. This isn't a time for vengeance.

This isn't a time for fear. This is a time to keep going, not to retreat, to mourn those who died, not to despair. It's a time for resolve, but not remorse. But most importantly, it's a time to unite.

TEN DAYS LATER I went to Abraham's Mosque in Newark to speak to the Muslim community in my state. I was a little concerned that the Muslims in Delaware had not stood up and condemned the attacks, but I think they had simply gone to ground. The constant references to Pearl Harbor had to remind them that one consequence of that long-ago bombing was the wholesale imprisonment of Japanese American citizens, with no due process whatsoever. Innocent and patriotic Muslim Americans were rightly worried they'd be made to answer for the 9/11 attacks. There had been some violent and unwarranted reprisals against Muslims in other states already. "Thank God, Delaware has not witnessed cases of raw, evil bigotry that violate everything for which our country stands," I said at the packed mosque that day. "Whenever I hear people try to blame the attacks in New York and Washington on the religion of Islam, I just wish I could reach into the hearts of the folks saying these things and make them understand how *wrong they are.* Whoever is guilty of these terrible crimes, whether it is Osama bin Laden or somebody else, one thing is for certain: By his very actions, by killing thousands of innocent people, he proved that he is no true Muslim."

The president had expressed similar sentiments already, and he'd pleaded with Americans to respect the peaceful Muslim population within our borders and without. In fact, in the weeks after 9/11, George W. Bush was acting like a president should; I suspected Secretary of State Powell had finally gained his full attention. When the administration satisfied itself and the world that bin Laden and his al-Qaeda terrorist network had been responsible for 9/11, they determined to take out the fundamentalist and repressive Taliban regime in Afghanistan that had offered safe haven and training grounds to the terrorists who had done the damage. But the president didn't rush into action. He offered the Taliban a chance to turn over Osama bin Laden and other al-Qaeda leaders. He drew up a bill of particulars against the Taliban, and he sent envoys to key capitals all over the world to make the case against the Taliban. And it wasn't just our longtime allies that the Bush administration meant to persuade; the president was talking to the Chinese, the Russians, and the Iranians.

He sent Powell's deputy to Pakistan to make sure President Pervez Musharraf knew exactly what we expected of him when we went to war next door in Afghanistan. There was a carrot involved and also a stick.

I did have one strange warning sign. On my way back to Wilmington one evening that fall, I ran into Richard Perle. Perle was a neoconservative and hardliner who in 2001 was chairing the Defense Policy Board, which was chartered to give "informed advice and opinion" to the secretary of defense and his chief deputies. I knew Perle wasn't shy about giving advice, so what he told me was unsettling.

The advisory board, according to Perle that night, was already pushing a plan to take out Iraqi dictator Saddam Hussein. The idea was to use the buildup toward war against the Taliban in Afghanistan as a feint. While the rest of the world focused on Afghanistan, the U.S. military would make a surprise attack on Baghdad. Saddam's own generals and the Iraqi people wanted so badly to be rid of Saddam, Perle insisted, that we could do it on the cheap. He explained that we could take out most of Saddam's heavy artillery with guided weapons. Then, as I recall him telling me, we'd drop seventeen thousand paratroopers into Baghdad one night, capture or kill Saddam, and wipe out his Republican Guard. The regular Iraqi military would then rise up and support us. When Perle wanted to know what I thought of his "decapitation plan," I didn't know what to say. It sounded absolutely insane to me. But I was worried this plan might actually be under consideration at the Defense Department, so I called somebody on my foreign policy staff and asked him to run the plan by someone who knew both the military and the region. A former head of CENTCOM (United States Central Command) told us that the idea was crazy and naïve, militarily and strategically. *What would they do after they parachuted into Baghdad?*

That Saddam Hussein had nothing to do with 9/11 apparently mattered not a whit to Perle. But I also knew Perle had some sway with Rumsfeld, and I knew he had the respect of Rumsfeld's chief deputy, Paul Wolfowitz. If this was the sort of fairytale advice Bush was getting from the neo-isolationist side of the San Andreas fault, I prayed that Secretary of State Powell was being persuasive.

And from what I could tell, he was. Bush seemed completely focused on toppling the Taliban in Afghanistan and on catching bin Laden and wiping out his al-Qaeda units. The president made sure the other NATO countries were up to speed on our plans for invading Afghanistan, and he also made it a point to keep Congress in the loop. When I was in meetings with Bush in the immediate aftermath of 9/11, he displayed none of the chest-thumping arrogance that I half-expected. He solicited both information and advice. He wasn't shy to ask questions and didn't seem to worry that asking revealed a lack of depth or knowledge. I think everybody in those meetings with him understood we were dealing with a new and different reality, and even the experts didn't have all the answers yet.

Some of those sessions went more than an hour, with the president peppering people with questions. He was particularly concerned with how the "Arab street" might react to a military move against the Taliban; he was getting advice that they might burn down U.S. embassies from Tunisia to Jakarta. From what I knew from years of dealing in the region, I told him, I didn't believe the Arab street would rise up against us if we were smart. Afghanistan was a justified war—we had presented a persuasive bill of particulars against the Taliban and al-Qaeda—but we really needed to be mindful of the need for vigorous public diplomacy and the need to get our message out not just to government leaders across the Muslim world but to the street, too. The president even asked me to draw up a proposal for investing in the infrastructure—satellites, stations, and hardware—and in the development of a message we could broadcast to countries with heavily Muslim populations.

George W. Bush had a reputation for impatience, but in the weeks immediately following the 9/11 attacks, I saw a president who was rational, thoughtful, resolute, and balanced. I saw a president who went to the American people and to the entire international community and made a compelling case for action in Afghanistan. When he gave the go-ahead for military action to wipe out the Taliban power base in Afghanistan, he had already made all the right moves to ensure the success of the operation and the cooperation of the rest of the world.

Two weeks into the fight in Afghanistan, it was clear that the military campaign was going to be a success. At an event at the Council on Foreign Relations, I made it a point to praise President Bush on his actions since the 9/11 attacks. "The vast majority of the foreign policy establishment, on the Democratic and Republican sides of the aisle, in fact share the view that up to now the president's done a pretty darn good job of assembling this multilateral force, resisting what were very strong entrees from parts of the administration to by-pass Afghanistan and go straight to Iraq. I think he's done well."

When I talked that night about our obligations in Afghanistan, I was pretty sure I was echoing what I'd heard from Secretary Powell and the president himself.

We *cannot* and we certainly *will* not walk away from 7 million displaced and desperate Afghans. We must do more to help the Afghan people, and we must do *far* more to make our aid visible across the Muslim world. . . . In the long term, we need to find a way to break the hold that the madrassas have had on a generation of young men. They will need to educate a generation of young women, to give them the tools necessary to seize the rights so cruelly denied them under Taliban rule. They'll need to de-mine the most heavily mined nation in the world. They'll need crop substitution programs to rid themselves of the title of the world's foremost producers of heroin and opium. They'll need wells, water purification centers, hospitals, out-patient clinics—even simple roads from one town to the next. I commend the president for promising $320 million in Afghan aid. In my opinion, this might be the best investment we could make. I say this notwithstanding the obstacles to achieving these goals that exist in a region that has not proved fertile for incubating democratic institutions. Clearly, we cannot do it alone. As demonstrated since September 11, it's even more obvious, at least to me, that our national interests cannot be furthered, let alone achieved, in splendid indifference to the rest of the world. . . .

Out of our dark grief our nation is newly united, and abroad we have new opportunities. As my mother says, "Out of every tragedy, if you look hard enough, you can find one good thing" . . . but we cannot squander this opportunity. I believe this president has made a genuine transition in his thinking. I hope I am not kidding myself. If he has, I think not only will he go down as a great president, I think we will have marked the beginning of a new era in international relations.

* 17 *

The Dark

THE SUN-SILVERED HIMALAYAS SHIMMERED OUT THE WINDOW of our small plane as we flew across Pakistan, from Lahore to Islamabad. Even at twenty thousand feet above sea level, it looked like our plane was riding currents well *below* the highest peaks to the north. There was something ominous and slightly forbidding about those mountains, which only increased our sense of the difficulty of this trip. We were flying toward our ultimate destination of Afghanistan, but with less than full cooperation from the Pentagon. The Department of Defense had been making it clear they were not interested in escorting a bunch of congressmen and senators through the war zone in Afghanistan. When a small congressional delegation had landed at Bagram Air Base north of the capital city of Kabul a few nights earlier, the Pentagon had kept them on a tight leash. They were confined to the base for the five hours they were in country; the chairman of Afghanistan's new interim government, Hamid Karzai, had to drive from Kabul in an armored convoy to meet with the group. When the leader of the delegation, Senator Joe Lieberman of Connecticut, was later asked what he'd seen of Afghanistan, he said he hadn't seen much: "It was dark."

I could appreciate the Pentagon's arguments: In January 2002, the Taliban regime seemed to be finished, but small fighting units were still inflicting damage on coalition troops and Afghani citizens alike. Military commanders were generally skeptical about diverting even a sliver of resources to security for elected officials. But I believed it was important for the chairman of the Foreign Relations Committee to get a firsthand look at the situation on the ground in Afghanistan.

The reports I'd been getting were all good. Fighting alongside the Northern Alliance, U.S. and coalition troops ended the rule of the Taliban in Afghanistan in less than two months. By the first days of 2002 we were mopping up the military operation and securing the country. We'd helped the Afghanis establish a new government under Karzai and started a campaign to raise billions of dollars from other countries to finance reconstruction of Afghanistan. Secretary Powell was making very public declarations that the United States had an obligation to stay and rebuild. We weren't going to "walk away," Powell said, "or leave the Afghan people in a lurch." And President Bush was continuing his tough talk about bringing Osama bin Laden and al-Qaeda in to answer for the deaths of nearly three thousand innocent civilians in New York and Washington. The rhetoric was crystal clear: The Bush Administration was going to stay the course in Afghanistan and hunt down the men responsible for 9/11.

I wanted a clearer picture of the security situation in Afghanistan, and I wanted to see and hear what it would take to rebuild the Afghan government, infrastructure, and economy. You can learn a lot just by being there; picking up little shards of story from people just trying to live their lives always helps fill in the whole picture. I also believed it was important for a Democrat to sit with Chairman Karzai and personally assure him that both the reconstruction effort and Karzai's new government had bipartisan support in the United States. Finally, I wanted to hear straight from Karzai's own mouth what he needed to give his new government a chance to succeed.

So I had chosen to go to Afghanistan on my own, without a big military escort or the fanfare big congressional delegations always attracted. It was really the only way to get in. I figured I could move more freely with a small group, so I was accompanied by two Foreign Relations Committee staff members, Jonah Blank and Puneet Talwar; my press person, Norm Kurz; and two military aides. Secretary of State Colin Powell clearly wanted me to make the trip, because his trusted deputy, Richard Armitage, made sure we had the resources we needed from the State Department. With the help of the State Department and the blessing of the director of Central Intelligence, George Tenet, Puneet and Jonah had planned the trip and made the security arrangements. We'd flown the first part of the trip commercial—from the United States, through Manchester, England, and then into Pakistan. We were given a small government plane for our forty-minute hop along the foothills of the Himalayas from Lahore to Islamabad. From there we'd be getting seats on the United Nations flight to Bagram Air Base. There was only one round-trip flight a day from Islamabad to Bagram, and that flight operated only three days a week. So looking out toward the mountains as we flew toward Islamabad, we were all anxious to be there on time.

We made it with no problem and even had time for a quick briefing from our ambassador in Pakistan before hopping on the U.N. flight. Our two military liaisons were dropped off in Islamabad, after being told they were strictly forbidden to travel with us into Afghanistan. This was contrary to the normal responsibilities of military officers accompanying congressional delegations on foreign visits; ordinarily they would be required to stay with us throughout the visit. But their orders seemed consistent with the Defense Department's lack of enthusiasm about my trip. So we flew toward Bagram without our lone tie to the U.S. military late on the afternoon of January 10, 2002, another cold, raw day on the plain amid the mountains of east central Afghanistan.

Bagram had been a Soviet air base in the long war fought here in the 1980s. Osama bin Laden had been a minor figure (despite his later self-aggrandizement) among the mujahideen fighters who helped repel the hated Soviet army and helped put an end to the myth of the Soviet military's invincibility. President Reagan had called them freedom fighters. The Soviet MiG fighter jets we saw lying pitifully broke and abandoned at the edges of the runway in Bagram were like a monument to that victory. But while that war was a source of enduring pride for Afghans, the country itself had been devastated by the viciousness of the fight. People who could afford to gave up and got out. The economy was left in tatters; warlords ruled the countryside, and the feared Taliban had stepped into the power vacuum and installed a repressive, fundamentalist regime that had proved a danger to the citizens of Afghanistan and a breeding ground and training center for terrorists intent on making punishing attacks throughout the world.

As we touched down at Bagram, I wondered if Afghans, ravaged by twenty-three years of war, had the energy and resolve to turn a new page. By the time my short trip was over, it was not the resolve of the Afghans that worried me.

A well-armed security detail from State piled us into two Chevy Suburbans tricked out with armor plating that could withstand high-caliber bullets, we were assured. I'm not sure they were pleased to be escorting my party, but Secretary of State Colin Powell was due in town right after me, so they were probably using our party as a dry run. As we got on the road to the capital city, the head of our security detail made his welcome-to-Afghanistan speech. "The ride will take about an hour," he said. "Once we make it through the pass, it will be a quick shot down to Kabul. I don't expect any problems, but if our car breaks down or we come under attack, and we have to get out of the car, whatever you do, do not leave the blacktop, because every inch of the way to that pass is mined."

The road to Bagram cut through a fertile agricultural area called the Shomali Plain. We didn't see a single farmer at work; the towns that dotted the way were abandoned by all but a few. Occasionally, out of the desolation, we'd see two or three herdless herdsmen walking along the road—they knew to stay on the blacktop, too—or a few children out playing in a quieted village. Whenever we spotted people on top of the huts up ahead, our security detail got a little tight. I could see them gripping their weapons a fraction closer. As we neared the figures, they almost always turned out to be young kids at play.

The traffic picked up as we got into Kabul. There were a few other cars on the road, a lot of bikes, and many more pedestrians who seemed to be wandering in an aimless and formless procession. Mounds of sand-colored rubble littered the streets and sidewalks. The horizon was a mass of blown-out buildings, but every once in a while we'd see a metalworking shop, a bicycle shop, or a kerosene dealer. Groups of men and boys wrapped in thin blankets clustered alongside the road and huddled at a bonfire struck from new-cut wood. Sometimes smaller children would break from the groups and make a run at our SUVs. They jumped up and down, dangerously close to our moving vehicles, hoping for near-worthless currency or a small gift. Our security team let us know we weren't going to be stopping and we weren't going to be rolling down our windows. So we rode through the streets in our impenetrable four-wheeled cocoon until we finally pulled up to the U.S. Embassy. Eighty or so Marines had set up a se-

cure perimeter around the building; guard stations, multiple barri-
cades, and sandbags ringed the well-worn embassy.

The embassy had been shuttered thirteen years earlier, set afire by
the Taliban as the war started, and reopened only a few days before
our arrival. The newly installed U.S. chargé d'affaires and his staff
had set up an office in the bowels of the building, but no matter what
part of the embassy we were in, the sour stench was overpowering, as
if nobody had bothered to clean the refrigerators on the way out all
those years before. The only running water in the entire building was
a barely heated trickle in the basement bathroom; "bucket flushes"
were the best we could hope for. Tom Friedman, the *New York Times*
columnist who was with us for part of that trip, took one look at the
embassy and bolted for his newspaper's nearby guesthouse. But I got
my own room, with a cot set among desks, and slept pretty well that
night.

The next morning we piled into our Suburbans and headed for a
meeting at the Ministry of Education, passing by one ruined building
after another. We passed a still-standing housing complex built by the
Soviets while they occupied Kabul. Twenty thousand refugees—many
from the Shomali Plain—had apparently left their homes when the
war started and packed into the two five-story buildings. So I decided
to stop in and see if I could learn anything. Our security detail grudgingly agreed to drive me through the complex, but they were less encouraging when I asked to get out. Americans under their guard
didn't do things like this, they said. They pointed to the unsecured
rooftops and the open windows facing the courtyard, explaining that
they couldn't adequately secure the area. But I got out anyway, and
people milling around the muddy courtyard started to follow me,
until I found myself in the middle of the courtyard with hundreds of
Afghanis gathered around. I'm always amazed at how happy people
are to see Americans; no matter where I've gone, from Bosnia to
Chad, people in the worst refugee camps imaginable always *expect*
America to be able to make things better *for them*. This was one of
those times when I thought I could make the promise to help and be
backed by the full power of the U.S. government. But warm feelings
for Americans were hardly universal. When I bent over and reached
out to one little boy who looked to be about seven, he recoiled in fear.

I've seen worse camps, but the refugees in the Soviet complex were
living in squalor. Electrical power in Kabul was sporadic, so the build-

ings had no heat and no lights. Food was scarce, and water was always suspect. Security was spotty because there was no police force and no standing army. In fact, I'd soon learn that civil servants hadn't been paid in about six months. As on all the streets in Kabul, men and boys with automatic weapons hovered at the edge of the crowd—and it was hard to tell if they were there to keep the peace or disturb it.

The security detail seemed more and more nervous as the crowd grew around me. I didn't think they were going to allow me much time, so I got right to the key question I had for these refugees, given the way they were living: Did they want to go back home? What if we provided mobile homes for them back at their rural villages?

We're not going back home, they told me. *They're still out there, the Taliban. We're not going back there until we know the Taliban is gone.* A new government in Kabul didn't solve the big problem. As these refugees explained it, the Taliban fighters had simply changed their turbans, taken their weapons, and melted into the general population or decamped to the mountainous regions. And when the Taliban fighters came back, they'd have new scores to settle. The refugees from the Shomali Plain wanted badly to return home, but they weren't going anywhere until they were sure the Taliban fighters were done for good.

Just about then one of the men in our security detail caught my eye. "It's time to go," he said. *"Now."* When we got back in the car, he explained that he'd seen some nervous teenage boys at the edge of the crowd who had guns they didn't know how to handle. They were afraid an accidental discharge would make problems they didn't want to get involved in.

Back in the vehicle heading back toward the Ministry of Education, we passed the University of Kabul. Some of the warlords in Afghanistan had been to school here; the next day we'd meet a man who had studied literature but now commanded two thousand soldiers. Things didn't work out as he'd planned. The university had been mounds of rubble since the war with the Soviets. Kabul, like much of Afghanistan, was a moonscape. NATO and the United States took a lot of heat about the damage our bombing had done in Kabul and the rest of Afghanistan, but the truth is, the country was a bombed-out shell before we ever arrived. Decades of civil strife, failed regimes, and struggles for power had made Kabul, a proud old city on the ancient Silk Road, virtually unlivable. Our job was to put it back together; police, hospitals, and schools were the first place to start.

Rasul Amin, the minister of education, agreed to take us to a school that was already back up and running. A sea of mud surrounded the school building, and there was no electricity in the classroom. They depended largely on sunlight, which was scarce on this gray winter day. The children sat in one cold, dank room. The students were mixed together across ages because none of the girls and very few of the boys had been able to attend regular schools since the Taliban came to power. So the twelve- and thirteen-year-olds had no more math or writing skills than the six- and seven-year-olds. Their books were thin, crumbling paperback notebooks; math was illustrated with martial examples: literally, 1 tank + 2 tanks = 3 tanks. Bayonets, rifles, missiles, and other weapons filled the pages. But the feeling of energy in the classroom was an almost physical sensation. This was an opportunity that most of these children had never imagined, and they were thrilled to be able to tell us what they were learning.

It would take so little money and effort to fix the schools and give the students real textbooks that I began to get excited about the possibilities. I really saw that we could teach these kids to dream again. "Do you think girls can grow up to be president?" I asked the group, and they just giggled. After a short visit with the children, I heard somebody say, "Time to go, Senator," and as I stood to leave I told the kids, "I have to go now."

"You can't go!" I heard someone say.

I looked up and saw a thirteen-year-old girl standing ramrod straight in the middle of the classroom, so brave and so determined. "America can't go," she said. "I must learn to read. I will be a doctor like my mother."

I wanted to walk over and hug her.

"No. No. No, honey," I said. "America is going to stay."

When I pressed Minister Amin about what he needed most for the schools, he was firm and certain. Textbooks and electricity could wait. What they needed was security. Without it, nothing could be built. Without it, nobody would be willing to send their children to school.

After the trip to the school, we went to the presidential palace to make a courtesy call on Hamid Karzai. The palace was a big, beautiful structure with tons of carved pink marble and handsome rugs. But it, too, was down at the heels and cold. The cash-shy new government could only afford to heat Karzai's personal living space and his immediate offices. We were ushered upstairs and into the warmer parts of the building, and Chairman Karzai made his entrance there. He was an elegant and dignified man wearing a heavy silk robe. The robe itself was a statement of solidarity in a fractured Afghanistan. Karzai wasn't wearing the traditional silks of his own Pashtun tribe, but the sort of robe worn by tribes in the Tajik and Uzbek areas.

He took us into his personal office and gave us green tea and plates of assorted nuts. The day's meeting was supposed to be a short hello because we had an official talk with Karzai and the key allies in his new government the next day. But the chairman could tell by the way we tucked into the pistachios that we were hungry, and he insisted we have lunch with him, which turned out to be a remarkable two-and-a-half-hour visit. For a man who had just turned forty-four, he was remarkably self-possessed. He seemed happy to answer any questions we had. I was curious if the majority of Afghans saw the U.S. and NATO forces as liberators or as just another occupying force doing further damage to the country. Karzai told his own story. From the beginning of the war it was clear to the warlords and religious leaders all over Afghanistan that Karzai was America's man. So he started getting requests for meetings, and the one that concerned him most came from ten mullahs from Kandahar. Kandahar was a Taliban stronghold and a religiously conservative area where the mullahs were thought to be in sympathy with even the most repressive of Taliban initiatives. Karzai believed they'd be coming in to try to beat him up about his alliance with America. Still, Karzai told us, he felt compelled to have the meeting. He'd need whatever meager support they'd be willing to give. So he sat down with them near the beginning of the holy month of Ramadan, around the time the bombs began falling on the Taliban.

After the "usual ten minutes of Afghan pleasantries," Karzai told us, the lead mullah of the group stood up and started talking about the American bombing campaign. The mullah reached into the sleeve of his garment and pulled out a rough, hand-drawn map of a village and a nearby al-Qaeda ammo dump. Karzai said he was sure the mullah was about to tell him that the Americans would surely hit the village, full of innocents, or that they'd hit the munitions, and the villagers would be blamed and tortured by Taliban soldiers. Instead, the mullah handed the map to Karzai, pointing out the ammo dump. *"Here,"* he said. *"Tell the Americans to bomb right here."*

The next day Chairman Karzai assembled most of his cabinet for another long lunch meeting, and he was a generous host under difficult circumstances. His government simply lacked basic comforts. Karzai actually suggested we steer clear of certain dishes of foods being served that day. In the middle of our lunch meeting, the already dim lights went out entirely, and we found ourselves sitting for a few moments in the dark. Karzai's ministers complained that they couldn't pay any of their workers. They weren't even able to pay the waiters serving us lunch that day. One cabinet minister was just hoping to be able to buy a desk soon. Karzai was straightforward and unembarrassed: They were in desperate need of cash. He wanted money that he could disperse for reconstruction projects among the tribal and ethnic factions that formed the Northern Alliance—the Pashtun, the Shia Hazara, the Uzbeks, and the Tajiks. Each of the big warlords in Afghanistan had a state sponsor he could turn to, from Pakistan to Iran to Turkey, but now was the time to begin to pull them from those separate orbits and bring them fully into the new government of Afghanistan. And if USAID (the United States Agency for International Development) continued to bypass Karzai and hand out money to every warlord in the countryside, the chairman and his ministers argued, there would be no incentive for them to play ball with Karzai's new central government. It would be like our federal government bypassing governors and giving money locally; there would be no way to make a rational statewide plan. The way things were working now, it seemed to me, he'd soon be reduced to being little more than the mayor of Kabul.

The other thing they desperately desired was some measure of security, and not just in Kabul. They wanted Mazar-e-Sharif, Herat, Kandahar, and other key locations secured as well—and the overwhelming majority of Karzai's administration wanted a multinational force on the ground to do it. If we didn't secure those spots, the Taliban would find the weak spots, and they'd be back with a vengeance. Even prominent members of the proud and indigenous Northern Alliance knew the international security force was not just a sound idea but a popular one. The Afghans had a long and proud tradition of repelling occupiers from their land, but the United States and its allies were not seen as a force intent on ruling the country. One former Northern Alliance leader told us that if a referendum were held in Kabul that day asking whether people preferred an international security force or power vested in the hands of the Northern Alliance, the people would vote for the international force. After so many years of fighting, the Afghanis were war weary and wanted the United States to lead a multinational force in securing their broken cities and villages.

Mornings in Kabul were never easy. With more than eight Marines encamped in and around the embassy, bathroom space was limited. Invoking senatorial privilege didn't seem fair to the soldiers who were trying to do their job in a strange land a long way from home, so I took my bucket of water and stood in line waiting to shower and shave like everyone else.

There were two striking things about the servicemen and servicewomen I met on the trip to Afghanistan. First, their morale was incredibly high. There was a real sense of mission among these soldiers. A story I heard from a young major from Delaware sort of encapsulated the spirit of our forces there. A pediatric hospital in Kabul lost power when its generator broke down, and the needed parts could not be purchased. Neither the Karzai government nor the U.S. Embassy could figure out how to come up with the $320 they needed to buy the replacement part. So while the patients in the hospital suffered, the Marines passed the hat, raised the money, got the part, and fixed the generator. They saw a problem and remedied it the quickest way they could.

The other thing the soldiers told me, up and down the chain of command, was that they needed more forces. The British were in charge of securing the city of Kabul, and the commander in charge of the International Security Assistance Force there, Major General John McColl, briefed me on the security situation. I had a sense of the difficulties from what I'd already seen on the streets, and McColl and his number two, whom I'd met in Kosovo a few years earlier, confirmed my unease. They put up maps of the city and gave us a quick tour of the ethnic and tribal breakdowns of the neighborhoods; then they showed us how the Brits, the French, and the Germans had divided responsibility by zones. General McColl was confident that the city could be secured so reconstruction and restoration could begin, but he was very clear that he needed more forces to nail it down and maybe more time than people first thought.

When I asked him how long he thought Parliament would be willing to keep their troops on the ground in Afghanistan, he said that depended largely on American resolve. *They're not going to let us stay unless the Big Dog is in the pen,* he said. *You guys pull out, we're not going to have support to stay.*

By the time we left Kabul for the ride back to Bagram, I was a lot more hopeful about the possibility of securing and rebuilding not only Kabul but large parts of the rest of Afghanistan. The project seemed to have strong international support, and Karzai showed wisdom, strength, and integrity. He had managed to deal the various tribes and ethnicities into the new government; they all had a stake in making it work. I believed if we supported Karzai and listened to what he needed, we could make this country safe and whole again.

Back at Bagram the next morning, I got a clearer sense of the progress of the pursuit of Osama bin Laden and al-Qaeda. Military officials there escorted me to a then classified facility where MPs were holding enemy prisoners captured in Afghanistan. The prison was a big beat-up hangar with the doors blown off, and once we got inside and my eyes adjusted to the low light, I could see an office up above with guards and sharpshooters lining the perimeter, looking down on their quarry—about 120 prisoners sprawled out on the big rectangular floor space. The floor was cut into a grid, and each section had a wooden plaque bearing its name: *Camp New York. Remember 9/11.* These were al-Qaeda fighters, the first I'd ever seen up close, and they looked like badasses. As I passed on the outskirts of the grid, many of the prisoners stared directly at me. None of them cowered. I've been in a lot of prisons, but these guys showed a ferocity and a hatred unlike any I'd ever seen.

The conditions were stark. Each POW was required to confine himself to his own four-by-eight-foot mat. They were fed and given blankets and coats to keep warm, but there was no heat in the open hangar. If they wanted to use the bathroom, there was a latrine up front. I suppose that these were some of the same guys who ended up in the military prison in Guantánamo.

After that little sightseeing tour, I was escorted to the facility where the al-Qaeda chasers were at work. The general in charge had set up an enormous open table, and he made the lead guy from every agency

322   ★   *Promises to Keep*

sit at the table. CIA, FBI, and military intelligence were all there, looking over one another's shoulders. There were no stovepipes; no one could keep information from the group. The laptops were all on the table. Everyone knew what everybody else was doing, and everyone knew what everybody else knew. That was the first time I'd ever seen that level of enforced information sharing, and it was the right way to do it. They had maps up on the walls tracking the progress of the Special Operations Forces on the hunt. The commander could point to the map and tell me where they had a patrol in Tora Bora. *We have 16 guys down in this area by the Pakistani border. We have 120 guys here.* They were all chasing bin Laden, and the commander really thought they could get him.

The men in that room also wanted more boots on the ground because there was a lot of difficult terrain to cover. They thought we should be internationalizing the operation and increasing the troop level. The French and Germans were among the countries offering to help with the pursuit. Apparently, Defense Secretary Donald Rumsfeld was blocking that move. He was making the argument that if we increased the number and internationalized, our ability to move would be somehow constrained; we'd have to coordinate every move, and that would slow us down.

We were scheduled to take the U.N.'s Sunday afternoon flight from Bagram back to Islamabad, but after making the drive from Kabul to the air base that morning, we started to hear rumors that the weather was so bad the plane wasn't even going to leave Islamabad. The fog hanging over the runway didn't give us much hope, but after about an hour waiting around, we heard sounds of an approaching jet. It was impossible to see the aircraft through the fog, and we listened as it circled once, then twice, then a third time before the pilots gave up and headed back to Pakistan. The next U.N. flight out was on Tuesday. We'd have to spend two more days in Kabul, and I was going to miss meetings with President Musharraf of Pakistan and Prime Minister Atal Bahari Vajpayee of India. Worse than that, there was no guarantee the fog would lift in a few days or a few *weeks*.

I went to the Marines operating the base and requested space on one of the next military supply planes that flew out of Bagram. We didn't need any special plane, I explained, just a few jump seats on a plane that was already leaving the airfield. A colonel arranged for us to get on the next one out. After a quick unscheduled trip back to

Kabul to do some television interviews, we found ourselves back at the airfield waiting for a C-130 cargo plane that was to land at ten that night and leave as soon as the supplies were off-loaded. The Marines explained the drill: Flight operations were bang-bang in Bagram because the Taliban fighters were still in the area taking pot-shots at aircraft. (I remember the words *Katyusha rocket* made a distinct impression at the time.) The Marines flew the cargo planes in under the cover of darkness, unloaded in a hurry, loaded up again, and then took off. It all happened in a matter of minutes; they never even bothered to shut off the engines.

We were waiting next to the runway at Bagram when the bad news came. Marine Colonel Bigelow told us what he knew. He appeared apologetic and slightly embarrassed, but he had his orders from on high: Senator Biden and his party were *not* allowed to fly on military transport. We were lucky to have access to a satellite phone, but I knew better than to call the Pentagon. So, standing in the cold just outside the colonel's operations trailer near a lonely tarmac in the middle of Central Asia, I called the Operations Center of the State Department and in less than a minute I had Secretary of State Colin Powell on the line. "Mr. Secretary," I said, "they said you kicked me off this plane."

"I didn't kick you off any plane," Powell said. "Rumsfeld! God-dammit!"

Then he asked me to put the colonel on the line. When we told Colonel Bigelow that the secretary of state was on the phone and would like to talk to him, the colonel came to attention at the mention of Powell's name, obviously thrilled to be speaking to the legendary man. "Yes, General," we heard him say. "No, General. . . . That's great, General." Bigelow came out of his tent grinning. Powell had called down to Central Command in Florida, and when he couldn't reach Secretary Rumsfeld, he beat up on Rumsfeld's deputy, Paul Wolfowitz, who approved our request. We were good to go.

So just before ten o'clock we were standing next to the tarmac in pitch dark. I couldn't make out the features of Puneet, Jonah, or Norm just a few feet away, but we did hear the engines of the cargo plane roaring onto the runway. As the Marines off-loaded the supplies, I noticed my guys hugging the men who had been our security detail throughout the trip; my staff members were so grateful, they were offering free lunches and an unlimited supply of beer when any member of the detail was next in Washington—a sentiment I shared. Then we were hustled onto the plane.

I was seated up in the cockpit near enough to see the night-vision goggles the pilots wore, and my staff guys—along with Tom Friedman—were strapped into red canvass jump seats. The airmen were moving in what seemed like perfectly controlled panic.

"What's going on?" Puneet asked out loud.

As we began our taxi down the runway with the cargo doors still open, somebody up by me answered him: "There's tracer fire just beyond the runway."

"What are we going to do?" Puneet said.

"Get the hell out of here!"

WHEN WE GOT back to Washington, I began to talk publicly about what needed to be done in Afghanistan. The headline was that so far Afghanistan was a real success. The Taliban appeared defeated, and we had al-Qaeda on the run. But I also made it clear that we had a long way to go and we had to act fast. We needed to get more U.S. forces on the ground. We needed to increase the international security force and get it out to the places where the warlords had long held sway; for this brief moment they would welcome outsiders. We had a lot of support all over the world, and we should be internationalizing the military effort, especially the chase for bin Laden. We needed his capture to be a success for the entire world. Rebuilding the Afghan infrastructure and economy wasn't like remaking Paris, but it would take real money and real commitment. And while we needed to hold the world accountable for reconstruction money, we couldn't wait for the international donor conference later that month; Karzai's interim authority needed some cold hard cash from the United States *now* so he could pay his civil servants and begin to provide things we take for granted here in America: electricity, food, clean water, and a prevailing sense of safety in the streets. If we didn't back our words of support with real deeds, we'd lose the support of the Afghan people. We needed to wipe out the poppy fields and give Afghani farmers a market for other crops.

The next time I saw President Bush, he was agreeable and still willing to listen; he was also noncommittal. When I pressed the need for more troops, he didn't sound encouraging. His people were telling him the Taliban were wiped out, perhaps, but those refugees from the

Shomali Plain I'd met knew better. *All due respect, Mr. President,* I told him, *but how many body bags did you count? You guys were saying the Taliban were thirty, forty, fifty thousand people. Okay, how many body bags. A thousand? Two thousand? Five? Where are they?*

Secretary of State Powell came back from his trip to Afghanistan a few days after me, and from what I was hearing, he was making similar recommendations to the president. In public the president was calling for a "Marshall Plan" for Afghanistan; he was saying we were going to finish the job. Armitage managed to get some cash to Karzai. There was talk that Powell's views were ascendant among Bush's foreign policy team. Reporters who called at the time were reminding me of my drumbeat of pre–9/11 criticism of the Bush administration on Star Wars and Kyoto and the rest. *Biden, weren't you wrong? This guy is a mainstream Republican internationalist. These guys are acting pretty well.* People were asking me if I thought the president had moved decisively out of the neoconservative unilateralist camp, and though I was encouraged, I couldn't say for sure. He seemed to be headed in that direction. I wanted to believe that he was moving that way. I certainly believed he was still in play.

That was a miscalculation.

Bush talk in January 2002 turned out to be the beginning of a pattern that would continue for the rest of Powell's tortured tenure in the Bush administration—a pattern I didn't fully see at the time. President Bush would give Secretary Powell the rhetoric he needed, but he was already surreptitiously giving Vice President Cheney and Secretary of Defense Rumsfeld the force and resources they requested for a new target. In essence, Powell and the State Department were as much in the dark as I had been on that sightless night on the tarmac in Bagram. As I look back on it, I have come to believe that no matter how close Powell was to the president, it seemed George W. Bush had a way of keeping his foreign policy hidden from his own secretary of state.

✳ 18 ✳

The Informed Consent of
the American People

IT STARTED TO COME CLEAR IN THE WEEKS AFTER I RETURNED: Bush was being swept away by the relatively smooth success in Afghanistan. Secretary of Defense Donald Rumsfeld seemed especially satisfied. He'd entered the Pentagon determined to remake the military into a fighting force that depended less on manpower and more on firepower. He was a great champion of expensive and lethal new weapons. Resistance to change was a given at the Pentagon. Nobody turned a battleship of that size and tradition very fast. I read somewhere that while I was giving a speech about terrorist threats on September 10, 2001, Secretary Rumsfeld was saying that the biggest threat to our national security was the Pentagon bureaucracy. But Rumsfeld appeared to me to be a guy who thrived on difficulty and conflict.

The attacks on September 11 gave him license to prove his point, and a test case. The force he sent into Afghanistan was a much smaller contingent than combat-tested officers such as General Powell would have sent in, but it worked in the short term. Big bombs and small troop force did the first job, which was to topple the Taliban, and the cost was minimal. Not a single American soldier was killed in combat from October through December 2001. And the "Arab Street" that had so worried the president didn't rise up in defense of the Taliban. But Bush's well-earned pride in that accomplishment started to harden into something less becoming.

The President continued to talk about his "Marshall Plan" rebuilding enterprise in Afghanistan, but the administration wasn't backing up the pledge with the necessary resources. The security forces didn't grow appreciably. I saw very little effort to reach out to other countries for help in the job. Rumsfeld continued to resist the notion of NATO forces joining the chase for bin Laden and refused to modify the rules of engagement to deal with the poppy fields and the heroin trade. What needed to be done on the ground to secure and rebuild Afghanistan was obvious. I'd seen it; Powell had seen it. Chairman Karzai and his ministers knew what needed to be done. The British general in charge of security in Kabul knew what needed to be done. So there was no doubt that Rumsfeld knew, too. But the administration just wasn't doing it. The Bush team was squandering an enormous opportunity.

I also noticed that there was less generosity to our allies. The Northern Alliance had fought hard and well, and NATO forces were indispensable. It was like Bush was back to going it alone again. The president had surprised just about everybody in Washington but the gurus at the conservative think tanks when he named the Axis of Evil—North Korea, Iran, and Iraq—and started making noise about the doctrine of preemption. And though Osama bin Laden and the Taliban were alive and well, there was starting to be chatter about the possibility of going to war in Iraq. The administration seemed uninterested in consulting with anybody in Congress, so at the end of February 2002 I started pushing a little bit. "This administration is, rightfully, very proud of how they've brought us from September 11 to the present day," I told the press. "I also think there's a little hubris at work here. . . . They're getting a little imperious about not sharing any ideas with anybody."

Not long after, the president invited me to the White House with other defense and foreign policy committee chairmen from both houses of Congress. But Bush was more on *send* than *receive*. At one point he focused in on me: *What's all this talk about hubris?*

I told the president that he was free to do what he wanted, but that he wasn't consulting with us at all these days. Bush started telling me that what I had just said wasn't true when Henry Hyde, a conservative Republican congressman and strong supporter of Bush, jumped in. *It is true, Mr. President,* he said. *I'm embarrassed in the Republi-*

*can caucus on Tuesdays. They ask me what the administration is
doing and I can't tell them. You don't talk to us anymore. Your people don't talk to us anymore.*

We'll take care of that, the president said. *Why don't you meet
once a week with Condi?*

No. Have her meet with Joe, Hyde said, shocking everyone in the
room. *He'll keep us informed.*

I did start meeting with National Security Advisor Condoleezza
Rice; she never really saw me once a week, and even when we did
meet, I didn't exactly feel like I was in the loop. I worked hard to keep
her informed about what I was doing with my Republican colleagues
on Foreign Relations, Chuck Hagel and Richard Lugar, to widen our
diplomatic dialogues with Iran and North Korea. I also kept her
briefed on what I was hearing in Afghanistan. I remember vividly
telling her that warlords were reasserting themselves, and we had to
do something to demonstrate our support of Karzai's central government. Otherwise, the warlords were going to go their own way and
the country was going to splinter again. She looked at me and basically said that the warlords have always been involved in Afghanistan
and there was nothing we could do about it.

I remember thinking, Whoa. Wait a minute. That's not what the
administration has been saying up to now. That pretty much ended
my hope that the White House was committed to help reconstruct
Afghanistan with a central government, a unified army, and an economy based on something other than poppy production. I walked out
of the office and said to my staff director on Foreign Relations that
the White House was changing policy.

Ever since my return from Afghanistan, a conversation I'd had
with one of Karzai's ministers had nagged at me. He'd been a little put
off that the administration had not given proper credit to the Northern Alliance's part in overthrowing the Taliban. He'd also been concerned that the United States was going to leave Afghanistan to its
own devices. The minister was pleased that the Taliban was out of
power but was worried that we'd declare instant victory and abandon
the new government and maybe come back with another three-week
blitzkrieg if the Taliban built back up enough to be a threat. He was
concerned that the United States was going to simply "drain the
swamp" when it filled up again. *We were with you,* he'd told me, *so
you've got to help us. And if you don't, we won't be with you next*

time. In January 2002, I felt comfortable reassuring the Afghan minister; I truly thought President Bush was going to do what he was saying—secure and rebuild Afghanistan. By the time I walked out of the meeting with National Security Advisor Rice a few months later, I was convinced the Bush administration was walking away from a promise.

Whatever Secretary Powell was saying at the time clearly wasn't getting through to the president. In fact, I thought the neoconservatives in the administration were very effectively seducing George W. Bush, essentially playing on his naïve belief that he could make us safe by spreading democracy around the world. So I had my staff begin educating me on what these neocons were all about. A couple of things were striking about the main practitioners within the Defense Department—led by Deputy Secretary Paul Wolfowitz. They were extremely intelligent and thoughtful people, and they had good intentions. Most were true believers in the mission of spreading democracy throughout the Middle East. They were also convinced that America had the wherewithal to do just that. It wasn't hard to see why an optimistic, ambitious, but woefully unprepared and uninformed president could get swept away by the vision. He just didn't know enough to know how hard that would be.

But I started to discern a dividing line within the Neocon camp as well, which separated Vice President Cheney and Defense Secretary Rumsfeld from the idealistic true believers. These two were more cynical in their views. They could give lip service to democratizing throughout the Middle East as long as it got them the military action they wanted, but they had no interest in expending serious resources to help a country like Afghanistan get up off its knees. Nation building, they made clear, was not on their agenda. They'd rather just come back in and "drain the swamp" whenever the Taliban began to look threatening again. When Senator Chuck Hagel and I introduced supplemental legislation for more money for Afghanistan, the administration argued against it.

As I read more of their seminal tracts, it became clear there was one place where the neocons found agreement, and that was in using force (and the threat of force) as the dominant tool in the struggle against terror. They really believed the way to avoid further and greater war was to exercise power in a way that frightened potential state sponsors of terrorists. What was the use of being the world's only military superpower, they asked, if political leaders were shy about demonstrating and exploiting our overwhelming force capabilities? "Shock and awe" was more than just a slogan. They believed they could scare rogue states into subjection.

Wolfowitz was constantly arguing that terrorists couldn't exist without state sponsors, that bin Laden and al-Qaeda had to have a state sponsor. They had strong theories about the terrible new world we lived in and identified the biggest threats—North Korea, Iran, and Iraq. Cheney even went so far as to trump up a false connection between Iraqi dictator Saddam Hussein and al-Qaeda's 9/11 plot. Toppling the Taliban had been a nice start for the Neocons, but they thought the way to handle the world's other malcontents and to avoid larger war was to take out one of the "axis of evil" leaders in a way that made the other malcontents quake. They wanted to leverage our nation's awesome military power in a way that sent a strong and unmistakable message: Enable terrorists and we'll wipe you out. And for many in the neocon movement, the effort to gather up allies and coalition partners in the war on terror only muddied the message. They figured that if we used our military power in the face of the disapprobation of the rest of the world, the dictators of potential rogue states would come to their senses. They'd understand that we meant business and wouldn't feel safe hiding behind European timidity or indifference. You're either with us, Bush liked to say of his "war on terror," or you're against us.

I thought the approach was enormously flawed. The facts on the ground showed that terrorist groups didn't base their training camps in countries with strong governments or dictators; they found safe haven in failed states and grew stronger in the vacuum of power. The other big mistake the neocons made, I believed, was to use threat and military force as the primary tool in the fight against terror. The aftermath of 9/11 had revealed a deep vein of sympathy for the United States in surprising places. My old teacher Governor Harriman would have seen this as an opportunity to engage. I was working hard with some of my Republican colleagues on the Senate Foreign Relations Committee to open a dialogue with our antagonists as well as our friends. With Condoleezza Rice's assent, Senator Hagel and I were working to reach out to Iran; Senator Lugar and I were talking about the need to engage directly with North Korea. We believed the only way to stop Kim Jong-Il from producing more weapons-grade plutonium was to start talks aimed at a nonaggression pact. That's what he really wanted. I was agitating to get the neocons to refrain from threatening "regime change," which turned out to be like asking a Catholic to renounce the Trinity.

In the meantime, because Bush had instructed Rumsfeld to start drawing up plans for the U.S. invasion of Iraq, there was a lot of noise about overthrowing Saddam Hussein. Of the three Axis of Evil countries Bush had identified, Iraq was the country that could put up the least military resistance, and I believed Cheney and Rumseld were pushing the president toward an invasion. The president had already laid out the Bush Doctrine, reimagining the rules for defending America: "For much of the last century, America's defense relied on the Cold War doctrines of deterrence and containment," he told the graduates of the United States Military Academy on commencement day, June 1, 2002, at West Point.

> In some cases, those strategies still apply. But new threats also require new thinking. Deterrence—the promise of massive retaliation against nations—means nothing against shadowy terrorist networks with no nation or citizens to defend. Containment is not possible when unbalanced dictators with weapons of mass destruction can deliver those weapons on missiles or secretly provide them to terrorist allies. . . . The war on terror will not be won on the defensive. We must take the battle to the enemy, disrupt his plans, and confront the worst threats before they emerge. In the world we have entered, the only path to safety is the path of action. And this nation will act. . . . Our security will require transforming the military you will lead—a military that must be ready to strike at a moment's notice in any dark corner of the world. And our security will require all Americans to be forward-looking and resolute, to be ready for preemptive action when necessary to defend our liberty and to defend our lives. . . . Along with our friends and allies, we must oppose proliferation and confront regimes that sponsor terror, as each case requires.

As they talked of preemptive action, administration officials were starting to build the case that Saddam Hussein was an imminent threat. After ten full years he was still flouting the U.N. demand that he disarm. We'd already had a briefing by DCI George Tenet and a few others concerning Saddam's stockpiles of weapons. There were tons of chemical and biological weapons as yet unaccounted for by the U.N. inspectors, and there were reports that he was trying to start up his moribund nuclear program. But Saddam had been pretty well bottled up by the world, and even if he were able to reconstitute a covert program to develop nuclear weapons, he was years away from having a bomb. I didn't think he posed any imminent threat, and I didn't think it was good policy to court war in Iraq to scare North Korea, Iran, Libya, and the like. So on July 31, 2002, I convened the Hearings to Examine Threats, Responses, and Regional Considerations Surrounding Iraq in the Senate Foreign Relations Committee. Like me, Republican Dick Lugar thought it was important to open up a national dialogue on Iraq to help inform all Americans. We meant to take a cold-eyed look at the threat that Saddam represented to the United States and our allies, the possible responses to that threat, and the consequences of pursuing each. "We have to ask how much military intervention would cost and consider its likely impact on our economy," Senator Lugar and I wrote in a joint op-ed on the opening day of the hearings. "And we need to determine what level of support we are likely to get from allies in the Middle East and Europe. . . . When Saddam Hussein is gone, what would be our responsibilities? This question has not been explored but may prove to be the most critical."

A month earlier the president had personally assured me "there is no plan" to take down Iraq, and I was confident Secretary of State Powell was trying to dissuade the president from an invasion. Powell played his cards close to the vest, and we didn't talk often, but sometimes when we'd discuss the reasons against the invasion, he'd say to me, *Call the president. Tell him what you just told me.* Still, I had the sense that Powell was losing ground. Ten days after Bush had told me there was "no plan," the *Washington Post* reported that the president had already "signed an intelligence order directing the CIA to undertake a comprehensive, covert program to topple Saddam Hussein, including authority to use lethal force to capture the Iraqi president." So I didn't ask the administration to send any witnesses, because I didn't want to force their hand. My intention in holding the hearings was to make public the disincentives to going to war in Iraq. I didn't want the president to get locked into going to war.

The two days of expert testimony were a good start at educating the country about the monumental difficulties of opening up another military front. I'll never forget the end of the closing statement of Anthony Cordesman, an expert on military strategy and the Middle East: "To be careless about this war, to me, would be a disaster. I am reminded of a quote about two thousand years old by [Bion of Smyrna]: 'Small boys throw stones at frogs in jest, but the frogs do not die in jest; the frogs die in earnest.' This is not a game, and it is not something to be decided from an armchair."

The strong consensus among weapons experts and former inspectors was that Saddam was not an imminent threat to the United States; he was five to ten years from a nuclear weapon. (If we wanted to worry about loose nukes, we should be worried about what was lying around in the former Soviet Union.) Nobody doubted the U.S. military's ability to dethrone Saddam fairly quickly, even given the dangers of chemical or biological weapons attacks, but the witnesses made it clear that we couldn't count on the sort of coalition we had in the Gulf War, and probably not even on the international support we had in Afghanistan. Turkey, which would be an important ally, was unlikely to be much help. Even our strong ally in the region, Saudi Arabia, wasn't going to put up real money. There remained strong international support for keeping Saddam in his box, but not for expending blood and treasure to overthrow his regime.

The most prescient testimony was about the aftermath of an invasion. Allies of the Iraqi exile Ahmed Chalabi offered reassuring assessments of the political situation on the ground. They said that we'd be treated as liberators, and that vast numbers of Iraqis would welcome the leadership of the Iraqi National Congress, Chalabi's exile government in waiting. But that view was not widely held among the people who knew the region. "We must be prepared to occupy the country and stay there for a very long time at very great expense in treasure but also in risk to lives," a senior fellow from the Council on Foreign Relations told the committee. ". . . A democratic Iraq of the kind that we talk about after Saddam will come about only if we are prepared to stay there for a very long time, accepting, in my view, very great risk of casualties and a threat to the territorial integrity of Iraq. A democratic regime is not going to have the capacity to keep that country together unless there is an American military force in the country that insists that it stay together, and we have to think about whether we really want to be the instrument." He thought it might require twenty years of American troops in Iraq. An informed economist thought the cost to reconstruct Iraq could run about $300 billion. Iraqi oil production would cover a fraction of those costs. And few thought we would be getting a lot of money from the rest of the world.

The experts foresaw real problems in the immediate aftermath of toppling Saddam. "If firm leadership is not in place in Baghdad on the day after, retribution, score-settling, and bloodletting, especially in urban areas, could take place," Professor Phebe Marr testified. The executive director of the Iraq Foundation predicted confusion but not chaos in the aftermath. "The system of public security will break down because there will be no functioning police force, no civil service, and no justice system. . . . It will be extremely important, both politically and operationally, to jump-start the Iraqi economy as quickly as possible and create opportunities for employment and to raise the standard of living in Iraq in a visible way. I cannot stress enough how important it is for Iraqis to see that their lives are better and not worse in a tangible, material way."

"Mr. Chairman," Senator Lugar said in the hearings, "let me just say that the testimony has led me to believe, first of all, that the need for planning in other parts of our government, in addition to the Defense Department, is extremely important. . . . Our efforts in Iraq cannot stop after the threat has been removed. It is in our national interests that a stable, peaceful Iraq emerges. I'm suggesting, to be provocative today, that we do have a plan. It must be more than a military plan, and it must result in attracting a broad coalition. If our statesmanship is adept, we will have the Russians aboard, the French will be with us, so will a lot of other people, and we will deal with the Iraq problem together."

One of the starker observations from the hundreds of pages of testimony was little more than an aside. "If the issue is about terrorism," said one Middle East expert, "then we have to remind ourselves that this is not likely to eliminate the motivation for terrorism in the Middle East. It may even increase it."

I worried above all that a war in Iraq would follow the Afghanistan model—quick victory and marginal efforts to secure and rebuild.

Given what Cheney and Rumsfeld had done in Afghanistan, I just didn't have confidence that the two men had any intention of doing what had to be done to reconstruct Iraq. I worried that it might become a second swamp they'd occasionally drain. "Given Iraq's strategic location, its large oil reserves, and the suffering of the Iraqi people, we cannot afford to replace a despot with chaos. It would be a tragedy if we removed a tyrant in Iraq," I said in the hearings, "only to leave chaos in its wake."

The hearings did start some discussion; and a lot of foreign policy adults weighed in. While Bush spent most of August on a working vacation at his ranch in Crawford, Texas, his father's former confidants began offering advice through the op-ed pages. Weeks after the hearings ended, George Herbert Walker Bush's national security advisor, Brent Scowcroft, cautioned the younger Bush in an editorial in the *Wall Street Journal*. "There is scant evidence to tie Saddam to terrorist organizations, and even less to the Sept. 11 attacks," Scowcroft wrote. "Indeed Saddam's goals have little in common with the terrorists who threaten us, and there is little incentive for him to make common cause with them. He is unlikely to risk his investment in weapons of mass destruction, much less his country, by handing such weapons to terrorists who would use them for their own purposes and leave Baghdad as the return address."

James Baker, the elder Bush's secretary of state, cautioned the president to build strong support in the world before he took on Saddam: "The costs in all areas will be much greater, as will the political risks, both domestic and international, if we end up going it alone or with only one or two countries."

Dick Lugar and I both felt the hearings had been a success—maybe too much of a success. On August 26, at a speech to the Veterans of Foreign Wars, Vice President Cheney began a public campaign to counter the case we'd made in the hearings, playing on irrational fears about Saddam Hussein's weapons capabilities and his intent to use them.

The Iraqi regime has in fact been very busy enhancing its capabilities in the field of chemical and biological agents. And they continue to pursue the nuclear program they began so many years ago. These are not weapons for the purpose of defending Iraq; these are offensive weapons for the purpose of inflicting death on a massive scale, developed so that Saddam can hold the threat over the head of anyone he chooses, in his own region or beyond. . . . Many of us are convinced that Saddam will acquire nuclear weapons fairly soon. . . . Simply stated, there is no doubt that Saddam Hussein now has weapons of mass destruction. There is no doubt he is amassing them to use against our friends, against our allies, and against us.

The divide between Powell and Cheney-Rumsfeld seemed wider than ever, and I couldn't tell for sure where the president was. Cheney's relationship with Bush was interesting to watch. You're in the room with the two of them, there's no doubt who's in charge—and that's George W. Bush. The president treats Cheney in much the same way he treats his Cabinet, his staff, and everybody in his orbit. I would not have been shocked to hear Bush say, "Dick, get me a cup of coffee," and see Cheney jump up and ask how he wanted it. When I was in meetings with the two of them, Cheney rarely spoke. He just sat like a bullfrog on a log, listening. But when everybody else left, Cheney stayed behind. I always assumed he gave the last words of advice.

With Bush at the center, the administration was still sending mixed signals. The president did make a strong step in the right direction by going to the United Nations on September 12 to make his case that the world had an obligation to make Saddam Hussein live up to his commitment to disarm following the Persian Gulf War in 1991. The *Washington Post* praised President Bush for challenging the United Nations to act: "To be meaningful, or credible in Baghdad," said a *Post* editorial, "any new action [by the United Nations Security Council] must set a deadline and authorize force in the event of defiance." I offered my public support of the president because I thought he did the right thing to call out Saddam. If international law was to mean anything, then it was time for the United Nations to enforce the ten-year-old resolution that called for Iraq to disarm in a way that could be verified by U.N. inspectors. "For more than a decade, Saddam has flouted the will of the international community, repeatedly reneging on his commitment to destroy Iraq's weapons of mass destruction capabilities," I said the day after his speech. "The president did the right thing by going to the United Nations and reminding it that Saddam Hussein is the world's problem and the U.N. has the obligation to act."

Around that time, some State Department officials started confiding their concerns about Cheney, Rumsfeld, and the neocons at Defense. "Damn those guys across the river [at the Pentagon]," one high-ranking State Department official complained to me on the phone. "They're f***ing nuts. They're crazy." But I still had confidence that the president could recognize what those officials at the State Department did and that Secretary Powell and high-ranking generals at the Pentagon could keep Bush from going to war unnecessarily in Iraq.

About a week after Bush's visit to the United Nations, the White House sent to Congress a draft resolution they wanted passed: "The President," it said, "is authorized to use all means that he determines to be appropriate, including force, in order to enforce the United Nations Security Council Resolutions referenced above, defend the national security interests of the United States against the threat posed by Iraq, and restore international peace and security in the region." The language was expansive; it literally meant that even after Saddam Hussein disarmed, the president could go to war over the refusal of Iraq to return prisoners from Bahrain. One of my Republican colleagues on the Foreign Relations Committee, Chuck Hagel of Nebraska, could only shake his head at the breadth of latitude the White House was asking Congress to deliver to the president. "It said the whole region!" Hagel would tell a reporter a few years later. "They could go into Greece or anywhere. Is central Asia in the region? I suppose! Sure as hell it was clear they meant the whole Middle East. It was anything. It was literally anything. No boundaries. No restrictions." Just prior to this, the White House was considering bypassing Congress. The White House counsel, Alberto Gonzales, had already sent a memo telling the president that he did not need a congressional resolution to take military action in Iraq.

Hagel, Lugar, and I immediately began working on a resolution with language that gave the president authority to use military force to disarm Saddam *only* if the Iraqi dictator refused to honor the U.N.'s demands that he disarm—and *only* after all other options had been exhausted. Our draft resolution obliged the White House to report its diplomatic progress at the United Nations to Congress and to make a hard case that Saddam's weapons were a "grave threat" to the

United States if he intended to go to war without the U.N.'s support. We also called for the White House to report to Congress his success in obtaining allies for any military action in Iraq. After sitting through the previous summer's hearings, the three of us wanted to make damn sure the American people understood the true costs of President Bush choosing to take us to war in Iraq. I wanted to make sure people knew about the dollar costs of military action—which the White House economic advisor had put at between $100 billion and $200 billion (a statement that cost him his job). Based on what I'd heard at our Foreign Relations Committee hearings, the price of securing the peace would be considerably higher. Given Bush's big tax cut, there would be a lot of domestic programs we would have to forgo—or considerable debt to pass down. The American people had the right to that information. And what Americans really deserved to know in weighing the options was how long we might find ourselves in Iraq. "We must be clear to the American people that we would be committing to Iraq for the long haul," I'd been saying since the hearings. "The 'day after' may well be the 'decade after.' "

The Biden-Lugar resolution picked up fans in a hurry. "Mr. Bush ought to accept it," the *Washington Post* said in an editorial on October 2, 2002. "It would unite Congress behind him and offer a responsible way forward. . . ." But when it became clear to the White House that our resolution was beginning to get strong bipartisan support in the Senate, Bush and Cheney (I learned much later) called on Trent Lott, the Republican leader: "Bush's order to me grew more emphatic," Lott wrote in his autobiography. "*Derail the Biden legislation,* he directed me, *and make sure its language never sees the light of day.*" He says he was also asked to make Dick Lugar see the White House point of view. About ten o'clock one night I got a call at home from Lugar, who wanted me to know that Bush administration officials had prevailed upon Democratic congressman Dick Gephardt to help them draft a more White House friendly resolution. Lugar said Lott and Bush were trying to pull him from our own resolution, but he implied that he was staying on. The Gephardt compromise language was moving fast, he told me, so he thought we had better pass Biden-Lugar out of the Foreign Relations Committee and to the full Senate at our regular business meeting the next day, or we might start to lose some of the Republicans who were ready to support us.

In order to get the resolution out of committee, I needed Democrats to vote for it. So I called Majority Leader Tom Daschle and asked him to host a meeting of the Democrats on the committee, which he did. We met in the majority leader's conference room the next morning, and I made my pitch for Biden-Lugar, pointing out the very real constraints it put on the president. Leader Daschle backed me. But Paul Wellstone of Minnesota said that as a matter of principle he couldn't support my resolution. The rest of the liberals on the committee said essentially the same thing. Sitting at the table I started to hear the lectures about principles.

Spare me the lectures, I said. *I thought our objective is to do all we can to avoid an unnecessary war. And you're telling me that if we give the president this authority, which radically constrains him compared to the resolution we're going to have to vote on, that you're being principled? Does anybody here think the White House doesn't have fifty-five votes for their resolution if we don't have an alternative?* I begged them to at least vote Biden-Lugar out of committee, but they made it clear they wouldn't do it—on principle. They wanted purity. I knew that if I didn't produce a large majority of Democrats, the more conservative Republicans would desert Biden-Lugar.

In the meantime, Senator Joe Lieberman signed on to the language that Gephardt had worked out with the White House. The Bush team got a lot of what they wanted, but not everything. Those of us who preferred the Biden-Lugar language were disappointed, but the president was giving personal assurances that he would try every avenue of diplomacy before he took the country to war. And it was clear that Powell and members of the Joint Chiefs were not eager to go to war in Iraq.

With that in mind, I decided to vote for the resolution. I said in my floor statement on October 10, 2002:

> We should support compelling Iraq to make good on its obligations to the United Nations—because while Iraq's illegal weapons of mass destruction programs *do not* pose an imminent threat to our national security, they will if left unfettered, and because a strong vote in Congress increases the prospects for a tough new U.N. resolution on weapons inspections, which in turn decreases the prospect of war. This is not a blank check to use force against Iraq for any

reason. It is an authorization to use force, if necessary, to compel Iraq to disarm, as it promised to do after the Gulf War. . . . This resolution does not make Saddam's removal its explicit goal. To have done so would risk alienating other countries who do not share that goal and whose support we need to disarm Iraq and, possibly, rebuild it. It would weaken our hand at the United Nations. . . . The United States has a singular capacity to act alone if necessary. We must—and this resolution does—preserve our right to do so. But acting alone in Iraq would cost us significantly more in lives lost, in dollars spent, and in influence dissipated around the world. Acting alone must be a last resort, not a defiant retort to those not yet convinced of our policy. . . . I also believe that we have time to deal [with Iraq] in a way that isolates Saddam, not the United States; that makes the use of force the final option—not the first one; that produces the desired results, not unintended consequences. . . . It is incumbent upon the United Nations and the United States Congress to help [the president] stay the course. The U.N. Security Council must deliver a tough new resolution that gives the weapons inspectors the authority they need to get the job done. The resolution should set clear deadlines for compliance. And it should make clear the consequences if Saddam Hussein fails to disarm, including authorizing willing U.N. members to use force to compel compliance. . . . It is also critical that Congress send the right message to the United Nations Security Council. Its members must not doubt our determination to deal with the problem posed by Iraq's weapons of mass destruction, including our willingness to use force if necessary. The stronger the vote in favor of this resolution, the stronger the likelihood that the Security Council will approve a tough resolution.

I believed the resolution passed by Congress provided the firm and united support Secretary of State Powell needed to be able to get the United Nations Security Council to pass and enforce a new resolution that got the inspectors back into Iraq, kept Saddam in his box, and thus avoided a war. I wasn't alone in that. I remember a call from Powell months after the vote when he was pushing to get a second United Nations resolution against Saddam Hussein. Powell had already unanimously won passage of a forceful resolution in the U.N.

Security Council in November 2002; his effort in the United Nations had been masterful and would turn out to be a true high point in the Bush presidency. A second resolution was going to be hard to get— and the hawks in the administration were not happy with the effort— but Powell wasn't giving up. *We might get this done,* Powell said to me in a determined tone. *We might be able to avoid a war. How bad would that be?*

★ 19 ★

My Mistake

I MADE A MISTAKE. I UNDERESTIMATED THE INFLUENCE OF Vice President Cheney, Secretary of Defense Rumsfeld, and the rest of the neocons; I *vastly* underestimated their disingenuousness and incompetence.

So George W. Bush went to war again, and just the way the neocons wanted him to—without significant international backing. The administration had not assiduously sought the support of the rest of the world, and it had not sought the informed consent of the American people. Vice President Cheney was banking largely on the support of the Iraqi people. "If your analysis is not correct and we're not treated as liberators but as conquerors, and the Iraqis begin to resist, particularly in Baghdad," Tim Russert asked the vice president on *Meet the Press* three days before the invasion began, "do you think the American people are prepared for a long, costly, and bloody battle with significant American casualties?"

Cheney said in reply:

Well, I don't think it's likely to unfold that way, Tim, because I really do believe that we will be greeted as liberators. I've talked with a lot of Iraqis in the last several months myself, had them to the White House. The president and I have met with them, various groups and individuals, people who have devoted their lives from the outside to trying to change things inside Iraq. And like Kanan Makiya, who's a professor at Brandeis, but an Iraqi, he's written great books about the subject, knows the country intimately, and is a part of the democratic opposition and resistance. The read we get on the people of Iraq is there is no question but what they want to get rid of Saddam Hussein, and they will welcome as liberators the United States when we come to do that.

Unfortunately, the Bush administration wasn't really talking to anybody inside Iraq. They were talking to Ahmed Chalabi, the Iraqi exile who ginned up evidence about the viability of Saddam's weapons programs and flat-out lied that his return with the American forces would be met with widespread approbation among the Iraqi population. I had been hearing the whispers that the Rumsfeld-Cheney-Wolfowitz axis had bought the Chalabi intelligence wholesale. Soon after the American forces took Baghdad and toppled the statue of Saddam, the consequences of relying on the unreliable Chalabi became apparent. We had plenty of troops to defeat the Iraqi army and not half enough to keep the peace. Secretary Rumsfeld simply had not made a plan for securing Iraq; he had ignored the Senate Foreign Relations Committee's recommendation that we would need five thousand to six thousand trained paramilitary police in the aftermath of the war. As the looting began in Baghdad, Rumsfeld waved it off. "Stuff happens!" he said at a press conference. "Freedom's untidy, and free people are free to make mistakes and commit crimes and do bad things. They're also free to live their lives and do wonderful things, and that's what's going to happen here."

A few days later I made a call to one of my key foreign policy staffers, Puneet Talwar, and caught him at a surprising place—the office where Paul Wolfowitz had convened a group of Iraqi expatriates to set up a postwar government operating out of Baghdad. My staff had been monitoring the postwar planning, but the existence of this facility had only come to Puneet's attention a few weeks earlier when somebody gave him a tape of a *60 Minutes* interview where Wolfowitz mentioned the group. It took Puneet nearly two weeks to get access to the facility, a well-kept secret that was an entire floor in one of the many defense contractor buildings in Crystal City. I just happened to call Puneet as he was making a tour there, and he was obviously alarmed by the amateurish goings-on. There were cubicles and partitions everywhere, he explained, sectioned into the various ministries-to-be in a new Iraqi government that would presumably be run by Chalabi. Letter-sized printer paper, turned horizontally, was taped to partition walls at fairly even intervals, announcing each office: MINISTRY OF DEFENSE, MINISTRY OF FINANCE, MINISTRY OF THE INTERIOR, and so forth. Puneet managed to talk to some of the expatriate "planners," though a number had already embarked for Kuwait. Emad Dhia, for instance, would soon be heading up a group in the U.S. Embassy called the Iraq Reconstruction and Development Council. The expatriates who remained were clearly pleased by Saddam's ouster, but their planning had only started in the months leading up to the March 2003 invasion and they didn't seem to know much about the functions of the various ministries to which they were going to be assigned in Baghdad. And none of them had the foggiest notion about the conditions on the ground in Iraq—either pre- or postinvasion. At that time Baghdad was burning. In fact, most government ministries were looted and still smoldering. So, these guys were getting ready to run or "advise" ministries that were being destroyed as they made their plans. These people, Puneet would say, "were not ready for prime time."

None of these Defense Department–sponsored people knew anything about the extensive study and plan for postwar Iraq prepared by the State Department. And nobody among Wolfowitz's shambling cadre of expats knew a thing about the State Department's proposed political plan for postwar Iraq. The United States was at war, and the San Andreas fault line that split the Bush administration's foreign policy team was wider than ever. But it now seemed clear where the president stood. Bush essentially put State on the sidelines in Iraq and handed Rumsfeld and Defense the task of securing and rebuilding. The shame was that the Senate Foreign Relations Committee and the State Department had predicted many of the problems we face today: the sorry state of the Iraqi infrastructure; the likelihood of postwar looting and resistance; the impossibility that Iraq's oil revenues would pay for reconstruction; the need for five thousand international police to help train the Iraqis; and, perhaps most lamentably, the folly of relying on exiles with no constituency in Iraq.

I never believed neocons like Wolfowitz were bad people; they had the best of intentions, and they truly wished to help the Iraqi people. Iraq and the rest of the world were better with Saddam deposed. But they seemed so absolutely in thrall to the ideological concepts they'd dreamed up in their think tanks over the past twenty years that they were completely untethered from the facts on the ground.

Jay Garner, who was put in charge of Iraq in the first weeks after Saddam's overthrow, started telling people that if the White House did have any plans to secure and rebuild Iraq, nobody shared them with him. Meanwhile, the USAID administrator was publicly claiming that we could rebuild Iraq at a cost of $1.7 billion. "That is our plan," he said.

On May 1, 2003, President Bush flew to an aircraft carrier in the peaceful waters off San Diego and—with a banner announcing MIS-SION ACCOMPLISHED behind him—announced that major combat operations in Iraq were over. Less than a month later the president announced, "We found the weapons of mass destruction." He was wrong.

When the man Rumsfeld picked to succeed Garner came to see me, I got really worried. He started off the meeting explaining to me all about Iraq and just what he was going to do to take the situation in hand. Paul Bremer was convinced about what he needed to do as the head of the Coalition Provisional Authority in Iraq, but his approach appeared to me to be wholly unburdened by any actual knowledge of the situation there. There was still no evidence of any reconstruction plan, so Dick Lugar and I decided to take a trip to Iraq to see and hear what was happening there. We asked Senator Chuck Hagel to go with us.

One of the first meetings we had in Baghdad was with Paul Bremer. A big part of our conversation was on the difficult question of how to handle the Iraqi military. We were all worried that Bremer's recent decision to disband the military would create a group of angry, unemployed men with military training. Bremer told us he'd recently decided to restore salaries to some of the lower-ranking officers, but not to recall the army. So now, I figured, we had angry, unemployed, *paid* men with military training. Then Bremer started talking about his plan to sell off state-owned industries, which seemed to me a benighted ideologically based decision that turned Iraq into an instant laboratory for Reaganomics in the Middle East. This made no sense at all; Iraq was little suited to this approach, and I thought the decision was apt to swell unemployment and provide more potential recruits for the insurgency.

At one point in the meeting I got fed up with Bremer's certainty about his own plans. *You've got a really tough job,* I told him. *If the Lord Almighty came down and gave us sixty percent of the right answers, we'd still have a less than even chance of making this work.* But Bremer was undaunted. He continued on, highlighting improvements in the security situation since he'd arrived in the country. In the two months since the statue fell, Bremer told us, the CPA had stood up thirty thousand Iraqi policemen. I was dubious; I'd spent enough time in Kosovo and Bosnia to know how long it takes to properly train police. So we made a visit to the Baghdad police academy to check on the progress. As we drove by the square where Saddam's statue had been toppled, I was thinking about our chances for a good outcome in Iraq. And I knew the Bush team would have to fundamentally change its plan if something good were to come of this invasion.

No matter what President Bush had done or whose advice he was taking, I wanted us to succeed in Iraq. Bush was the only one who could really make it happen. His success was America's success, and his failure was America's failure. In June 2003, I still thought we had an opportunity to leave Iraq better than we had found it. I never believed we could make a liberal democracy there, but I was convinced we could make a country with a loosely federated government in which all the major communities—Shia, Sunni, and Kurd—had a stake and a piece of the oil revenues; a country where the rights of the minority Sunni were respected; a country that was not a breeding ground or a haven for terrorists; and a country that was not a threat to us or its neighbors.

Taking a measure of the police force was, for me, the surest way to judge the first steps. I've long believed that security is the base requirement of any government. Everything follows from security. In its absence, reconstruction would not be able to go forward, and ordinary citizens would not put their faith in the government. In its absence, the very real fissures among the Iraqi population would become more pronounced. I was struck and cheered by the simple fact that few Iraqis went out of their way to identify themselves to us as Shia or Sunni on that first visit, but there were already Iraqi leaders exploiting sectarianism—to pull Shi'ites from Sunnis, Sunnis from Kurds, and on and on. We didn't have much time to get it right. And I was not heartened by what I saw at the main site of the police training.

Bernard Kerik was in charge of the training program at the time, but he was nowhere to be found. The physical plant of the place was the first red alert. The interior of the building was gutted down to the studs, with the electrical wiring and plumbing hanging out for all to see. One of the American officials at the facility explained the situation: Baghdad had had plenty of police before the war, but the veterans of that force would be little help because they were really just Saddam Hussein's well-armed goons. I recall the training official pointing to a five- or six-story apartment complex nearby and explaining that had there been a murder in that building, for instance, they'd put up a notice at the front desk of the building telling everybody to report to the police station. Anybody who didn't show up, Saddam's police would probably kill them. And everybody knew that. They were, we were told, little more than a hit squad. They had no investigative capacity. They had no patrol cars. There was no training along the lines we require of a police officer in the United States. Most didn't even know how to direct traffic.

When I asked how long it would take to stand up a force of seventy-five thousand professionals, I was told five years and five thousand more professional trainers. When I asked if they had adequate prison space, I was told it would take at least two years, maybe three, if the funding came through. At one point the trainees were called out to the parade grounds to give a little demonstration for us. As the orders were shouted in Arabic, the recruits fell in in an earnest but ragtag way. It would have been funny in a Keystone Kops sort of way had it not been so tragic. I couldn't help thinking that these men were either incredibly brave or absolutely desperate for a salary. I still think about them today, in their brand-new blue-on-blue uniforms, marching around that courtyard, and I've wondered how many of them are still alive; the police became the first and most visible targets of insurgents and sectarian militia groups. Before we left, we asked an Iraqi officer what they needed most. He told me they needed green uniforms.

"But you have brand-new uniforms," I said.

"Saddam's force wore green," he said. "People will only listen to us if we wear green."

I walked out of that police station worried about our prospects in Iraq. The early efforts were a disaster.

The United States and British forces were doing incredible work, but they simply didn't have enough troops to secure Iraq and keep its population safe. When we got back home I began agitating for more

forces in Iraq and better police training. I also called on the administration to ask other countries to share the extraordinary burden that
fell to our soldiers. Over the next year, on NBC, CNN, and the Senate floor, in Senate hearings, and in private meetings with administration officials, I spoke as loudly as I could, because I believed we didn't
have time to waste:

> Our experts tell us we need fifty-five hundred police now, European
> police. We need twenty-five thousand more troops now. And it ei-
> ther means they're going to be ours, ours alone, or we're going to
> do it with other people. And the only way you do it with other peo-
> ple is you want to share the burden, you got to share some of the
> decisions too. . . . There is a need for fifty-five hundred European
> crack police, *gendarmes,* to be brought in to maintain the peace and
> security for the citizens, stop the looting, make the traffic lights
> work, investigate the murders and the rapes, while we are training
> eighty thousand new police officers . . . so I implore the president
> to get over his feelings about the Europeans, the French, the Ger-
> mans in particular, and seek their assistance, because I believe they
> are ready to assist. They need to be asked. . . . We need another
> thirty thousand forces from other countries to help alleviate the
> strain on our forces. . . . We need more troops. We need more cops.
> We need more civilian affairs people. We were woefully unpre-
> pared, but we have incredible people there now. They don't have
> the resources.

I made another check on the police training program about a year
later, on a congressional trip led by Democratic Senate leader Tom
Daschle. Rumsfeld had boasted of having put 210,000 Iraqis—police
and army—in uniform, so I scheduled a visit to the main training facility, which by then was in the middle of the Jordanian desert. A private contractor was running the training program, and the officials
walked our congressional delegation through a big auditorium where
the new recruits were getting classroom training. In the classroom, inside this hangar, the echo was so bad it was hard to hear somebody
ten feet away.

We were briefed by a very able American woman and a Canadian
Mounted Policeman who were running the training there, as well as
an official from the Jordanian police who was there to assist. When

they started to tell us what a grand and successful program they were running, I cut them off, walked over, and closed the door. They'd been talking about a six- to eight-week training program to prepare these men for the streets. "Please don't do this to us," I said. "Okay?" Then I asked them to tell us the truth about the situation. They didn't have time to do real training. "This program's not worth a damn, is it?"

And one of them said, basically, "No, it's not."

For the police force in Jordan, recruits trained for five months; for the force in Canada, recruits trained for six months. And all over the world new police were mentored for at least six months by veteran officers. This program was simply inadequate.

Every eight weeks the trainers were to put a thousand Iraqis on planes and fly them to the training facility in Jordan. Out of a thousand scheduled to go, just more than seven hundred generally showed up. There were no physicals or psychological exams. Nine of every hundred recruits were illiterate. Occasionally they'd find out that one of the recruits was a convicted felon or even a murderer, and they'd have to send him back home, too.

We peppered the training officials with questions.

Do you know whether they report to the police stations?
No.
Do you have any follow-up mentoring?
No.
Do you have any notion what happens to them?
No.

They didn't even really know if the trainees ever made it to a police station at all. The training program officials confided that what they really needed was a sixteen-week schedule and a six-month follow-up mentoring program. At one point the Canadian thanked us for funding new automobiles for the Iraqi police. He said he had hoped to be teaching evasive driving here in Jordan, but most of the recruits had never driven, so mainly what they did was teach the men how to move the cars out of the road so they didn't block traffic.

In the spring and summer of 2004 the insurgency was surging. Deaths of American soldiers and Iraqi civilians were rising steadily, with no end in sight. The death toll for Americans was climbing toward a thousand. Still, Rumsfeld was insisting we were making good progress, and he continued to maintain that the United States had put 210,000 Iraqis in uniform.

There were times I really felt pangs of sympathy for the president. Not only was he uninformed and out of his depth, but the advisors he leaned on were cooking him. In the first place, Rumsfeld was making false and dangerous statements about security forces—and the statements were politically inane. If it was true that the Iraqis now had 210,000 security forces, I said at the time, why did we have 130,000 troops in the country? How could we justify sending America's sons and daughters?

Of course, a small percentage of American families were asked to sacrifice. The burden of the war was falling on the middle-class and poor Americans who make up the overwhelming bulk of the fighting forces in Iraq. The soldiers I met in the Middle East went to Iraq gladly and performed heroically in a deteriorating and frustrating situation. They were sent to Iraq ill-equipped, undertrained for the mission, and undermanned to counter an insurgency that the Defense Department bosses had dismissed. On one of my trips to Iraq I met a big bald-headed badass Marine officer who was trying hard to get more troops. "Damn these guys, Senator," he told me. "The first thing you learn in war college is counterinsurgency. Counterinsurgency—you sweep and hold. I'm sending these boys out there in Anbar Province, and they're kicking ass. They sweep through, clear the insurgents, and then they leave. We can't keep them there to hold the ground because we don't have enough troops. They can't occupy. They can't guard the perimeter. They can't prevent infiltration. The insurgency builds back up, and a couple more of our kids get killed sweeping the same area again. It's all a function of numbers."

When I traveled the country, I sensed that Americans were torn between their instinct to support our president in a time of war and a nagging doubt that he had a workable plan to get the measure of security in Iraq that would allow us to bring the troops home safely. Every time I visited Iraq, the situation on the ground got worse. I'd go with a congressional delegation and we'd arrive at the Baghdad airport in a corkscrew landing to be less of a target. Soldiers would hustle us off a C-130, wrap us up in body armor, and put us in a Black Hawk helicopter with two soldiers and machine guns hanging out the sides. We'd fly at 150 miles per hour, a hundred feet over Baghdad, over the redundant layers of giant cement walls, and into "the Green

Zone." Then they'd drive us in serpentine fashion at 40 miles per hour to meetings in the four-square-mile safe zone. We were no longer allowed to get out of the car and stand around; in fact, we weren't permitted to leave the car unless the specially trained security team opened the car door. And this was in the "safe zone"!

Even when their own generals began to raise red flags about the growing problem of sectarian violence—and the CIA began warning that Iraq could be on a path to civil war—the civilian leaders at Defense refused to rethink their strategy. Things never got better, and Rumsfeld and Cheney never got any wiser. It became increasingly clear that those two men had eroded our country's claim to any moral high ground by flouting the Geneva Conventions. They forced policy decisions that allowed the hideous prisoner abuse at Abu Ghraib in Iraq and encouraged the mistreatment of Muslim prisoners at our facility in Guantánamo in Cuba. I wasn't shy about hammering Rumsfeld. Soon after Abu Ghraib broke in April 2004, people started asking me if I thought Rumsfeld should be fired. And I said, unequivocally, Yes. *Were I president, I would fire him. Obviously, it's the president's decision, but what ever happened to the gentlemanly notion of accountability?* I thought that was sort of an ultimate Republican test. *Just as a matter of honor the secretary would offer his resignation. And the reason he should step down is it makes it virtually impossible to get any other nations to work with us. They don't want to work with him.*

Not long after, I found myself in a room with President Bush and Vice President Cheney, talking about Iraq, when the president all of a sudden said, *Why do you keep picking on Rummy?* I could tell he wasn't just making small talk; he seemed angry. *Mr. President,* I said, *all due respect, let's get something straight: I didn't call for his resignation. I was asked were I president what would I do. And I said I would fire him.*

President Bush asked why I'd do that, and I looked at Cheney. *Mr. Vice President,* I said, *full disclosure: Were you not a constitutional officer, I'd fire you, too. Simple reason, Mr. President: Can you name me one piece of substantial advice given about the war in Iraq that's turned out to be true? That's why, Mr. President.*

Cheney just sat there, rocking, not saying a word.

Recently, at a birthday party for a colleague's wife, I found myself on a back patio with Senator Lugar and Colin Powell. While the hostess was calling us inside, Powell seemed intent on staying on the patio to talk. He was complaining that the White House was attacking him for calling for the closing of the Guantánamo prison. *These damn guys,* I remember him saying. *They're mad at me now. They're all over my ass.*

We started reminiscing about dealing with Bush in the lead-up to the Iraq invasion, and Powell was shaking his head, saying how he had thought he had the president swayed: *I think I have him. I think he agrees. And then he goes the opposite way. I don't know what's wrong with him.* The way Powell figured it, he was just getting beat by Rumsfeld and Cheney.

I remember that night thinking how Powell was kidding himself about Bush, like he still had to rationalize to himself that he'd been outmaneuvered in a political game by these two shrewd old hands; he still wouldn't recognize that President Bush had simply made the wrong decisions. In a way I'd been doing the same thing as Powell— shifting blame to Bush's handpicked minions. But in the end the president—and the president alone—is culpable. I do not question George W. Bush's motives. And I recognize how tough the job was in Iraq. As I'd said to Bremer, if the Lord Almighty had given the president every right answer for every tough decision he faced in Iraq, we'd still only have a slightly better than average chance of getting Iraq right. It was that hard; I still feel that way. But I believe that President Bush failed to lead. History will judge him harshly not for the mistakes he made—we all make mistakes—but for the opportunities he squandered.

I still maintain that the costliest mistake the president made was his unwillingness to level with the American people about what would be required to prevail in Iraq. He never seemed willing to ask any but a small percentage to make a real sacrifice to win the war. He didn't tell them that well over one hundred thousand troops would be needed for many years. He didn't tell them that the cost could surpass $300 billion. He didn't tell them that even after paying such a heavy price, success was not assured because no one had ever succeeded before at forcibly remaking a nation, let alone an entire region.

Instead, he took us to war essentially alone, before it was necessary, on the heels of the biggest and most lopsided tax cut in history, with half the troops we needed to succeed. The Bush administration sent in teams to hunt nonexistent weapons of mass destruction, and left hundreds of tòns of munitions unguarded until they were simply carried off by potential insurgents. The administration never took the time to understand the difficulty of reconciling the Shi'ite majority, who had bled for so long under Saddam, and the Sunni minority, who had ruled, let alone the Kurds, who control most of the oil in Iraq but live in fear of an invasion from Turkey, and a strong central government in Baghdad.

The president cut the French, Germans, and Russians out of reconstruction contracts; and rejected overtures from President Chirac of France, who told me of his willingness to put troops in Iraq if Bush had been willing to cede some control to NATO.

Even in the summer of 2004, as his campaign against John Kerry was joined in earnest, George W. Bush still had the power to make Iraq the world's problem and not just our own. That is the power of the American presidency. But it would have required mending relationships he had broken in the run-up to the invasion and maybe even showing some humility. The demands of leadership had never been more daunting, but the potential rewards remained high. "I'm sure there are people around the president who will tell him to reject the [notion of reaching out to the world]," I said that summer.

They'll tell him that reaching out will make him look weak, that it will be an admission of failure. I would say to them the hour for hubris and arrogance is long past. It's time for leadership. And right now only the president of the United States can provide it. . . .

For the world to follow, we must do more than rattle our sabers and demand allegiance to our vision simply because we believe we are right. We must provide a reason for others to aspire to that vision. And that reason must come with more than the repetition of a bumper-sticker phrase about freedom and democracy. It must come with more than the restatement of failed policy. It must come with the wisdom to admit when we are wrong and resolve to change course and get it right.

✳ 20 ✳

Why?

I REALLY BELIEVED THE AMERICAN PEOPLE WOULD VOTE for a new president in the 2004 election; in the Democratic nominee they were getting a man who had experience and character. John Kerry had served in the United States Senate for nearly twenty years, and he'd been deeply involved in foreign affairs for all those years. More important, he knew what it really meant to send young men into battle, and he knew a president should not do it lightly, or without a clear and defined mission that was backed by the country. John is a decorated war hero who had served with valor in Vietnam. He had not only bravely served his country as a young soldier, but he'd had the guts to stand up to the Nixon administration and tell the American people what was happening to soldiers and civilians in Vietnam.

Jill and I were at home the night of the election and we stayed up late watching returns. When she finally gave up and went to bed, I still held on to the slim hope that Kerry could win. As the night went on, it became clear he would not. But I stayed up all night, flipping fitfully from station to station. I felt terrible for John, but I also felt really worried for the country. John had talked of making me his secretary of state, and I believed we had a real handle on how to fix the situations in Afghanistan, in Iraq, and in diplomatic circles around the globe. I knew the first steps I'd take in Iraq to refocus our efforts on providing physical and economic security for Iraqis and basics like electricity, fuel, and sewage removal. I'd put a swift end to the neocon fantasy of quickly and decisively remaking an Iraq in our image; privatizing industries and building democratic institutions were distant goals that we could not impose on this fragile and decimated country. I also knew which key Republican leaders I could count on to build real bipartisan support, and I felt I knew where to find the common ground where they could be with us.

The 2004 election seemed to be another opportunity that George W. Bush frittered away; the campaign should have been a platform for him to reach out to Democrats. But the president and his political team used the Iraq war as another chance to drive a wedge between Americans—as if anybody who wasn't with them all the way was unpatriotic, unsupportive of the troops, or soft on terror, as if to be against them was to fail to keep America's best interests at heart.

That ethic of division had permeated Washington since the 1994 Republican takeover of Congress—and it's a tragically corrosive agent in our politics, in our institutions, and in our daily lives. What makes the partisanship so debilitating is that it's not confined to one party and, despite what so many pundits say, it's much more than a political tool to win elections. It has shaped our culture and our national dialogue. We've lost our ability to disagree without being disagreeable, and to argue substance without questioning the basic decency of the people on the other side of the line. The partisanship rips at the bonds of affection that tie the country state to state, political party to political party, citizen to citizen.

I didn't sleep that election night and was still at the television when Jill came down the next morning at six. She walked across the kitchen to our TV room, and when I looked up, I could see her standing at the edge of the room, facing me. "What happened?" she asked.

"It's over," I said. "We lost."

I watched Jill as she stood in the doorway, visibly upset, and I really didn't know what to say. I knew she couldn't believe the country had elected George Bush again. But I couldn't help thinking there was something more than that upsetting her. Had John Kerry won the election, it would have closed off the question of my running for president of the United States. And I think it upset her that the question was back on the table. I was pretty sure I knew where she stood. Jill had had only one thing in mind. Her instinct was to protect me and to protect our family—and she understood that my running for the Democratic presidential nomination in 2008 meant the entire Biden family would have to make big sacrifices.

IN THE WEEKS after John Kerry's defeat, Jill knew I was thinking about running in 2008, but we never really talked about it, even when we were alone. I didn't dare bring it up at our annual Thanksgiving trip to Nantucket just a few weeks after the 2004 election. The trip was a tradition of Jill's making; ever since we were first dating, that trip had been the time we got away as a family and closed off the world. In the beginning it was just Jill, Beau, Hunter, and I driving up to a rental house. A few years later, our daughter, Ashley, was born. On the drive up, Jill and I would help our children work on their Christmas lists. Jill would cook a big Thanksgiving dinner and we'd sit around playing board games, talk about life, and just be together. By 2004, we had to caravan up. We had two daughters-in-law now, and four grandchildren. In the evenings after dinner the kids would go out for a walk and Jill and I would stay in and look after the little ones. Jill would spread out catalogs and help them make their Christmas lists.

Politics seemed so far away from Nantucket those evenings, and my family was healthy and happy. And our children and our grandchildren all genuinely *wanted* to be with us. I looked at Jill and remembered that day so long ago in the U.N. chapel when she was a nervous young bride who had given me back my life. What we had nearly thirty years later was beyond what I'd hoped for that day. Whatever happened from here on out, Jill and I had accomplished all the big things, and we'd done it together.

JUST AFTER THANKSGIVING I made my fourth trip to Iraq, with three of my Senate colleagues—Chuck Hagel, Dianne Feinstein, and Lincoln Chafee. What I saw was disheartening. The disconnect between the administration's rhetoric back in Washington and the reality on the ground was greater than it had ever been. The president kept insisting that "freedom is on the march." In fact, the so-called Sunni dead-enders were digging in and launching more frequent attacks against our troops, who were dying in greater numbers. Al-

Qaeda, which had not been in Iraq before the war, was getting a real foothold in the west, threatening to turn the country into what I called a "Bush-fulfilling prophecy." And sectarian tensions were starting to heat up. By virtually every measure, the country seemed to be going backward: there were fourteen-hour blackouts in Baghdad, raw sewage in the streets rose above the hubcaps of the Humvees, oil production fell below prewar levels. There were no jobs and far too many guns and explosives—some eight hundred thousand tons in the thousands of ammo depots we hadn't secured for lack of a plan and sufficient numbers of troops.

I was happy to get out of Iraq and head home for Christmas. It was night, and we filed into the C-130 transport plane on the tarmac at the Baghdad airport. Usually we'd share the cavernous, hollowed-out plane with soldiers who were shipping out, civilians taking leave, and huge crates of supplies. This time the plane was empty except for a long metal box draped with an American flag, secured tightly to the floor. For a long minute we stood without talking, paying a silent tribute to the unknown soldier in the coffin. We'd be his—or her—companions for the final trip home. We took our seats in the straps rigged up along the sides of the plane. I was sitting next to Tony Blinken, my staff director on the Foreign Relations Committee, who has a brilliant grasp of foreign policy, talking about the report we'd write about the trip. The props started turning and the cabin went totally dark as a security precaution. We couldn't talk above the noise. The pilot hurtled the plane into the air. After all those trips into and out of the Balkans and then Iraq, I was used to the corkscrew takeoffs and landings. But about a minute into the flight there was a huge flash of white light outside the window that briefly illuminated the cabin. Instantly the plane went almost completely vertical, or so it seemed, and then into a sharp drop, the engines whining and straining. Then we leveled off. In the dark Tony grabbed my arm and yelled in my ear: "What the heck was that?"

"I don't know," I said. "Maybe it's the military's idea of in-flight entertainment."

A little while later, the copilot came down from the cockpit: "Sorry about the commotion. The surface-to-air-missile warning system was triggered and we had to go evasive."

"So, did someone take a shot at us?" I asked.

"We don't know for sure—but it happens."

Two hours later we touched down in Jordan. I called Jill.

"I'm out of Iraq and I'm coming home."

THE NEXT TIME the entire Biden family was together was just before Christmas. Beau, Hunter, Ashley, and the rest of our family always come home a few days early, so we can celebrate the birthday of
our oldest granddaughter, Naomi. A few nights before Christmas, we
had a big birthday party at the Lake House, and when Jill and I finished cleaning the kitchen and went upstairs to bed, she said to me, in
an alarmingly nonchalant fashion, "We're having a family meeting tomorrow morning in the library. We need to talk to you about something." Then, as is her way, she rolled over and went to sleep.

Of course, I couldn't sleep at all. I got up and went down the stairs
in the dark and into the now-empty library and stared pacing around.
I knew what this meeting was going to be about—the presidential race.
I had been making noise about running. There were things I believed I
could do for the country—things I felt prepared to do for the country—and for the first time in my career I wasn't sure I could do them
as a United States senator. But I was already anticipating what my family would tell me the next morning. *We have so much already. The
family is so strong. Remember how they treated you in 1987. Why invite more pain and heartache? Why take the risk?* I could almost hear
my children in my head. *You can't do this, Dad. We don't want you to
go through this again. We don't want to go through this again.* I found
myself sitting in my library, getting a little angry. But I knew what I
had to do the next morning. I kept telling myself I couldn't lose my
temper the next day. I couldn't get angry. If they don't want me to run,
I thought, I can't run. It's not an arguable point. I'd be asking them to
sacrifice too much privacy, too much time. I owed it to them to honor
their wishes. When I trudged up to bed some time later, I was calmer.

When I showered and dressed and went down to the library the
next morning, everybody else had assembled. They put me in a
wingchair next to a fireplace. Jill, my sister, Val, Beau, Hunter, and
Ashley were arrayed on the couches around me. My longtime friend
and advisor Ted Kaufman was there, too. In my head I kept reminding myself: *You're the father. Be graceful. No matter what, don't lose
your temper.*

"We've been meeting," Jill said, and I realized they'd really thought about how to say this to me.

Then I heard Jill again. "I want you to run this time," she said. "It's up to you, but we'll support it."

For a second I couldn't speak. "Why?"

"We think you can unite the country," Jill said. "We think you're the best person to pull the country together."

✶ 21 ✶

Promises to Keep

"ARE WE GOING TO BE OKAY?"

A woman in Dubuque, Iowa, put it to me just that directly in one of my early campaign events. It's the theme of most of the questions I get these days, and I believe it bespeaks an anxiety in the country that goes well beyond the fear of another terrorist attack inside our borders. I hear every day from men and women who feel less secure about their future, less secure in their jobs, less secure in their ability to protect their own children, and, after the Bush administration's stunning foreign policy blunders, more alone in the world than at any time in our long history. George W. Bush and Dick Cheney have dug us into a very deep hole.

So are we going to be okay? It's not a simple question. But as I look back at the lessons I've learned in my career in politics and government—as I look back at the story of my life—the answer is pretty clear to me: Nothing in my experience has made me doubt the remarkable promise of this country that I saw as a young person who *aspired* to a life in public service. And my years in the Senate have made me less cynical about the heart of this nation and its institutions.

I think of two specific stories separated by many years and many miles. One involves my former colleague John Stennis, who had already represented Mississippi in the United States Senate for twenty-five years when I was first elected in 1972. Senator Stennis's retirement in 1988 opened up a commodious and much-coveted office in the Russell Building; by then I had enough seniority to make a claim on it. So before he left town, I stopped by to say a good-bye to my old friend and, frankly, to look around his offices. John Stennis was in a wheelchair by then, having lost a leg to cancer. He was impeccably dressed, sitting at his long mahogany conference table. When I walked in, he motioned me to a leather chair at the table. "Sit down, Joe. Sit down."

And as I sat down, he said, "Remember the first time you came to see me, Joe?" And I shook my head. I didn't remember. So he recalled for me the story of a thirty-year-old senator-elect from Delaware coming to his office to pay respects in 1972. Stennis sort of chuckled when he reminded me that when he'd asked me why I'd run for the Senate, I seemed to have forgotten his long record as a segregationist and blurted out, "Civil rights, sir."

"I was a pretty smart young fellow then, wasn't I, Mr. Chairman?" I said.

"Joe, I wanted to tell you something then that I'm going to tell you now," Stennis said. "You're going to take this office, aren't you?"

"Yes sir, Mr. Chairman."

"Good, good," he said, and he began to run his hand back and forth across the smooth, polished mahogany. "You see this table, Joe? This table was the flagship of the Confederacy from 1954 to 1968. We sat here, most of us from the Deep South, the old Confederacy, and we planned the demise of the civil rights movement. And we lost. And, Joe, now it's time that this table go from the possession of a man who was against civil rights to a man who was for civil rights."

I wasn't sure what to say, so I got up and thanked him, and as I moved to the door, Senator Stennis said, "And Joe, one more thing. The civil rights movement did more to free the white man than the black man."

He could see me looking at him, confused, and he pounded on his chest. "It freed my soul," he said. "It freed my soul."

In the years I'd known him, John Stennis turned away from his segregationist past. There are a whole lot of people who see his transformation as a journey of political expedience. I choose to see it as a journey of the heart—a sincere desire to reflect the more generous instincts of Mississippians, and to honor the aspirations of *all* Americans. By his own account, John Stennis was personally enlarged by his service in the Senate. That is the power of the institution and the true strength of our federal government. Men and women who serve in

Washington come into contact with folks from all over the country—of all races, religions, and political orientations. And those who are willing to look for the good in their fellow public servants, as Senator Mike Mansfield advised me to do when I first arrived in the Senate, become better people and more able legislators.

The other event happened more recently, in a place that couldn't be farther from the marbled halls of the United States Senate. In June 2006, at the tail end of a trip back to Iraq. I took a detour to visit a refugee camp in Chad in West Africa. The desert camp was home to thousands of families who had fled the genocidal violence of the neighboring Darfur region. There were already thirty thousand people in this one camp, I was told, and that number was growing. Estimates had it that around three hundred thousand people had been forced to flee their homes in Darfur. We landed on an airstrip that was really just a dirt road in the middle of a desert. Two long lines of boulders defined the edges of the runway. There wasn't so much as a scrub tree to be seen. We rolled to a bumpy stop, and as I stepped out of the plane, a young African aid worker emerged from the settling dust and extended his hand. He said, "Thank you, American, for coming."

He escorted me into an open area amid the thousands of tents, where young families swarmed around me. I couldn't understand a single word they said, but I saw in their eyes that same look I saw in Bosnia, and in Kosovo in the 1990s, when we saved tens of thousands from the slaughtering hand of Slobodan Milosevic. It was the same look I'd seen just a few days earlier in Iraq among the Shi'ites who no longer had to hide from Saddam Hussein's Baathist thugs who had killed well over a hundred thousand of them in the decades before. It was the look of hope and of expectation, as if America could make a difference in their lives. The people in the camp in Darfur would have reacted the same way to any American official who visited. Those refugees didn't see a middle-aged guy in a rumpled pair of pants getting off that plane. They saw, vaguely outlined in that swirling dust, the promise of America.

And it struck me in that moment that sometimes we in America don't understand how important we are to the rest of the world—not just because of our military power and our foreign aid, but because of the values we hold dear: compassion, honesty, integrity of thought, generosity, freedom, and hope. We sometimes forget that the United States of America stands as a reminder to billions and billions of people that there is a better place in the world. We sometimes forget that America is the one country in the world that still shimmers, like that "shining city on the hill," as a promise of a brighter tomorrow.

In the last six and a half years the divisiveness and shrill partisanship of the Bush administration has dimmed the bright light of that promise and effectively drowned out the truest, deepest voice of our citizenry. Bush and Cheney have encouraged us to act out of naked self-interest and suggested that if we do the rest will take care of itself. And we all know that in a nation as rich, as free, as powerful as ours, the road to self-interest is often the easy road to take. It's certainly the most tempting. Democrats have been too timid, too quiet, in calling attention to the corrosive tendencies of that ethic.

But as I travel the country lately, I hear a new voice rising. I hear the voice of people who are tired of watching the future sold short for a quick profit; I hear the voice of people who are tired of seeing the benefits of democracy and capitalism unjustly distributed to the favored few, whether the favored few have asked for them or not. I hear the voice of people calling for a future in which *every* American is more secure in life and liberty and more able to pursue happiness. I hear the voice of people willing to make sacrifices today to achieve that kind of tomorrow. It's time for a president to listen to that rising voice and to amplify it. It's time for a president who can point the American people to the future within their reach, tell them what it will take to get there, and vigilantly remind them why it's worth fighting for. It's time for a president to stand up and remind the American people that we have promises to keep—promises to the world, promises to one another, promises to our children and to our grandchildren. In rededicating ourselves to the hard work of fulfilling those promises, we restore America as the hope of the world and the vision of a brighter future.

We must first trust ourselves enough to imagine a future befitting the strongest country the world has ever known. I see a world with a stable Iraq wherein its people are safe and prosperous, its borders secure, its landscape free of terrorist training grounds, and the countries in the region and in the rest of the world are invested in its success. That is the only way to sufficiently honor the sacrifice of that young soldier in the flag-draped coffin whom I rode with on a transport plane out of Iraq—along with nearly thirty thousand other American men and women who have sacrificed life, limbs, or mental well-being in the fight in Iraq. That's a promise we must make to those men and women, and a promise we are obliged to keep.

I see a future in which we have discovered and developed renewable energy sources so we can loosen ourselves from the grip of the oil oligarchs in the Middle East and reverse global warming. As the richest and most prosperous country in the history of the world, we are obliged to lead the development of new energy technologies that protect the environment.

I see a future in which every American family has health insurance, and every father and mother go to bed at night secure in the knowledge that a catastrophic illness or accident will not bankrupt them. I see a future in which every American child has access to preventive health care and to primary and secondary schools that prepare him or her for a successful life. I see a future in which cost can *never* be a barrier for any young person whose educational achievement has merited admittance to college. These are the promises we must make to our children. These are not someone else's children—they are our children, America's children, blood of our blood, bone of our bone, the sinew that binds us. We have always counted on the next generation to carry forward the goals we fail to reach in our own time, and if we don't protect the health and the dreams of *all* of our children, we are betraying our own best intentions.

I see a future in which pensions are secure and private corporations honor *all* the promises they have made to their retirees; a future in which Social Security is fully funded and solvent for generations to come. I see a future in which the richest among us are happy to pay their fair share of taxes because they recognize the benefits of investing in our national well-being.

And I see a future in which Americans remember that when we value what we hold in common above all else, there is nothing we cannot achieve. We won't do it as blacks or as whites, as southerners or as northerners. We won't do it as rich or as poor, as men or as women—we won't even do it as Democrats or as Republicans—but as a people of faith, together, listening to our own best voice, remembering that we have promises to keep.

The vision of that future is what keeps me going because it is absolutely within our reach. I'm optimistic about our chances for one simple reason: Americans want to be better. John Stennis's story of redemption, like a thousand other less public transformations I have seen, is proof enough that Americans want to be good, and want to be good to one another.

WHEN I GOT back from the campaign trip that took me through Dubuque, I came walking in my front door with my overnight bag full of dirty clothes slung over my shoulder, happy to be home. "Well," Jill said as she welcomed me back, "we're into it now." I'd been away from home four nights in a row, and the schedule for next week looked about the same. But it was good to see Jill smiling anyway.

We talked about whom we might see for dinner that night and I finally said, "You know what? We haven't talked for a while. Let's just you and I go to dinner." So we went out to a little restaurant for some pasta and Jill started asking me how it went on the road. She wanted to know details, event by event: How many people showed up? What did they want to talk about? How was the response? And I told her it went really well. A lot of people were showing up, and they were interested in the issues that I knew best and the response was great.

"Well, what do you think?" she said, which really meant: Does it seem possible, winning the nomination?

"I'm not sure, but I feel pretty good out there," I said. "And there's something different about running this time. I can see how I govern. I can picture myself sitting in the Oval Office. I can picture who I'd pick up the phone and call to help me run the government. I can picture the first decisions I'd make."

That's the strange irony and the 180-degree turn I feel as compared with the first time I ran for the presidential nomination. In 1987 I couldn't yet visualize myself doing the job of a president, but by the end of that campaign I could picture in my head how I'd get the nomination. When I started to campaign in 2005, it was the reverse. Doing the job I could see. I was absolutely prepared for that. But I wasn't yet entirely sure how to get my message through the media din that surrounds voters.

Jill broke in. "Look, the thing that's going on with you that I like," she said, "is whether you win or lose, this is going to work out fine."

"How's that?" I wondered.

"You're going to give it your best shot," she said. "And you're going to go out there and run for the right reasons, and tell people why you should be president . . . and we'll be okay."

ACKNOWLEDGMENTS

This book could not have been written without the help of Mark Zwonitzer. Mark helped to refine and arrange the stories I wanted to tell into an overall narrative. He not only transcribed and polished them but helped to fact-check stories, many of which occurred decades ago. Mark is a talented writer, friend, and confidant.

ABOUT THE TYPE

This book was set in Sabon, a typeface designed by the well-known German typographer Jan Tschichold (1902–74). Sabon's design is based upon the original letter forms of Claude Garamond and was created specifically to be used for three sources: foundry type for hand composition, Linotype, and Monotype. Tschichold named his typeface for the famous Frankfurt typefounder Jacques Sabon, who died in 1580.